Lecture Notes in Computer Science 6106

Commenced Publication in 1973
Founding and Former Series Editors:
Gerhard Goos, Juris Hartmanis, and Jan van Leeuwen

Jorge Real   Tullio Vardanega (Eds.)

Reliable
Software Technologies –
Ada-Europe 2010

15th Ada-Europe International Conference
on Reliable Software Technologies
Valencia, Spain, June 14-18, 2010
Proceedings

 Springer

Volume Editors

Jorge Real
Universidad Politécnica de Valencia, DISCA-ETSINF
Camino de Vera s/n, 46022 Valencia, Spain
E-mail: jorge@disca.upv.es

Tullio Vardanega
University of Padua, Department of Pure and Applied Mathematics
Via Trieste 63, 35121 Padua, Italy
E-mail: tullio.vardanega@math.unipd.it

Library of Congress Control Number: 2010927689

CR Subject Classification (1998): D.3, D.2, F.3, C.2, H.4, C.3

LNCS Sublibrary: SL 2 – Programming and Software Engineering

ISSN   0302-9743
ISBN-10   3-642-13549-8 Springer Berlin Heidelberg New York
ISBN-13   978-3-642-13549-1 Springer Berlin Heidelberg New York

springer.com

© Springer-Verlag Berlin Heidelberg 2010
Printed in Germany

Typesetting: Camera-ready by author, data conversion by Scientific Publishing Services, Chennai, India
Printed on acid-free paper   06/3180

Preface

The 15th edition of the International Conference on Reliable Software Technologies – Ada-Europe 2010—took place in the attractive venue of Valencia, deservedly making Spain the most visited country in the conference series. Previous editions of the conference were held in Switzerland (Montreux 1996 and Geneva 2007), United Kingdom (London 1997 and York 2005), Sweden (Uppsala 1998), Spain (Santander 1999 and Palma de Mallorca 2004), Germany (Potsdam 2000), Belgium (Leuven 2001), Austria (Vienna 2002), France (Toulouse 2003 and Brest 2009), Portugal (Porto 2006), and Italy (Venice 2008).

The conference represents the main yearly event promoted by Ada-Europe, in cooperation with ACM SIGAda. This third visit to Spain acknowledges the fact that Ada-Spain is the largest national association of Ada-Europe, and is a major contributor to Ada-Europe's activities. This year the conference was organized by members of the Instituto de Automática e Informática Industrial (AI2) and the Departamento de Informática de Sistemas y Computadores (DISCA) of the Universidad Politécnica de Valencia.

The year 2010 is important for Ada: this is the year when the new amendment to the language (known as Ada 2012) is taking its definitive shape. The conference program was not unaware of this fact, and these proceedings reflect it by including papers about multicore programming in Ada, along with an overview of the key elements of the Ada 2012 amendment in the making.

The scientific program of the conference, which feeds these proceedings, also included sessions devoted to software dependability, critical, real-time and distributed systems, and language technology, all under the more general heading of "Reliable Software Technologies." This program is the result of a thorough selection process of 17 submissions out of 42 received from authors of 19 different countries.

The conference was enriched with three keynote talks delivered by prestigious speakers, whose insightful contributions opened the central days of the conference:

- Theodore Baker (Florida State University, USA), a long-time contributor to Ada and a leading researcher in real-time systems, opened the conference by reviewing the state of the art in multiprocessor real-time scheduling in his talk entitled "What to Make of Multicore Processors for Reliable Real-Time Systems?"
- Pedro Albertos (Universidad Politécnica de Valencia, Spain), a leading figure of the automatic control community, explored the relationship between implementation and performance of control algorithms in a talk entitled "Control Co-design: Algorithms and Their Implementation"
- James Sutton (Lockheed Martin, USA), a worldwide expert software architect, in his talk "Ada: Made for the 3.0 World," analyzed the fitness of Ada

for the so-called 3.0 World, where complexity and chaos are appeased, and both can be used to the user's advantage.

These proceedings give account of the first two keynote talks by including papers contributed by their respective authors. Both papers appear in the "Keynote Talks" section.

As a forum that aims to connect academic with industrial knowledge and experience around reliable software technologies, the conference also included an interesting series of industrial presentations whose proceedings will appear in forthcoming issues of Ada-Europe's *Ada User Journal*. That part of the conference program included:

- "HRT-UML and Ada Ravenscar Profile: A Methodological Approach to the Design of Level-B Spacecraft Software," by R. López, A. I. Rodríguez from GMV, Spain
- "Applying Model-Driven Architecture and SPARK Ada – A SPARK Ada Model Compiler for xtUML," by E. Wedin from Saab, Sweden
- "Ada 95 Usage Within the Airbus Military Advanced Refuelling Boom System," by I. Lafoz from Airbus Military, Spain
- "Ada 95 Usage Within the Airbus Military Generic Test Environment System," by B. Lozano from Airbus Military, Spain
- "Implementing Polymorphic Callbacks for Ada/C++ Bindings," by M. Sobczak from CERN, Switzerland
- "A Reusable Work Seeking Parallel Framework for Ada 2005," by B. Moore from General Dynamics Canada
- "Database Programming with Ada," by F. Piron from KonAd GmbH, Germany
- "Future Enhancements to the U.S. FAA's En-Route Automation Modernization (ERAM) Program and the Next Generation Air Transportation System (NextGen)," by J. O'Leary from FAA, USA, and A. Srivastava from Northrop Grumman IT, USA
- "System Architecture Virtual Integration Case Study," by B. Lewis from U.S. Army Aviation and Missile Command, USA
- "Lessons Learned from the First High Assurance (EAL 6+) Common Criteria Software Certification," by D. Kleidermacher from Greenhills Software, USA
- "An Introduction to ParaSail: Parallel Specification and Implementation Language," by S. T. Taft from SofCheck, USA

The conference also scheduled a series of tutorials that, once more, gave participants the opportunity to learn about particular approaches, techniques and tools aimed at the development of reliable software. The program was formed by the following nine tutorials, all given by recognized experts in the relevant areas:

- "Developing High-Integrity Systems with GNATforLEON/ORK+," by J. A. de la Puente and J. Zamorano from the Technical University of Madrid, Spain

- "Software Design Concepts and Pitfalls," by W. Bail from The MITRE Corporation, USA
- "Using Object-Oriented Technologies in Secure Systems," by J.P. Rosen from Adalog, France
- "Hypervisor Technology for Building Safety-Critical Systems: XtratuM," by I. Ripoll and A. Crespo from Universidad Politécnica de Valencia, Spain
- "How to Optimize Reliable Software," by I. Broster from Rapita Systems Ltd, UK
- "Developing Web-Aware Applications in Ada with AWS," by J.P. Rosen from Adalog, France
- "MAST: Predicting Response Times in Event-Driven Real-Time Systems," by M. González Harbour from University of Cantabria, Spain
- "SPARK: The Libre Language and Toolset for High-Assurance Software," by R. Chapman from Altran Praxis Ltd, UK
- "C#, .NET and Ada: Keeping the Faith in a Language-Agnostic Environment," by B. Brosgol and J. Lambourgh from AdaCore, USA and France

The conference success heavily depended on the active and generous contribution of a number of individuals and organizations. All of them deserve our most sincere gratitude. We especially thank all who submitted quality contributions that enabled us to offer an attractive and technically sound program. Of course we are most grateful to all attendees, who made the conference thrive. The Organizing Committee was formed by Albert Llemosí, Tutorial Chair, who conjured a high-quality tutorial program; Erhard Plödereder, Industrial Chair, who coordinated the elaboration of the industrial program; Ahlan Marriott in his role as Exhibition Chair; and Dirk Craeynest, serving as Publicity Chair. The members of this committee met with the Program Co-chairs in Valencia to make the final program selection and composition.

The organizers are also grateful to the members of the Local Organizing Committee at the Universidad Politécnica de Valencia, Francisco Blanes, Sergio Sáez, and José Simó. The Program and Industrial Committees did a splendid job at raising submissions and providing quality reviews that aided in the difficult task of eliciting the final contents of the conference. Last but not least, we wish to express our gratitude to the exhibitors at the conference, at the time of writing: AdaCore, Altran Praxis, Atego and Ellidiss; and the sponsors: Ministerio de Ciencia e Innovación of the Spanish Government, Consellería d'Educació of the Generalitat Valenciana, Universidad Politécnica de Valencia and its entities Departamento de Informática de Sistemas y Computadores, Escuela Técnica Superior de Ingeniería Informática, and Instituto de Automática e Informática Industrial.

June 2010   Jorge Real
                                                                                      Tullio Vardanega

Organization

The 15th International Conference on Reliable Software Technologies – Ada-Europe 2010—was organized by Ada-Europe and Universidad Politécnica de Valencia, in cooperation with ACM SIGAda.

Organizing Committee

Conference Chair:	Jorge Real
	(Universidad Politécnica de Valencia, Spain)
Program Co-chairs:	Jorge Real
	(Universidad Politécnica de Valencia, Spain)
	Tullio Vardanega
	(Università di Padova, Italy)
Tutorial Chair:	Albert Llemosí
	(Universitat de les Illes Balears, Spain)
Industrial Chair:	Erhard Plödereder
	(Universität Stuttgart, Germany)
Exhibition Chair:	Ahlan Marriott
	(White Elephant GmbH, Switzerland)
Publicity Chair:	Dirk Craeynest
	(Aubay Belgium & K.U.Leuven, Belgium)

Program Committee

Alejandro Alonso	José-Javier Gutiérrez	Erhard Plödereder
Ted Baker	Andrew Hately	Jorge Real
John Barnes	Peter Hermann	Alexander Romanovsky
Johann Blieberger	Jérôme Hugues	Jean-Pierre Rosen
Jørgen Bundgaard	Hubert Keller	Ed Schonberg
Bernd Burgstaller	Albert Llemosí	Sergio Sáez
Alan Burns	Kristina Lundqvist	Theodor Tempelmeier
Rod Chapman	Franco Mazzanti	Jean-Loup Terraillon
Dirk Craeynest	John McCormick	Santiago Urueña
Alfons Crespo	Julio Medina	Tullio Vardanega
Juan A. de la Puente	Stephen Michell	Francois Vernadat
Raymond Devillers	Javier Miranda	Andy Wellings
Franco Gasperoni	Daniel Moldt	Daniel Wengelin
Michael González	Laurent Pautet	Jürgen Winkler
Harbour	Luís Miguel Pinho	Luigi Zaffalon

External Reviewers

Björn Andersson	Ilya Lopatkin	José Ruiz
Etienne Borde	Yannick Moy	Jayakanth Srinivasan
Pierre-Emmanuel Hladik	Florent Peres	Thomas Wagner
Didier Le Botlan	Jose Quenum	

Sponsoring Institutions

The organizers of the conference are grateful to the exhibitors and sponsors of the conference.

Exhibitors, at the time of writing:
   AdaCore
   Altran Praxis
   Atego
   Ellidiss Software

Sponsors:
   Ministerio de Ciencia e Innovación, Spanish Government (project TIN2009-06669-E)
   Consellería d'Educació, Generalitat Valenciana
   Universidad Politécnica de Valencia (program PAID-03-09)
   Departamento de Informática de Sistemas y Computadores, UPV
   Escuela Técnica Superior de Ingeniería Informática, UPV
   Instituto de Automática e Informática Industrial, UPV

Table of Contents

Real-Time Systems

Language Technology

Distribution and Persistency

What to Make of Multicore Processors for Reliable Real-Time Systems?

Theodore P. Baker[*]

Florida State University, Tallahassee FL 32306, USA
baker@cs.fsu.edu
http://www.cs.fsu.edu/~baker

Abstract. Now that multicore microprocessors have become a commodity, it is natural to think about employing them in all kinds of computing, including high-reliability embedded real-time systems. Appealing aspects of this development include the ability to process more instructions per second and more instructions per watt. However, not all problems are amenable to parallel decomposition, and for those that are, designing a correct scalable solution can be difficult. If there are deadlines or other hard timing constraints the difficulty becomes much greater.

This paper reviews some of what is known about multiprocessor scheduling of task systems with deadlines, including recent advances in the analysis of arbitrary sporadic task systems under fixed-priority and earliest-deadline first scheduling polices. It also examines critically the foundations of these theoretical results, including assumptions about task independence and worst-case execution time estimates, with a view toward their practical applicability.

1 Introduction

Over the past decade, the microprocessor industry has been moving increasingly toward symmetric multicore architectures. The introduction of the AMD dual-core Opteron, in 2004, was followed closely by the Intel dual-core Pentium D and the IBM dual-core Power5 processor. Increases in feature *density* predicted by Moore's Law appear to be sustainable for at least a few more generations, but increases in processing *speed* do not. Pipelining and speculative execution appear to have reached a point of diminishing returns. Clock rates also seem to have reached a limit, as power consumption increases at approximately the cube of clock frequency. Manufacturers have decided that the way to extract improvements in performance from further advances in miniaturization is through the use of multiple processors of moderate power, executing in parallel [38]. Two- and four-core processors are already a commodity, eight-core processors have been delivered, and "terra-scale" computing is predicted [30].

What will we make of these new processors? This question should be on the minds of developers of every kind of software. Appealing prospects include

---

[*] This paper is based upon work supported in part by the National Science Foundation under Grant No. EHS-0509131.

J. Real and T. Vardanega (Eds.): Ada-Europe 2010, LNCS 6106, pp. 1–18, 2010.

the ability to process more instructions per second and more instructions per watt. However, not all problems are amenable to parallel decomposition, and for those that are, designing a correct scalable solution can be difficult. If there are deadlines or other hard timing constraints the difficulty becomes much greater.

This paper seeks to convey an appreciation of the gap that exists between what is known in theory about the problem of scheduling ideal multiprocessors to meet deadlines, and the behaviors of actual multicore processors. It begins with a sampling of theoretical research that appears as if it should be applicable to this problem. It then questions the foundations of these theoretical results, including assumptions about processor architecture, task independence and worst-case execution time estimates, with respect to their applicability to current and future generations of multicore processors in high-reliability real-time systems. It finally expands the focus to consider the directions that programming languages and software design methodologies may need to go in order to better exploit multicore technology.

2   Scheduling Theory Foundations

Scheduling theory is based on abstract models of workloads and processors. A great many different models have been studied. This paper focuses on just one type of workload model and one type of processor model.

Task workload models. In real-time scheduling theory, a *task* is an abstraction for a source of a potentially infinite sequence of *jobs*. A job is a schedulable computation with a finite *execution time*. Other parameters of each job include a *release time* and a *deadline*. Each task has a set of *scheduling parameters* that constrain the execution times, arrival times, and deadlines of the sequences of jobs that it may generate. The jobs of each task are required to be executed serially, using only one processor at a time.

A *task* in scheduling theory may be used to model an execution of a sequential thread of control, such as an Ada task[1], in software. Jobs correspond to bursts of computation between wait states. The execution time of a job is the amount of processor time used during one such burst of computation, the release time is the arrival time of the event that triggers the transition from waiting to competing for execution, and the completion time is the time of the next transition to a wait state.

This paper focuses primarily on periodic and sporadic task systems. A *sporadic task system* is a set $\tau = \{\tau_1, \tau_2, \ldots, \tau_n\}$ of tasks, each characterized by a triple (p_i, e_i, d_i) where: p_i is the minimum separation between release times of the jobs of the task, also known as the *period* of the task; e_i is an upper bound on the execution time for each job of the task, also known as the *worst-case*

---

[1] This overloading of the word "task" can lead to erroneous reasoning, since not all Ada tasks can be modeled as scheduling theory tasks. In this paper "task" always means a scheduling theory task, except in the phrase "Ada task". "Thread" is used for Ada tasks and other similar threads of control.

execution time (WCET); and d_i is the *relative deadline*, which is the length of the scheduling window of each job. A periodic task system is said to have *implicit deadlines* if $d_i = p_i$ for every task, *constrained deadlines* if $d_i \leq p_i$, and *arbitrary deadlines* if there is no such constraint. A *periodic task system* is like a sporadic task system except that the separation between release times of τ_i must be equal to p_i. Additional parameters are sometimes specified, such as the release times of the first job of each task, and an upper bound on release time jitter.

Real systems often do not fit the periodic or sporadic model, or have any other sufficient constraints on the patterns of arrivals and execution times of jobs to support schedulability analysis. One way of accommodating such workloads is to queue their jobs to be executed by a *server task*. The server task is scheduled according to an algorithm that limits the amount of processor time that the server can consume within any given time interval, by imposing a *budget*. In effect, the natural job boundaries of the aperiodic workload are redrawn by the server scheduling mechanism, which ends the current "job" of the server whenever it reaches the limit of its budget, and releases a new "job" whenever the server's budget is extended. Sporadic Server [44] and Constant Bandwidth Server [1] are examples of such *bandwidth-limiting algorithms*, which allow the worst-case behavior of a server to be modeled by a sporadic task in most contexts.

Identical multiprocessor models. This paper focuses on multiprocessor platforms with a set of identical processors and shared memory with uniform access speed. Every job is presumed to be executable on any processor, with no difference in worst-case execution time between processors.

The above models leave out many ugly details of real systems, including release time jitter and overheads such as context-switches and migrations of tasks between processors, in order to make analysis more tractable. When applying the theory, one must add sufficient margins to the task parameter values to account for such differences between reality and the model[2].

3   Scheduling Algorithms and Tests

A *schedule* is an assignment of jobs to processors, varying over time. A schedule is *feasible* if it satisfies all the constraints of the workload, including job deadlines. A collection of jobs is said to be feasible if there exists a feasible schedule for it. For practical purposes schedules must be computable by a *scheduling algorithm*. A particular workload is said be *schedulable* by a given algorithm if the algorithm always finds a feasible schedule.

Scheduling algorithms can be dichotomized as static *vs.* dynamic, off-line *vs.* on-line, and preemptive *vs.* nonpreemptive. Priority-based on-line schedulers are

---

[2] Narrowing these margins would appear to require accounting explicitly for circular dependences between actual job execution times and decisions made by on-line schedulers. A critical concern in the application of any such analysis would be potential instability under execution time variations caused by factors other than the scheduler.

classified according to how priorities are allowed to vary. Rate Monotonic (RM) scheduling, in which tasks with shorter periods are assigned higher priorities, is an example of a *fixed-task-priority* (FTP) scheduling algorithm. Earliest-deadline-first scheduling is an example of a *fixed-job-priority* (FJP) algorithm. PD^2[2] is an example of a *dynamic priority* algorithm. *Within this paper, all on-line scheduling algorithms are assumed to be applied in preemptive mode.*

A *schedulability test* tells whether a particular workload is schedulable by a given algorithm. A schedulability test is *sufficient* for a given class of workload and processor models if passing the test guarantees the workload is schedulable. It is *exact* if it also only fails when there is some sequence of jobs consistent with the workload model that is not schedulable.

One of the subtleties of multiprocessors is that certain intuitively appealing scheduling algorithms are subject to "*anomalies*", in which a schedulable system becomes unschedulable because of some apparently harmless change, such as earlier-than-expected completion of a job. A good scheduling algorithm should continue to schedule a task system satisfactorily if actual tasks behave better than the specifications under which the system was validated, or if the specifications of tasks are changed in a direction that reduces the overall workload. This property, named "*sustainability*" in [14], has been shown to hold for some multiprocessor scheduling algorithms and tests, but not for others (*e.g.* [9]).

Anyone making a choice of scheduling algorithm for an application should consider several factors, including: (1) sufficient generality to cover the variety of workload types expected in the application; (2) flexibility to handle the changes in task specifications that are expected over the lifetime of the application; (3) compatibility with the operating system that will be used; (4) run-time determinism or repeatability, as an adjunct of system testability and reliability; (5) sustainability of the algorithm and the available schedulability tests for it; (6) effectiveness of the scheduling algorithm in scheduling jobs to complete within deadlines; (7) effectiveness of the available schedulability tests. Studies of real-time scheduling theory mostly focus on the last two issues, but for practical purposes it is important to consider all of them. It is also important to consider the last two as a pair, since *a scheduling algorithm can only be trusted to schedule a particular task system correctly if it has been verified to do so.*

There are several empirical ways to evaluate multiprocessor scheduling algorithms and tests. One is to compute the success ratio on large numbers of randomly generated task systems (*e.g.* [8]). This can provide useful information if the characteristics of the task sets considered are similar to those expected for a given class of applications. It may be the only way to compare some combinations of scheduling algorithms and schedulability tests. Such experiments can be especially informative if the task parameter values used in the tests are adjusted to take into account the measured overheads of an actual implementation (*e.g.* [22])[3].

---

[3] Running schedulability tests on random task sets is not the same as simulating actual task system executions. The latter is not a valid way to verify schedulability for multiprocessor systems since the "critical instant" property (*c.f.* [34]) no longer holds.

Analytic ways to evaluate scheduling algorithms and tests include "speedup factors" (*e.g.* [12]), which are out of scope for the present paper, and *utilization bounds*. The *utilization* u_i of a task τ_i is the ratio e_i/p_i of its execution time to its period. A *utilization bound* for a scheduling policy is a function β such that each task system τ is guaranteed to be schedulable if $u_{\mathrm{sum}}(\tau) <= \beta(\tau)$, where u_{sum} is the sum of the utilizations of all the tasks in the system. The bound is *tight* if there are unschedulable task systems with $u_{\mathrm{sum}}(\tau)$ only infinitesimally larger than $\beta(\tau)$.

A *density bound* is an extension of the notion of utilization bound, for task systems that have other than implicit deadlines ($d_i \neq p_i$). The definition of density bound is the same as utilization bound, except that the utilization u_i is replaced by the *density*, defined as $\delta_i \stackrel{\mathrm{def}}{=} e_i / \min(d_i, p_i)$.

This paper uses utilization bounds and density bounds to provide insight into the relative effectiveness of various methods of multiprocessor scheduling, not because they tell the whole story, but because they can be stated concisely, can be compared easily, and there are examples of sufficient schedulability tests.

Care must be taken when interpreting such bounds, since they can be misleading. Both pertain only to schedulability of <u>worst-case</u> (pathological) examples[4]. Empirical studies have shown that much higher utilization levels can be achieved for most task systems.

4 Static Scheduling

Historically, the analysis of scheduling for multiprocessors focused first on static scheduling techniques, in which a finite schedule is computed off-line. Static scheduling has been studied extensively in the literature of operations research and discrete mathematics. Although optimal static scheduling is known to be NP-hard for all but a few simple classes of problems [46], it is still practicable for real-time task systems of moderate size. Moreover, for practical purposes optimal scheduling is not required; any schedule that satisfies the application constraints will do.

There is a wealth of theory and published practical experience on static scheduling of multiprocessors. One representative example is [48], which reports success in optimal multiprocessor scheduling for periodic systems with deadlines, precedence, and exclusion constraints. A more recent one is [31], which shows how to approximate optimal scheduling using linear programming.

---

[4] Care must also be taken when applying a utilization or density bound outside the constraints of the model for which it has been proven. Some of the original published proofs only mention periodic task systems. There is a pattern of these analyses remaining valid for sporadic tasks, because good scheduling algorithms are sustainable under later job release times that do not violate the sporadic minimum separation constraint. Another pattern is of utilization bounds extending to density bounds. One should not assume any such extension is valid without checking that it has been proven.

Static schedules have several virtues. They can handle complex forms of constraints and achieve a high degree of optimization. Optimizations can be applied to a variety of criteria, including output jitter, power, and memory. They can eliminate the need for software locking, by scheduling access to shared resources during non-overlapping time intervals. They can also minimize buffering and dataflow blocking, such as between producers and consumers. Though static schedules are intrinsically periodic, they can be adapted to handle sporadic and aperiodic workloads by means of a periodic server. Since the schedule repeats, behavior observed during a few periods of testing is a valid predictor of behavior over longer periods of time. Static scheduling may also prove to be a practical necessity for accurate analysis of the effects of task-dependent interference between processors on WCET.

Static scheduling does have shortcomings, including a tendency to over-allocate processor time, and fragility with respect to run-time variations in workload and longer-term changes in system specifications. Static scheduling may be impracticable for systems in which the release times and execution times of jobs are highly variable or cannot be predicted with confidence. In the single-processor domain, the limitations of static scheduling have led to widespread adoption of priority-based on-line scheduling algorithms.

However, where the workload is sufficiently predictable, static scheduling may still be the best way to achieve reliable high performance from a multicore processor. Moreover, with multiple cores one can apply static scheduling to an appropriate subset of the system functionality, on a subset of the processors, and apply dynamic scheduling to the rest.

5   Partitioned Dynamic Scheduling

Until recently, partitioned scheduling was widely held to be the only way to use multiprocessors for embedded real-time systems. It is a very natural and convenient bridge from single-processor dynamic scheduling to a multiprocessor platform. By assigning each task to one processor, statically, and then applying a dynamic local scheduling algorithm and schedulability test, one achieves some of the predictability of a static schedule and some of the flexibility of a dynamic scheduler, without having to develop any new scheduling algorithms or schedulability tests. Finding a partition that is feasible locally on each processor may be accepted as a sufficient system-level schedulability test, if the tasks are sufficiently independent. Sustainability of the schedulability analysis carries over from the single-processor local scheduling algorithm.

Optimal assignment of tasks to processors is a form of bin-packing problem, which is NP-hard, but optimality is not required. The First-Fit-Decreasing-Utilization partitioning algorithm has been cited as being very effective in some publications. However, in practice one would want to use an ordering heuristic that takes into account addition considerations, including localization of data sharing, balancing data flow rates between cores, and distributing excess processor capacity among the processors.

Since the allocation of processing resources is forced to be done fixed-size chunks, partitioned scheduling is generally not *work conserving*; that is, a processor may be idled while tasks eligible for execution on other processors are not able to execute. This can result in partitioning failures at low utilization levels, and even when partitioning is successful the idling of processors can result in longer average-case response times and lower total system throughput than with global scheduling.

For partitioned preemptive Earliest-Deadline-First (EDF) scheduling, a utilization bound of $\frac{m\lfloor 1/u_{\max}(\tau)\rfloor+1}{\lfloor 1/u_{\max}(\tau)\rfloor+1}$ for m processors was derived in [36]. For the unrestricted case where $u_{\max}(\tau) = 1$ this reduces to $(m+1)/2$. The proof is for periodic task systems only. This worst-case utilization bound is tight in the sense that a scheduling algorithm that does not vary priority within a single job cannot achieve a utilization bound higher than $(m+1)/2$ on m processors, whether scheduling is partitioned or global. That is easy to see by considering a set of $m+1$ tasks, each with processor utilization infinitesimally larger than 50% [4].

For partitioned RM, a utilization bound of $(n-1)(2^{1/2}-1) + (m-n+1)(2^{1/(m-n+1)}-1)$ for m processors and n tasks was derived in [35]. For large n, this reduces to $(m+1)(2^{1/2}-1)$. This result was proven to be tight for "reasonable" partitioning schemes based on the single-processor RM utilization bound as a test of schedulability, and the proof has been claimed to extend to all partitioning schemes. The proof is for periodic task systems only.

Partitioned scheduling can handle periodic and sporadic task sets, and can also handle aperiodic workloads scheduled under a bandwidth-limiting server mechanism. Several authors have studied partitioning algorithms for these more general workload models, but a description of those results does not fit within the scope of the present paper.

An advantage of partitioned scheduling is that efficient single-processor locking mechanisms such as SRP [5] can be applied for resources that are only shared by tasks on the same processor, and higher-overhead global locking mechanisms can be reserved for resources shared across processors. Space limitations here permit only the barest summary of research on protocols for global locks, which is still inconclusive. The most appropriate locking protocol for global resources will depend on (1) whether task scheduling is partitioned or global, (2) the priority model, and (3) the length of critical sections. However, a central consideration in all cases is to minimize idle processor time caused by tasks awaiting global locks. One approach, used by the Distributed Priority Ceiling Protocol (D-PCP) [40], is to bind each globally shared resource to a single processor and execute sections on it via remote procedure calls to a high priority server on that processor. An alternative approach, used by the Multiprocessor Priority Ceiling Protocol (M-PCP) [40], Multiprocessor Stack Resource Protocol (M-SRP)[25], and Flexible Multiprocessor Locking Protocol (FMLP) [20], is to raise tasks holding global locks to nonpreemptible local priority. It was shown in [37] that using the same priorities for local scheduling and service order on global locks could be harmful for overall system schedulability, as compared to service based on tasks' tolerance for blocking, or even FIFO. The M-SRP and FMLP adopt FIFO service. The FMLP additionally optimizes short-wait locks by using bare spin-locks. The performances of some of these algorithms in actual implementations on multiprocessors are reported in [21,41,26].

Unfortunately, critical sections are not the only kind of blocking that can occur in a real system. Dataflow blocking can occur, in which one task waits for data or buffer space to be produced by another. This kind of blocking does not require idling the processor in a single-processor system or with global scheduling, because whenever one task has to wait for another to perform an action the scheduler can give the processor of the waiting task to the awaited task. In contrast, if the waiting task and the awaited task are on different processors, the waiting task's processor may become idle. This idle time can reduce system throughput in the short term, which can cause congestion later, resulting in missed deadlines. If care is not taken in assigning deadlines or priorities across processors, a third task may preempt the awaited task on its processor, resulting in potentially unbounded blocking. Appropriate buffering can reduce data flow blocking, but the partitioning algorithm still needs to pay attention to matching average data flow rates across processors.

A partitioning of tasks among processors may be fragile. If the execution time of one task increases, there is no limit to the range of the potential side effects. Repartitioning and lock protocol changes may be necessary. The effects may cascade across every processor. Fragility may be reduced by distributing excess capacity evenly across processors.

While it may seem wasteful to only use 50% of of the theoretical processing capacity of a system, thinking in terms of the worst-case utilization bound may not be so bad. Pushing for high utilization of cores on multicore processors may be just as bad for performance as pushing disk and memory utilization to high levels on single-processor systems. For reasons explained in Section 8, trying to schedule all processors at 100% capacity is likely to be counter-productive, as job execution times can grow with greater intercore contention for data paths and memory access. Moreover, idle cores need not necessarily translate to wasted power.

Partitioned scheduling is easy to implement. The partitioning is done off-line. The on-line component is low-overhead because of the per-processor task ready-queues, which incur less contention for concurrent access and can be protected by a lighter-weight locking mechanism than is required to maintain a global ready-queue.

Test coverage with partitioned scheduling will be better than with a globally scheduled system, because of the reduction in the number of possible combinations of concurrent task activities on different processors. Execution times should also be more predictable, for the preceding reason and also because of the absence of migration events.

6   Task Splitting

An inherent limitation of all partitioned scheduling schemes is that each task must execute entirely on one processor. This constraint makes optimal partitioning

NP-hard, and prevents a pure partitioned scheduling algorithm from achieving a utilization bound greater than $(m+1)/2$.

Recent research has attacked this limitation using *task splitting* techniques. These algorithms deviate from the strict partitioned model by allowing limited planned migration of a few tasks, typically up to $m-1$ tasks for m processors. The partitioning algorithm assigns tasks to processors in some heuristic order. When it reaches a point where adding another task to a given processor would cause a local deadline miss it splits that task in two, assigning a fraction to the given processor that will fit without causing any missed deadlines, and migrating the remainder to another processor. This approach is able to get past the $(m+1)/2$ limit on utilization bounds for partitioned fixed-job-priority scheduling.

Several task splitting techniques have been proposed. One noteworthy recent example is [29], which demonstrates that a partitioned fixed-task-priority (FTP) scheduling algorithm can achieve the utilization bound $mn(2^{1/n} - 1)$ on m processors. This is of special interest because it equals the worst-case RM utilization bound for a single processor. Another recent example is [32], which is based on preemptive EDF local scheduling and obtains a utilization bound of $m(4\sqrt{2} - 5)$ on m processors, or about 65% of the total processing capacity.

So far, it does not seem that any of these techniques has been tested in an implementation, so there remain questions about their practicability.

7   Global Scheduling

As an alternative to partitioned scheduling, a dynamic scheduling algorithm may be applied in global mode, where all tasks compete for execution on all processors. Global dynamic scheduling can be work-conserving, which can result in better scheduling performance than partitioned scheduling. In fact, there is a very simple global dynamic scheduling algorithm that can meet all deadlines at utilizations up to 100%.

The key to understanding how to get 100% processor utilization and still meet deadlines with the workload and processor models described here is to recognize the importance of keeping all processors busy. It is easy to keep a single processor busy, by never idling the processor if there is work to be done; this can be achieved without constraining the order in which jobs are executed, and so there is no conflict with executing jobs in deadline order, and no problem achieving all deadlines up to 100% processor utilization. With more than one processor, the situation changes. The job execution order can affect the ability to keep all processors busy. For example, if a dual-processor scheduler has two short jobs and one long job ready, and decides to execute the short jobs first, it may end up later with one processor idle. The problem is that a single job cannot use additional processors[5]. One way to work around this limitation is to split up the job's execution and interleave it serially with other tasks. Suppose

---

[5] Unless, of course, one breaks out of the task model and codes jobs for parallel execution. This is one of the weaknesses of the task model, discussed further in Section 9.

the processor time can be split up into small enough units that each task τ_i can be assigned a fraction u_i of a processor between its release time and its deadline. Such a scheduler is optimal in the sense of never missing a deadline for a feasible task system, and can achieve 100% utilization without missing deadlines on implicit-deadline periodic task systems.

While this ideal processor sharing model is impracticable to implement, [15] showed that the same utilization bound can be achieved by a quantum-based time-slicing approximation. A number of variants of this proportional fair-share (Pfair) scheduling concept have been explored. One variant, called PD^2, is work-conserving and has been shown to be optimal for the scheduling of independent asynchronous implicit-deadline periodic tasks [2].

A criticism of the Pfair approach is that by slicing time finely it incurs a large scheduling overhead. Brandenburg *et al.* [22] performed experiments using an implementation of the PD^2 algorithm on a variant of the Linux operating system kernel using an 8-core Sun "Niagara" processor. They measured the scheduling overheads on a few examples, and then applied schedulability tests to large numbers of randomly generated task systems with shared resources and critical sections. Potential dataflow blocking was not taken into account. The task execution times were adjusted to allow for scheduling overheads, and schedulability tests were modified to take into account blocking times due to critical sections. The experiments showed that that PD^2 had serious problems with high preemption and migration costs until the scheduler was modified to stagger the time-slicing points of the processors across the cores, so that quantum expirations no longer occurred synchronously on all processors. Even with this improvement, PD^2 did not seem to perform as well as partitioned EDF, except for systems with tasks near the 50% utilization region (which is known to be pathological for partitioning algorithms), and without a high degree of global resource sharing. However, it is difficult to say whether such experiments will accurately predict performance in any particular application.

Global applications of EDF and RM were neglected for decades after Dhall [24] showed that the utilization bound on m processors is 1 (as if the system had only one processor). The proof is a pathological case involving m low-utilization (*light*) periodic tasks and one high-utilization (*heavy*) task with slightly longer period. Fortunately, closer study of this phenomenon over the past seven years revealed ways of obtaining much better performance.

A global EDF utilization bound of $m - (m-1)u_{\max}(\tau)$ was derived in [45,27]. This shows that worst-case behavior only occurs for large values of the maximum individual task utilization $u_{\max}$. The bound can be shown to be tight by generalization of the Dhall example. However, it is not an exact schedulablity test, and other forms of tests have done much better in experiments with random task systems [8]. The global EDF utilization bound extends to a density bound for sporadic task systems with arbitrary deadlines. In this more general form it has been called the "density test" for global EDF schedulability.

For global RM, a utilization bound of $\frac{m}{2} - (\frac{m}{2} - 1)u_{\max}(\tau)$ was derived [17]. It also extends to a density bound.

Variants of EDF have been designed with higher utilization bounds for systems with large u_{max}. An algorithm called EDF-US[ζ] gives top priority to jobs of tasks with utilizations above threshold ζ and schedules jobs of the remaining tasks according to their deadlines [45]. It achieves a utilization bound of $(m + 1)/2$, which is tight.

Similar variants of RM have also been proposed. RM-US[ζ] gives higher priority to tasks with utilizations above ζ [4,7]. A RM-US utilization bound of $\frac{m+1}{3}$ is proven in [17]. A tight bound is not known, though [39] argued that the optimum value of ζ is approximately 0.3748225282.

Another recently discovered FTP priority assignment algorithm, known as SM-US[ζ] and based on ordering tasks by slack, has been shown to have a utilization bound of $m(2/(3 + \sqrt{3}))$ on m processors, or approximately 38% of the total processing capacity [3].

Despite the low worst-case utilization bounds, fixed-job-priority algorithms have several advantages. They perform fewer context switches than the Pfair methods, and hence have lower scheduling overhead. They can achieve more precise control over timing, by using interval timers that are finer grained than the overhead of quantum-based scheduling methods would permit. In the case of fixed-task-priority, support already exists in most operating systems, including Linux.

Although the fixed-job-priority (FJP) algorithms do not have any practicable exact schedulability tests,[6]. there is a steadily growing collection of practicable *sufficient-only* tests for FJP scheduling policies, including the utilization bounds cited above and a number of more accurate tests that cannot be described within the space limitations here. Examples for EDF include [6,16,11,18] and examples for FTP include [7,17,13]. These tests are difficult to compare. They generally cannot be strictly ranked in scheduling effectiveness, in the sense that there are examples of schedulable task systems that are recognized as schedulable by each test that are not recognized as schedulable by others. Some definitely appear to be more effective than others, on the average, for randomly chosen task systems. Some have good speed-up factors but do not perform well on the average. Some have been shown to be sustainable, some have been shown to be unsustainable, and the sustainability of others remains unknown. Other important properties, including the effects of blocking due to critical sections have not been studied well. So, it is likely to take several more years of study for any consensus to emerge on which of these tests are most useful in practice.

Global scheduling is more difficult to implement than partitioned scheduling. The shared dispatching queue is a bottleneck which becomes more serious as the number of cores grows[7]. The interprocessor interrupts needed to trigger scheduling on other processors are also costly. However, experiments with implementations of several global scheduling algorithms, including PD^2 and global EDF, in a variant of

---

[6] The only known exact tests are based on exhaustive exploration of the scheduling state space, are limited to integer time values, and have unacceptable growth in time and space [10,28].

[7] The standard Linux kernel maintains per-core task dispatching queues, and only performs migrations at longer intervals, for this reason.

the Linux kernel have been reported, and the performance looks good [22]. Adding support for the RM-US and EDF-US hybrids would be extremely simple, and would increase scheduling effectiveness without adding any overhead.

Testing is likely to be more difficult for globally scheduled systems, unless explicit interprocessor synchronization points are inserted to reduce timing variations. That is, introduction of task migrations on top of preemptions increases hugely the number of different combinations of potential parallel interactions that may occur between tasks.

Another current area of weakness of global scheduling is the handling of critical sections. Intrinsically, global scheduling will incur greater overhead for lock and unlock operations than partitioned scheduling, because using light-weight local locking protocols for some critical sections is not an option. Moreover, the state of knowledge regarding suitable protocols for globally scheduled systems is behind that for partitioned systems. This author is unaware of any experiments with global scheduling analogous to those cited for partitioned scheduling in [26,21,41], but conjectures that when such experiments are done they will reveal that allocating global locks in scheduling priority order (as in [43,42]) out-performs FIFO service if scheduling priorities or deadlines are applied globally. Likewise, global application of scheduling priorities should also result in reduced blocking if the SRP's highest-locker priority is assigned to global lock holders, rather than the M-SRP's total nonpreemptibility.

8   Cracks in the Foundations

Despite progress in theoretical understanding of real-time scheduling on multiprocessors, there is cause for concern about the validity of the theory for actual systems. The problem is that real multicore processors do not fit the assumptions of the models on which the theory is based.

One false assumption is that jobs running on different processors have independent execution times. Concurrent jobs can already interfere on a single processor, but the interferences occur around context switch points, which are not very frequent and can be bounded. On a multiprocessor, cache and memory bus conflicts between jobs can occur throughout the jobs' executions. Even predicting context switching costs is potentially more complicated on a multiprocessor, as the cost of a switch will depend on whether it includes migration between processors, whether the migration crosses cache domains, and what other tasks do to the cache between context switches. For example, [22] reports cases, on an 8-core processor with shared L2 cache, where the cost of migration was less than the cost of preemption. They attributed this effect to migration allowing a preempted task to resume executing sooner than if it had been forced to wait for its previous processor to become available again, and so incurring less loss of cache affinity. Besides concurrent cache contention and task migrations, other dynamic factors that can affect execution times include prefetching-hardware contention, memory-controller contention, and memory-bus contention. These are reported to account for variations in execution time of "60%, 80% and sometimes 100%" between executions of the same program [19].

A second false assumption is that the execution time of a job will be independent of which core executes it and when. One example is reported in [47], where an undocumented asymmetry with respect to memory bandwidth between the cores on an Intel Xeon 5345 quad-core processor resulted in differences of up to 400% in completion times of identical jobs running in parallel on different cores. Another example is the "Turbo Boost" feature of the Intel^{TM} Core i7^{TM} processor, which varies the execution speed of each core in response to developing hot spots within the chip [23].

The central false assumption, which underlies both of those above, is that one can schedule processors to meet deadlines effectively while entirely ignoring the on-chip bus and memory network. The emerging picture is that with more cores the primary scheduling bottleneck shifts from the processors to the resources that move information between them. Scheduling the cores without accounting for this network is naïve and unlikely to produce satisfactory outcomes.

A few efforts have been made at static WCET analysis that predicts and accounts for cache misses on multicore processors. The methods appear to be intrinsically limited, by growth of the number of combinations of potentially interfering concurrent computations that must be considered, to very simple task and hardware models. None appear to have been tested against actual performance of a real system.

Perhaps the most ambitious WCET analysis attempt so far is [33]. It assumes the workload is specified as a finite set of jobs assigned statically to processors, which are related by precedence constraints. The system is represented graphically as a UML-like "message sequence chart", which shows how jobs trigger releases of other jobs across processors over time. The example studied is a two-core processor with private 2KB direct-mapped L1 cache and shared set-associative L2 cache with associativity ranging from 1 to 4 and size ranging from 1KB to 16KB. The analysis only considers instruction cache. The tasks are assumed to be scheduled by priority, but given the way the analysis process iteratively refines estimates of earliest start times and latest completion times along with the job WCET estimates, it could just as well produce a static schedule. So, this work supports consideration of static scheduling.

It is going to be very difficult to find WCET bounds for multicore machines that are simultaneously trustworthy and not absurdly high, and it is likely to become more difficult as one moves from static to partitioned to global scheduling. The lack of good WCET estimates is likely to severely limit practical applications of hard-real-time scheduling theory for multicore processors. Obtaining useful guarantees of hard deadlines at significant levels of system loading may just be impracticable.

9   Predictions

Supposing that the claims above about multicore processors are valid – including growing difficulties with execution time variability and bottlenecks within the on-chip – where are we headed? With the acknowledgment that this is a case of piling speculation upon speculation, here are some predictions.

The end of hard real time? There will be increasing pressure to design real-time systems that are "softer" in order to accommodate the increasing difficulty of obtaining reliable WCET estimates and the resultant decrease in precision and trustworthiness of schedulability analyses. Where hard deadlines cannot be avoided, designers will need verify them under conservative assumptions. Softer real-time tasks will need to get by with statistical performance estimates, derived from testing and static analysis based on observed execution times. The system scheduling policy will need to enforce bandwidth limitations on all tasks accurately enough support the requirements of the tasks with hard deadlines.

If it turns out that processors are no longer the system bottleneck, and if power can be saved while they are idle, achieving high processor utilization will be less important. Queuing theory and the utilization-bound results suggest that as the number of cores and the number of tasks go up, work flow will increasingly approximate a fluid – so long as individual tasks are small. Dedicating a core to a task that is too large to fit this model or has a very strict deadline may be wiser than trying to push processor utilizations to some limit that is believed to be safe based on an unrealistic theoretical model.

As suggested in Section 5, the time may be coming when the processor allocation problem resembles the memory and disk allocation problems. If so, it may be time to adopt similar management strategies, such as allocating time in equal quanta to better fit the fluid model, and allowing a reasonable amount of spare capacity to even out the flow.

Threads considered harmful? There will be pressures to re-think the thread-based concurrent programming paradigm. The concept of a thread as the basic unit of concurrent programming and the idea of threads sharing their entire address space seem to be firmly entrenched in programming languages, operating systems, and programming culture. However, if the rules of microprocessor architecture are changing, it may be time for these conventions to change also.

We should look closely at the current thread model with respect to demand for on-chip network bandwidth, ability to handle fine-grained concurrency, and inappropriate scheduling constraints.

Threads enforce more serialization than is required for some applications. Thinking in terms of threads has led researchers in scheduling theory to constrain the jobs of each task to be executed serially, and use only one processor at a time. If these constraints stand in the way of fully exploiting the parallel execution possibilities of a multiprocessor, pressure will build to relax them.

With enough processors, it becomes profitable to split jobs into smaller units that can run in parallel. The ability to split a job requires forethought in the software's design and coding, but the number of ways in which a job is split is a performance-tuning and scheduling decision, which depends on the hardware configuration and the rest of the workload. It is not clear that such details should be hard-coded into the software. It is not clear, either, that fine-grained parallelism introduced solely as an opportunity for performance improvement should be expressed using the same programming constructs as are used to express mandatory elements of asynchrony and concurrency derived from the problem domain, or be burdened by their heavier-weight semantics.

Several problems with threads come from *implicit* sharing of their entire memory space. If the programming language and operating system make it easy for threads to share variables, programmers will access variables from multiple threads without careful consideration, or even without awareness of doing it. This is bad, since variable sharing has negative consequences for software reliability, performance, and schedulability analysis. The more shared memory accesses a task makes, the more load it puts on the data paths between processors, caches, and memory, and the longer and more variable its execution times become. The more variables are shared intentionally the more chance for errors in synchronization, and of course every instance of unintentional sharing is a ticking bomb.

What to do in Ada? It is a good time to take inventory of the Ada language, to see what it provides for constructing reliable highly concurrent real-time software using multicore processors. What does the language have that helps or hurts? It is good that Ada has a well developed concurrent programming model. However, some specifics may not be so good. Should the language be changed, or should a particular style of usage be developed for multicore systems? Questions to consider include:

- How can we reduce casual memory sharing, and make intentional memory sharing more visible, with a view to modeling and managing the flows of data between cores?
- How can we design software that can make use of additional cores as they become available, without redesigning and re-coding, and in a way that is amenable to schedulability analysis?

Ada already has several features that make data sharing visible, including task entry parameters, protected objects, and the package sharing model of the Distributed Systems Annex. Would it be practical to program in Ada under the restriction that these be the *only* avenues for data sharing between threads? Would this be enough?

It might help to adopt an event-driven programming style, in which all computations are explicitly broken into jobs, which are queue-able data objects, executed by virtual servers. The servers could be implemented as Ada tasks. A system could be tuned by allocating multiple servers to a single queue, or having a single server serve multiple queues. Having the jobs carry much of their own data may reduce memory contention between cores. If the primary flows of data are via job objects, the flow of data between cores may be modeled and managed in terms of the flow of jobs. In this context, it may also be time to take a second look at the "featherweight task" model of [5] as well as other ways of expressing parallelism at a finer grain and with lower overhead than current Ada tasks.

These are just a few initial considerations. Inventive minds, with further practical experience using multicore processors, will surely think of more.

References

1. Abeni, L., Buttazzo, G.: Integrating multimedia applications in hard real-time systems. In: Proc. 19th IEEE Real-Time Systems Symposium, Madrid, Spain (December 1998)
2. Anderson, J., Srinivasan, A.: Mixed pfair/ERfair scheduling of asynchronous periodic tasks. In: Proc. 13th EuroMicro Conf. on Real-Time Systems, Delft, Netherlands, June 2001, pp. 76–85 (2001)
3. Andersson, B.: Global static-priority preemptive multiprocessor scheduling with utilization bound 38%. In: Baker, T.P., Bui, A., Tixeuil, S. (eds.) OPODIS 2008. LNCS, vol. 5401, pp. 73–88. Springer, Heidelberg (2008)
4. Andersson, B., Baruah, S., Jonsson, J.: Static-priority scheduling on multiprocessors. In: Proc. 22nd IEEE Real-Time Systems Symposium, London, UK, December 2001, pp. 193–202 (2001)
5. Baker, T.P.: Stack-based scheduling of real-time processes. Real-Time Systems 3(1), 67–100 (1991)
6. Baker, T.P.: An analysis of EDF scheduling on a multiprocessor. IEEE Trans. on Parallel and Distributed Systems 15(8), 760–768 (2005)
7. Baker, T.P.: An analysis of fixed-priority scheduling on a multiprocessor. Real Time Systems (2005)
8. Baker, T.P.: A comparison of global and partitioned EDF schedulability tests for multiprocessors. In: Int. Conf. on Real-Time and Network Systems, Poitiers, France, June 2006, pp. 119–127 (2006)
9. Baker, T.P., Baruah, S.K.: Sustainable multiprocessor scheduling of sporadic task systems. In: 21st Euromicro Conference on Real-Time Systems, ECRTS 2009, July 2009, pp. 141–150 (2009)
10. Baker, T.P., Cirinei, M.: Brute-force determination of multiprocessor schedulability for sets of sporadic hard-deadline tasks. In: Tovar, E., Tsigas, P., Fouchal, H. (eds.) OPODIS 2007. LNCS, vol. 4878, pp. 62–75. Springer, Heidelberg (2007)
11. Baruah, S.K.: Techniques for multiprocessor global schedulablity analysis. In: Proc. Real-Time Systems Symposium, December 2007, pp. 119–128. IEEE Computer Society Press, Los Alamitos (2007)
12. Baruah, S.K.: An improved EDF schedulability test for uniform multiprocessors. In: Proc. 16th IEEE Real-time and Embedded Technology and Applications Symposium (April 2010)
13. Baruah, S.K.: Schedulabilty analysis of global deadline-monotonic scheduling. Technical report, University of North Carolina, Dept. of Computer Science (2010)
14. Baruah, S.K., Burns, A.: Sustainable scheduling analysis. In: Proc. 27th IEEE Real-Time Systems Symposium (RTSS 2006), Rio de Janeiro, Brasil, December 2006, pp. 159–168 (2006)
15. Baruah, S.K., Cohen, N., Plaxton, C.G., Varvel, D.: Proportionate progress: a notion of fairness in resource allocation. Algorithmica 15, 600–625 (1996)
16. Bertogna, M., Cirinei, M., Lipari, G.: Improved schedulability analysis of EDF on multiprocessor platforms. In: Proc. 17th EuroMicro Conf. on Real-Time Systems, Palma de Mallorca, Spain, July 2005, pp. 209–218 (2005)
17. Bertogna, M., Cirinei, M., Lipari, G.: New schedulability tests for real-time task sets scheduled by deadline monotonic on multiprocessors. In: Anderson, J.H., Prencipe, G., Wattenhofer, R. (eds.) OPODIS 2005. LNCS, vol. 3974, pp. 306–321. Springer, Heidelberg (2006)

18. Bertogna, M., Cirinei, M., Lipari, G.: Schedulability analysis of global scheduling algorithms on multiprocessor platforms. IEEE Trans. on Parallel and Distributed Systems 20(4), 553–566 (2009)
19. Blagodurov, S., Zhuravlev, S., Lansiquot, S., Fedorova, A.: Addressing shared resource contention in multicore processors via scheduling. Technical report, Simon Fraser University (2009)
20. Block, A., Leontyev, H., Brandenburg, B., Anderson, J.H.: A flexible real-time locking protocol for multiprocessors, August 2007, pp. 47–56 (2007)
21. Brandenburg, B., Anderson, J.: A comparision of the M-PCP, D-PCP, and FMLP on LITMUS^{RT}. In: Baker, T.P., Bui, A., Tixeuil, S. (eds.) OPODIS 2008. LNCS, vol. 5401, pp. 105–124. Springer, Heidelberg (2008)
22. Brandenburg, B., Calandrino, J.M., Anderson, J.H.: On the scalability of real-time scheduling algorithms on multicore platforms: A case study. In: Proc. 29th IEEE Real-Time Systems Symposium, December 2008, pp. 157–169 (2008)
23. Charles, J., Jassi, P., Ananth, N.S., Sadat, A., Fedorova, A.: Evaluation of the of the Intel Core i7 Turbo Boost feature. In: IEEE Workload Characterization Symposium, pp. 188–197 (2009)
24. Dhall, S.K., Liu, C.L.: On a real-time scheduling problem. Operations Research 26(1), 127–140 (1978)
25. Gai, P., Lipari, G., Natale, M.D.: Minimizing memory utilization of real-time task sets in single and multi-processor systems-on-a-chip. In: Proc. 22nd IEEE Real-Time Systems Symposium, December 2001, pp. 73–83 (2001)
26. Gai, P., Natale, M.D., Lipari, G., Ferrari, A., Gabellini, C., Marceca, P.: A comparison of MPCP and MSRP when sharing resources in the janus multiple-processor on a chip platform. In: Proc. 9th IEEE Real-Time and Embedded Technology and Applications Symposium, May 2003, pp. 189–198 (2003)
27. Goossens, J., Funk, S., Baruah, S.K.: Priority-driven scheduling of periodic task systems on multiprocessors. Real Time Systems 25(2-3), 187–205 (2003)
28. Guan, N., Gu, Z., Deng, Q., Gao, S., Yu, G.: Exact schedulability analysis for static-priority global multiprocessor scheduling using model-checking. In: Obermaisser, R., Nah, Y., Puschner, P., Rammig, F.J. (eds.) SEUS 2007. LNCS, vol. 4761. Springer, Heidelberg (2007)
29. Guan, N., Stigge, M., Yi, W., Yu, G.: Fixed-priority multiprocessor scheduling with Liu & Layland's utilization bound. In: Proc. 16th IEEE Real-Time and Embedded Technology and Applications Symposium (April 2010)
30. Intel Corporation. Terra-scale computing program (2009), http://techresearch.intel.com/articles/Tera-Scale/1421.htm
31. Jansen, K., Porkolab, L.: Linear-time approximation schemes for scheduling malleable parallel tasks. In: Proceedings of the 10th Annual ACM-SIAM Symposium on Discrete Algorithms, pp. 490–498 (1999)
32. Kato, S., Yamasaki, N.: Portioned EDF-based scheduling on multiprocessors. In: Proc. 8th ACM International Conference on Embedded Software (EMSOFT 2008), pp. 139–148. ACM Press, New York (2008)
33. Li, Y., Suhendra, V., Liang, Y., Mitra, T., Roychoudhury, A.: Timing analysis of concurrent programs running on shared cache multi-cores, December 2009, pp. 57–67 (2009)
34. Liu, C.L., Layland, J.W.: Scheduling algorithms for multiprogramming in a hard real-time environment. Journal of the ACM 20(1), 46–61 (1973)
35. Lopez, J.M., Diaz, J.L., Garcia, D.F.: Minimum and maximum utilization bounds for multiprocessor rate monotonic scheduling. IEEE Trans. Parallel and Distributed Systems 15(7), 642–653 (2004)

36. Lopez, J.M., Garcia, M., Diaz, J.L., Garcia, D.F.: Worst-case utilization bound for EDF scheduling on real-time multiprocessor systems. In: Proc. 12th EuroMicro Conf. Real-Time Systems, pp. 25–33 (2000)
37. Lortz, V.B., Shin, K.G.: Semaphore queue priority assignment for real-time multiprocessor synchronization. IEEE Trans. Software Engineering 21(10), 834–844 (1995)
38. Lowney, G.: Why Intel is designing multi-core processors. In: SPAA 2006: Proc. 18th ACM symposium on Parallelism in Algorithms and Architectures, pp. 113–113. ACM, New York (2006)
39. Lundberg, L.: Analyzing fixed-priority global multiprocessor scheduling. In: Proc. 8th IEEE Real-Time and Embedded Technology and Applications Symposium, San Jose, CA, USA, pp. 145–153. IEEE Computer Society, Los Alamitos (2002)
40. Rajkumar, R., Sha, L., Lehoczky, J.P.: Real-time synchronization protocols for multiprocessors. In: Proc. 9th IEEE Real-Time Systems Symposium, pp. 259–269 (1988)
41. Ras, J., Cheng, A.M.K.: An evaluation of the dynamic and static multiprocessor priority ceiling protocol and the multiprocessor stack resource policy in an SMP system. In: Proc. 15th IEEE Real-Time and Embedded Technology and Applications Symposium, pp. 13–22 (2009)
42. Santiprabhob, C.S.C.P., Baker, T.P.: Reducing priority inversion in interprocessor synchronization on a fixed-priority bus. Technical report, Florida State University, Dept. of Computer Science, Tallahassee, FL (August 1991)
43. Santiprabhob, P., Chen, C.S., Baker, T.P.: Ada run-time kernel: The implementation. In: Proceedings of the 1st Software Engineering Research Forum, November 1991, pp. 89–98 (1991)
44. Sprunt, B., Sha, L., Lehoczky, L.: Aperiodic task scheduling for hard real-time systems. Real-Time Systems 1(1), 27–60 (1989)
45. Srinivasan, A., Baruah, S.: Deadline-based scheduling of periodic task systems on multiprocessors. Information Processing Letters 84, 93–98 (2002)
46. Stankovic, J.A., Spuri, M., Natale, M.D., Buttazzo, G.: Implications of classical scheduling results for real-time systems. IEEE Computer 28, 16–25 (1994)
47. Tuduce, I., Majo, Z., Gauch, A., Chen, B., Gross, T.R.: Asymmetries in multi-core systems – or why we need better performance measurement units. In: Exert 2010: The Exascale Evaluation and Research Techniques Workshop (March 2010)
48. Xu, J.: Multiprocessor scheduling of processes with release times, deadlines, precedence, and exclusion relations. IEEE Trans. Softw. Eng. 19(2), 139–154 (1993)

Control Co-design: Algorithms and Their Implementation*

Pedro Albertos[1],[**], Alfons Crespo[1], José Simó[1], and Adel Fernández[2]

[1] Instituto de Automática e Informática Industrial
Universidad Politécnica de Valencia
P.O. Box. 22012, E-46071, Valencia, Spain
{pedro,alfons,jsimo}@aii.upv.es
[2] Departamento de Automática y Computación
Inst. Superior Politécnico José Antonio Echeverría, La Habana, Cuba
adel@electrica.cujae.edu.cu

Abstract. This paper deals with the new approach in the design of hard real-time control applications where the control requirements as well as computing and communication constraints should be jointly taken into account to design a control application. Resource distribution and limitation, safety requirements and autonomy lead to the need of the so called co-design, where the integral problem of the design of the control structure, algorithm and its implementation should be tackled together. Along these lines, after a motivation, the interlacing between both design issues is analyzed and new concepts and architectures are proposed.

Keywords: real-time constraints, control safety, control structure, embedded control systems, networked control systems, event-based control systems, control kernel, control effort, time delays.

1 Introduction

Traditionally, control designers and software engineers work separately. The former conceive the control algorithms based on the required performance and the process knowledge, regardless of their subsequent implementation [10], whereas the software engineers deal with the control code without looking after the impact of the code execution in the control performance [7]. But their activities are interlaced and both designs should be jointly treated, mainly if the control tasks share resources with some other activities and these resources are limited. The real-time (RT) control design and implementation should be reviewed from both perspectives [14], [28] and a co-design approach should be adopted.

To this end, global requirements on control applications in time critical environments, such as automotive, aerospace or flight control, where multiple

---

* This project has been partially granted by Consellería de Educación under PROMETEO project number 2009-0268 as well as CICYT project SIDIRELI: DPI2008-06737-C02-01/02.
** Currently on leave at the Industrial Control Centre, University of Strathclyde, Glasgow, granted by the Ministerio de Educación (PR2009-0268).

J. Real and T. Vardanega (Eds.): Ada-Europe 2010, LNCS 6106, pp. 19–40, 2010.

interactive control loops are implemented, should be reviewed to extract their main requirements. Special attention should be devoted to new and widespread control scenarios where the controller is not anymore implemented in a dedicated computer without resources constraints, but sharing and competing for computing, storage and communication facilities with several other tasks. Embedded control systems [3], networked control systems [16] and event-based control systems [9] challenge the design of the control and its implementation where architectural issues play a relevant role in the controlled system performance [21]. Main issues in control co-design [8], other than control algorithms themselves, are the communication (networking) issues, the hybrid behavior, RT constraints in computing and scheduling, multi-mode operation and safety constraints. There is a need of support for RT activities, device drivers access, fault tolerance and distribution [20] with special emphasis on the minimal use of hardware and software. In this context, new software development models and middlewares ([27], [11]) are proposed to deal with quality of service of control performance as well as computing, communications and power resources availability. The ultimate goal of this technology is to allow the separation of complex control systems design from the RT tasks dynamic reconfiguration. Some key concepts interacting with both, the control performance and the control implementation, such as the control effort [5] or the control kernel [2] are emphasized and some general directions in the co-design are summarized.

Let us consider some examples:

Automotive. The so-called electronic car should rather be termed as automatic control car. A number of devices are located everywhere in different parts of the car to measure speed, temperature, flow, lightness, sliding... Initially most information provided by these devices was used for monitoring, to be displayed to the driver. At present instead, all these measurements are

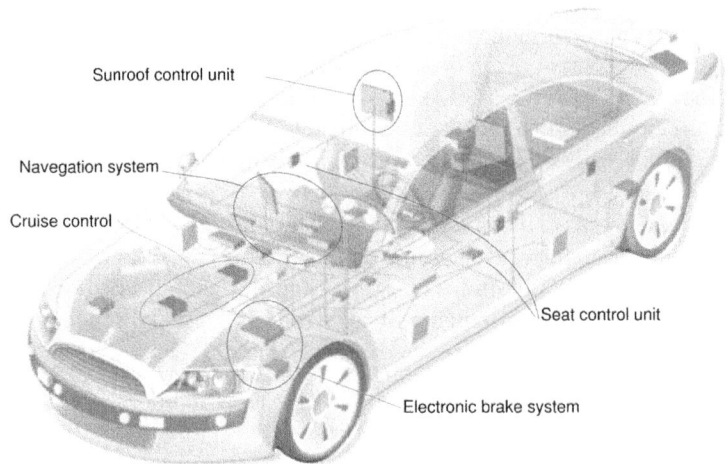

Fig. 1. A car with multiple distributed sensors

increasingly used to control many processes. They include servo braking (even brake-by-wire), computer assisted steering, traction control systems, active suspension, besides all the climate control, and invisible engine control, fuel efficiency and pollution control systems and the trusted cruise control. Some cars include collision avoidance systems and automated parallel parking. The information is distributed, and so is the actuation combining data from different sensors to elaborate the control actions (see Figure 1). And there are several local control units but there is a central control unit to coordinate all the activities. Anti-sliding control, speed control, engine control... do not work independently and according to the time and resources availability, the "best possible" control action is sent to the actuators.

The control, computer and communication network infrastructure in a car is substantial. At the present state of the art it may be viable to consider an internal wireless network rather than a wired network, purely from a fuel efficiency point of view (less cables = less weight = more fuel efficiency).

Aerospace and flight control. The continuous improvement in aerospace control should rely on integrated control systems seeking a variety of goals: flight control, control of power units, engine controls, utility systems, data fusion and concentration... All this requires a modular approach to design with upgradeable units and reusable components providing a fast and reliable operation, fault tolerance, reconfigurability and minimal resource requirements. Working in a harsh environment, the control must operate under different scenarios with variable availability of signals, power and general resources. In this context, special tools to rapid development and testing of the control solutions are required: design requirements translation at different levels, control design, code generation and testing.

Platforms to develop and test embedded control solutions have been proposed elsewhere [12]. We have built a very modular system involving the use of simulation facilities (Matlab®), RT development tools (Linux and Partikle[1]) and simple communication facilities to design and test control strategies for helicopters.

Industrial systems. Applications in the process industry are not in general as time demanding as the previous ones, but the number of signals, the distribution of subprocesses, sensors and actuators and the need to reduce the wiring and increase the reliability and safety of the applications also ask for a joint design of the control and its implementation. Networked and coordinated control are crucial issues in the process industry.

---

[1] PaRTiKle is a small footprint RT operating system designed for use in embedded systems. PaRTiKle [24] is especially well suited, but not limited, to work in combination with XtratuM technology. XtratuM [18] is a bare-metal hypervisor for RT systems that provides spatial and temporal isolation to many operating systems running as partitions. Several partitions can run simultaneously under RT constraints on top of the hypervisor. It is especially useful when a strong isolation of critical code is required.

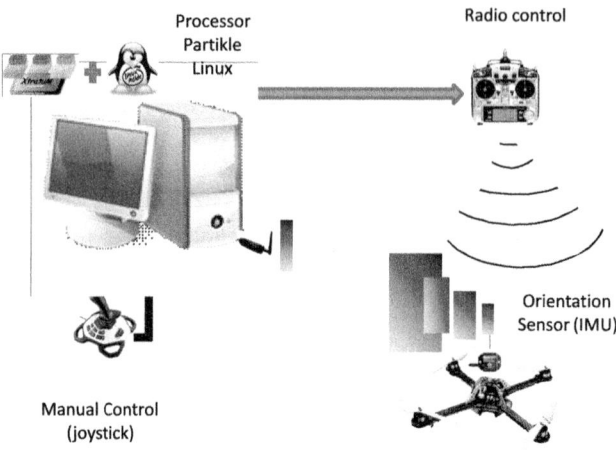

Fig. 2. A platform for prototypes development

The paper is structured as follows. In the next section, the computing requirements for control applications are reviewed. Then, the control algorithm requirements for an efficient RT implementation are discussed. New control scenarios with a space distributed operation have been developed recently. This is the topic of the next section, where networked systems and control over the network raise new challenges. Merging altogether, the need of simultaneously design the control and its implementation, the co-design, appears as the logical frame for the design of most RT control applications in the near future.

2   Computing Requirements for Control Applications

A standard periodic control loop implementation written in Ada 95 has the scheme shown in figure 3. The code is composed of two parts: specification and implementation. In the specification part the parameters associated with the task (initial-time, period and phase) are defined, while in the implementation part an infinite loop that executes at each period the actions related to the control (get external values, calculate the action value, send it, and compute global state) is included. This sequence may be changed or some tasks can be skipped according to the availability of resources.

This code corresponds to a classical control scheme where the computation of the control action can be undertaken using traditional techniques. However, more and more applications require complex computation and the use of exhaustive algorithms (unbounded algorithms) that can compromise the responsiveness of the system. If this is the case, the computation time should be split into a fixed (mandatory) part and an optional part (improvement).

The main requirements on SW/HW to run a control application are:

```
task Level_Control (initial_time, period, phase: TIME);

task body Level_Control is
level : Sensor_Value;
action : Actuator_Value;
reg : Regulator;
next_period : TIME;        -- period task attribute

begin
Define_Regulator(reg, par1, par2, ...);
....
delay until (initial_time + phase);
next_period := initial_time + phase;
loop
  level := get_level_sensor();
  Regulator_evaluate(reg, level, action);
  -- operations to improve the regulator results
  send_actuator(action);
  -- operations to evaluate the global state
  --operations to prepare the data for the next sampling
  -- operations of updating the global data base
  delay until next_period;
  next_period := next_period + period;
end loop;
...
end Level_Task;
```

Fig. 3. Standard control-loop implementation in Ada 95

– To have a quick an secure dispatch of a control action.
– To get a basic "picture" of the current situation.
– To compute a simple and fast control action to be improved if resources are available.
– To switch to the appropriate control mode, based on the resources availability.
– To reconfigure under detected faults.

To always provide a control action to the process, there should be a basic task organizing the back-up pile of control actions, by either pre-assignment or as a result of a batch computation. For instance, in model predictive control the algorithm computes a sequence of control actions to be applied at the next time instants, unless they are updated at the next sampling period. This default backlog should be stored and used, if no option to get better suggestions is available.

Not all the signals being treated have the same relevance (see next section). Thus, the system should give priority to those signals providing the fundamental knowledge about the current situation and the actions to be computed and delivered. In this sense, on-line rescheduling should allow to give the highest priority to these signals and their related treatment. This will ensure a safe operation of the control system.

In order to keep the process under control at any moment, a control action should be delivered at due time to the process. To that end, simple and fast control algorithms, probably not too performing but providing an adequate response, should be implemented with high priority, to be executed at the time required by the controlled process. If there is more time or, in general, more resources, a better action could be evaluated and the simplest one would be discarded.

Task mode management is related to the organization of tasks in different modes of operation. Several tasks included in a mode cooperate in the system control when some external conditions stand. For instance, under normal operation of a cruise navigation control, tasks involved in this mode take control of the different control loops, visualization and monitoring. If the system state changes and the system has to be managed in a different way, a mode-change event is raised and the operating system should stop the tasks involved in the previous mode and start those involved in the new mode. Tasks can be included in several modes with the same or different timing constraints. A mode change protocol is the method to implement this task switch. Protocols have to be efficient guaranteeing the system schedulability during the change phase [13], [17], [26].

Fault tolerance management is related to the detection and management of abnormal situations, such as missing data, emergency control or components fault. Error detection is a service that should be regarded as a basic functionality to achieve fault tolerance. Error management should advise in detail how the error or fault has to be handled, but it is more application dependent. Fault tolerance involves both questions, the detection of faults and, depending on the fault nature, its management or its propagation to the application.

RT control applications are paradigmatic applications where hard RT issues should be taken into account. They are reactive systems, gathering information from the environment, processing it and providing some actions in due time. And the information processing is done by sharing many resources with some other applications which also can be as demanding as them. Moreover, these applications may run in uncertain scenarios where operating conditions may change.

New trends in the control implementation regards infrastructure abstraction by means of middleware (Mw) components. Communication Systems such as DDS (Data Distribution System) [23],[22] provide the abstraction of communication details driving the data flow by specified QoS (Quality of Service) requirements. Data-centric approaches like DDS are specially well suited to develop event-based control systems (see Section 4.3). Using a publish/subscribe model, control applications can optimize the bandwidth usage but the control theory required to develop this kind of applications needs further development and maturity. In a similar way, the execution environment can be provided by middleware by using virtual machine technologies, i.e. RT Java (RTSJ).

Objects and agents can be deployed in a distributed execution platform also with the support of specific middleware like ORBit, PolyORB, RT-Corba or ACE+TAO[2]. In a similar way some research is focused on the definition of a

---

[2] These open source middlewares can be downloaded from the corresponding web pages, like [25].

middleware abstraction of basic control services: the Control Kernel (see Section 5). This abstraction provides an execution environment to deploy control applications.

In summary, let us consider the final picture of a software infrastructure supporting control applications as a bundle of interacting middlewares (Real-Time and Control Kernel) with the following desirable features:

- Real-time Mw: Data-centric and event-based communications driven by QoS and QoC (Quality of Control), specific time meta-information (time-stamps, temporal fire-walls, actual delays), Real-time Object Brokers, Redundancy support, Execution introspection in terms of QoC, delays and resources involved (bandwidth, computing time, power).
- Control Kernel Mw: Sampling, acting, signals holding, controller's switching management, default and "emergency" actions support, QoC management.
- Operating System: Real-time scheduling with dynamic load support, power management, fine-grained timing.

3   Control Algorithmic Requirements for RT Implementations

The execution of a control algorithm is not a unique activity and its parts may have different treatment, also depending on the environment. Let us discuss in some detail the issues involved in the RT implementation of the control algorithm.

3.1   Control Activities

In classic control design there are a number of basic assumptions about the control implementation [6], [7]:

- The data acquisition system is providing the required data.
- The actuators' drivers timely deliver the control actions.
- The CPU computes on-time the control action.
- The data required to perform the computations are stored in the memory.
- The sampling pattern is regular (constant, synchronous and uniform for any control task).
- The control goals as well as the control algorithms are fixed and well defined.
- Power supply is guaranteed.

It is difficult to guarantee the fulfilment of these assumptions in autonomous distributed control applications.

In digital control, the code to implement the control algorithm only takes a few lines but there are many other control related activities which are crucial to properly implement the control. The activities carried out in running a control algorithm should be analyzed and those which are more critical should be guaranteed under no matter which conditions the system is operating. Moreover, to run a control application in a safe mode, the following requirements should be fulfilled:

- A safe control action should be delivered at any required time to the process. This action may be the result of a detailed computation or simply a safe back-up command such as: *do nothing*.
- A supervisory control must make executive decisions and propose actions such as: *switch controllers, disconnect*, etc.
- A control action should be computed based on gathered data and a predefined algorithm: *On-Off, PID*[3], *Robust, Adaptive*, etc.
- Some data should be recorded, displayed, stored, updated.
- Communication links with other activities should be provided.

Not all activities have the same importance. It is evident that if there is no reaction to the process the computed control action becomes irrelevant.

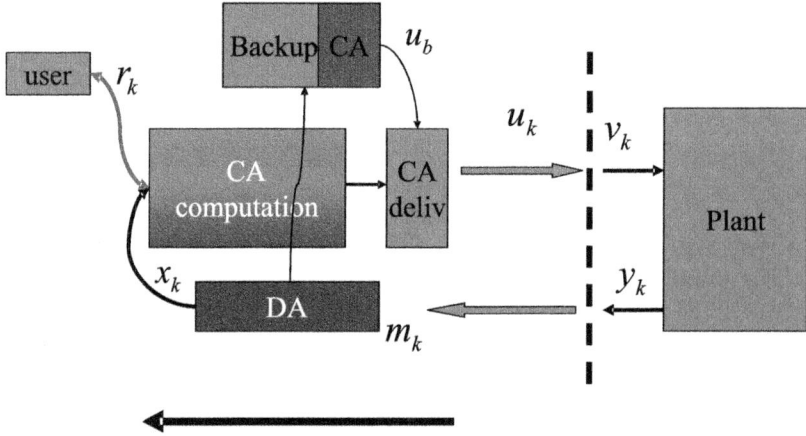

Fig. 4. Control activities

The activities shown in figure 4 can be ranked in order of relative importance as follows:

1. Assure the execution of a control action (CA) delivering. At least,
   - a safe back-up, or
   - a back-up based on previous (stored) data (defining the process situation).

   That is, there is always an action to be sent to the process. This action may be just a safe action (disconnect, open, close, etc) or it may depend on the current situation. It could be an emergency control action or, for instance, a previously computed suboptimal action.
2. Data acquisition of essential data, and then

---

[3] PID stands for Proportional-Integral-Derivative controller. See [4] for a basic overview of control concepts.

3. Compute (and deliver) a safe control action based on current data. If fresh data are gathered, the decision can be refined and updated, improving the safe control action or it can be decided to
4. Instigate a change of operation mode. This may require
   - Alarm treatment
   - Change to a new controller (structure and parameters)
   - Deliver a proper (back-up) control action.

Under normal operation, without resources constraints, these activities will be complemented by the following:

- Get the full set of required data and process it.
- Compute the current control action and deliver it.
- Evaluate and select the most appropriate control structure (i.e. which are the variables and the controllers involved in computing the control action).
- Communicate with the environment, other systems and/or the operator.
- Coordinate with higher decision levels.

Other than the control action delivering, the mode changing protocol and the fault treatment, a number of local decisions should be taken with a high priority:

- Detect missing data. Missing data should be replaced by estimated data. If it is not possible, a mode change should be initiated, in order to use a control structure not requiring the missing data.
- Evaluate control performance. This will allow the monitoring of the control task to decide if the control is properly working or some extra action should be taken.
- Determine the control action to be issued. Alternative controllers may compute different control actions. It should be decided which action is the most convenient to be applied and delivered to the process.
- Change the operating mode. As a result of any of the previous decisions.
- Compute back-up signals (CA and outputs). Have some alternatives ready in case there is some incident in the next sampling periods.

3.2 Models, Signals and Controllers

Most control algorithms are designed by using model-based approaches. That is, the controller design procedure uses in some way an abstraction, a model of the process to be controlled. Obviously, the more complex the process model is the more complex the controller results. And a complex controller implementation requires more computing resources, availability of a larger number of signals and usually a longer computation time.

In hard RT control applications alternative controllers based on different models should be available so as to use the most appropriate according to the current resource availability.

In the control action computation, some signals are fundamental and some others are complementary. Also, there may be different representations of the same variable depending on its accuracy, estimation procedure or time print. The quality of the signals will also determine their use. Missing data are usually replaced by old data, and are updated by extrapolation or prediction algorithms.

To compute the control action different controllers may be used. Each controller is characterized by its complexity (the number of operations required for its computation), the information required to run it (parameters and involved variables) and its computing time. The system must be able to decide the controller to be used as well as the required pre- and post- computing treatment of the involved signals.

3.3   Control Action Relevance: The Control Effort

In the sequential execution of multitasking activities as a result of simultaneously controlling several variables, that is dealing with multiloop control, there are inherent delays and jitter between the sampling of process signals and the delivering of control actions.

In digital control, the control loop is open in between two updates of the control input. Thus both delays and jitter influence the control performance. This influence[4] depends on the changes the controller produces in the controlled plant dynamics. In fact, if there is a soft control the absence of control action is not necessarily significant, but if we pretend to strongly change the plant behavior by the control action, then any delay will modify the result. In general, the stronger the change in dynamics is the worse the effect of any unaccounted delay. There are different ways to determine the relevance of a signal. In a qualitative way, the most relevant signal is that whose failure provokes the highest performance degradation in the system.

In this framework, it is interesting to introduce the concept of *control effort* as a measure of the change in the plant dynamics the control action produces[5]. Assume a multivariable process, with p measurements being stabilized/controlled by means of m control actions. Among these variables $(m + p)$ the most relevant one is the one that leads to a less stable behavior, if disconnected.

Altogether, the signals to be more accurately computed are those involving the greater control effort but also related to the more relevant controlled signals.

3.4   Control Algorithm

As a result, the design of the control algorithm must be able to adapt parameters and data of the controller as well as to reconfigure the control structure based on:

- New jitters and delays due to the rescheduling.
- Changes in the sampling period, due to changes in the resources availability.
- Model reduction of the process and/or controller, also due to changes in the resources and specially in the event of missing data.

---

[4] In some special cases this influence may be positive [1] but, in general, the control performance is degraded.

– Power availability, to change to simplest controllers if a lack of energy is
  expected in the next future.

Moreover, for many autonomous RT control applications, changes in operation
mode and environment should be accounted for in the equations of the control
algorithm.

There are several approaches to control algorithm design. First, to try to maxi-
mize the determinism of the control algorithm computation, avoiding looping and
options. This will result in a perfectly schedulable algorithm. If some flexibility is
introduced, then a robust design allowing to cope with different scenarios would
be required. The price we pay for that is a conservative and less performant control. Next step is to introduce a dynamic (active) robustness by changing the frame
according to the situation (i.e., gain scheduling). The best performing approach,
from the control viewpoint, but also the more demanding from the computing
viewpoint is to implement feedback scheduling [15], that is, to schedule the different activities based on current measurements taken on the process.

4   Challenging Control Scenarios

As already mentioned, new control scenarios have emerged. In particular, dealing with resource constraints (embedded control systems), distributed resources
(networked control systems) and non uniform/periodic sampling (event-driven
control). Let us discuss the main features of these new scenarios.

4.1   Embedded Control Systems

Most of the warnings and concerns discussed above apply to the design of Embedded Control Systems (ECS). RT control applications on embedded systems
require the best use of the available computation resources. The main advantages
they offer include the reduced price and size, broadening the scope of possible
applications: mass-production systems due to the cost reduction and specific accurate applications for their reduced size and high performance. But the most
important problem is the limited computational capabilities they can use. Short
sampling periods and non-delayed control actions which warrant better control
performance cannot be ensured.

Hence, one of the most important issues is related with the reliable and optimal use of the computational resources and what the resource shortage involves
in the design and implementation of the control algorithms. For these applications, it is not always possible to implement the control by using general
purpose operating systems because of the particular requirements in terms of
delays and jitter limitation. Thus, the control computations should be implemented as RT tasks being executed under a specific RT scheduling policy. In
this sense, the basic common features of ECS can be summarized as: compact
and reduced size, autonomy, reconfigurability, safety, fault tolerance and ability
to work under missing data operation conditions. In the end, one CPU, with its

own power supply, must control a number of variables in an uncertain environment. The problems to be considered are related to implementation, workload and resources sharing, and control performance degradation.

From the implementation point of view the same resources, and in particular the CPU, must be shared between different tasks. As a result of this competition for the CPU, time delays and jitter affect the activation times of tasks, which in turn has an effect on the performance of the control algorithm. Working in a changeable environment, the control goals and options may change and the control algorithms should be adequate to new scenarios. Thus, alternative control algorithms should be ready to get the control of the process. The changeable scheduling and data availability determines that variable delays should be considered, [14]. The synchronicity of signals cannot be ensured anymore. Any embedded control system should be proved to be reliable and safe operation should be ensured.

From a computational point of view low-cost algorithms should be designed to use as little computation time and memory as possible, and an easy update of information should be provided to allow for the shortest time in controller changes. Control algorithms should be split in mandatory and optional tasks, the later being only run if time is available. Switching between different control scenarios requires to consider supervisory levels, and resource saving claims for memory saving (storing only what is necessary) and optimal data transfer. On the other hand, for safety reasons hardware redundancy may be implemented if its cost, size and involved complexity is affordable and fault detection, isolation and system reconfigurability should be provided to allow an autonomous behavior.

ECS algorithms should be designed by using the most appropriate process model, with different levels of detail. Thus model reduction techniques should be considered to simplify either the plant model or the designed controller. As already mentioned, supervisory control is required to decide about the most suitable operation mode. This implies the design of hybrid controllers, taking care of the transfer between modes of operation. It is well known that, in general, the performance of the digital control degrades if the sampling period increases. Thus, if resources are available, the control tasks periods should be reduced and this implies changes in the controller parameters as well as in the stored information. One mandatory feature of ECS is a safe operation. Thus, control algorithms should provide always a control action, even under adverse conditions such as data missing, faults or lack of computation time to compute the most convenient control action.

Also, as discussed in the sequel, non regular sampling should be considered.

4.2   Networked Control Systems

A new order of complexity arises when the the control system is spread over a network of computing-sensing-acting devices (nodes) linked through different networking technologies.

Each node may house different devices, see figure 5, acting locally or through the network. In this scenario the RT analysis must be extended to take into account the

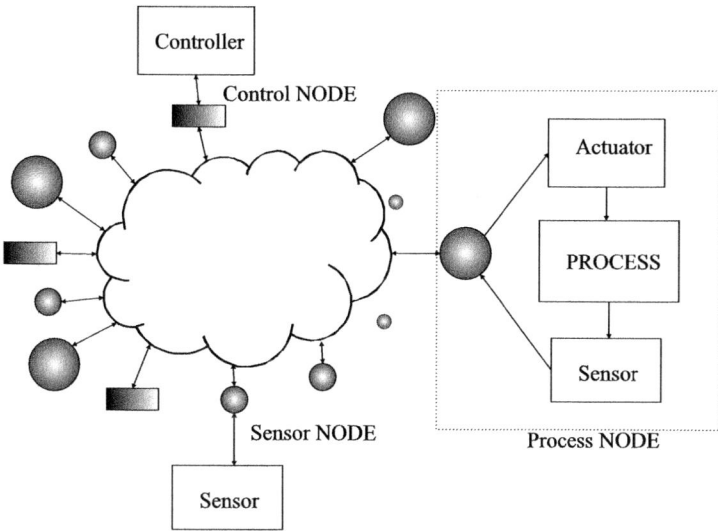

Fig. 5. Networked processes, processors, sensors and actuators

delays introduced by the communication infrastructure. Additionally, if some RT communication infrastructure is available, a scheduling plan for the involved buses should be obtained to ensure delay bounds. Given the specification of control tasks and the capabilities of computing and communication infrastructures, the off-line scheduling analysis should follow the next rough steps:

1. Identification of control tasks and mapping between tasks and processing nodes. After this mapping, the worst case execution time (WCET) of each task can be computed as resulting from the target processing architecture.
2. Identification of shared information and bus scheduling. Once the bus access protocols and scheduling have been determined the worst case for communication delays can be obtained.
3. Tasks scheduling for each node. If some task cannot meet its deadline, return to Step 1 and reassign tasks to nodes.

This approach has some weak aspects:

- The final implementation of the entire control system is too rigid. Tasks are assigned to nodes in the way that the movement of tasks among nodes or the inclusion/rejection of tasks from nodes should be foreseen at the design stage and modeled as "operation modes". Each operation mode provides a different scheduling scenario that must be analyzed off-line following the above mentioned three steps. Moreover, tasks belonging to each operation mode should be pre-loaded in affinity nodes in order to be ready to run if the operation mode changes. This fact usually leads to a memory over-consumption that impacts the hardware requirements. The design complexity can be assumed when the operation modes are well defined and the number of them is not too high taken into account the design resources and perhaps business bounds for design cost. This design complexity becomes intractable when the physical system to be controlled is highly dynamic and reconfigurable. In these cases a hierarchical decomposition of the problem must be made with, again, a consequent increase in design complexity.

Although from the computational point of view, the problems derived from the "operational modes" decomposition can be overcome, the main criticism to this approach comes from the control engineering field. The main problem here is the "mode switching" procedure. Engineers can ensure a stable performance of the controllers running in each mode but it is hard to ensure stability during the switching time, even more if the switching is random. New components should be included in the architecture to manage the mode switching in closed loop.

- As for the memory, the communication and processing specifications should be defined by the peak of load found among all operation modes (and perhaps influenced by the switching strategy). This leads to an increase of the cost of the computing infrastructure. This cannot be avoided but regarding the general low resource usage, systems should integrate into the scheduling components power management techniques as fine grained as possible in order to spend energy only when needed. This is especially important in nodes using wireless technology and battery powered.

- The maximum delay for a data transaction over the communication infrastructure provided by the off-line analysis is enough to feed schedulability analysis and verify that control deadlines are satisfied. But, again from the control engineering point of view, this maximum delay cannot be used to align samples in time and correct the control action by taking into account explicitly the real delay in the controller computations. In this context, communication technologies providing time meta-information together with data are very valuable.

4.3   Event-Driven Control

Regular sampled data systems are very popular. First because their mathematical treatment is well established and there are many control analysis and design techniques for them. Also, because digital control has been traditionally implemented in computer-based systems with a time driven operation. These two conditions match perfectly and excellent results are reported in the literature. Problems arise if there is lack of resources. Regular sampling implies the repeating of the control cycle at every period. It does not matter if it is needed or not, and it does not take into account if the sampling frequency is the one the control performance requires. The first change in this scenario is when the processed signals have different power spectrum. In this case they do not need to be sampled at the same rate. Then, multirate systems become a necessity, optimizing the use of the sensors, actuators and computing units. But we can go further. We can compute the control action just when it is needed. This is the basis of the so called *event-driven* control systems.

As summarized in the work of K. Åström [9], regular sampled data are unfeasible when dealing with distributed, asynchronous and multi time scale systems. In these cases, the control should be updated anytime an event is detected,

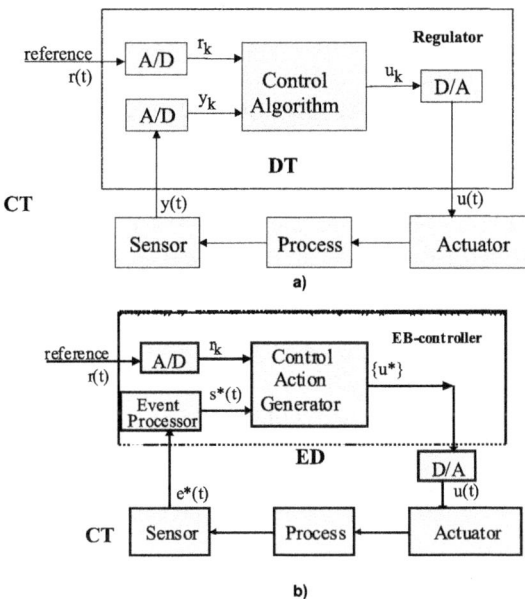

Fig. 6. Basic control loop: a) regular sampled data; b) event-driven

analyzed and a new control action is generated. In this conceptual case the control structure is different, as depicted in figure 6.

The sensor can be a local virtual sensor, processing the measurements and detecting an event signal $e^*(t)$ to be sent to the controller. The event processor determines $(s^*(t))$ what should be done and fires the control action generator. This block is a kind of "generalized hold" generating the series of signals u^* (it could be just a permanent one) to be sent to the actuator as far as no new event appears. In this way, the communication load is highly reduced and it only happens upon the occurrence of an event. As discussed in the next section, both the event detection and the storage of the future control actions can be done at a lower (the kernel) level.

There is a lot of work to do in this area and new tools to analyze the stability and performance of event-driven controllers should be developed. What is undoubtable is that this is the right approach to save resources without degrading performance.

5 Control Co-design: The Control Kernel

To fulfill the basic and common features of software applications, the kernel of a RT operating system (RTOS) provides an "abstraction layer" that hides from the application the hardware details of the target processor on which it runs. This permits the development of portable applications. Moreover, it ensures the execution of the most important activities.

In a similar way, the control kernel concept [2] can be interpreted as the basic services to be provided in order that the control application can be safely performed. This also requires to define which are the basic and most important control activities, in any control application, as outlined in Section 3.1.

The control kernel will be run with high priority. Its main goals are [2]:

1. To provide a flexible interface to manipulate the gathered information (including the registration and elimination of sensors) from a control application at execution time. In this way, it is possible to reconfigure the application under changing environments.
2. To provide a flexible interface to manipulate actuator devices, including their registration and elimination.
3. To keep control over the system in all situations. Each control subsystem must be able to autonomously control its corresponding part within the system.
4. The control kernel should be robust and adaptable to changing situations. Furthermore, it should detect fault conditions in sensors, actuators, communication networks, etc.

5.1   Main Features of the Control Kernel

As the processors operation has a sequential behavior, some basic activities should be implemented at a low level and with high priority to guarantee the availability of the resources they need and a timely response. Furthermore, as the ultimate platform where the controller will be implemented can change in the sense of computational resources, it is necessary to use a layered structure to accomplish the basic requirements of the control system.

The control kernel should be able to interact with the environment (sensors, actuators, communication channels), the OS and exchange information with the control algorithm implemented at application level. Also, it should cluster all common jobs of the control activities related to any variable, such as the data acquisition and the delivering of the control action [19].

Figure 7 shows these interactions, where the following abbreviations stand for:

- ADQ: Samples of variables.
- REF: Control references.
- ESM: Outputs, references and inputs estimation.
- CO: Control commands, including
  - Controller commuting
  - Change of controllers' parameters.
- SCA: Sending of control actions.
- SDI: State and diagnostic of inputs.

Taking into account the elements analyzed in section 3.1 the proposed architecture should have a *supervisor component* at the control kernel level. It will permit to apply each control strategy at the needed time and to carry out the following actions:

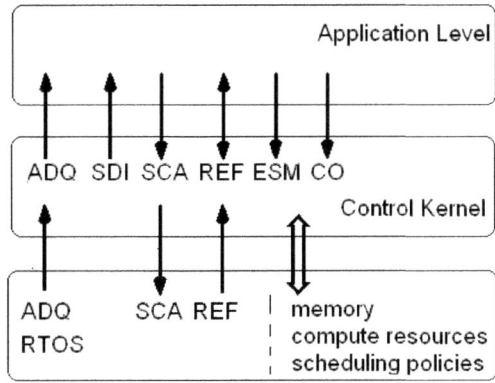

Fig. 7. Layers and interactions of the control kernel

1. To check the control variable measurements.
2. To check the control performance index.
3. To switch controllers.
4. To change the parameters of the controllers.
5. To send the estimated control actions.

The control kernel should have access to a set of alternative control actions from where it is possible to select and send the most appropriate one to the process. The algorithms corresponding to the most complex control strategies (i.e. optimal control, adaptive control, predictive control and intelligent control) should be run at the application level because they need a larger processing capacity. Other control strategies such as PID (all variants) or simple state feedback control will be allocated at the control kernel level and they will be identified as basic controllers. It is worth clarifying that the full control algorithm is not a part of the control kernel because it depends on the process to be controlled. This makes it possible to assure that the control kernel behaves deterministically because it is possible to determine with good precision the time required to compute the control action.

5.2   A Distributed Control Kernel Implementation

The control kernel should be conceived in a modular way, allowing a distributed implementation as well as different levels of complexity depending on the application. To this end, a distributed embedded control model can be defined as composed by two node types: *Light nodes* and *Service nodes* (see figure 8). Service nodes are powerful embedded computers running a full featured RTOS and complete networking with I/O capabilities. Light nodes are small and low power consumption processors with limited computing and networking capabilities but complete I/O features.

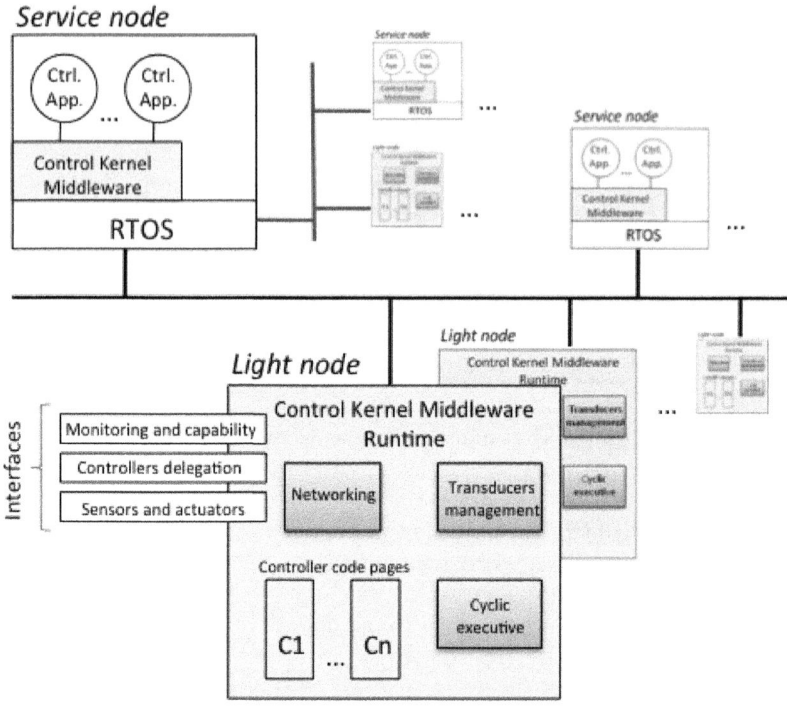

Fig. 8. Architecture of the distributed control kernel

Control applications run in service nodes on top of a fully featured *Control Kernel Middleware* (CKM). This middleware provides for abstractions and functionalities related to RT execution of control tasks, access to sensors and actuators, and communications management. The programming model of the CKM follows the concept of code delegation. In this sense, a control application delegates the execution of some control code to the CKM that provides computational resources to execute it. Note that a control task, once inside the CKM, can run on whatever service node of the DCS that has access to the communications space of the task.

Light nodes are a cost-effective solution to have some computing resources as close as possible to each actuator. This is mandatory in order to reduce the non-determinism in the time of delivering control actions to the controlled process. Light nodes run a retail of the CKM: *the CKM Runtime*. This Runtime communicates with the CKM offering interfaces for management, sensing and acting and code upload. Features of the CKM Runtime include network interfacing to sensors and actuators and controller code pages upload. A light node can be used as a simple slave component to interface the DCS or it can run local controllers in a cyclic executive environment.

Any controller of a control application that has been delegated to the CKM with attached native code page for the light node type, can be delegated to this

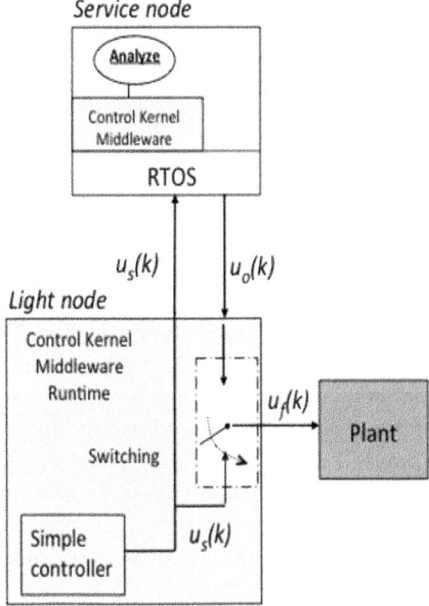

Fig. 9. Light nodes ensure that always exist a control action to be sent to the process $(u_o(k)$ or $u_s(k))$

light node by uploading this codepage and asking for switching. Controller pages can be uploaded through the CKM Runtime without any interference with the controllers currently running in the node. The uploaded pages are activated for running by the switching mechanism provided by the CKM Runtime.

In particular, service nodes may include supervising and optimizing control activities and light nodes can run activities to drive the system to a safe state or run a simple algorithm that guarantees a minimum of stability in the system at any time.

Let us consider the model depicted in figure 9. Two nodes are defined for this control kernel structure:

- The service node produces high-quality control responses $(u_o(k))$ which are sent to the light node to be applied on the plant. If $u_o(k)$ is not received or it has some delay, then the light node will apply his calculated control action $u_s(k)$.

- The light node controls directly the process and the service node only monitors and analyzes the sensory data and the control action $u_s(k)$ to determine if it is suitable. It ensures that there always exists a control action $(u_f(k))$ to be sent to the process. This signal may be just a safe action (disconnect, open, close, unchange, etc.) or the result of a simple calculus (computed locally in the node) $(u_s(k))$ or it may be the signal calculated $(u_o(k))$ and received from a service node.

When $u_o(k)$ is not detected or it is wrong, immediately the signal $u_f(k)$ is switched to a safe signal $u_s(k)$. This switching may be executed into a light or a service node. Under these circumstances, the service node can determine if it is necessary to change and delegate new code into the light node to execute other controller.

6   Discussion and Conclusions

In this work a biased analysis of the co-design of control algorithms and their implementation has been presented, mainly from a control viewpoint.

Initially, the requirements from both the control and computing perspective have been reviewed and some relevant application areas have been visited to emphasize the embedded character of many applications as well as the need for development platforms capable of speeding up the design and validation of integrated and complex RT control applications.

To fully develop a demanding RT control application, other than the end user requirements the constraints imposed by the implementation environment should be taken into account to get the best possible performance and, in any case, a safe operation. This co-design approach is always convenient but it becomes necessary if dealing with new control developments where resources are scarce, operating conditions are very changeable and there is a great uncertainty in the achievable results. In this sense, embedded control systems, with high autonomy and resources constraints, and networked control systems, with distributed and shared resources, are emblematic frameworks. And these settings are pervading most control applications.

The first consequence of this analysis is the re-structuring of the control algorithm implementation. It is not anymore a cyclic loop to be repeated periodically. The relevance of activities and signals should be pointed out. The most fundamental activities should be scheduled at a very low level and priority should be given to the most relevant signals. This leads to the concept of control effort and evokes the need for a basic layer, the control kernel, to execute the fundamental activities.

To save resources, all the activities leading to compute the control action should be only performed if needed, and in many cases there is a waste of resources to compute a control action being the same as the previous one or easily predicted from it. In this framework, event-based control systems offer a way to go. Unfortunately, the control theory required to design event-controlled plants is still in its dawn, and much effort should be devoted to reach the maturity that regular sampled-data-based approaches offer to the designers. Also from the communications viewpoint, event-based behavior is quite natural and new developments of communication systems, like DDS, go in this direction.

Let us conclude by emphasizing the concept of control kernel. This layer, implemented as a middleware in the control application, allows for greater reliability, reusability, transportability and safety in the design and operation of RT control applications.

References

1. Albertos, P.: Phase-conditionally stable systems. Systems & Control Letters 55, 803–808 (2006)
2. Albertos, P., Crespo, A., Simó, J.: Control Kernel: a Key concept in Embedded Control Systems. In: IFAC Conf. on Mechatronics (2006)
3. Albertos, P., Crespo, A., Vallés, M., Ripoll, I.: Embedded control systems: some issues and solutions. In: 16th IFAC World Congress (2005)
4. Albertos, P., Mareels, I.: Feedback and Control for Everyone. Springer, Heidelberg (2010)
5. Albertos, P., Olivares, M.: Time Delay Limitations in Control Implementation. In: European Control Conference, Karlsrue, Germany (1999)
6. Albertos, P., Vallés, M., Cuenca, A., Valera, A.: Essential control in Embedded Control Systems. In: IFAC Symp. On Cost Oriented Automation, Havana, Cuba (2007)
7. Årzén, K.-E., Cervin, A.: Control and Embedded Computing: Survey of Research Directions. In: Proc. 16th IFAC World Congress, Prague, Czech Republic (2005)
8. Årzén, K.-E., Cervin, A., Eker, J., Sha, L.: An Introduction to Control and Scheduling Co-Design. In: Proceedings of the 39th IEEE Conference on Decision and Control, Sydney, Australia (2000)
9. Åström, K.J.: Event based control In Analysis and Design of Nonlinear Control Systems. In: Honour of Alberto Isidori, vol. 147, pp. 127–147. Springer, Heidelberg (2007)
10. Åström, K.J., Wittenmark, B.: Computer controlled systems. Prentice Hall, Englewood Cliffs (1997)
11. Baliga, G., Kumar, R.: A Middleware for Control Over Networks. In: Decision and Control. European Control Conference, pp. 482–487 (2005)
12. Banning, R., Roesch, M., Morgan, A.: Improved Embedded Flight Control System Design Oricess using Integrated System Design/code Generation Tools, pp. 134–138. IEEE, Los Alamitos (1994)
13. Bertrand, D., Déplanche, A., Faucou, S., Roux, O.H.: A Study of the AADL Mode Change Protocol. In: Proceedings of the 13th IEEE international Conference on on Engineering of Complex Computer Systems. ICECCS, pp. 288–293. IEEE Computer Society, Washington (2008)
14. Cervin, A.: Integrated Control and Real-Time Scheduling. PhD Thesis. Departament of Automatic Control, Lund Institute of Technology, Lund, Sweden (2003)
15. Cervin, A., Ecker, J., Bernhardsson, B., Årzén, K.-E.: Feedback feedforward scheduling of control tasks. Real Time Systems 23(6), 25–53 (2002)
16. Chow, M.-Y., Tipsuwan, Y.: Network-Based Control Systems: a Tutorial. In: The 27th Annual Conference of the IEEE Industrial Electronics Society, pp. 1593–1600 (2001)
17. Crespo, A., Albertos, P., Vallés, M., Lluesma, M., Simó, J.: Schedulability issues in complex embedded control systems. In: IEEE International Symposium on Computer-Aided Control Systems Design, Munich, Germany (2006)
18. Crespo, A., Ripoll, I., Masmano, M., Arberet, P., Metge, J.J.: XtratuM an Open Source Hypervisor for TSP Embedded Systems in Aerospace. Data Systems In Aerospace DASIA, Istanbul, Turkey (2009)
19. Fernández, A., Vallés, M., Crespo, A., Albertos, P., Simó, J.: Middleware for Control Kernel Implementation in Embedded Control Systems. In: The 17th IFAC World Congress, Seoul, Korea (2008)

20. Kopetz, H.: Real-time systems: design principles for distributed embedded applications. Kluwer Academic Publishers, Dordrecht (1997)
21. Lee, E.A.: Cyber Physical Systems: Design Challenges. In: International Symposium on Object/Component/Service-Oriented Real-Time Distributed Computing, ISORC (2008)
22. OMG: Data Distribution Service for Real-Time Systems, v1.1. Document formal/2005-12-04 (2005)
23. Pardo-Castellote, G.: OMG Data-Distribution Service: architectural overview. In: Proceedings of 23rd International Conference on Distributed Computing Systems Workshops, Providence, USA, vol. 19-22, pp. 200–206 (2003)
24. Peiró, S., Masmano, M., Ripoll, I., Crespo, A.: PaRTiKle OS, a Replacement for the Core of RTLinux-GPL. In: 9th Real Time Llinux Workshop, Linz, Austria, Real-Time Systems Group, Polytechnic University of Valencia, p. 6 (2007)
25. PolyORB.: Distributed applications and middleware, http://polyorb.ow2.org/
26. Real, J., Crespo, A.: Mode Change Protocols for Real-Time Systems: A Survey and a New Proposal. Real-Time Systems 26(2), 161–197 (2004)
27. Schantz, R.E., Loyall, J.P., Rodrigues, C., Schmidt, D.C., Krishnamurthy, Y., Pyarali, I.: Flexible and Adaptive QoS Control for Distributed Real-Time and Embedded Middleware. In: Endler, M., Schmidt, D.C. (eds.) Middleware 2003. LNCS, vol. 2672, Springer, Heidelberg (2003)
28. Xia, F., Sun, Y.: Control-Scheduling Codesign: A Perspective on Integrating Control and Computing. NO.S. 1, 1352 (2006)

Dispatching Domains for Multiprocessor Platforms and Their Representation in Ada

Alan Burns and Andy Wellings

Department of Computer Science
University of York, UK
{burns,andy}@cs.york.ac.uk

Abstract. Multiprocessor platforms are becoming the norm for more powerful embedded real-time systems. Although Ada allows its programs to be executed on such platforms it provides no explicit support. If Ada is going to be an effective language for multiprocessor real-time systems then it needs to address the mapping issue that will allow the programmer to express their requirements for task to processor affinity. A number of different mapping and scheduling approaches are advocated in the scheduling literature. The primitives in the language should allow these schemes to be directly supported. In this paper we propose extensions to Ada 2005 to introduce the notion of dispatching domains, and we show how these can be used to implement two example multiprocessor scheduling approaches.

1 Introduction

One of the challenges facing real-time systems is how to analyse applications that execute on multiprocessor systems. Although current schedulability analysis techniques are in their infancy, approaches are beginning to emerge. In this paper, we consider the support that Ada can give to allow applications to be able to benefit from these new techniques. The facilities described in this paper originated from ideas developed at the International Real-Time Ada Workshop (IRTAW 14) in September 2009[1].

An increasing number of embedded applications are now executed on multiprocessor and multicore platforms. For non-real-time programs, it is usually acceptable for the mapping of tasks to processor (we shall use the term CPU in this paper) to be implementation defined and hidden from the program. For real-time programs, this is not the case. *The control of affinities is as important as the control of priorities.*

A difficulty with targeting language abstractions to multiprocessor systems is that there is more than one multiprocessor architecture. In addition, the facilities that operating systems provide to exploit the parallelism in the architecture vary with no accepted standards. Moreover, there is more than one method of representing parallel code in languages. In this paper we consider symmetric multiprocessors – SMPs (homogeneous MPSoCs), we assume base-line operating system facilities such as those

---

[1] The IRTAW series of workshops are unlike most workshops in that ideas are developed from submitted position papers. One of the main themes of IRTAW 14 was to develop proposed extensions to Ada 2005 to allow programs to exploit multiprocessor systems. The related position papers are [6,9,11,15,13,14]. This paper refines and develops the initial proposals.

J. Real and T. Vardanega (Eds.): Ada-Europe 2010, LNCS 6106, pp. 41–53, 2010.

available with the Linux 2.6 kernel, and concurrency constructs such as the Ada task and protected object.

The paper is structured as follows. We first briefly review the current provisions within Linux and the Ada language for multiprocessor execution. We then consider the basic requirements that any change to the language must try and address. In Section 4 we propose a set of language modifications that are aimed at satisfying these requirements. Two illustrations of the usage of these facilities are provided in Section 5. Some conclusions are then given.

2   Current Facilities

2.1   Linux

Since kernel version 2.5.8, Linux has provided support for SMP systems [8] via the notion of CPU affinity. Each process in the system can have its CPU affinity set according to a CPU affinity mask. The CPU affinity mask of a process determines the set of CPUs on which it is eligible to run.

```
#include <sched.h>

int sched_setaffinity(pid_t pid, unsigned int cpusetsize,
    cpu_set_t *mask);

int sched_getaffinity(pid_t pid, unsigned int cpusetsize,
    cpu_set_t *mask);

void CPU_CLR(int cpu, cpu_set_t *set);
int CPU_ISSET(int cpu, cpu_set_t *set);
void CPU_SET(int cpu, cpu_set_t *set);
void CPU_ZERO(cpu_set_t *set);
```

A CPU affinity mask is represented by the cpu_set_t structure. Four macros are provided to manipulate CPU sets. CPU_ZERO clears a set. CPU_SET and CPU_CLR respectively add and remove a given CPU from a set. CPU_ISSET tests to see if a CPU is part of the set. The first available CPU on the system corresponds to a cpu value of 0, the next CPU corresponds to a cpu value of 1, and so on. A constant CPU_SETSIZE specifies a value one greater than the maximum CPU number that can be stored in a CPU set.

sched_setaffinity sets the CPU affinity mask of the process whose ID is pid to the value specified by the mask. If the process specified by pid is not currently running on one of the CPUs specified in mask, then that process is migrated to one of the CPUs specified in mask. This action is performed by a high priority kernel thread called the migration thread (there is one thread per CPU)[5]. If necessary, an interprocessor interrupt is sent to force a reschedule on another processor.

sched_getaffinity allows the current mask to be obtained.

An error is returned if the affinity mask contains no processors that are physically in the system, or if `cpusetsize` is smaller than the size of the affinity mask used by the kernel.

The affinity mask is actually a per-thread attribute that can be adjusted independently for each of the threads. The value returned from a call to `gettid` (get thread id) can be passed in the argument `pid`.

Two final points are worth making. The first is that unless the Real-Time Preemption patch is installed then preemptive priority-based scheduling across processor cannot be guaranteed. The second point is that the set of CPUs that are allocated to a process can be constrained externally to that process. Hence, the set passed to `sched_setaffinity` is filtered by the Linux kernel so that only the allowed CPUs are used. This allowed set can be changed asynchronously using the "cpuset virtual file system"[7].

Other operating systems provide slightly different facilities, but the Linux support is typical of what can be expected.

2.2   Ada

The Ada Reference Manual allows a program's implementation to be on a multiprocessor system. However, it provides no direct support that allows programmers to assign their tasks onto the processor in the given system. The following ARM quotes illustrate the approach.

> "NOTES 1 Concurrent task execution may be implemented on multicomputers, multiprocessors, or with interleaved execution on a single physical processor. On the other hand, whenever an implementation can determine that the required semantic effects can be achieved when parts of the execution of a given task are performed by different physical processors acting in parallel, it may choose to perform them in this way." ARM Section 9 par 11.

This simply allows multiprocessor execution and also allows parallel execution of a single task if it can be achieved, in effect, "as if executed sequentially".

> "In a multiprocessor system, a task can be on the ready queues of more than one processor. At the extreme, if several processors share the same set of ready tasks, the contents of their ready queues is identical, and so they can be viewed as sharing one ready queue, and can be implemented that way. Thus, the dispatching model covers multiprocessors where dispatching is implemented using a single ready queue, as well as those with separate *dispatching domains*." D.2.1 par 15.

This allows the full range of partitioning identified below. However, currently the only way that an implementation can provide the mechanisms to allow programmers to partition their tasks amongst the available processors is via implementation-defined pragmas, or non-standard library packages. For example, GNAT uses a pragma called `Task_Info` and an associated package `System.Task_Info` which provides platform specific information.

3   Basic Requirements

The primary real-time requirement for supporting the execution of Ada tasks on SMPs is to manage the mapping of tasks to processors. We assume that we are concerned with real-time code, in which case the execution of any task can be view as a sequence of invocations or *jobs*. Between jobs, the task is blocked, waiting either for an event (typically an external interrupt) or for a future time instance[2].

To cater for the allocation/mapping of tasks/jobs to processors, two basic approaches are possible:

1. **Fully Partitioned** – each task is allocated to a single processor on which all its jobs must run; and
2. **Global** – all tasks/jobs can run on all processors, jobs may migrate during execution.

There are many motivation for choosing either global or partitioned allocation, some of these motivations come from issues of scheduling [2]. These details are not significant here, what is important is that the Ada language should be able to support both schemes.

From these schemes, two further variants are commonly discussed: for global scheduling, tasks are restricted to a subset of the available CPUs; and for partitioned scheduling, the program can explicitly change a task's affinity and hence cause it to be moved at run-time.

Restricting the set of CPUs on which a task can be globally scheduled supports scalability – as platforms move to contain hundreds of CPUs, the overheads of allowing full task migration become excessive and outweigh any advantage that might accrue from global scheduling. Controlled changing of a task's affinity has been shown to lead to improved schedulability for certain types of application [12,1].

There may be other non-real time requirements for a mapping facility. For example, coscheduling where tasks *must* run in parallel is sometimes quoted as a requirement for high performance computing [10]. Alternatively, there is often a perceived need to have a group of tasks share access to a processor's data cache. The programmer doesn't care which processor they run on as long as it is the same processor. In both these cases, the tasks are tightly coupled and regularly exchange data. From a real-time perspective, the former can be achieved (approximately) by setting the priorities of the tasks to the same value. The later can only be achieved by fixing the tasks to a single processor (or a set of globally scheduled processors that have a common cache). We note that analysis models for these two use cases (with their strict definitions) have yet to be derived.

In the following discussions, in keeping with the terminology in the current Ada Standard, we will use the term *processor dispatching domain* (or just *dispatching domain*) to represent a group of processors across which global scheduling occurs. A task is said to be *assigned* to a dispatching domain; and if it is partitioned to execute on just one CPU, it said to be *set* to that CPU.

---

[2] Of course, this view of an Ada task is not explicitly enforced by the Ada language semantics. Rather, tasks should follow this convention to be amendable to schedulability analysis.

4   Language Modifications

We propose facilities to allow the processors allocated to an Ada program to be partitioned into a number of *non-overlapping* dispatching domains. Every task is scheduled within a dispatching domain. A task may also be assigned to execute on just one CPU from within its associated dispatching domain. We assume that the set of processors allocated to a program is not changed during its execution. Any external change to the set is outside the control of the Ada program and is likely to result in erroneous program execution. The following issues are addressed:

- representing CPUs and CPU sets,
- representing dispatching policies and dispatching domains,
- identifying interrupt affinities,
- ceiling priorities and locking.

Although the these proposals are designed to support SMP systems, the goal is that they should be applicable to more general systems such as those with different CPU speeds and/or those with non-uniform memory access times[3]. *All the facilities discussed here are on a per-partition basis.*

4.1   Representing CPUs and CPU Sets

First, a simple representation of the multiprocessor platform is required. A simple integer type is used to represent the range of CPUs (CPU_Range). These definitions are give here in a child package of System, although they could just be added to System:

```
package System.Multiprocessors is
   type CPU_Range is range 0 .. <implementation-defined>
   function Number_Of_CPUs return CPU_Range;
end System.Multiprocessors;
```

Typically, operating systems provide a means of specifying a collection of CPUs using a bitset. Here, we provide a private type in a child package[4].

```
package System.Multiprocessors.CPU_Sets is

   type CPU_Set is private;
   Default_CPU_Set : constant CPU_Set;   -- includes all processors

   procedure Zero(Set: in out CPU_Set);
   procedure All_Set(Set: in out CPU_Set);
   procedure Set_One(Set: in out CPU_Set; Processor : CPU);
   procedure Clear(Set: in out CPU_Set; Processor : CPU);
   procedure Set_Many(Set: in out CPU_Set; Processors : CPU_Set);
```

---

[3] Platforms containing processors with different instruction sets are not considered here. The assumption is that they are best addressed using the Ada *partition* concept, and treated more like distributed systems than multiprocessor systems.

[4] As the Ada language evolves to support other architectures such as NUMA and cc-NUMA, further data structures may need to be introduced; for example, the processor domain and the node domains that are defined in Linux.

```
   procedure Clear(Set: in out CPU_Set; Processors : CPU_Set);
   function Is_Set(Set: in CPU_Set; Processor : CPU) return Boolean;

private
   ...
end System.Multiprocessors.CPU_Sets;
```

We note that for SMPs, a simpler representation is possible using just a subrange within
CPU_Range.

4.2   Representing Dispatching Policies and Dispatching Domains

Dispatching Policies

Ada supports a range of dispatching options all from within a priority-based dispatching
framework. These are defined in a hierarchy of packages rooted in the Ada.Dispat-
ching package. Each of the policies can be applied across the whole priority range
or within bands of priorities. The dispatching policy is set using pragmas and applies at the partition level. To extend this framework to allow the dynamic creation
of dispatching domains, it is first necessary to have a more formal definition of a
dispatching policy as a predefined type within the language. Here, we introduce this
type (Dispatching_Domain_Policy) in the Ada.Dispatching package. We
also define a subtype to represent the policies that can be used with priority-specific
dispatching.

```
with System; use System;
package Ada.Dispatching is
   pragma Pure(Ada_Dispatching);

   Dispatching_Policy_Error : exception;

   type Dispatching_Domain_Policy is private.

   type Policy is (Priority_Specific_Dispatching,
                   Non_Preemptive_FIFO_Within_Priorities,
                   FIFO_Within_Priorities,
                   Round_Robin_Within_Priorities,
                   EDF_Across_Priorities);

   subtype Priority_Specific is Policy range
     FIFO_Within_Priorities .. EDF_Across_Priorities;

   procedure Set_Policy(DDP : in out Dispatching_Domain_Policy;
                        P : Policy);

   procedure Set_Priority_Specific_Policy(
               DDP : in out Dispatching_Domain_Policy;
               P : Priority_Specific; Low : Priority; High : Priority);
   -- raises Dispatching_Policy_Error if
   --    DDP has not been set to Priority_Specific_Dispatching, or
   --    High is not greater than Low, or
   --    any priority from Low to High had already been set
```

```
private
  -- not defined by language
end Ada.Dispatching;
```

A series of calls of the final procedure allows the program to construct the required priority-specific allocations.

We note that a more extendible representation of these policy types is possible.

Dispatching Domains

Although this proposal allows the dynamic creation of dispatching domains, there is one main restriction. This is the dispatching policy for the domain must be specified at the time the domain is created. Once specified it cannot be changed.

The following package (defined here as an extension to `Ada.Dispatching`) allows the group of CPUs to be partitioned into a finite set of non-overlapping `Dispatching_Domains`. One dispatching domain is defined to be the `System` dispatching domain; the environmental task and any derived from that task are allocated to the `System` dispatching domain by default. Subprograms are defined to allow new dispatching domains to be created and their scheduling policies defined.

Tasks can be assigned to a dispatching domain and be globally scheduled within that dispatching domain according to the defined scheduling policy for its priority level. Alternatively they can be assigned to a dispatching domain and set to a specific CPU within that dispatching domain. Tasks cannot be assigned to more than one dispatching domain, or set to more than one CPU.

```
with Ada.Task_Identification; use Ada.Task_Identification;
with Ada.Real_Time; use Ada.Real_Time;
with System.Multiprocessors; use System.Multiprocessors;
with Ada.Dispatching; use Ada.Dispatching;
with System; use System;
package Ada.Dispatching.Domains is

   type Dispatching_Domain is private;

   System_Dispatching_Domain : Dispatching_Domain;

   function Create(PS : in CPU_Set;
     DDP : in Dispatching_Domain_Policy) return Dispatching_Domain;
   -- Checks to see if the processors are in the system
   -- dispatching domain; if so, remove from system scheduling
   -- domain and add to the new domain, set the scheduling policy
   -- for the domain
   -- raise Dispatching_Policy_Error
   --     if the system cannot support global scheduling
   --       of the processors identified in PS, or
   --     if processors not in system dispatching domain, or
   --     if in system scheduling domain but has a task set, or
   --     if the allocation would leave the system dispatching domain
   --       empty, or
   --     if Dispatching_Domain_Policy has not been assigned
```

```
function Get_CPU_Set(DD : Dispatching_Domain) return CPU_Set;
function Get_Dispatching_Domain(T : Task_Id := Current_Task)
         return Dispatching_Domain;

procedure Assign_Task(DD   : in out Dispatching_Domain;
                      T  : in Task_Id := Current_Task);
-- raises Dispatching_Domain_Error if T is already assigned
-- to a dispatching domain

procedure Assign_Task(DD   : in out Dispatching_Domain;
                      P : in CPU_Range;
                      T : in Task_Id := Current_Task);
-- raises Dispatching_Domain_Error if P not in DD or if
-- T is already assigned

procedure Set_CPU(P : in CPU_Range; T : in Task_Id := Current_Task);
-- raises Dispatching_Domain_Error if P not in current DD for T

procedure Free_CPU(T : in Task_Id := Current_Task);

function Get_CPU(T : in Task_Id := Current_Task) return CPU_Range;
-- returns 0 if T is not set to a specific CPU

procedure Delay_Until_And_Set_CPU(
    Delay_Until_Time : in Ada.Real_Time.Time; P : in CPU_Range);
-- raises Dispatching_Domain_Error if P not in
-- current DD for calling task

private
  -- not defined by the language
end Ada.Dispatching.Domains;
```

The required behaviour of each subprogram is as follows;

- Create – Creates a dispatching domain with a dispatching policy. The identified CPUs are moved from the System dispatching domain to this new domain. A CPU cannot be moved if it has a task assigned to it. The System dispatching domain must not be emptied of CPUs as it always contains the environmental task[5].
- Get_CPU_Set and Get_Dispatching_Domain – as their names imply.
- Assign_Task – There are two Assign_Task procedures. One allocates the task just to a dispatching domain (for global scheduling) the other allocates it to a dispatching domain and sets a specific CPU within that dispatching domain (for partitioned scheduling).
- Set_CPU – sets the task to a specified CPU. The task will now only execute on that CPU.
- Free_CPU – removes the CPU specific assignment. The task can now execute on any CPU within its dispatching domain.
- Get_CPU – returns the CPU on which the designated task is assigned.
- Delay_Until_And_Set_CPU – delays a task and then sets the task to the specified CPU when the delay expires. This is needed for some scheduling schemes.

---

[5] Note, there still is only one environmental task. There is no requirement for parallel elaboration of an Ada partition.

In addition to these two packages there are two new pragmas required to control the affinity of tasks during activation:

```
pragma Dispatching_Domain (DD : Dispatching_Domain);
pragma CPU (P : CPU_Range);
```

The following points should be emphasized.

- All dispatching domains have the same range of priorities (`System.Any_Priority`).
- The 'System' dispatching domain, `System_Dispatching_Domain`, is subject to the policies defined using the configuration pragmas: `Task_Dispatching_Policy` and `Priority_Specific_Dispatching`.
- A task has, by default, the dispatching domain of its parent. If the parent is assigned to a processor, then so is the child task.
- A task that wishes to execute, after a delay, on a different CPU and with a different deadline (for EDF scheduling) must use a Timing Event.

Finally, there are a number of implementation characteristic that must be documented, and there will be certain implementation advice useful to include in the ARM. For example the CPU(s) on which the clock interrupt is handled and hence where delay queue and ready queue manipulations (and user code - Timing Events) executed must be documented. As there is no scheduling between dispatching domains an implementation is recommended to have distinct queues per dispatching domain. If the Ada environment is being implemented on a system that has predefined dispatching domains, the details of these domains should also be documented.

4.3 Interrupt Affinities

Ada programs identify interrupt handlers using pragmas within protected objects. Although interrupts may be directed (on some architectures) to particular CPUs, the assumption here is that their Ada handlers (the associated protected objects) are accessible from all CPUs as they simply reside in main memory.

There is, however, a need to know on which CPU interrupt code will execute. Hence the following should be added:

```
function Get_CPU(I: Interrupt_Id) return CPU_Range;
-- returns 0 if interrupt is handled by more than one CPU
```

4.4 Ceiling Priorities and Locking

The current Ada mechanism for accessing protected objects from multiple CPUs is not fully defined by the language. Instead, implementation advice is given. In this, the assumption is that tasks will busy-wait (spin) at their active priorities for the lock (although other implementations are allowed). This is not changed by the proposals in this paper.

However, the non-lock optimization that is typically used in uniprocessor implementation is no longer viable on a multiprocessor platform. Generally, protected objects require a real lock in this environment unless all user tasks accessing the object are set to the same CPU.

The following guidelines on setting ceiling priorities can be given:

- For global scheduling – setting the ceiling priority of a protected object that is *only* accessed within a single dispatching domain can use the usual approach of setting ceilings to max priority of the accessing tasks plus 1 (note it must be plus 1 for global scheduling to work).
- Fixed tasks – Where tasks are fixed to a processor in the same dispatching domain, care must be taken and the interaction between tasks and protected object must be understood when setting the ceilings. It is probably safest to force non-preemptive execution of protected subprograms by setting the ceiling to the highest priority. It may also be advantageous to spin at this ceiling level as well.
- For protected objects shared between dispatching domains, the protected objects must run non-preemptively. This is because there is no relationship between the priorities in one allocation domain and those in another.

It should also be noted that on multiprocessor systems:

- Nested protected object locks can cause deadlock (there are some schemes in the literature to avoid this – for example for each chain another lock must be acquired first[4]).
- Chain blocking is possible.
- In the absence of deadlock, blocking can be bounded.

Programmer control over ceilings allows protocols such as non-preemptive execution of 'shared' POs to be programmed. No further language provision is required.

5   Examples

To illustrate the expressive power of the facilities advocated in this paper we will outline how two particular scheduling schemes can be programmed. Further examples of the use of the basic model is presented in [3], which can be found in the same proceedings as this paper.

5.1   Task-Splitting

Here we will use only the system dispatching domain but we will set tasks to execute on specific processors.

This scheme, called *task-splitting*, has gained some attention recently[12,1] as it attempts to combine the benefits of static and global partitioning. The scheme uses EDF scheduling on each CPU with task-partitioning for most tasks. A small number of tasks are however allowed to migrate at run-time, they execute for part of their execution time on one CPU and then complete on a different CPU. For N CPUs, there are N-1 split tasks.

Consider a dual-processor system with therefore just one split task. This task, `Split`, will be assumed to have a period of 20ms and a relative deadline equal to its period. The worst-case execution time of the task is 3.2ms. The splitting algorithm (the details are not relevant here) calculates that the task should execute on CPU 1 for 1.7ms (within a deadline of 5ms) and then switch to CPU 2 to execute its remaining 1.5ms (within its final relative deadline of 20ms).

It uses a `Timer` to change the task's processor allocation and deadline of the task once it has executed for 1.7ms. This is achieved by the following protected object:

```ada
with Ada.Dispatching.EDF; use Ada.Dispatching.EDF;
with Ada.Dispatching.Domains; use Ada.Dispatching.Domains;
...
protected Switcher is
  procedure Register(ID : Task_ID; E : Time_Span);
  procedure Handler(TM :in out Timer);
private
  Client : Task_ID;
  Extended_Deadline : Time_Span;
end Switcher;

protected body Switcher is
  procedure Register(ID : Task_ID; E : Time_Span) is
  begin
    Client := ID;
    Extended_Deadline := E;
  end Register;

  procedure Handler(TM :in out Timer) is
    New_Deadline : Deadline;
  begin
    New_Deadline := Get_Deadline(Client);
    Set_Deadline(New_Deadline + Extended_Deadline,Client);
      -- extends deadline by fixed amount passed in as E
    Set_CPU(2,Client);
  end Handler;
end Switcher;
```

The task itself would have the following outline.

```ada
pragma Task_Dispatching_Policy(EDF_Across_Priorities);
with Ada.Dispatching.EDF; use Ada.Dispatching.EDF;
with Ada.Dispatching.Domains; use Ada.Dispatching.Domains;
...

task Split is
  pragma Relative_Deadline(Milliseconds(5));
  pragma Priority (15); -- computed from deadline of task
  pragma CPU(1);
end Split.

task body Split is
  Id : Task_ID := Current_Task;
  Switch : Timer(ID'Access);
  Next : Time;
  First_Phase : Time_Span := Microseconds(1700);
  Period : Time_Span := Milliseconds(20); -- equal to full deadline
  First_Deadline : Time_Span := Milliseconds(5);
  Temp : Boolean;
```

```
begin
  Switcher.Register(ID,Period-First_Deadline);
  Next := Ada.Real_Time.Clock;
  loop
    Switch.Set_Handler(First_Phase,Switcher.Handler'Access);

    -- code of application

    Next := Next + Period;
    Switch.Cancel_Handler(Temp); -- to cope with task
                                 -- completing early (ie < 1.7ms)
    Set_Deadline(Next+First_Deadline);
    Delay_Until_And_Set_CPU(Next,1);
    -- a Timing Event could be used to combine the last two operations
  end loop
end Split;
```

5.2 Two Separate Domains

Here we consider a system with 8 or more processors, the first 4 are to be placed in one dispatching domain (the default) and will employ fixed priority dispatching (i.e. the default dispatching policy). The other processors will be placed into a second domain employing a partitioned scheme in which the lower 20 priorities are to be used for EDF scheduling and the others for fixed priority scheduling.

Here we provide the library package that will set up the second domain. The relevant predefined packages are assumed to be present.

```
procedure Set_Up(Second_Domain : out Dispatching_Domain);
  DP : Dispatching_Domain_Policy;
  CP : CPU_Set;
begin
  Set_Policy(PP, Priority_Specific_Dispatching);
  Set_Priority_Specific_Policy(PP, EDF_Across_Priorities,
    Priority'First, Priority'First + 20);
  Set_Priority_Specific_Policy(PP, FIFO_Within_Priority,
    Priority'First+21, Priority'Last);

  Zero(CP); -- clear mask
  for CPU in 5 .. Number_Of_CPUs loop
    Set_One(CP, CPU);
  end loop;

  Second_Domain := Create(CP,DP);
end Set_Up;
```

6 Conclusions

Historically, Ada has always taken a neutral position on multiprocessor implementations. On the one hand, it tries to define its semantics so that they are valid on a multiprocessor. On the other hand, it provides no direct support for allowing a task set to be partitioned. This paper has presented a set of facilities that could gain wide support and would help Ada system developers migrate their programs to what is becoming the default platform for embedded real-time systems.

The assumptions underlying the proposals made in this paper is that an Ada program has access to a fixed set of CPUs on the execution platform. Any external changes to the set of available processors is outside the control of the Ada program and is likely to result in erroneous program execution.

Acknowledgements

The ideas presented in this paper were initially suggested by the authors and then refined by the participants at the IRTAW 14 and in conjunction with the Ada Rapporteur Group. We gratefully acknowledge their contributions.

References

1. Andersson, B., Bletsas, K.: Sporadic multiprocessor scheduling with few preemptions. In: Euromicro Conference on Real-Time Systems (ECRTS), pp. 243–252 (2008)
2. Andersson, B., Jonsson, J.: Fixed-priority preemptive multiprocessor scheduling: to partition or not to partition. In: Proceedings of the International Conference on Real-Time Computing Systems and Applications (2000)
3. Andersson, B., Pinho, L.M.: Implementing multicore real-time scheduling algorithms based on task splitting using Ada 2012. In: Real, J., Vardanega, T. (eds.) Ada-Europe 2010. LNCS, vol. 6106, pp. 54–67. Springer, Heidelberg (2010)
4. Block, A., Leontyev, H., Brandenburg, B.B., Anderson, J.H.: A flexible real-time locking protocol for multiprocessors. In: Proceeding of the 13th IEEE International Conference on Embedded and Real-Time Computing Systems and Applications, RTCSA 2007 (2007)
5. Bovet, D.P., Cesatí, M.: Understanding the Linux Kernel, 3rd edn. O'Reilly, Sebastopol (2006)
6. Burns, A., Wellings, A.J.: Supporting execution on multiprocessor platforms. In: Proceeding of the 14th International Workshop on Real-Time Ada Issues (IRTAW 14) (to appear)
7. Linux Kernel Documentations. CPUSets. Technical report (2008), http://linux.mjmwired/kernel/Documentation/cpusets.txt
8. Linux Manual Page. sched_setaffinity(). Technical report (2006), http://linux.die.net/man/2/sched_setaffinity
9. Michell, S., Wong, L., Moore, B.: Realtime paradigms needed post Ada 2005. In: Proceeding of the 14th International Workshop on Real-Time Ada Issues, IRTAW 14 (2005) (to appear)
10. Ousterhout, J.K.: Scheduling techniques for concurrent systems. In: Proceedings of Third International Conference on Distributed Computing Systems, pp. 22–30 (1982)
11. Ruiz, J.: Towards a ravenscar extension for multiprocessor systems. In: Proceeding of the 14th International Workshop on Real-Time Ada Issues (IRTAW 14) (to appear)
12. Shinpei, K., Nobuyuki, Y.: Portioned edf-based scheduling on multiprocessors. In: EMSOFT, pp. 139–148 (2008)
13. Wellings, A.J., Burns, A.: Beyond Ada 2005: allocating tasks to processors in smp systems. In: Proceedings of IRTAW 13, Ada Letters, vol. XXVII(2), pp. 75–81 (2007)
14. Wellings, A.J., Malik, A.H., Audsley, N.C., Burns, A.: Ada and cc-numa architectures. what can be achieved with Ada 2005? In: Proceeding of the 14th International Workshop on Real-Time Ada Issues (IRTAW 14) (to appear)
15. White, R.: Providing additional real-time capabilities and flexibility for Ada 2005. In: Proceeding of the 14th International Workshop on Real-Time Ada Issues (IRTAW 14) (to appear)

Implementing Multicore Real-Time Scheduling Algorithms Based on Task Splitting Using Ada 2012

Björn Andersson and Luís-Miguel Pinho

CISTER-ISEP Research Centre,
Polytechnic Institute of Porto, Portugal
bandersson@dei.isep.ipp.pt, lmp@isep.ipp.pt

Abstract. Multiprocessors, particularly in the form of multicores, are becoming standard building blocks for executing reliable software. But their use for applications with hard real-time requirements is non-trivial. Well-known real-time scheduling algorithms in the uniprocessor context (Rate-Monotonic [1] or Earliest-Deadline-First [1]) do not perform well on multiprocessors. For this reason the scientific community in the area of real-time systems has produced new algorithms specifically for multiprocessors. In the meanwhile, a proposal [2] exists for extending the Ada language with new basic constructs which can be used for implementing new algorithms for real-time scheduling; the family of task splitting algorithms is one of them which was emphasized in the proposal [2]. Consequently, assessing whether existing task splitting multiprocessor scheduling algorithms can be implemented with these constructs is paramount. In this paper we present a list of state-of-art task-splitting multiprocessor scheduling algorithms and, for each of them, we present detailed Ada code that uses the new constructs.

Keywords: Ada, multiprocessors, multicores, real-time scheduling.

1 Introduction

Despite multiprocessors, in the form of multicores, becoming the norm in current computer systems, their use for applications with real-time requirements is non-trivial. The reason is that although a comprehensive toolbox of scheduling theories is available for a computer with a single processor, such a well-established comprehensive toolbox is currently not available for multicores.

One of the emerging and most interesting classes of multiprocessor scheduling algorithms today is called task-splitting scheduling algorithms [3-9]. With such an algorithm, most tasks are assigned to just one processor, whilst a few tasks are assigned to two or more processors and may migrate in a controlled manner (the migration may be performed in the middle of the execution of a job) so that at every instant, such a task never executes on two or more processors simultaneously. This class is appealing because the algorithms in this class (i) cause few (and provably small number of) preemptions and (ii) can be proven to be able to schedule task sets to meet deadlines even at high processor utilizations.

J. Real and T. Vardanega (Eds.): Ada-Europe 2010, LNCS 6106, pp. 54–67, 2010.

The Ada community has shown an increasing interest in real-time scheduling on multicores [2,10,13] and a proposal exists [2] for extending the language for real-time scheduling on multicores. Our initial opinion was that the proposed extension seemed useful for implementing task splitting, but it is important to fully evaluate its appropriateness considering the task splitting scheduling algorithms that have already been published.

Therefore, in this paper, we present Ada code for implementing a subset of the current task splitting scheduling algorithm. From the extensive set of previously published algorithms, we have selected the ones [4,8,9] that perform best (in terms of being able to schedule tasks at high utilization and generating few preemptions), and that allow showing how different types of approaches can be programmed in Ada. We would like to note, nevertheless, that the algorithm in [3] could be also used, but it may require very small execution segments at highly precisely specified time intervals, something which is difficult to achieve in practice.

We find that the new proposal [2] is sufficient for implementing those task splitting algorithms [4,8,9] that we believe are useful to designers. Attaining efficient implementations of them may require a new timing construct however.

The remainder of this paper is organized as follows. Section 2 presents the system model and gives an overview of the algorithms. Section 3 presents the recently proposed language extension. Sections 4 to 6 present Ada programs for the dispatchers of the task splitting algorithms. Section 7 provides conclusions.

2   System Model and Algorithm Overview

We consider the problem of scheduling a set of tasks $\tau = \{\tau_1, \tau_2, \ldots, \tau_n\}$ on m processors. A task τ_i is characterized by T_i, D_i, and C_i with the interpretation that the task τ_i releases a (potentially infinite) sequence of jobs such that (i) the time between two consecutive jobs of the same task is at least T_i and (ii) each job must complete C_i units of execution within at most D_i time units from the release of the job. We assume that a job cannot execute on two or more processor simultaneously. We also assume that a processor cannot execute two or more jobs at the same instant. We assume that a job needs no resource (such as shared data structures) other than a processor for execution.

We distinguish between three types of task sets:

- In an implicit-deadline task set, each task τ_i has $D_i = T_i$;
- In a constrained-deadline task set, each task τ_i has $D_i \leq T_i$;
- In an arbitrary-deadline task set, each task τ_i is not constrained by the above ($D_i = T_i$ or $D_i \leq T_i$).

In this paper, we focus on algorithms for constrained-deadline task sets. In order to understand task splitting algorithms, let us consider the following example.

Example 1. Consider three tasks to be scheduled on two processors. Each task τ_i has $T_i = D_i = 1$ and $C_i = 0.51$. We can assign task τ_1 to processor 1 and task τ_3 to processor 2 and then let task τ_2 be assigned to both processors 1 and 2; we say that τ_2 is a *split task*. This splitting should be done in a controlled manner; for example do the splitting of τ_2 so that τ_2 requires 0.379 units of execution on processor 1 and 0.131 units of execution on processor 2. Since τ_2 is assigned to two processors, it is important that dispatchers on each processor ensure that τ_2 never executes on two or more processors simultaneously.   □

In task splitting algorithms, there are three approaches for ensuring that a split task does not execute on two or more processors simultaneously:

- Slot-based split-task dispatching;
- Job-based split-task dispatching;
- Suspension-based split-task dispatching.

Slot-based split-task dispatching is used in [4, 5, 7]. Figure 1 shows the idea. Time is organized into timeslots of equal size and these timeslots are synchronized across all processors. The time interval of a timeslot is partitioned into three sub-time-intervals, one in the beginning of the timeslot, one in the middle of the timeslot and one in the end of the timeslot. A split task is assigned to the beginning sub-time-interval of one processor and the end sub-time-interval of another processor; these time intervals must be dimensioned so that the task meets its deadline and so that there is no overlap in time between the subintervals.

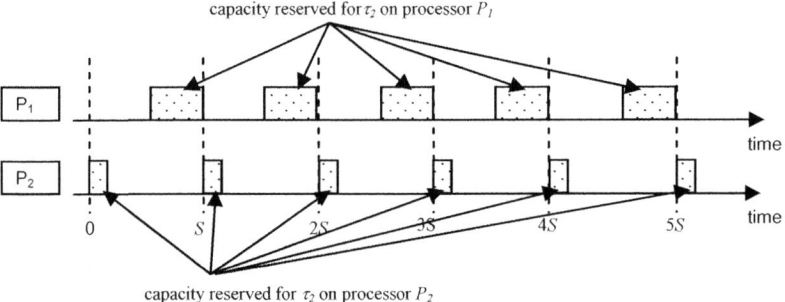

Fig. 1. Slot-based split-task dispatching: How to perform run-time dispatching of a task that is assigned to two processors. A white rectangle with black dots indicates capacity reserved for task τ_2.

τ_2 is a split task. When a job of τ_2 arrives, it executes on processor 1 and then it migrates to processor 2.

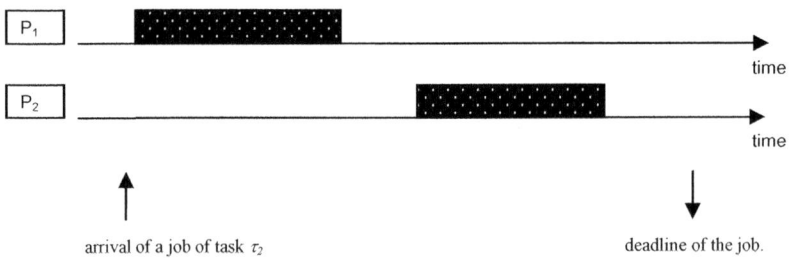

Fig. 2. Job-based split-task dispatching: How to perform run-time dispatching of a task that is assigned to two processors. A dark rectangle with white dots indicates execution of the job of task τ_2.

Job-based split-task dispatching is used in [8, 9]. Figure 2 shows the idea. There are no timeslots. Instead, when a job is released, a certain condition is setup specifying when the job should migrate to another processor. This condition can be that a certain amount of time has elapsed since the release of the job (used in [9]) or that a certain amount of execution has been performed by the job (used in [8]).

Suspension-based split-task dispatching is similar to job-based split-task dispatching but the default case is that all pieces of a job are ready all the time on all processors to which the split task is assigned. But when the job executes on one processor, it suspends the job on the other processors.

Slot-based split-task dispatching and job-based split task dispatching are areas of active research in the real-time systems research community. The slot-based split-task dispatching offers higher utilization bounds whereas the job-based split task dispatching offers fewer preemptions.

Suspension-based split-task dispatching is not possible in the proposed Ada model for multiprocessors, since there is a single ready queue within the same allocation domain. It is also currently not explored in the real-time systems research community. The authors believe this is because suspension-based split-task dispatching provides utilization bounds and preemption bounds similar to the job-based split-task dispatching but with the suspension-based split-task dispatching there is the drawback that it can happen that an event (say a release of a job) on processor 1 causes a context switch on processor 2 which in turns causes a context switch on processor 3 and so on.

Hence, we will only discuss (i) slot-based split-task dispatching and (ii) job-based split-task dispatching, because we believe they are most relevant for software developers.

3 Language Extensions

Burns and Wellings have proposed in [2, 10] language extensions for real-time scheduling on multicores, which after discussion in the International Real-Time Ada Workshop [13] have been proposed for the upcoming Ada revision [14]. This section presents the proposed extension, but limited to what is necessary for implementing the task splitting algorithms (more details on this proposal can be found in [16]).

The proposed extension defines appropriate packages for handling the set of CPUs available to the program, and the creation of non-overlapping dispatching domains:

```
package System.MultiProcessors is
   type CPU_Range is range 0..<implementation-defined>;
   function Number_Of_CPUs return CPU_Range;
end System.MultiProcessors;

package System.MultiProcessors.CPU_Sets is
   type CPU_Set is private;
   Default_CPU_Set : constant CPU_Set;
   procedure All_Set( Set: in out CPU_Set);
end System.MultiProcessors.CPU_Sets;

package Ada.Dispatching is
   type Dispatching_Domain_Policy is private;
   -- other declared types and subprograms not shown here
end Ada.Dispatching;
```

```
package Ada.Dispatching.Domains is
   type Dispatching_Domain is  private;
   System_Dispatching_Domain: Dispatching_Domain;

   -- other declared subprograms not shown here

   procedure Set_CPU(P : in CPU_Range;
                     T : in Task_Id := Current_Task);

   procedure Delay_Until_And_Set_CPU(
                     Delay_Until_Time : in Ada.Real_Time.Time;
                     P : in CPU_Range);
end Ada.Dispatching_Domains;
```

Procedure Set_CPU is fundamental for task splitting as it allows to dynamically change the allocation of tasks to specific CPUs.

Although not used in this paper, the capabilities for supporting more than one dispatching domain are very interesting for other approaches. For example, it is also important for some partitioned cluster approaches (such as in [7]) since it allows detecting incorrect assignment of tasks to processors. Also, it is useful for improving the performance of algorithms that do not use task splitting. For example, global scheduling with EDF suffers from poor ability to meet deadlines for certain task sets but this effect can be mitigated by subdividing processors into disjoint dispatching domains and applying global scheduling with EDF on each dispatching domain (such an approach is sometimes called *clustered-global EDF* [12]).

4   Slot-Based Split Tasks Dispatching

The algorithm described in this section is the one in [4], and it is shown in Figure 1. The algorithm is intended for implicit-deadline sporadic tasks. The left column of page 4 in [4] gives a good description of the dispatching algorithm. In this section, we reformulate it with the proposed Ada extensions.

To illustrate task splitting, we will consider a task set $\tau=\{\tau_1, \tau_2, \tau_3\}$ to be scheduled on two processors. The tasks are characterized as $T_1=100$ ms, $T_2=200$ ms, $T_3=400$ ms, $D_1=100$ ms, $D_2=200$ ms, $D_3=400$ ms and $C_1=51$ ms, $C_2=102$ ms, $C_3=204$ ms.

Recall that the algorithm depends on a timeslot; the size of the timeslot is $TMIN/\delta$, where $TMIN$ is the minimum of T_i of the task set and the parameters δ can be chosen by the user. We choose $\delta=4$ and apply it to the example above and this gives us that the timeslot has a duration of 25 ms. Also, the algorithm depends on a parameter SEP which specifies how much we can fill-up a processor when we (i) assign tasks to processors and (ii) split tasks. Using Equation 27 in [4] tells us for $\delta=4$ that $SEP=0.889$.

The task assignment/splitting algorithm in [4] gives us the following (for $\delta=4$, $SEP=0.889$). Task τ_1 is assigned to processor 1; task τ_3 is assigned to processor 2; task τ_2 is assigned to both processor 1 and to processor 2 and the splitting of this task is specified by two variables, *hi_split* and *lo_split*, with values $hi\_split[1]=0.379$ and $lo\_split[2]=0.131$. Intuitively, this means that 37.9% of the processing capacity of processor 1 will be used for task τ_2 and analogously 13.1% of the processing capacity of processor 2 will be used for task τ_2. Together these figures (37.9% and 13.1%) give us the utilization of the task τ_2 (51%).

Recall that the timeslot duration is 25 ms. Due the unknown phasing of the task arrival related to the slot start, the algorithm specifies that a reserve on processor 1 for task τ_2 should occupy a fraction $hi\_split[1]+2\alpha$ of the duration of the timeslot and a reserve on processor 2 for task τ_2 should occupy a fraction $lo\_split[2]+2\alpha$ of the duration of the timeslot. (The value of α is computed based on δ; see Equation 9 in [4]; in this example α becomes 0.02786.) Therefore, the duration of the reserve for processor 1 becomes 4.668 ms and for processor 2 becomes 10.868 ms.

The code is as follows:

```ada
pragma Priority_Specific_Dispatching (EDF_Across_Priorities, 1, 10) ;
pragma Priority_Specific_Dispatching (FIFO_Within_Priorities, 11, 12);

with Ada.Real_Time.Timing_Events; use Ada.Real_Time.Timing_Events;
with Ada.Task_Identification; use Ada.Task_Identification;
with Ada.Dispatching.Domains; use Ada.Dispatching.Domains;
with System.Multiprocessors; use System.Multiprocessors;
with Ada.Real_Time; use Ada.Real_Time;
with Ada.Dispatching.EDF; use Ada.Dispatching.EDF;
with Ada.Asynchronous_Task_Control; use Ada.Asynchronous_Task_Control;

Period_Task_1               : constant Time_Span:=Milliseconds( 100);
Min_Inter_Arrival_Task_2 : constant Time_Span:=Milliseconds( 200);
Period_Task_3               : constant Time_Span:=Milliseconds( 400);

Deadline_Task_1             : constant Time_Span:=Milliseconds( 100);
Deadline_Task_2             : constant Time_Span:=Milliseconds( 200);
Deadline_Task_3             : constant Time_Span:=Milliseconds( 400);

Execution_Time_Task_1       : constant Time_Span:=Milliseconds(  51);
Execution_Time_Task_2       : constant Time_Span:=Milliseconds( 102);
Execution_Time_Task_3       : constant Time_Span:=Milliseconds( 204);

TMIN : constant Time_Span := Milliseconds( 100);
Time_Slot_Delta : constant integer := 4;
Time_Slot_Length : constant Time_Span := TMIN / Time_Slot_Delta;
Alpha : constant float := 0.02786; -- this is computed based on
                                   -- Time_Slot_Delta

CPU_1 : constant CPU_Range := 0;
CPU_2 : constant CPU_Range := 1;
Reserve_Phase_1_Task_2 : constant Time_Span:= Microseconds( 4668);
Reserve_Phase_2_Task_2 : constant Time_Span:= Microseconds(10868);

Start_Time : Time := Clock;

type Current_Phase is (Not_Released, Phase_1, Suspended, Phase_2);


protected type Sporadic_Switcher is
    pragma Priority(12);
    procedure Register(ID : Task_ID; Phase_1_CPU, Phase_2_CPU: CPU_Range;
                       Phase_1_Reserve, Phase_2_Reserve : Time_Span);
    procedure Handler(TM :in out Timing_Event);
    procedure Release_Task;
    procedure Finished;
    entry Wait;
private
    Released: Boolean := False;
    Switch_Timer: Timing_Event;

    Client_ID : Task_ID;
    Client_Phase_1_CPU, Client_Phase_2_CPU   : CPU_Range;
    Client_Phase_1_Reserve, Client_Phase_2_Reserve : Time_Span;
```

```
      Client_Current_Phase : Current_Phase;

      End_of_Phase_1, Start_of_Phase_2, End_of_Slot: Time;
   end Sporadic_Switcher;

   task Task_1 is
      pragma Priority (1);
   end Task_1;

   task Task_2 is
      pragma Priority (11);
   end Task_2;

   task Task_3 is
      pragma Priority (1);
   end Task_3;

   protected body Sporadic_Switcher is
      procedure Register(ID : Task_ID; Phase_1_CPU, Phase_2_CPU: CPU_Range;
                         Phase_1_Reserve, Phase_2_Reserve : Time_Span) is
      begin
         Client_ID := ID;
         Client_Phase_1_CPU := Phase_1_CPU;
         Client_Phase_2_CPU := Phase_2_CPU;
         Client_Phase_1_Reserve := Phase_1_Reserve;
         Client_Phase_2_Reserve := Phase_2_Reserve;
      end Register;

      procedure Handler(TM :in out Timing_Event) is
      begin
         case Client_Current_Phase is
            when Not_Released =>
               Set_CPU(Client_Phase_2_CPU, Client_ID);
               Switch_Timer.Set_Handler(End_of_Slot, Handler'Access);
               Client_Current_Phase := Phase_2;
               Released := True;
            when Phase_1 =>
               Client_Current_Phase := Suspended;
               Switch_Timer.Set_Handler(Start_of_Phase_2, Handler'Access);
               -- between slots - do nothing just set timer, alternative would
               -- be to lower priority to a "background" level priority
               -- more work conservative but we decided to maintain the algorithm as
               -- is in the original paper
               Hold(Client_ID); -- This call puts the task to sleep; it will not
-- execute on any CPU until "continue" has been
                                -- performed on it.
            when Suspended =>
               Set_CPU(Client_Phase_2_CPU, Client_ID);
               Switch_Timer.Set_Handler(End_of_Slot, Handler'Access);
               Client_Current_Phase := Phase_2;
               Continue(Client_ID);
            when Phase_2 =>
               Set_CPU(Client_Phase_1_CPU, Client_ID);
               Switch_Timer.Set_Handler(End_of_Phase_1, Handler'Access);
               Client_Current_Phase := Phase_1;
         end case;
      end Handler;


      procedure Release_Task is    -- called by someone else or by interrupt
         Number_of_Slots: Integer;
         Release_Time, Slot_Start: Time;
      begin
         -- calculate parameters

         Release_Time := Clock;
         Number_of_Slots := (Release_Time - Start_Time) / Time_Slot_Length;
         Slot_Start := Start_Time + Time_Slot_Length * Number_of_Slots;
```

```
      End_of_Phase_1 := Slot_Start + Client_Phase_1_Reserve;
      Start_of_Phase_2 := Slot_Start + Time_Slot_Length - Client_Phase_2_Reserve;
      End_of_Slot := Slot_Start + Time_Slot_Length;

      -- decide if release or not depending of phase
      if Release_Time >= Slot_Start and Release_Time < End_of_Phase_1 then
         Set_CPU(Client_Phase_1_CPU, Client_ID);
         Switch_Timer.Set_Handler(End_of_Phase_1, Handler'Access);
         Client_Current_Phase := Phase_1;
         Released := True;
      elsif Release_Time >= Start_of_Phase_2 and Release_Time < End_of_Slot
then
         Set_CPU(Client_Phase_2_CPU, Client_ID);
         Switch_Timer.Set_Handler(End_of_Slot, Handler'Access);
         Client_Current_Phase := Phase_2;
         Released := True;
      else
         -- between slots - do nothing just set timer
         -- alternative would be to lower priority to a "background" level
         -- priority
         -- more work conservative but we decided to maintain the
         -- algorithm as is in the original paper
         Client_Current_Phase := Not_Released;
         Switch_Timer.Set_Handler(Start_of_Phase_2, Handler'Access);
      end if;
   end Release_Task;

   procedure Finished is
      Cancelled: Boolean;
   begin
      -- cancel the timer.
      Switch_Timer.Cancel_Handler(Cancelled);
   end Finished;

   entry Wait when Released is
   begin
      Released := False;
   end Wait;

end Sporadic_Switcher;


task body Task_1 is
   Next : Time;
begin
   Next := Ada.Real_Time.Clock;
   Set_CPU( CPU_1 );
   loop
      Delay_Until_and_Set_Deadline( Next, Deadline_Task_1);
      -- Code of application
      Next := Next + Period_Task_1;
   end loop;
end Task_1;


My_Switcher: Sporadic_Switcher;

task body Task_2 is
begin
   My_Switcher.Register(Current_Task,
                        CPU_2, CPU_1,
                        Reserve_Phase_1_Task_2,
                        Reserve_Phase_2_Task_2);
   loop
      My_Switcher.Wait;
      -- Code of application
      My_Switcher.Finished;
   end loop;
end Task_2;
```

```
task body Task_3 is
   -- similar to Task 1
end Task_3;
```

We can make three observations. First, the non-split tasks, task 1 and task 3 have very simple code; they are basically programmed like we would have done if we wanted to implement partitioned EDF. Second, implementing task 2 requires some extra work. First of all, split tasks execute in the processor which they are currently allocated in preference to other tasks. Therefore, a priority level was created for the split task (priority 11), higher than the band for the regular EDF tasks.

Note also that the algorithm in [4] was designed for sporadic tasks, therefore a protected type is created to simultaneously control the release of the sporadic and to control the allocation of the task to the processors, depending on the phase within the slot. When the task is released (procedure Release_Task), first it is necessary to determine in what phase of the slot the release instant occurred. If it is within the interval reserved in a specific processor (Phase 1 – CPU 2; Phase 2 – CPU 1) then the task is allocated to that processor, and immediately released. Note that if the release instant is between the reserved slots, the task is not released. In all cases, a timer is armed for the next instant that the task attributes need to be changed.

When the timer handler is called, it changes the allocation of the task, or, if it is the end of the first phase, it needs to suspend the task with asynchronous task control. A better approach (for improving average responsiveness) would be to decrease the priority of the task to the EDF band (with a Deadline of Time'Last) or to create a background tasks lower priority band, which would allow the task to execute if the processor is idle. However, the task is suspended in order to maintain the equivalence to the algorithm of [4].

In the code-example above, we let tasks 1 and 3 arrive periodically and task 2 arrive sporadically. The algorithm allows any subset of tasks to arrive periodically and any subset of tasks to arrive sporadically however. For example, Task_1 can easily be changed so that it arrives sporadically as well; changes needed for doing so are listed below:

```
protected PO_for_Task_1 is
   pragma Priority(1);
   procedure Release_Task;
   entry Wait;
private
   Released: Boolean := False;
end PO_for_Task_1;

protected body PO_for_Task_1 is
   procedure Release_Task is   -- called by someone else or by interrupt
   begin
      Released := True;
   end Release_Task;

   entry Wait when Released is
   begin
      Released := False;
   end Wait;
end PO_for_Task_1;

task body Task_1 is
begin
```

```
    Set_CPU( CPU_1 );
    loop
        PO_for_Task_1.Wait;
        -- Code of application
    end loop;
end Task_1;
```

Note that the protected object used for releasing Task 1 has the same priority (pre-emption level) of the task as we are assuming that the release event is only within CPU_1. If that was not the case, the preemption level would need to be higher [15] than the priority of Task 1, as in the case of the switcher protected object.

For arbitrary-deadline sporadic tasks, although different off-line scheduling algorithms are used [5], the algorithm for dispatching is the same as for implicit-deadline, with only the parameters being calculated differently.

5 Job-Based Split Tasks Dispatching for Implicit-Deadline Sporadic Tasks

The algorithm described in this section is the one in [9]. The text in the right column of page 3 in [9] describes the dispatching algorithm. The algorithm is based on configuring different priorities for each phase of the split task. The task starts to execute in one CPU, and after a certain clock time its affinity is changed to the second CPU, with a different priority.

To illustrate task splitting, we will consider the same task set as in Section 4; consider a task set $\tau=\{\tau_1, \tau_2, \tau_3\}$ to be scheduled on two processor. The tasks are characterized as $T_1=100$ ms, $T_2=200$ ms, $T_3=400$ ms, $D_1=100$ ms, $D_2=200$ ms, $D_3=400$ ms and $C_1=51$ ms, $C_2=102$ ms, $C_3=204$ ms. The approach in [9] uses a rule called HPTS (Highest Priority Task Splitting) and therefore, task τ_1 is split between processor 1 and processor 2. (Note that this is different from Section 4, where task τ_2 was split between two processors.). Task τ_2 is assigned to processor 1; task τ_3 is assigned to processor 2 and task τ_1 is split between processor 1 and processor 2.

The splitting of task τ_1 is done such that (i) the first piece of τ_1 has execution time 49 ms, relative deadline 49 ms and is assigned to processor 1 and (ii) the second piece of τ_1 has execution time 2 ms, relative deadline 51 ms and is assigned to processor 2. It is easy to see that the sum of the execution times of these pieces of task τ_1 is C_1 and the sum of the relative deadlines of the pieces of task τ_1 is D_1.

In this section, we formulate the algorithm with the new Ada constructs. For brevity we just show the main differences to the previous section.

The code is as follows:

```
pragma Task_Dispatching_Policy(FIFO_Within_Priorities);
with System; use System;
with Ada.Dynamic_Priorities; use Ada.Dynamic_Priorities;
-- includes and constants similar to the previous section
-- The constants are used for task 2
C_First_Phase   : constant Time_Span:=Milliseconds(49);
C_Second_Phase  : constant Time_Span:=Milliseconds( 2);
D_First_Phase   : constant Time_Span:=Milliseconds(49);
D_Second_Phase  : constant Time_Span:=Milliseconds(51);

Priority_Task1_First_Phase  : constant Priority := 20;
Priority_Task1_Second_Phase : constant Priority := 19;
```

```
Priority_Task2 : constant Priority := 18;
Priority_Task3 : constant Priority := 17;

protected body Job_Based_Switcher is
    procedure Register( ID : Task_ID; Phase_1_CPU, Phase_2_CPU: CPU_Range;
                        Phase_1_C, Phase_2_C, Phase_1_D, Phase_2_D: Time_Span;
                        Phase_1_Prio, Phase_2_Prio: Priority) is
    begin
        -- ... just update protected data
    end Register;

    procedure Handler(TM :in out Timing_Event) is
    begin
        -- in this algorithm, handler is just called in the end of phase 1
        Set_CPU(Client_Phase_2_CPU, Client_ID);
        Set_Priority(Client_Phase_2_Prio, Client_ID);
    end Handler;

    procedure Release_Task is
    begin
        -- calculate parameters

        Release_Time := Clock;
        End_of_Phase_1 := Release_Time + Client_Phase_1_D;

        -- set first phase parameters
        Set_CPU(Client_Phase_1_CPU, Client_ID);
        Set_Priority(Client_Phase_1_Prio, Client_ID);

        -- set timer
        Switch_Timer.Set_Handler(End_of_Phase_1, Handler'Access);

        -- release
        Released := True;
    end Release_Task;

    procedure Finished is
        Cancelled: Boolean;
    begin
        -- cancel the timer.
        Switch_Timer.Cancel_Handler(Cancelled);
    end Finished;

    entry Wait when Released is
    begin
        Released := False;
    end Wait;

end Job_Based_Switcher;

My_Switcher: Job_Based_Switcher;

task body Task_1 is
begin
    My_Switcher.Register( ... );
    loop
        My_Switcher.Wait;
        -- Code of application
        My_Switcher.Finished;
    end loop;
end Task_1;
```

In this approach, the dispatching algorithm performs the migration at a certain time relative to the arrival of a job. Thus, both Release_Task and Handler procedures are much simpler. The first simply calculates the time to arm the timer, setting the parameters of the first phase (CPU and priority), whilst the second just changes these parameters. Note that we use fixed-priority scheduling of the task as proposed in [9].

6 Job-Based Split Tasks Dispatching for Constrained-Deadline Sporadic Tasks

The algorithm described in this section is the one in [8]. Figure 6 on page 6 in [8] gives a good description of the dispatching algorithm. The algorithm is very similar to the algorithm in Section 5 but differs in that (i) it uses EDF instead of RM on each processor and (ii) it performs migration when the job of a split task has performed a certain amount of execution. Therefore, there is no need for the mechanism to migrate the split task to know the arrival time of a job of a split task. Also, there are no timeslots.

The code is as follows:

```ada
pragma Task_Dispatching_Policy(EDF_Across_Priorities);

protected My_Job_Based_Switcher is
   pragma Priority(Ada.Execution_Time.Timers.Min_Handler_Ceiling);
   procedure Register(ID : Task_ID; Phase_2_CPU : CPU_Range);
   procedure Budget_Expired(T : in out Ada.Execution_Time.Timers.Timer);
private
   Client_ID : Task_ID;
   Client_Phase_2_CPU : CPU_Range;
end My_Job_Based_Switcher;


protected body My_Job_Based_Switcher is
   procedure Register(ID : Task_ID; Phase_2_CPU: CPU_Range) is
   begin
      -- ... just update protected data
   end Register;

   procedure Budget_Expired(T : in out Ada.Execution_Time.Timers.Timer) is
   begin
      -- similarly to previous section,
      -- handler is just called in the end of phase 1
      Set_CPU(Client_Phase_2_CPU, Client_ID);
   end Budget_Expired;

end My_Job_Based_Switcher;

task body Task_2 is
   Next : Time;
   My_Id : aliased Task_Identification.Task_Id:= Task_2'Identity;
   The_Timer : Ada.Execution_Time.Timers.Timer(My_Id'Access);
   Cancelled: Boolean;
begin
   My_Job_Based_Switcher.Register( ... );
   Next := Ada.Real_Time.Clock;
   -- note that we do not assign the task to any processor
   -- We will do it later in the loop below
   loop
      Delay_Until_and_Set_Deadline( Next, Deadline_Task_2);
      Set_CPU(Phase_1_CPU, My_ID);
      Ada.Execution_Time.Timers.Set_Handler(The_Timer, C_First_Phase,
                          My_Job_Based_Switcher.Budget_Expired'Access);
      -- Code of application
      Ada.Execution_Time.Timers.Cancel_Handler(The_Timer, Cancelled);
      Next := Next + Period_Task_2;
   end loop;
end Task_2;
```

The code for execution-time monitoring that we use follows to some extent the idea on page 7 in [11]. But expiry of our handler for execution time monitoring does not need to notify the task (task 2) and this simplifies our code.

It should also be noted that the algorithm in [8] allows a task to be split between more than two processors. Our Ada code can be extended to that case by letting the handler `Budget_Expired` set up a new execution-time monitoring, with a call to `Set_Handler`.

7 Conclusions

We have seen details on how task splitting algorithms can be implemented using the recently proposed Ada extensions. In terms of efficiency, we expect this Ada code to be acceptable on multicores with a small number of cores. For very large multicores, the mechanism for migrating a task may impose a significant sequential bottleneck and for such platforms, a direct implementation of the task splitting algorithms in the Ada run-time may be needed. Also, if clocks and timers are available in just one (or in a reduced set of) processor(s), local timers are needed for better efficiency, particularly for more sophisticated algorithms such as the one in Section 4; an approach with user-defined clocks could be looked after. Nevertheless, multicore scheduling is still in its beginning, therefore it is still too soon to determine which algorithms to support.

Acknowledgments. This work was partially funded by the Portuguese Science and Technology Foundation (Fundação para a Ciência e a Tecnologia - FCT) and the European Commission through grant ArtistDesign ICT-NoE-214373.

References

1. Liu, C.L., Layland, J.W.: Scheduling Algorithms for Multiprogramming in a Hard-Real-Time Environment. Journal of the ACM 20, 46–61 (1973)
2. Burns, A., Wellings, A.: Supporting Execution on Multiprocessor Platforms. In: Proc. of 14th International Real-Time Ada Workshop (2009)
3. Andersson, B., Tovar, E.: Multiprocessor Scheduling with Few Preemptions. In: Proc. of The 12th IEEE International Conference on Embedded and Real-Time Computing and Application, pp. 322–334 (2006)
4. Andersson, B., Bletsas, K.: Sporadic Multiprocessor Scheduling with Few Preemptions. In: Proc. of 20th Euromicro Conference on Real-Time Systems, pp. 243–252 (2008)
5. Andersson, B., Bletsas, K., Baruah, S.K.: Scheduling Arbitrary-Deadline Sporadic Task Systems on Multiprocessors. In: Proc. of 29th IEEE Real-Time Systems Symposium, pp. 385–394 (2008)
6. Andersson, B., Bletsas, K.: Notional Processors: An Approach for Multiprocessor Scheduling. In: Proc. of 15th IEEE Real-Time and Embedded Technology and Applications Symposium, pp. 3–12 (2009)
7. Bletsas, K., Andersson, K.: Preemption-light multiprocessor scheduling of sporadic tasks with high utilisation bound. In: Proc. of 30th IEEE Real-Time Systems Symposium (2009)

8. Kato, S., Yamasaki, N., Ishikawa, Y.: Semi-Partitioned Scheduling of Sporadic Task Systems on Multiprocessors. In: Proc. of 21st Euromicro Conference on Real-Time Systems (ECRTS 2009), pp. 249–258 (2009)
9. Lakshmanan, K., Rajkumar, R., Lehoczky, J.: Partitioned Fixed-Priority Preemptive Scheduling for Multi-Core Processors. In: Proc. of 21st Euromicro Conference on Real-Time Systems, pp. 239–248 (2009)
10. Wellings, A., Burns, A.: Beyond Ada 2005: Allocating Tasks to Processors in SMP Systems. In: Proc. of 13th International Real-Time Ada Workshop (2007)
11. Ada Issue 307 Execution-Time Clocks (2006), http://www.sigada.org/ada_letters/apr2006/AI-00307.pdf
12. Brandenburg, B., Calandrino, J., Anderson, J.: On the Scalability of Real-Time Scheduling Algorithms on Multicore Platforms: A Case Study. In: Proceedings of the 29th IEEE Real-Time Systems Symposium, December 2008, pp. 157–169 (2008)
13. Burns, A., Wellings, A.J.: Multiprocessor Systems Session Summary. In: 14th International Real-Time Ada Workshop (IRTAW-14)
14. Managing affinities for programs executing on multiprocessor platforms, AI-167 (2009) http://www.ada-auth.org/cgi-bin/cvsweb.cgi/ai05s/ai05-0167-1.txt?rev=1.1.
15. Rajkumar, R., Sha, L., Lehoczky, J.P.: Real-time synchronization protocols for multiprocessors. In: Proceedings 9th IEEE Real-Time Systems Symposium, pp. 259–269 (1988)
16. Burns, A., Wellings, A.J.: Dispatching Domains for Multiprocessor Platforms and their Representation in Ada. In: Real, J., Vardanega, T. (eds.) Ada-Europe 2010. LNCS, vol. 6106, pp. 41–53. Springer, Heidelberg (2010)

Preliminary Multiprocessor Support of Ada 2012 in GNU/Linux Systems

Sergio Sáez and Alfons Crespo

Instituto de Automática e Informática Industrial,
Universidad Politécnica de Valencia,
Camino de vera, s/n, 46022 Valencia, Spain
{ssaez,alfons}@disca.upv.es

Abstract. The next release of the Ada language, Ada 2012, will incorporate several new features that address current and future software and hardware issues. One of these features is expected to be explicit support for multiprocessor execution platforms. This work reviews the enhancements at the language level required to support real-time scheduling over symmetric multiprocessor platforms, and the corresponding support at the operating system level. It analyses the preliminary support for these features within the Linux kernel and proposes a set of language extensions that will provide the required functionalities. Multiprocessor implementation aspects of other Ada language constructs such as *timing events*, *execution time clocks* and *interrupt management* are also analysed.

Keywords: Symmetric Multiprocessor Platforms, Linux kernel, Ada 2012.

1 Introduction

Real-Time and embedded systems are becoming more complex, and multiprocessor/multicore systems are becoming a common execution platform in these areas. Although schedulability analysis techniques for real-time applications executing over multiprocessor platforms are still not mature, some feasible scheduling approaches are emerging. However, in order to allow these new techniques to be applied over existing real-time multiprocessor operating systems, a flexible support has to be provided at the kernel and user-space levels.

Ada 2005 allows real-time applications to be executed on multiprocessor platforms in order to exploit task-level parallelism, but no direct support is provided to allow the programmer to control the task-to-processor mapping process. In order to achieve a predictable behaviour in a real-time multiprocessor platform, the system designer must be able to control the task-to-processor allocation process and, in general, the processor assignment of any executable unit with dynamic behaviour, such as timers and interrupt handlers.

At the last International Real-Time Ada Workshop (IRTAW 14) some of these multiprocessor issues were addressed. Ada extensions were proposed to cope with open issues in the scope of real-time application over symmetric multiprocessor

J. Real and T. Vardanega (Eds.): Ada-Europe 2010, LNCS 6106, pp. 68–82, 2010.

platforms (SMP) [1]. However, no specific real-time multiprocessor operating system was considered during this analysis.

This paper analyses the existing support in the GNU/Linux platform to implement the multiprocessor extensions of the Ada language that are likely to be integrated in the forthcoming Ada 2012. Some features of Ada 2005 that are poorly supported in the GNU/Linux platform are also considered. The work reviews the scheduling approaches that can be used to design real-time multiprocessor systems, the programming functionalities required and some of the proposed Ada interfaces for making use of these approaches at the application level. Once the Ada RTS requirements have been analysed, the current support to implement these extensions in the GNU/Linux platform is studied and simple extensions at library and kernel level[1] are proposed for those features that are still missing. Kernel and library support for execution-time clocks, group budgets and interrupt handling over multiprocessor platforms are also considered.

The rest of this paper is organised as follows: the next section deals with multiprocessor task scheduling in real-time systems, and the requirements at the language and kernel level to address the presented approaches. Section 3 addresses execution time clocks and group budget issues over the GNU/Linux platform. Interrupt affinities and timing events are addressed in section 4. The paper finishes with some conclusions and proposals for future work.

2 Multiprocessor Task Scheduling

A real-time system is composed of a set of tasks that concurrently collaborate to achieve a common goal. A real-time task can be viewed as an infinite sequence of job executions. Each job is activated by an event, such as an external interrupt from a physical device or an internal clock event. It is assumed that a job does not suspend itself during its execution. A task is suspended only at the end of a job execution, waiting for the next activation event. Even so, the system scheduler can preempt a job execution in order to execute a higher priority task.

2.1 Multiprocessor Scheduling Approaches

In order to predictably schedule a set of real-time tasks in a multiprocessor platform several approaches can be applied. One classification based on the capability of a task to migrate from one processor to another is shown next:

Global scheduling. All tasks can be executed on any processor and after a preemption the current job can be resumed in a different processor.
Job partitioning. Each job activation of a given task can be executed on a different processor, but a given job cannot migrate during its execution.
Task partitioning. All job activations of a given task have to be executed in the same processor. No job migration is allowed.

---

[1] During this work Linux kernel 2.6.31 and GNU C Library *glibc* 2.10 have been used.

Depending on whether the choice of the target processor is carried out *on-line* or *off-line*, six possible approaches arise. Static schedulability analysis techniques that ensure timely execution of the task set in all of them have not yet been developed. Neverthless, new techniques are continuously emerging with improved support for several of these approaches: new global scheduling schedulability tests for fixed [2] and dynamic priorities [3], task splitting approaches [4], etc. Since it is not expected that a commercial Real-Time Operating System (RTOS) would implement each possible on-line scheduling algorithm at the kernel level, the RTOS support has to be focused on a flexible *System Call Interface* that makes it possible to implement the required services at the application or run-time level [5,6].

Next subsections analyse the required kernel functionalities that must be provided to implement these approaches at the user-space level, possible extensions of the Ada Standard Libraries, and the available support for these functionalities that is present in the Linux kernel and glibc library.

2.2   Required Functionalities

In order to allow efficient implementations of multiprocessor scheduling approaches at the user-space level, a RTOS must provide a flexible kernel programming interface and a set of administration tools. These facilities must allow the system architect to design predictable real-time applications, despite of the current unavailability of accurate schedulability analysis techniques. Depending on the scheduling approach followed to map the real-time task set into the platform processors, the functionalities required from the RTOS may vary.

On one hand, if target processors for every active entity (task or job) are determined off-line, the resulting decisions are typically coded into the application as is done with other real-time task attributes (priority, deadline, etc.) Thus, the application code needs an adequate Application Programming Interface (API) to specify the target processor for each active entity. In the case of a task partitioning approach, the target processor can be specified before thread creation, by means of thread attributes, or during the task initialisation code by means of direct processor allocation. However, if the job partitioning approach is used, the task is responsible for setting the processor to be used by the next job at the end of the execution of the current one. Next section shows examples of both approaches using a possible Ada interface. The requirements for a full off-line global scheduling approach, i.e. a cyclic multiprocessor executive, is out of the scope of this work.

On the other hand, when the target processor for a given active entity is determined on-line, i.e. during normal system execution, the processor allocation decisions are normally carried out by a privileged task or by the system scheduler. In a user-space implementation, this privileged task acts as an Application-Defined Scheduler (ADS)[5] and has to use the API offered by the OS kernel to allocate application tasks into specific processors. In this case, although other kernel mechanisms could be required to allow this application-level scheduling, e.g. normal and execution time timers, the API to specify a target processor would be quite similar. The only difference with respect to the off-line case is that the ADS thread must be able to specify the target processor for the rest of the application threads.

It is also possible that a mixed on-line/off-line approach be required by a given real-time task set, such as an application with several operating modes. In this case, an off-line task partitioning approach could be applied on each operating mode, but an on-line mode change manager should be able to modify the target processor of any system task during a mode change. Fortunately, this mixed approach does not require any additional kernel functionality with respect to pure on-line or off-line approaches.

Finally, an additional possibility is to use different scheduling approaches on each processor of the execution platform. In such a way, the available processors could be partitioned in different mutual-exclusive processor sets, applying to each subset a different scheduling approach. This possibility only requires additional functionalities from the OS kernel if at least one of the scheduling approaches used in a processor subset is the global scheduling approach, and the global scheduler is implemented at the kernel-level. In this later case, the application should be able to specify that a given set of tasks is going to be globally scheduled but that the set only can use a subset of the available processors. Once the processors subset is specified, the OS scheduler decides *when* and *where* each task is executed within the specified processor subset. No additional API is required if the processors partition is performed and managed at user-space.

Therefore, the functionalities expected from the OS to implement the presented multiprocessor scheduling approaches can be summarised as follows:

R.1. The ability to specify the target processor of the current task or a different task.
R.2. The ability to change the execution processor immediately, or to specify the target processor for the next activation of a task.
R.3. The ability to specify a unique target processor or a subset of the available ones for a given task.

2.3 Ada Programming Interface

In the last International Real-Time Ada Workshop several different Ada interfaces were proposed to cover the scheduling approaches presented above. The main differences between these proposals reside in the abstractions presented at application level. This section shows a set of similar interfaces to cope with the multiprocessor scheduling approaches and their requirements presented above.

The current behaviour of Ada applications over multiprocessor execution platforms defaults to the global scheduling approach. GNAT[2] provides a basic support for switching from global scheduling to off-line task partitioning by means of **pragma** Task_Info. Apart from this basic support, a possible interface to address task partitioning at the application level is shown by Listing 1.

---

[2] GPL 2009 version of GNAT compiler from AdaCore has been used in this work as the reference implementation of native Ada Run-Time System. www.adacore.com

Listing 1. Basic multiprocessor support

```
package Ada_System is
   type Processor is range ...;  -- implementation-defined
   type Processor_Set is array (Processor) of Boolean;

   Any_Processor : constant Processor := ...;
end Ada_System;

with Ada.Task_Identification; use Ada.Task_Identification;
with Ada_System; use Ada_System;
package Ada_System_Scheduling is
   ...
   function Get_Available_Processors return Processor_Set;
   procedure Set_Processor(P: Processor; T : Task_Id := Current_Task);
   function Get_Processor(T : Task_Id := Current_Task) return Processor;
end Ada_System_Scheduling;
```

This interface provides support for requirement **R.1** allowing the current task to change its execution processor or the processor of another task. However, to support job partitioning a given task needs to establish its next target processor. If procedure Set_Processor is supposed to be a scheduling point, i.e., it changes the execution processor immediately, a different procedure will be required to perform a deferred processor assignment. Since it makes no sense to perform the complicated process involved in changing the execution processor of the current task just before getting suspended, some deferred processor assignment procedure is required to support the job partitioning approach efficiently.

Following the example of *deadline assignment and delay until* of Ada 2005, a deferred processor assignment could be established as shown by Listing 2.

Listing 2. Processor assignment and **delay until** procedure

```
procedure Delay_Until_And_Set_Processor(DT: Ada.Real_Time.Time;
                      P: Processor; T: Task_Id:= Current_Task);
```

However, given that the use of Delay_Until_And_Set_Something procedures will be incompatible with the procedure Delay_Until_And_Set_Deadline, already defined in Ada 2005 (D.2.6) [7] we propose instead the procedure shown in Listing 3.

Listing 3. Deferred processor assignment procedure

```
procedure Set_Next_Processor(P: Processor; T : Task_Id := Current_Task);
```

This procedure makes it possible to establish the next target processor to be used when the task Task_Id is awakened again to start its next job execution. In this way, the next processor assignment can be combined with any **delay until** construct or Delay_Until_And_Set_Something procedure. Both procedures Set_*_Processor will cover requirement **R.2** described above. Listing 4 shows a periodic task with job partitioning that makes use of the deferred processor assignment and **delay until** construct.

Listing 4. Periodic task with job partitioning based on **delay until**

```
with Ada_System; use Ada_System;
with Ada_System_Scheduling; use Ada_System_Scheduling;
task body Periodic_With_Job_Partitioning is
   type List_Range is mod N;
   Processor_List :  array (List_Range) of Processor
                  := (...);   -- Decided at design time
   Processor_Iter :  List_Range := List_Range'First;
   Next_Processor: Processor;
   Next_Release   : Ada.Real_Time.Time;
   Period         : Time_Span := ...;
begin
   Task_Initialize ;
   Next_Release := Ada.Real_Time.Clock;
   Set_Processor(Processor_List( Processor_Iter ));   -- Processor for first  activation
   loop
      Task_Main_Loop;
      -- Next job preparation
      Processor_Iter  := Processor_Iter 'Succ;
      Next_Processor := Processor_List(Processor_Iter );
      Next_Release := Next_Release + Period;
      Set_Next_Processor(Next_Processor);
      delay until Next_Release;
      -- Alternatively: Delay_Until_And_Set_Processor(Next_Release, Next_Processor);
   end loop;
end Periodic_With_Job_Partitioning;
```

In this example, a periodic task uses a recurrent list of the processors where its jobs will execute. The cyclic processor list is supposed to be computed at design time using an off-line job partitioning tool. In this way, task migrations between processors are determined in a predictable way at job boundaries. If Set_Processors procedure was used before **delay until** construct, then the task would perform an unnecessary processor migration just before getting suspended for the next job activation.

A different approach to implement the job partitioning scheme without requiring deferred processors assignments is the use of Timing_Events to implement periodic, sporadic and/or aperiodic task as proposed in [8]. In this case, the Timing_Event handler can change the target processor of the periodic task using Set_Processor before releasing it (requirement **R.1**). Listing 5 shows a periodic task using job partitioning and Timing_Events to implement a periodic release mechanism[3].

---

[3] Original code extracted from Real-Time Ada Framework [8].

Listing 5. Periodic task with job partitioning based on Timing_Events

```
with Ada_System; use Ada_System;
with Ada_System_Scheduling; use Ada_System_Scheduling;
package body Release_Mechanisms.Periodic is
  protected body Periodic_Release is
    entry Wait_For_Next_Release when New_Release is
    begin
      ...
      New_Release := False;
      ...
    end Wait_For_Next_Release;

    procedure Release(TE : in out Timing_Event) is
    begin
      Next := Next + S.Period;
      Set_Processor(S.Next_Processor, S.Get_Task_Id);  -- Set next job processor
      New_Release := True;                             -- Activates the job
      TE.Set_Handler(Next, Release'Access);
    end Release;
  end Periodic_Release;
  ...
task type Periodic_With_Job_Partitioning (S: Any_Task_State;
                                          R: Any_Release_Mechanism) is
    pragma Priority(S.Get_Priority);
end Periodic_With_Job_Partitioning;

task body Periodic_With_Job_Partitioning is
    type List_Range is mod N;
    Processor_List : array (List_Range'First .. List_Range'Last) of Processor
                  := (...);  -- Decided at design time
    Processor_Iter : List_Range := List_Range'First;
    Next_Processor: Processor;
begin
    S. Initialize ;
    Set_Processor(Processor_List( Processor_Iter ));  -- Processor for first  activation
    loop
       S.Code;
       -- Next job preparation
       Processor_Iter := Processor_Iter'Succ;
       Next_Processor := Processor_List(Processor_Iter );
       S.Set_Next_Processor(Next_Processor);
       R.Wait_For_Next_Release;
    end loop;
end Periodic_With_Job_Partitioning;
```

Finally, to cover requirement **R.3** and allow the construction of processor partitions to restrict global scheduling to a subset of the available processors the notion of *scheduling allocation domains* [1] has been proposed. The interface to be added to Listing 1 is similar to the one shown in Listing 6.

Listing 6. Scheduling domain management interface

```
package Ada_System_Scheduling is
  type Scheduling_Domain is limited private;

  function Create(PS : Processor_Set) return Scheduling_Domain;
  function Get_Processor_Set(SD : Scheduling_Domain) return Processor_Set;
  procedure Allocate_Task(SD: in out Scheduling_Domain;
                          T : Task_Id := Current_Task);
  procedure Deallocate_Task(SD: in out Scheduling_Domain;
                            T : Task_Id := Current_Task);
  function Get_Scheduling_Domain(T : Task_Id := Current_Task)
                                            return Scheduling_Domain;

  ...
end Ada_System_Scheduling;
```

2.4   GNU/Linux Support

Although the Linux kernel is a general purpose OS, its real-time behaviour and its expressive features are being continuously improved, making it possible to build *hard-enough* real-time applications for some environments. However, the glibc-kernel tandem on GNU/Linux systems still lacks of some of the features required by Ada 2005 (e.g. EDF scheduling[4]). This gives rise to an incomplete native implementation of the Ada RTS over this platform.

However, this is not the case for multiprocessor scheduling support. The scheduling scheme in the Linux kernel is based on a static priority policy for real-time processes and a variable quantum round-robin scheduling algorithm for normal processes, as proposed by POSIX 1003.1b [9]. Each processor has its own *run queue* with a separate *process queue* per priority level: the first 100 priority levels for real-time processes (SCHED_FIFO and SCHED_RR POSIX scheduling policies) and the next 40 priority levels for normal processes (SCHED_NORMAL). The lower the priority level, the higher the process priority. These real-time priority levels are exposed in reverse order to the applications[5] that can use real-time priorities in the range $[1, 99]$[6].

In spite of the per-processor run queue internal structure of the Linux kernel, processes are allowed to migrate from one processor to another. In this way, the default scheduling approach of a real-time process inside the Linux kernel is global scheduling based on static priorities. However, the Linux kernel offers a flexible interface that covers almost any requirement for implementing real-time multiprocessor scheduling approaches presented in section 2.1.

The Linux kernel interface for multiprocessor scheduling control is twofold. On one hand, an administrative tool in the form of *cpuset file system* makes it

---

[4] A new EDF scheduling class is being developed for new releases of Linux kernel.
[5] Real-time priority values exposed to applications put the internal priority levels upside-down: the higher the priority value, the higher the task priority.
[6] The real-time process queue with the highest priority is reserved for Linux kernel internal processes.

possible to organise the processor and memory placement for SMP and NUMA architectures [10]. These *cpusets* provide a mechanism for assigning a set of CPUs and memory nodes to a set of tasks, and for establishing a set of useful features to configure the behaviour of heterogeneous multiprocessor platforms.

On the other hand, a programming interface is also provided by means of kernel system calls. This API allows the specificantion of the set of processors that are to be used by a given thread, but they are subordinated to the configuration performed with the *cpuset* mechanism. Functions provided by the Linux kernel to support scheduling requirements presented in section 2.2 are shown in Listing 7.

Listing 7. CPU-related Linux kernel system calls

```
#define _GNU_SOURCE
#include <sched.h>
#include <linux/getcpu.h>
int  sched_setaffinity (pid_t pid, size_t cpusetsize, cpu_set_t *mask);
int  sched_getaffinity (pid_t pid, size_t cpusetsize, cpu_set_t *mask);
int  getcpu(unsigned *cpu, unsigned *node, struct getcpu_cache *tcache);
```

These functions allow a real-time application to select between global scheduling, specifying multiple processors in its affinity map `mask`, and the task partitioning approach, using single processor affinity maps. There are a set of equivalent functions that allow the use of thread identifiers or thread attributes to specify the target task. Using this system call interface an Ada RTS can implement almost the full interface proposed in section 2.3. However, as the system call function sched_setaffinity immediately enforces the process identified by `pid` to be executed on a processor belonging to its affinity map, deferred processor assignment required by the job partitioning approach still remains unsupported. The next subsection suggest a Linux kernel extension to support Ada procedures Set_Next_Processor or Delay_Until_And_Set_Processor.

2.5   Required Linux Kernel Extensions

The required functionality to allow deferred affinity changes implies simple changes at kernel and glibc level. The suggested extension is to modify the internal system call kernel function sched_setaffinity to accept an additional flag parameter that specifies when the affinity change will be performed. If the new flag indicates *deferred change*, sched_setaffinity function avoids immediate task migration by skipping the invocation to migrate_task(). In this case, the processor switch will be automatically performed when the corresponding thread becomes suspended and removed from the current processor *run queue*. The new implementation of this system call will be faster than the previous one for deferred processor assignments and will carry almost no penalty when immediate task migration is used. The new system call function prototype is shown in Listing 8.

Listing 8. Linux kernel system calls modifications

```
#define SCHED_SET_IMMEDIATE 1
#define SCHED_SET_DEFERRED 2
long sched_setaffinity (pid_t pid, const struct cpumask *in_mask, const long flag);
```

At the glibc library level the kernel system call will be separated into two wrapper functions shown in Listing 9, for backward compatibility reasons.

Listing 9. Glibc library level extensions

```
/* The old one use SCHED_SET_IMMEDIATE flag */
int sched_setaffinity (pid_t pid, size_t cpusetsize, cpu_set_t *mask);
/* The new one use SCHED_SET_DEFERRED flag */
int sched_setnextaffinity (pid_t pid, size_t cpusetsize, cpu_set_t *mask);
```

Once these simple extensions are applied to the kernel and glibc library, all the multiprocessor scheduling approaches reviewed in section 2 can be implemented, and the proposed Ada interfaces can be incorporated within the native Ada RTS for GNU/Linux platform.

3   Execution Time Clocks, Timers and Group Budgets

The Ada Reference Manual provides a language-defined package to measure execution time of application tasks in section D.14 [7]. However, GNAT GPL 2009 does not implement execution time clocks in the native RTS for the GNU/Linux platform. This section examines whether the current Linux kernel and glibc library have enough facilities to implement the Ada.Execution_Time package and its child packages Timers and Group_Budgets, and the corresponding multiprocessor extensions.

Recent Linux kernel and glibc library implement several clocks that make it possible to measure time in different ways. Among the currently supported clocks, we find CLOCK_THREAD_CPUTIME_ID that performs high-resolution measurements of the CPU-time consumed by a given thread. The interface functions shown in Listing 10 provide the *clock identifier* of a given thread and read its CPU-time clock and resolution.

Listing 10. GNU/Linux support functions for execution time clocks

```
#include <pthread.h>
#include <time.h>
int pthread_getcpuclockid(pthread_t thread, clockid_t *clock_id);
int clock_getres (clockid_t clk_id, struct timespec *res);
int clock_gettime(clockid_t clk_id, struct timespec *tp);
```

These functions and the definition of the `timespec` structure are enough to implement the package Ada.Execution_Time on the GNU/Linux platform. However, the manual pages about these functions advise about possible bogus results if the implied thread is allowed to migrate between processors with different clock sources, since the processor running frequencies could be slightly different. SMP platforms based on multicore processors should not suffer from this kind of clock drifts.

In the same way, the Linux kernel implements POSIX timers, which implement all the functionalities required by package Ada.Execution_Time.Timers. The function prototypes in C are shown in Listing 11.

Listing 11. POSIX timers in Linux kernel

```
#include <signal.h>
#include <time.h>
int timer_create( clockid_t  clockid , struct sigevent *evp, timer_t *timerid );
int timer_settime(timer_t timerid , int flags , const struct itimerspec *new_value,
                  struct itimerspec * old_value );
int timer_gettime(timer_t timerid , struct itimerspec *curr_value );
int timer_delete ( timer_t  timerid );
```

However, the Linux kernel defines an additional notification mechanism that can be specified in struct sigevent on timer creation: SIGEV_THREAD_ID. This new mechanism makes it possible to notify a specific thread when the timer expires. As described in previous sections, a thread can have a specific processor affinity map. This notificationfacility can be used by the Ada RTS to create a set of server tasks that manage timer expirations on a per-processor or per-scheduling domain basis. With This structure we can add specific multiprocessor support in package Ada.Execution_Time.Timers in order to set the processor where the protected procedure defined by the Timer_Handler will be executed. The notification thread will directly depend on the target processor specified for the timer handler execution. Based on the previously proposed interfaces, Timer type could be extended as shown by Listing 12.

Listing 12. Extensions to execution time timers

```
with Ada_System; use Ada_System;
with Ada_System_Scheduling; use Ada_System_Scheduling;
package Ada.Execution_Time.Timers is
   ...
   procedure Set_Scheduling_Domain(TM : in out Timer;
                                   SD: access all Scheduling_Domain);
   function Get_Scheduling_Domain(TM : Timer) return Scheduling_Domain;
   procedure Set_Processor(TM : in out Timer; P: Processor);
   function Get_Processor(TM : Timer) return Processor;
end Ada.Execution_Time.Timers;
```

On the other hand, although the Linux kernel computes the execution time of the group of threads that composes a process, no additional groups of threads can be defined without disrupting process unity. So, to directly support group budgets under GNU/Linux systems, a completely new set of kernel system calls and the corresponding support will have to be added.

4   Interrupt Affinities

In a general purpose OS like GNU/Linux system the interrupt management rarely can be performed at user-space level. What is intended as interrupt management in Ada RTS on UNIX systems is to manage the *software interrupts* or *signals* as defined by the POSIX standard.

4.1   Hardware Interrupts and POSIX Signals

Adding multiprocessor support to POSIX signals management is somehow problematic, since the standard specifies that signals are sent to a process as a whole. Because of this, to establish on which thread and in which processor is a signal handler to be executed does not have a straightforward solution. A possible interface and an implementation that will allow the specification of the processor or execution domain where a signal handler would be executed is presented bellow.

In order establish an interrupt affinity the package Ada.Interrupts can be extended as follows:

Listing 13. Explicit multiprocessor support for Ada Interrupts

```
with Ada_System; use Ada_System;
with Ada_System_Scheduling; use Ada_System_Scheduling;
package Ada.Interrupts is
   ...
   procedure Set_Scheduling_Domain(Interrupt : Interrupt_ID;
                                   SD: Scheduling_Domain);
   function Get_Scheduling_Domain(Interrupt : Interrupt_ID)
                                        return Scheduling_Domain;
   procedure Set_Processor(Interrupt : Interrupt_ID; P: Processor);
   function Get_Processor(Interrupt : Interrupt_ID) return Processor;
end Ada.Interrupts;
```

The proposed implementation on a GNU/Linux system is similar to that proposed for handlers of execution time timers in section 3. One thread is attached to each processor in the system where a signal handler can be executed[7]. Then, all the signals are blocked on all threads allowing these signal handler threads to catch pending signals by means of the POSIX function sigwaitinfo. The prototypes of the functions involved are shown in Listing 14.

Listing 14. POSIX functions to mask and wait for signals

```
#include <pthread.h>
#include <signal.h>
int pthread_sigmask(int how, const sigset_t *newmask, sigset_t *oldmask);
int sigwaitinfo (const sigset_t *set, siginfo_t *info);
```

The value of the `sigset_t` set for a given thread represents the set of signals that have been assigned to the processor on which the thread is allocated. Signals

---

[7] Some processors could be reserved for non-real-time applications.

allocated only to a scheduling domain as a whole will be present on the signal sets of every signal handler thread of that domain.

Although hardware interrupt handlers cannot be attached at user level in GNU/Linux systems, it could be interesting to have a programming interface that allow an Ada real-time application to establish the processor affinity of such interrupts. As an example, a real-time application could be interested in allocating all its real-time tasks in a subset of the available processors and to move non real-time related hardware interrupts to another processors.

The Ada interface will remain as shown in Listing 13, but to support hardware interrupts the package Ada.Interrupt.Names needs to be extended with new interrupt identifiers. As interrupt lines (numbers) change from one system to another, a generic interrupt identifiers could be defined as shown by Listing 15.

Listing 15. Hardware interrupt Ada names

```
package Ada.Interrupts.Names is
   ...
   HW_Interrupt_0 : constant Interrupt_ID := ...;
   HW_Interrupt_1 : constant Interrupt_ID := ...;
   ...
end Ada.Interrupt.Names;
```

A Linux kernel over an Intel x86 platform will require at least 224 hardware interrupt identifiers, although some of them are reserved for internal kernel use. The Linux kernel offers a simple interface through its `proc` virtual file system [11] to change the affinity of a hardware interrupt. The processor affinity mask of an interrupt # can be established by writing the corresponding hexadecimal value on `/proc/irq/IRQ#/smp_affinity` file.

4.2   Timing Events

The standard package Ada.Real_Time.Timing_Events is also strongly related to interrupt management. It allows a user-defined protected procedure to be executed at a specified time. This protected procedure is normally executed at Interrupt_Priority 'Last in real-time applications. When such applications execute in a multiprocessor platform, with more and more code being moved to timing event handlers, it will be useful to allow the programmer to specify the processor where a timing event handler will be executed. A possible extension to support this functionality in Timing_Event type is shown in Listing 16.

Listing 16. Multiprocessor support for timing events

```
with Ada_System; use Ada_System;
with Ada_System_Scheduling; use Ada_System_Scheduling;
package Ada.Real_Time.Timing_Events is
   ...
   procedure Set_Scheduling_Domain(TM : in out Timing_Event;
                                   SD: access all Scheduling_Domain);
   function Get_Scheduling_Domain(TM : Timing_Event) return Scheduling_Domain;
```

procedure Set_Processor(TM : **in out** Timing_Event; P: Processor);
function Get_Processor(TM : Timing_Event) **return** Processor;
end Ada.Real_Time.Timing_Events;

To support a multiprocessor platform, an event-driven server task can be allocated on every available processor and execution domain. When procedure Set_Handler was invoked, the timing event information will be queued on the appropriate server task that will finally execute the handler code.

5   Conclusions

Some of the proposed extensions of Ada 2012 have been analysed, mainly in relation to multiprocessor platforms. The proposed Ada interfaces have been reviewed and the required support from the underlying execution platform has been studied. Existing support for the required features at Linux kernel and GNU C Library level have been analysed, and simple extensions proposed to support unaddressed requirements. Also simple Ada interfaces and implementations have been proposed to allocate any kind of execution units (timer and interrupt handlers) to specific platform processors.

After this analysis, a preliminary support of presented features has been considered feasible and we have started the corresponding implementation at the library and kernel level. We will presentExperimental results of the ongoing implementation in the near future.

Acknowledgement. This work was partially supported by the Spanish Ministerio de Ciencia y Tecnología (MCYT) under grant TIN2008-06766-C03-02 and ITEA2 06038.

References

1. Burns, A., Wellings, A.: Multiprocessor systems session summary. In: 14th International Real-Time Ada Workshop, IRTAW-14 (2009)
2. Baruah, S.K., Fisher, N.: Global fixed-priority scheduling of arbitrary-deadline sporadic task systems. In: Rao, S., Chatterjee, M., Jayanti, P., Murthy, C.S.R., Saha, S.K. (eds.) ICDCN 2008. LNCS, vol. 4904, pp. 215–226. Springer, Heidelberg (2008)
3. Baruah, S.K., Baker, T.P.: Schedulability analysis of global EDF. Real-Time Systems 38(3), 223–235 (2008)
4. Andersson, B., Bletsas, K.: Sporadic multiprocessor scheduling with few preemptions. In: 20th Euromicro Conference on Real-Time Systems, pp. 243–252 (2008)
5. Aldea Rivas, M., González Harbour, M.: POSIX-compatible application-defined scheduling in MaRTE OS. In: 14th Euromicro Conference on Real-Time Systems, pp. 67–75 (2002)
6. Aldea Rivas, M., Miranda González, F.J., González Harbour, M.: Implementing an application-defined scheduling framework for ada tasking. In: Llamosí, A., Strohmeier, A. (eds.) Ada-Europe 2004. LNCS, vol. 3063, pp. 283–296. Springer, Heidelberg (2004)

7. Taft, S., Duff, R., Brukardt, R., Ploedereder, E., Leroy, P. (eds.): Ada 2005 Reference Manual: Language and Standard Libraries. Springer, Heidelberg (2005) ISO/IEC 8652:1995(E) with Technical Corrigendum 1 and Amendment 1
8. Wellings, A.J., Burns, A.: Real-time utilities for Ada 2005. In: Abdennahder, N., Kordon, F. (eds.) Ada-Europe 2007. LNCS, vol. 4498, pp. 1–14. Springer, Heidelberg (2007)
9. IEEE Std 1003.1b-1993: IEEE Standard for Information Technology: Portable Operating Sytem Interface (POSIX). Part 1, system application program interface (API) — amendment 1 — realtime extension (1994)
10. Derr, S., Jackson, P., Lameter, C., Menage, P., Seto, H.: Cpusets. Technical report ftp.kernel.org Documentation/cgroups/cpusets.txt
11. Molnar, I., Krasnyansky, M.: SMP IRQ affinity. Technical report ftp.kernel.org Documentation/IRQ-affinity.txt

Practical Limits on Software Dependability: A Case Study

Patrick J. Graydon, John C. Knight, and Xiang Yin

University of Virginia, Charlottesville VA 22903, USA
{graydon,knight,xyin}@virginia.edu

Abstract. The technology for building dependable computing systems has advanced dramatically. Nevertheless, there is still no *complete* solution to building software for critical systems in which *every* aspect of software dependability can be demonstrated with high confidence. In this paper, we present the results of a case study exploration of the practical limitations on software dependability. We analyze a software assurance argument for weaknesses and extrapolate a set of limitations including dependence upon correct requirements, dependence upon reliable human-to-human communication, dependence upon human compliance with protocols, dependence upon unqualified tools, the difficulty of verifying low-level code, and the limitations of testing. We discuss each limitation's impact on our specimen system and potential mitigations.

1 Introduction

The past several decades have seen dramatic advances in technology for building dependable computing systems. Proof of software functionality, for example, has advanced from a costly manual exercise to a tool-aided endeavor that is becoming practical for ever-larger systems [13,22]. Using languages such as SPARK Ada and approaches such as Correctness-by-Construction, it is possible to prove that even large systems are demonstrably free of entire classes of defects including unhandled runtime exceptions, inadvertent memory overwrites, flow errors, and buffer overflows. These advances have not, however, provided practitioners with a *complete* solution to building software for ultra-critical systems in which *every* aspect of software dependability can be demonstrated with high confidence.

In this paper, we present the results of a case study conducted to explore the practical limitations on software dependability. In prior work, we implemented software for a specimen life-critical medical device and a developed a rigorous argument showing how evidence arising from our effort supports the conclusion that the software we developed is fit for use in the context of that device [6]. In this work, we analyze that argument and extrapolate from its weaknesses a set of practical limitations on the assurance of software dependability.

We describe the development effort and artifacts upon which our case study is based in section 2 and the case study process in section 3. In section 4, we discuss the limitations that we discovered, the effect of each upon the case study target, and any potential mitigations we are aware of. We discuss related work in section 5 and conclude in section 6.

J. Real and T. Vardanega (Eds.): Ada-Europe 2010, LNCS 6106, pp. 83–96, 2010.

2   The UVA LifeFlow LVAD MBCS

In prior work [6], we introduced Assurance Based Development (ABD), an engineering approach to the synergistic creation of software and assurance of the software in the form of rigorous argument. In order to assess ABD and its unique process synthesis mechanism, we conducted a case study development of Magnetic Bearing Control Software (MBCS) for a safety-critical system, the University of Virginia's LifeFlow Left Ventricular Assist Device (LVAD). The details of this case study are reported elsewhere [6].

2.1   The UVA LifeFlow LVAD

LifeFlow is a prototype artificial heart pump designed for the long-term (10–20 year) treatment of heart failure. LifeFlow has a continuous-flow, axial design. The use of magnetic bearings and careful design of the pump cavity, impeller, and blades reduce the damage done to blood cells, thus reducing the potential for the formation of dangerous blood clots. Fig. 1 shows the placement of the pump, the batteries and the controller, a cross-section of the pump, and the overall structure of the controller. Control of the magnetic suspension bearings is provided, in part, by software running on a Freescale MPC5554 microcontroller. Table 1 summarizes the MBCS requirements.

2.2   The MBCS Development Process

As part of the case study evaluation of ABD, we developed an implementation of the MBCS and completed a formal verification of its functionality. Briefly, our software development process included:

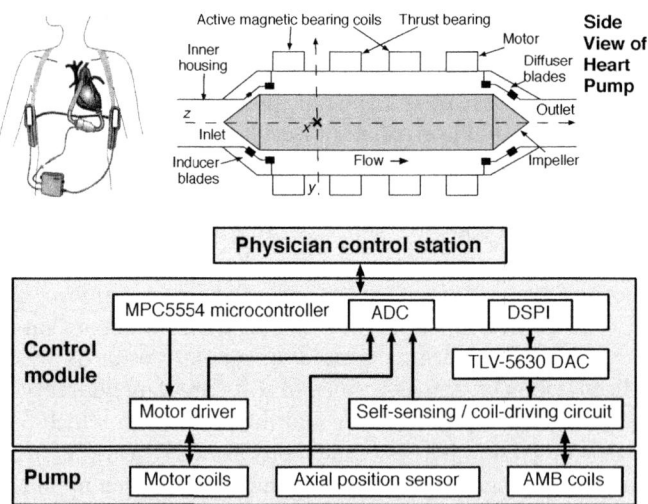

Fig. 1. LifeFlow structure and use

Table 1. Magnetic bearing control software requirements

Functionality	1. Trigger and read Analog-to-Digital Converters (ADCs) to obtain impeller position vector u.
	2. Determine whether reconfiguration is necessary. If so, select appropriate gain matrices $\mathbf{A}$, $\mathbf{B}$, $\mathbf{D}$, and $\mathbf{E}$.
	3. Compute target coil current vector y and next controller state vector x:
	$$y_k = \mathbf{D} \times x_k + \mathbf{E} \times u_k$$ $$x_{k+1} = \mathbf{A} \times x_k + \mathbf{B} \times u_k$$
	4. Update DACs to output y to coil controller.
Timing	Execute control in hard-real-time with a frame rate of **5 kHz**.
Reliability	No more than 10^{-9} failures per hour of operation.

1. Development of a formal specification in PVS [19] and an informal argument showing that this specification refines the requirements.
2. Design of a cyclic executive structure to manage the real-time tasks.
3. Design of the bearing control task routines by functional decomposition.
4. Implementation of the MBCS in SPARK Ada.
5. Implementation of bootstrap code in PowerPC assembly language.
6. Use of AdaCore's GNAT Pro compiler [1] to target the bare microcontroller.
7. Formal verification that the implementation refines the functional specification using the PVS proof checker and the SPARK tools in accordance with our Echo verification approach [21,22].
8. Machine analysis of Worst-Case Execution Time (WCET) and stack usage.
9. Requirements-based functional testing to Modified Condition / Decision Coverage (MC/DC) [9] was planned but not completed because of limited resources. For the purposes of this study, we proceeded as if the testing had been completed and the expected evidence gained. Had the testing proved impossible to conduct as planned, we would have revised our testing plans, possibly resulting in more limited testing evidence.

The resulting software consisted of 2,510 lines of SPARK Ada, of which 579 implement the control calculations and 114 implement the main program and cyclic executive structure, with much of the remaining code implementing interfaces to the MPC5554's functional and peripheral units. The software also includes implementations of the `memcpy` and `memset` library routines called from compiler-generated code and a bootstrap routine consisting of 106 PowerPC assembly language instructions.

2.3   The MBCS Fitness Argument

The MBCS fitness argument, recorded in the graphical Goal Structuring Notation (GSN) [11], explains how evidence from the MBCS development effort

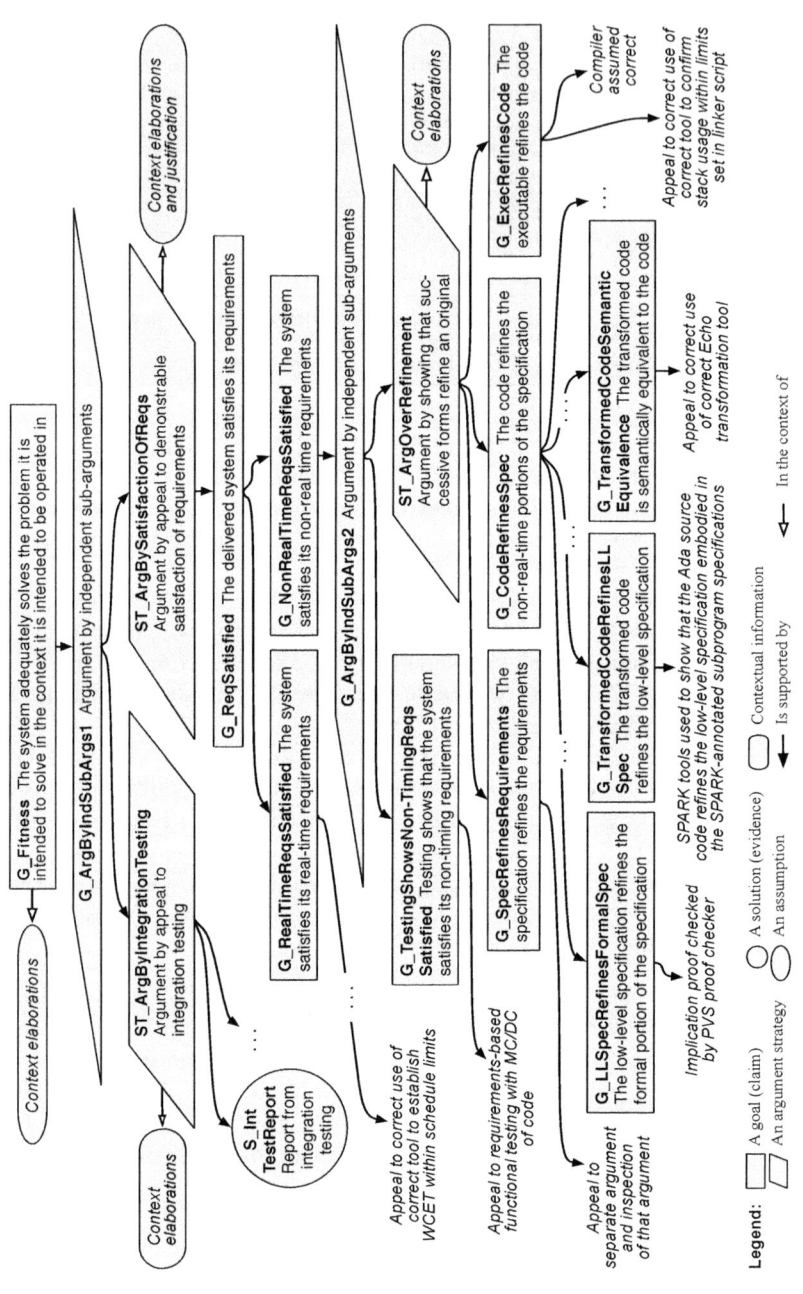

Fig. 2. Excerpt from the LifeFlow MCBS fitness argument

supports the claim that the MBCS is fit for use in the context of the LifeFlow LVAD. Fig. 2 illustrates the general form of the argument, which contains 348 GSN elements. After operationally defining "fit for use in the context of the MBCS" to mean demonstrably satisfying the given software requirements, the argument decomposes requirements obligations into real-time and non-real-time requirements. Our argument that the real-time requirements of the MBCS have been met rests largely upon the use of a WCET analysis tool to ensure that scheduled tasks complete within their scheduled execution periods. We use two independent lines of support to show that the MBCS's non-real-time requirements have been satisfied. The first is an appeal to requirements-based functional testing with MC/DC, and the second is a refinement argument based on our Echo approach to practical formal verification [22].

3   Case Study Process

Our case study evaluation of the practical limitations on software dependability was based upon and driven by the MBCS fitness argument. Dependability is irreducibly a system property: software by itself cannot do any harm to people, equipment, or the environment and so cannot be "unsafe." In order for safety to be a consideration, software has to be operating as part of a complete system for which damage is possible. When a system includes software, that software must have certain properties if the system is to be adequately dependable. Limitations on software dependability preclude demonstrating that software possesses such properties, and such limitations thus present threats to a software fitness argument's conclusion.

We identified two forms of threat to the MBCS fitness argument: (1) assumptions in the argument, such as the assumption that the PVS proof checker will not accept an invalid proof; and (2) reasoning steps in which the premises do not actually *entail* the claim, such as the argument that requirements-based functional testing with MC/DC supports the claim that the system meets its functional requirements. For each threat, we: (a) identified the general limitation of which the identified threat was a specific instance; (b) evaluated the limitation's impact on to the MBCS fitness argument; and (c) enumerated any potential mitigations of which we were aware.

We do not claim that the list of limitations presented in section 4 is complete. Other development efforts might be subject to limitations that did not affect the MBCS effort, and others might find limitations in the MBCS effort that we overlooked. The range and impact of the limitations facing this effort, however, are one indication of the challenges of dependable software engineering generally.

4   Limitations Discovered

In this section, we present the limitations uncovered by our case study. These limitations, which overlap somewhat, are pervaded by three major themes:

1. Dependence upon fallible human beings.
2. Incomplete or immature tools or technologies.
3. Techniques that cannot *practically* ensure the needed dependability.

4.1   Reliance upon Correct Requirements

The correctness of the requirements is assumed in many software development efforts. Unfortunately, requirements gathering depends unavoidably on fallible human beings. Requirement defects do occur: the majority of software defects in critical embedded systems, in fact, stem from requirements defects [18].

MBCS manifestation. The correctness of the requirements is assumed in 336 of 348 elements (97%) of the MBCS fitness argument. With the exception of an appeal to integration testing, the MBCS software fitness argument contends that the MBCS is fit for use in the context of the LifeFlow LVAD system because the MBCS meets the requirements imposed upon it by that system.

Potential mitigations. Many techniques have been suggested and used to re-duce the incidence of requirements defects. Requirements can, for example, be structured in such a way as to make omissions and contradictions more obvious, thereby increasing the likelihood that they will be caught and corrected [10]. Prototypes can be built to demonstrate an understanding of the requirements so that stakeholders have the opportunity to correct misconceptions. None of these techniques, however, will yield demonstrably adequate requirements.

Requirements for embedded software are derived from the design of the system in which the software is embedded. This replaces reliance upon a subject matter expert to enumerate requirements with a reliance upon the derivation process. Embedded software requirements can be no more trustworthy than the process used to derive them: defects in hazard analysis, fault tree analysis, Haz-Op studies, or FMECA could all contribute to erroneous software requirements.

4.2   Reliance upon Reliable Human-to-Human Communication

The construction of software requires precise communication of complex concepts, frequently between people with different backgrounds and expertise. Systems engineers, for example, must communicate software requirements completely and correctly to software engineers. Such communication again relies upon fallible humans and is fraught with the potential for error. In the worst case, the recipient of communication will be left with an understanding other than that which the originator intended *and will be unaware of the error.*

MBCS manifestation. The MBCS fitness argument does not explicitly address the sufficiency of human-to-human communication. The argument does, how-ever, reference 16 documents written in whole or in part in natural language, including the requirements, the specification, test plans, inspection protocols, various reports, and tool manuals. Of these, the strength of the main fitness claim rests most heavily upon correct understanding of the requirements. The potential for a misunderstanding of the requirements is mitigated somewhat by the use of an independent test team: unless the test team and the drafters and reviewers of the specification made the same mistake, the miscommunication would likely result in either a failed test case or a falsely failing test case.

Potential mitigations. The use of formal languages can partially address this problem. However, while formal semantics define precisely one meaning for a given formal text, it is impossible to formalize *all* engineering communication. Since formal languages are semantically void, natural language is unavoidable even if its use is restricted to binding formal tokens to real-world meanings.

Research has addressed the problem of communication deficiencies in engineering. The CLEAR method, for example, addresses misunderstandings of the terms used in requirements by building definitions that are demonstrably free of certain classes of common defects [8,20]. Unfortunately, we are aware of no method that can demonstrably reduce the incidence of miscommunication to an adequate level when the consequences of miscommunication are severe.

4.3 Reliance upon Understanding of the Semantics of Formalisms

In every software development effort, human beings read and write artifacts in at least one formal language, such as a programming language or specification language. Even if these languages contained no deliberate ambiguities (e.g. unspecified integer storage sizes in C), and even if their specifications were not given in natural language, the engineering processes surrounding them require fallible humans to accurately identify the meaning of each artifact written in them. As a result, a developer's misunderstanding of a language's semantics could lead to error. For example, a developer writing a formal specification in Z might forget which decorated arrow symbol corresponds with which type of relationship and so express a relationship other than that intended. Such errors become hard to reveal if the same misunderstanding is propagated to multiple artifacts (e.g. the specification and the source code) during development.

MBCS manifestation. Several formal artifacts appear in the MBCS fitness argument: the PVS specification, SPARK annotations, Ada and assembly language source code, the linker script, annotations for the WCET and stack usage analysis tools, and various tool configurations. Of these, the strength of the main fitness claim rests most heavily upon human understanding of the formal specification. While the result of a misunderstanding of the semantics of Ada or of the SPARK annotation language should be caught during Echo formal verification, there is no more authoritative artifact against which the specification can be mechanically checked.

Potential mitigations. Developers should be adequately trained and skilled in the languages that they employ, but training cannot guarantee perfect understanding. Mechanical verification of each formal artifact against a more authoritative artifact cannot address errors in the most authoritative artifacts. Moreover, the use of independent personnel in inspections and hand proofs, while helpful, cannot guarantee a sufficiently low rate of misunderstanding-based errors.

4.4   Reliance upon Reviews or Inspections

Reviews or inspections, properly performed, can be an effective tool for finding and eliminating defects [14]. Unfortunately, inspections, however performed, are performed by fallible humans and cannot *guarantee* the absence of a defect.

MBCS manifestation. We rely upon inspection to validate: (1) a separate argument showing that the specification refines the requirements; (2) the loop bounds and other configuration of the WCET tool; (3) the hand-generated bootstrap code; (4) the linker script; (5) the (non-SPARK) `memset` and `memcpy` routines; (6) the hardware interface routines, some written in assembly language; and (7) our usage of floating-point arithmetic.

In our fitness argument, shown in Fig. 2, the refinement sub-argument rooted at **ST_ArgOverRefinement** relies solely upon inspection to establish the correctness of non-SPARK code, including the absence of side effects that would invalidate the assumption of non-interference made during formal verification of the remaining code. However, functional testing evidence complements this sub-argument as shown in the figure.

Potential mitigations. Inspections can be limited to specific parts of specific artifacts, focused on answering specific questions, and structured so as to force a thorough and systematic examination of the artifacts [14]. While these improvements increase the overall rate at which inspectors find specific kinds of defects in specific work products, their use cannot justify concluding with high confidence that the inspected work products are free of the defects in question.

4.5   Reliance upon Human Compliance with Protocols

In many software development efforts, fallible human developers are required to precisely follow certain protocols. A configuration management protocol, for example, might require that a developer use configuration management software to label the version of source code to be built or ensure that the build machine is configured with the required version of the compiler and any libraries used. These protocols establish important properties, e.g. which versions of the source artifacts correspond with a given version of the executable. Should the developer fail to follow the protocol precisely, the property might not be established.

MBCS manifestation. The MBCS fitness argument requires human compliance with: (1) an integration testing protocol; (2) an argument review protocol; (3) a configuration management protocol; and (4) source code and tool configuration inspection protocols. In the cases of (1), (2), and (4), compliance is forced by requiring developers to sign off on the completion of protocol steps. Compliance with the configuration management protocol is cited in many areas of the fitness argument, as the protocol is used to guarantee that the various testing and analysis activities were conducted on the correct version of the correct artifact.

Potential mitigations. Checklists and sign-off sheets can help to ensure that developers are aware of the responsibilities imposed upon them by a protocol. However, even if they are taken seriously rather than treated as meaningless paperwork, a developer might still misunderstand the protocol's implications and sincerely indicate compliance without actually establishing the needed property.

4.6   Reliance upon Unqualified Tools

The fitness of software often relies on one or more of the tools used in its production. A defective compiler, for example, might produce an unfit executable from source code that has been mechanically proven to refine a correct formal specification. Clear and convincing evidence that tools are demonstrably fit for the use to which they are put is, unfortunately, rarely available. Even when available, such evidence will necessarily be limited in the same ways as evidence of the fitness of any software product.

MBCS manifestation. The MBCS fitness argument contains 14 instances of a "correct use of correct tool" argument pattern, explicitly denoting reliance upon the WCET tool, the test coverage tool, the test trace collection mechanism, the test execution and reporting tool, the PVS theorem prover, the Echo specification extractor [22], the SPARK Examiner, the SPARK POGS tool, the SPADE Simplifier, the SPADE proof checker, the Echo code transformer [22], the stack usage tool, the compiler (including its Ada compiler, PowerPC assembler, and linker), and the disassembler. In some of these cases, a defect in the tool or its configuration is unlikely to result in unfit software. A defective Echo transformer, for example, would be unlikely to produce transformed source code that did not preserve the semantics of the original and yet satisfied formal proofs of functional correctness. In other cases, correctness of a given tool is relied upon more heavily. The only provisions we made for catching an error introduced by a defective compiler, for example, are the functional and integration testing.

Potential mitigations. Ideally, developers of critical software systems would be able to choose from a range of tools, each accompanied by assurance of correctness that is adequate given the use to which the tool will be put. In the absence of such tools, developers must employ a development process in which an error introduced by an unqualified tool is adequately likely to be caught.

4.7   Reliance upon Tools That Lack Complete Hardware Models

Ideally, an embedded system developer would specify the desired system behavior in terms of signals visible at the boundary between the computer and the larger system and then use mechanical tools to prove that the software, running on the target computer, refines that specification. Unfortunately, the present generation of analysis tools typically models the hardware more abstractly and cannot easily be used to verify software functionality in this complete end-to-end sense.

MBCS manifestation. As part of the Echo formal verification to which we subjected the MBCS, we documented the behavior required of the implementation's subprograms using SPARK annotations. We then used the SPARK tools to prove that our implementations satisfied these specifications. (We used PVS proofs to complete the verification by showing that the subprograms, taken together, refine the formal specification.)

Unfortunately, this approach did not allow us to verify all aspects of the MBCS's hardware interface routines. We could not prove, for example, that a loop waiting on a hardware flag indicating the completion of analog-to-digital conversion would terminate in bounded time. Such a proof would require knowledge that the writes to memory-mapped variables that preceded the blocking loop would cause the hardware to set the flag in question in bounded time. Lacking an end-to-end solution for formally verifying this code, we relied upon a combination of testing and inspection to establish the needed properties.

Potential mitigations. Formal models of the behavior of computing hardware almost certainly exist, as they would be indispensable in the verification of the hardware. If these models could be extracted and translated into a form that could be used by software verification tools, it might be possible to extend formal verification to routines that interact with peripherals.

We note that a complete approach to end-to-end formal verification of embedded software might require using multiple tools. Tools such as the SPARK tools, which are based on a pre- and post-condition model, might need to be complemented by a tool such as a model checker that supports Linear Temporal Logic modeling. Such a combination would allow us to prove a more complete set of properties provided techniques were developed to permit the synergistic operation of the proof systems and a machine checked synthesis of the results.

4.8   The Unavoidable Use of Low-Level Code

High-level languages operate on an abstract model of the machine. When this model is inadequate, either because it does not permit control over some aspect of machine state that has been abstracted away or because efficiency needs preclude the use of a compiler, developers must write code in a low-level language such as the target assembly language. The verification technique chosen for the high-level code may not be applicable to this low-level language, the nature of which might limit the available analysis tools and techniques.

MBCS manifestation. We used the GNAT Pro Ada compiler to target the bare microcontroller with no Ada run-time library. While this obviated the need to procure a suitably-qualified operating system and standard libraries, it created the need for a startup routine that would configure the microcontroller to the state required for executing compiler-generated code. Our startup routine, written in PowerPC assembly language, configured the memory controller and enabled the microcontroller's floating-point unit. This choice also obliged us to supply implementations of the `memcpy` and `memset` library routines that are called by compiled code. Because implementing these routines required using access types, they had to be coded in plain Ada rather than SPARK Ada and verified via inspection (and testing) rather than formal verification.

Potential mitigations. Verification of assembly-level code and hardware interactions has been shown to be feasible [2,3]. A hybrid verification using multiple tools and techniques would allow the developer to exploit the unique capabilities of each tool, again with the difficulty of showing that the combination of techniques selected permits complete verification of the entire program.

4.9   The Ability to Verify Floating-Point Arithmetic

Functional requirements for computations are often conceived of in terms of real-valued or integer-valued arithmetic, but digital computers can only implement arithmetic on finite types. In the case of integer arithmetic, the practical distinction is well understood by programmers, who take care to allocate enough storage to handle the largest and smallest values a given variable might take on. The distinction between real-valued arithmetic and its floating-point approximation is less-well understood by average programmers. Even if each step is required to be correct by the IEEE-754 standard, the floating-point semantics (rounding and exceptions) might make the behavior of a program difficult to foresee and analyze.

MCBS manifestation. The Echo approach to formal verification treats floating-point arithmetic as if it were real-valued arithmetic with a bounded range. It tells us that our implementation does not use one variable when another was meant or multiplication where addition was meant. It cannot, however, tell us whether single-precision floating-point arithmetic is adequately precise for this application. We are forced to assume that it is.

Potential mitigations. Using floating-point computation to adequately substitute for real-valued arithmetic is quite complicated. Programmers might know rules of thumb such as "don't test for equality" and "avoid adding numbers of vastly-dissimilar exponent," but most programmers are not experts in the numerical field and we should not rely on the programmers' knowledge to produce correct floating-point arithmetic. Formal methods have been successfully used both for hardware-level and high-level floating-point arithmetic. If the rounding and approximation semantics are built into verification condition generation for the source code, one might be able to reason about the bound between floating-point results and the real-value results that they approximate. Such a technique does exist [4] and has been demonstrated to be useful for small C programs.

4.10   Reliance upon Testing

Requirements-based testing is used in all software projects to establish that the software meets its requirements, either alone or in parallel with formal verification evidence. Demonstrably adequate testing, however, is difficult or impossible for many critical software projects for several reasons:

1. Toy examples aside, *complete* input space coverage is unattainable. Furthermore, testing sufficient to establish high levels of reliability is infeasible [5].
2. The strength of testing evidence is limited by the degree to which one can trust the test oracle not to pass a test that should fail.
3. Instrumentation of the tested software might be required, making it uncertain that the results apply to the software which will be released.
4. Special computing hardware might be required, making it uncertain that the results apply to software running on the target hardware.
5. Test sequencing and test result collection tools may be defective.
6. Human developers may fail to follow the testing protocol faithfully.

MBCS manifestation. Functional testing evidence *complements* formal verification evidence in the MBCS fitness argument as shown in Fig. 2. We avoid instrumentation and assume that standard precautions such as the use of skilled, independent testers and test kit with an established history are sufficient. Since the functional correctness of the MBCS is *also* established by formal verification, some risk that the functional testing will miss an error can be tolerated.

Potential mitigations. Much has been written on the subject of testing, and there are many ways in which testing can be improved in one respect or another. However, we are aware of no approach to testing that can positively establish functionality where ultra-high levels of assurance are required.

4.11 Reliance upon Human Assessment of Dependability

Were the evidence of dependability perfect — the requirements, test results, and so on completely trustworthy — there would still be practical limitations on the degree to which adequate dependability could be assured. Safety cases and other rigorous assurance arguments have gained attention recently as a means of uniting and explaining dependability evidence, but the technology for validating such arguments is both immature and reliant upon fallible humans.

MBCS manifestation. Our confidence in the fitness of the MBCS rests entirely upon the sufficiency of its fitness argument. If the fitness argument were to contain a logical fallacy, for example, this confidence might be misplaced.

Potential mitigations. Validation of assurance arguments is an area of active research interest. Researchers have proposed argument review techniques [12] and taxonomies of argument fallacies to avoid [7]. In addition, research into improving the dependability of natural language communication in other domains [8] might prove useful if adapted to arguments. Nevertheless, we are aware of no approach than can positively establish the soundness of the assurance argument.

5 Related Work

The related work in specific areas of limitation have been discussed in section 4. The practical and theoretical limits of software dependability assurance have been the subject of numerous papers and discussions, e.g. [15,16,17], and the limitations discussed in this paper are known in isolation or related groups. Our contribution lies in analyzing the MBCS fitness argument to derive the dependability limitations affecting the MBCS and to assess the impact of each.

6   Conclusion

Analysis of our assurance argument revealed 11 major practical limitations on software dependability that affected our specimen software development effort. Each of these limitations embodied one or more of three themes: (1) dependence upon fallible human beings; (2) incomplete or immature tools or technologies; and (3) techniques that cannot *practically* ensure the needed dependability.

While time and investment may mitigate problems embodying only the second theme, the first and third themes reflect fundamental problems. Addressing these limitations in a given engineering effort requires structuring the development process so that the resulting weaknesses in dependability assurance are compensated for by the use of complementary efforts.

This case study demonstrates a significant benefit of assurance arguments: they convey comprehensively and intuitively precisely what the dependability of each software system depends upon. Furthermore, an argument explicitly documents where developers are relying upon the independence of evidence.

Acknowledgement

We thank Brett Porter of AdaCore and the AdaCore corporation for their support of the MBCS project, Paul Allaire and Houston Wood for details of the Life-Flow LVAD, and Kimberly Wasson for her constructive criticism. Work funded in part by National Science Foundation grants CNS-0716478 & CCF-0905375.

References

1. AdaCore: GNAT Pro High-Integrity Family. http://www.adacore.com/-home/products/gnatpro/development_solutions/safety-critical/
2. Alkassar, E., Hillebrand, M.A., Leinenbach, D.C., Schirmer, N.W., Starostin, A., Tsyban, A.: Balancing the load. Journal of Automated Reasoning 42(2), 389–454 (2009)
3. Alkassar, E., Schirmer, N., Starostin, A.: Formal pervasive verification of a paging mechanism. In: Tools and Algorithms for the Construction and Analysis of Systems, pp. 109–123 (2008)
4. Boldo, S., Filliatre, J.C.: Formal verification of floating-point programs. In: Proceedings of the 18th IEEE Symposium on Computer Arithmetic (ARITH 2007), pp. 187–194. IEEE Computer Society Press, Washington (2007)
5. Butler, R., Finelli, G.: The infeasibility of experimental quantification of life-critical software reliability. IEEE Trans. on Software Engineering, 66–76 (1991)

6. Graydon, P.J., Knight, J.C.: Software process synthesis in assurance based development of dependable systems. In: Proceedings of the 8th European Dependable Computing Conference (EDCC), Valencia, Spain (April 2010)

7. Greenwell, W., Knight, J., Holloway, C., Pease, J.: A taxonomy of fallacies in system safety arguments. In: Proceedings of the 2006 International System Safety Conference (ISSC 2006), Albuquerque, NM, USA (July 2006)

8. Hanks, K., Knight, J.: Improving communication of critical domain knowledge in high-consequence software development: An empirical study. In: Proceedings of the 21st International System Safety Conference, Ottawa, Canada (August 2003)

9. Hayhurst, K.J., Veerhusen, D.S., Chilenski, J.J., Rierson, L.K.: A practical tutorial on modified condition / decision coverage. Technical Memorandum TM-2001-210876, NASA, Hampton, VA (May 2001)

10. Heninger, K.L.: Specifying software requirements for complex systems: New techniques and their application. IEEE Transactions on Software Engineering 6(1), 2–13 (1980)

11. Kelly, T.: A systematic approach to safety case management. In: Proc. of the Society for Automotive Engineers 2004 World Congress, Detroit, MI, USA (2004)

12. Kelly, T.: Reviewing assurance arguments — a step-by-step approach. In: Proceedings of the Workshop on Assurance Cases for Security — The Metrics Challenge, Dependable Systems and Networks (DSN) (July 2007)

13. Klein, G., Elphinstone, K., Heiser, G., Andronick, J., Cock, D., Derrin, P., Elkaduwe, D., Engelhardt, K., Kolanski, R., Norrish, M., Sewell, T., Tuch, H., Winwood, S.: seL4: Formal verification of an OS kernel. In: Proc. of the 22nd ACM Symposium on Operating Systems Principles, Big Sky, MT, USA (October 2009)

14. Knight, J.C., Myers, E.A.: An improved inspection technique. Communications of the ACM 36(11), 51–61 (1993)

15. Laprie, J.C., Le Lann, G., Morganti, M., Rushby, J.: Panel session on limits in dependability. In: Highlights from Twenty-Five Years, Twenty-Fifth International Symposium on Fault-Tolerant Computing, June 1995, pp. 608–613 (1995)

16. Littlewood, B.: Limits to dependability assurance — a controversy revisited. In: Companion to the proceedings of the 29th International Conference on Software Engineering (ICSE 2007), Washington, DC, USA (2007)

17. Littlewood, B., Strigini, L.: Validation of ultrahigh dependability for software-based systems. Communications of the ACM 36(11), 69–80 (1993)

18. Lutz, R.R.: Analyzing software requirements errors in safety-critical, embedded systems. In: Proc. of the IEEE International Symposium on Requirements Engineering (RE 1993), San Diego, CA, USA (January 1993)

19. SRI International: PVS specification and verification system, http://pvs.csl.sri.com/

20. Wasson, K.S.: CLEAR requirements: improving validity using cognitive linguistic elicitation and representation. Ph.D. thesis, University of Virginia, Charlottesville, VA, USA (May 2006)

21. Yin, X., Knight, J., Nguyen, E., Weimer, W.: Formal verification by reverse synthesis. In: Harrison, M.D., Sujan, M.-A. (eds.) SAFECOMP 2008. LNCS, vol. 5219, pp. 305–319. Springer, Heidelberg (2008)

22. Yin, X., Knight, J.C., Weimer, W.: Exploiting refactoring in formal verification. In: Proc. of the 39th Annual IEEE/IFIP International Conference on Dependable Systems and Networks (DSN 2009), Lisbon, Portugal (June 2009)

Program Verification in SPARK and ACSL: A Comparative Case Study

Eduardo Brito and Jorge Sousa Pinto

Departamento de Informática / CCTC
Universidade do Minho, Braga, Portugal
{edbrito,jsp}@di.uminho.pt

Abstract. We present a case-study of developing a simple software module using contracts, and rigorously verifying it for safety and functional correctness using two very different programming languages, that share the fact that both are extensively used in safety-critical development: SPARK and C/ACSL. This case-study, together with other investigations not detailed here, allows us to establish a comparison in terms of specification effort and degree of automation obtained with each toolset.

1 Introduction

In recent years, deductive program verification based on contracts and JML-like annotation languages has been a very active and fruitful area of research. The state of the art of currently available tools has been greatly advanced with the use of SMT provers and other automatic proof tools targeted for verification.

The SPARK [1] programming language and toolset offers program verification capabilities as part of a wider array of static analyses aimed at the development of high-integrity software. The SPARK reality is different from that faced by verification tools for general-purpose languages, since the SPARK language itself is so restricted (as imposed by the specific application domains in which it is used) that some of the big verification challenges (to name one: the manipulation of data structures in the program heap) are not even present.

Curiously, our industrial research partners who work in the safety-critical context (more specifically, in the development of real-time, embedded applications) are mainly interested in two programming languages: SPARK and C. This may sound surprising, as one can hardly think of two imperative languages that stand farther away from each other in terms of safety restrictions, but it is a reality. Prompted by this fact, we present in this paper an attempt to compare SPARK with C in terms of the programming and annotation languages, as well as the currently available verification tools. Naturally, this comparison only makes sense for a subset of C that excludes features that are absent in SPARK.

Let us recall two fundamental differences between both programming languages, in addition to the safety issues: C has very little support for abstraction, whereas SPARK, which is a subset of Ada, explicitly supports abstract data types, as well as refinement. In SPARK specification contracts are part of the language; in C we resort to the external ACSL [3] specification language.

J. Real and T. Vardanega (Eds.): Ada-Europe 2010, LNCS 6106, pp. 97–110, 2010.

Our goals are (i) to explain the differences involved in coding a very simple software module when full verification is an issue; (ii) to evaluate the relative difficulty of establishing the safe execution of programs in both platforms (we expect it to be easier in SPARK, as a consequence of the language design); and (iii) to assess how the verification tools compare in terms of automatic proof.

The paper can be used by readers familiar with either ACSL (or other JML-like language) or SPARK, as a quick introduction to the other platform, and as a general introduction to verified development in both languages. We believe this to be a useful contribution towards promoting the use of such tools.

2   Background

The goal of deductive program verification is to *statically* ensure that a program performs according to some intended specification, resorting to the axiomatic semantics of the programming languages and tools like theorem provers. Typically, what is meant by this is that the input/output behaviour of the implementation matches that of the specification (this is usually called the *functional* behaviour of the program), and moreover the program does not 'go wrong', for instance no errors occur during evaluation of expressions (the so-called *safety* behaviour). Related approaches that do not concern us here are *dynamic verification* (which considers a single run of a program), *software model checking* (based on the exploration of a limited state space), and *extended static checking* (which abandons correctness and completeness for the sake of automation). Neither of these offer as high an assurance degree as deductive verification.

The idea of a software *contract* – consisting, for each procedure / method, of a precondition that should be established by the caller and a postcondition that must be established by the callee – was initially meant to be used as part of a software development cycle that relies on dynamic verification. The code is compiled by a special compiler that introduces run-time checks for the contracts in the code, that will be executed at call-time and at return-time. Since these conditions are checked dynamically, they must be written as boolean expressions in the syntax of the programming language, which may include calls to other methods or functions defined as part of the same program.

Figure 1 shows a typical specification of a bounded stack that can be found in many tutorials on the design by contract approach to software development [13]. The figure contains an informal description of each operation on stacks, and in some cases a contract consisting of a precondition and a postcondition. Notice that methods count, capacity, and isFull occur in several preconditions and postconditions. In fact, the first two are not usually given as part of a stack's interface, and their presence is justified by their use in other methods' contracts.

In general, annotation languages include two features that can be found in postconditions in this example: the possibility of referring to the value of an expression in the pre-state (old_count() for count), and of referring to the return value (Result). The preconditions state that some stack operations cannot be performed on an empty or a full stack, while the postconditions partially specify

- `nat count()` – Returns the number of elements currently in the stack.
- `nat capacity()` – Returns the maximum number of elements that the stack may contain.
- `boolean isEmpty()` – Returns information on whether the stack is empty.
  Postcond: `Result = (count() = 0)`
- `boolean isFull()` – Returns information on whether the stack is full.
  Postcond: `Result = (count() = capacity())`
- `int top()` – Returns the top of the stack.
  Precond: `not isEmpty()`
- `void pop()` – Removes the top of the stack.
  Precond: `not isEmpty()`; Postcond: `count() = old_count() - 1`
- `void push(int n)` – Pushes item n onto the stack.
  Precond: `not isFull()`; Postcond: `count() = old_count() + 1 and top() = n`

Fig. 1. Stack operations

the functional behaviour of the methods. This is straightforward for `isEmpty` and `isFull`. For `push` the postcondition ensures that the element at the top of the stack on exit is indeed the pushed value, and the stack count is increased with respect to its initial value; for `top` the contract simply states that the count is decreased. It is implicit that the stack remains unmodified, with the exception of its top element when performing a push or pop operation.

Although program verification based on preconditions and postconditions pre-dates design by contract by decades, it has been revitalized by the growing popularity of the latter and the advent of specification languages like JML [10], intended to be used by different tools ranging from dynamic checking to test-case generation, static analysis and verification. In contract-based program verifica-tion each procedure C is annotated with a contract (Precond: P; Postcond: Q); checking its correctness amounts to establishing the validity of the Hoare triple $\{P\}\,C\,\{Q\}$ [8]. A program is correct if all its constituent annotated procedures are correct. The verification process follows the mutually recursive nature of pro-grams: in proving the correctness of procedure f that invokes procedure g, one simply assumes the correctness of g with respect to its contract. In a deductive framework, correctness of a program can be established by the following steps.

1. Annotating the source code with specifications in the form of contracts (for every procedure / function / method) and invariant information for loops;
2. Generating from the code, with the help of a *verification conditions generator* tool (VCGen for short), a set of first-order proof obligations (verification conditions, VCs), whose validity will imply the correctness of the code; and
3. Discharging the verification conditions using a proof tool. If all VCs are valid then the program is correct.

ACSL/Frama-C and SPARK. Frama-C [3] is a tool for the static analysis of C programs. It is based on the intermediate language Jessie [11] and the multi-prover VCGen Why [7]. C programs are annotated using the ANSI-C Specifi-cation Language (ACSL). Frama-C contains the **gwhy** graphical front-end that allows to monitor individual verification conditions. This is particularly useful when combined with the possibility of exporting the conditions to various proof tools, which allows users to first try discharging conditions with one or more automatic provers, leaving the harder conditions to be studied with the help of an interactive proof assistant. For the examples in this paper we have used the Simplify [6] and Alt-Ergo [5] automatic theorem provers. Both Frama-C and ACSL are work in progress; we have used the Lithium release of Frama-C.

SPARK on the other hand is both a language and a toolset. The language is a strict subset of the Ada 95 standard, with some added anotations, designed with predictability and safety in mind. What we mean by strict is that every SPARK program is a valid Ada 95 program. This is very important since the SPARK toolset does not provide a compiler, relying instead on existing Ada compilers. A clearly defined semantics for the SPARK subset of Ada 95 is obtained by imposing a set of rules that precisely define a set of programming practices and limitations that do not depend on specific aspects of the compiler.

Because SPARK was created mainly to be used in the context of critical embedded and real-time systems, it imposes some restrictions that may seem too harsh, but are in fact fairly standard in those scenarios. For instance in embedded systems it is usually important to know the exact memory footprint of the programs, so dynamic memory allocation is forbidden in SPARK. Also, pointers / pointer operations and recursion are not present in SPARK.

The most relevant tools in the toolset are the Examiner, the Simplifier, and the interactive Proof Checker. The Examiner is responsible for checking if the Ada code is compliant with the set of restrictions imposed by SPARK, including the consistency of programs with respect to data and information flow annotations. It also contains the VCGen functionality responsible for generating the proof obligations. The Simplifier tool simplifies and attempts to automatically discharge the verification conditions, with the help of user-supplied rules. Although not a powerful automatic theorem prover of the same nature as those used by Frama-C, it is a carefully designed tool that incorporates many years of experience in simplifying typical VCs. The Proof Checker is the manual, interactive prover. For this work we have used SPARK GPL edition 2009, V. 8.1.1.

3   Bounded Stack: Specification

We use the bounded stack example to illustrate the differences between the verified development of a small software module in SPARK and C/ACSL. We first discuss a few modifications of the typical DbC specification in Figure 1. If we think algebraically in terms of the usual stack equations:

$$top(push(n, s)) = n \qquad\qquad pop(push(n, s)) = s$$

Only the first equation is ensured by the contracts of Figure 1. Note that the contracts for push and pop do not state that the methods preserve all the elements in the stack apart from the top element; they simply specify how the *number* of elements is modified. We will strengthen the specification by introducing a *substack* predicate, to express the fact that a stack is a substack of another. The notion of substack together with the variation in size allows for a complete specification of the behaviour of these operations. Equally, the contracts for top, isEmpty, and isFull must state that these methods do not modify the stack (i.e. they have no side effects, which is not stated in Figure 1).

Additionally, we add to the specification an initialisation function that creates an empty stack. Also, we consider that the operations count and capacity are not part of the interface of the data type (they are not available to the programmer). In both specification languages count and capacity will be turned into the *logical functions* count_of and cap_of that exist only at the level of annotations, and are not part of the program. These logical functions are sometimes also called *hybrid functions* because they read program data. In ACSL they are declared inside an axiomatic section at the beginning of the file. Note that no definition or axioms can be given at this stage for the logical functions.

In SPARK (as in Ada) the specification and implementation of a package are usually placed in two separate files: the *package specification* (.ads) and the *package body* (.adb) containing the implementation. Packages are separately

```
package Stack
--# own State: StackType;
is
   --# type StackType is abstract;
   --# function Count_of(S: StackType) return Natural;
   --# function Cap_of(S: StackType) return Natural;
   --# function Substack(S1: StackType; S2: StackType) return Boolean;

   MaxStackSize: constant := 100;

   procedure Init;
   --# global out State;
   --# derives State from;
   --# post Cap_of(State) = MaxStackSize and Count_of(State) = 0;

   function isEmpty return Boolean;
   --# global State;
   --# return Count_of(State) = 0;

   function isFull return Boolean;
   --# global State;
   --# return Count_of(State) = Cap_of(State);

   function Top return Integer;
   --# global State;
   --# pre Count_of(State) > 0;

   procedure Pop;
   --# global in out State;
   --# derives State from State;
   --# pre 0 < Count_of(State);
   --# post Cap_of(State) = Cap_of(State~) and Count_of(State) = Count_of(State~)-1 and
   --#      Substack(State, State~);

   procedure Push(X: in Integer);
   --# global in out State;
   --# derives State from State, X;
   --# pre Count_of(State) < Cap_of(State);
   --# post Cap_of(State) = Cap_of(State~) and Count_of(State) = Count_of(State~)+1 and
   --#      Top(State) = X and Substack(State~, State);
end Stack;
```

Fig. 2. Stack SPARK specification

compiled program units that may contain both data and code and provide encapsulation. Figure 2 shows the specification file for the Stack package; `StackType` is an abstract type that is used at the specification level and will later be instantiated in a package body. In the package specification a variable `State` of type `StackType` stands for an abstract stack, i.e. an element of the ADT specified. This will be refined in the body into one or more variables of concrete types.

The specification of a bounded stack in ACSL is given in Figure 3. For the sake of simplicity we choose to use a global stack variable, but stacks could equally be passed by reference to the C functions. A crucial difference with respect to the SPARK specification is that ACSL has *no support for refinement* (and neither has C, of course). Thus in the figure the `typedef` declaration is left unfinished. The reader should bear in mind that it will not be possible to reason about stacks without first providing a concrete implementation. Whereas in SPARK/Ada one can have different implementations in different body files for the same package specification file, in C those implementations would have to be obtained using the file in the figure as a *template* that would be expanded.

Some language features are directly reflected in the two specifications. The SPARK function `Init` will always produce an empty stack with capacity given by the constant `MaxStackSize`, since dynamic allocation is not possible. In the C version it takes the desired stack capacity as argument. Also, we take advantage of SPARK's type system and set the type returned by functions `Cap_of` and `Count_of` to `Natural` rather than `Integer` (since the number of elements cannot be negative). C's type system is much less precise, thus integers are used instead, but note the use of the `integer` ACSL logical type (for logical functions only).

Concerning the two specification languages, different keywords are used to identify preconditions (`pre`, `requires`) and postconditions (`post`, `ensures`), as well as the return values (`return`, `\result`). Also, ACSL offers the possibility of using optional *behaviours* in specifications, which permits the association of more than one contract to a function. For instance the behaviour `empty` (resp. `not_empty`) of function `isEmpty` corresponds to the precondition that the current count is zero (resp. not zero), specified with an *assumes* clause. Behaviours allow for more readable specifications and for more structured sets of VCs.

C functions may in general have side effects, whereas SPARK functions are by definition *pure*: they are not allowed to modify the global state or to take parameters passed by reference. Thus the SPARK functions `isEmpty`, `isFull`, and `top` are not allowed to modify the state of the stack, which is an improvement (obtained for free) with respect to the contracts in Figure 1. In ACSL functions can be annotated with *frame conditions* that specify the modified parts of the state (variables, structure fields, array elements, etc). The frame conditions of the above three pure functions are written `assigns \nothing`. Appropriate verification conditions are generated to ensure the validity of each frame condition.

A consequence of the previous difference is that SPARK allows for program functions to be used in assertions, whereas in ACSL this is forbidden because of the possibility of side effects. This is reflected in different treatments of the `Top` function in both languages: in the SPARK specification `Top` is a program function

```
typedef ... Stack;
Stack st;

/*@ axiomatic Pilha {
  @ logic integer cap_of{L} (Stack st) = ...
  @ logic integer top_of{L} (Stack st) = ...
  @ logic integer count_of{L} (Stack st) = ...
  @ predicate substack{L1,L2} (Stack st) = ...
  @ } */

/*@ requires cap >= 0;
  @ ensures cap_of{Here}(st) == cap  && count_of{Here}(st) == 0;
  @*/
void init (int cap);

/*@ assigns \nothing;
  @ behavior empty:
  @    assumes count_of{Here}(st) == 0;
  @    ensures \result == 1;
  @ behavior not_empty:
  @    assumes count_of{Here}(st) != 0;
  @    ensures \result == 0;
  @*/
int isEmpty (void);

/*@ assigns \nothing;
  @ behavior full:
  @    assumes count_of{Here}(st) == cap_of{Here}(st);
  @    ensures \result == 1;
  @ behavior not_full:
  @    assumes count_of{Here}(st) != cap_of{Here}(st);
  @    ensures \result == 0;
  @*/
int isFull (void);

/*@ requires 0 < count_of{Here}(st);
  @ ensures \result == top_of{Here}(st);
  @ assigns \nothing;
  @*/
int top (void);

/*@ requires 0 < count_of{Here}(st);
  @ ensures cap_of{Here}(st) == cap_of{Old}(st) &&
  @         count_of{Here}(st) == count_of{Old}(st) - 1 &&
  @         substack{Here,Old}(st);
  @*/
void pop(void);

/*@ requires count_of{Here}(st) < cap_of{Here}(st);
  @ ensures cap_of{Here}(st) == cap_of{Old}(st) &&
  @         count_of{Here}(st) == count_of{Old}(st) + 1 &&
  @         top_of{Here}(st) == x && substack{Old,Here}(st);
  @*/
void push (int x);
```

Fig. 3. Stack ACSL specification: operation contracts

and it is used in the postcondition of Push, whereas in ACSL a new logical function top_of is used; its relation with the top program function is established by a postcondition of the latter. In addition to logical / hybrid functions, ACSL offers the possibility of having *predicates* to be used in annotations; they may be either defined or else declared and their behaviour described by means of axioms. In SPARK a predicate must be declared as a logical function that returns a boolean. This is reflected in the declarations of substack in both languages.

In ACSL it is possible to refer to the value of an expression in a given program state, which is extremely useful in any language with some form of indirect memory access. In fact, all hybrid functions and predicates *must* take as extra arguments a set of *state labels* in which the value of the parameters are read, even if this set is singular. Thus, for instance, whereas in SPARK the substack predicate takes two stacks as arguments, and is invoked (in the postconditions of Pop and Push) with arguments State and State~, where the latter refers to the state of the stack in the pre-state, the ACSL version takes as arguments a single stack variable st and two state labels L_1, L_2 , with the meaning that the value of st in state L_1 is a substack of the value of st in state L_2. It is then invoked in annotations making use of predefined program labels *Here* (the current state) and *Old* (the pre-state in which the function was invoked).

In SPARK the procedures Init, Pop, and Push have data flow annotations with the meaning that the state of the stack is both read and modified, and the new state depends on the previous state (and for Push also on the argument X). In functions, the --# global State; data flow annotation simply means that these functions read the state of the stack. At this abstract level of development, it is not possible to specify with either SPARK data flow annotations or ACSL frame conditions that the procedures do not modify some *part* of the state (e.g. pop and push preserve the capacity). This has then to be done using postconditions.

Reasoning about Specifications in SPARK. A major difference between both languages is that in SPARK it is possible to reason in the absence of concrete implementations. To illustrate this, we will define a procedure that swaps the values of two variables using a stack. The relevant package and body are shown in Figure 4. Running the SPARK Examiner on this file produces 9 verification conditions, of which, after running the SPARK Simplifier, only one is left unproved. This VC is generated from the postcondition of Swap, which is only natural since we haven't given a definition of substack.

The SPARK Simplifier allows users to supply additional rules and axioms, in the FDL logical language, in a separate file. The following SPARK rule states that two equally sized substacks of the same stack have the same top elements.

```
ss_rule(1) : stack__top(S1) = stack__top(S2) may_be_deduced_from
 [stack__count_of(S1) = stack__count_of(S2), stack__substack(S1,S3), stack__substack(S2,S3)].
```

Unfortunately, even with this rule, the Simplifier fails to automatically discharge the VC, so the user would be forced to go into interactive proof mode (using the SPARK Proof Checker) to finish verifying the program. Alternatively, the following rule allows the Simplifier to finish the proof automatically:

```
with Stack;
--# inherit Stack;
package SSwap is
  procedure Swap(X, Y: in out Integer);
    --# global in out Stack.State;
    --# derives Stack.State, X, Y from Stack.State, X, Y;
    --# pre Stack.Count_of(Stack.State) <= Stack.Cap_of(Stack.State)-2;
    --# post X = Y~ and Y = X~;
end SSwap;

package body SSwap is
  procedure Swap(X, Y: in out Integer)
    is
    begin
       Stack.Push(X); Stack.Push(Y);
       X := Stack.Top; Stack.Pop;
       Y := Stack.Top; Stack.Pop;
    end Swap;
end SSwap;
```

Fig. 4. Swap using a stack

```
ss_rule(3) : stack__top(S1) = stack__top(S2) may_be_deduced_from
   [stack__count_of(S3) = stack__count_of(S2)+1, stack__count_of(S1) = stack__count_of(S3)-1,
    stack__substack(S1,S3), stack__substack(S2,S3)].
```

This also illustrates a technique that we find very useful with the Simplifier: writing special purpose rules that follow the structure of the computation. In this example we have simply mentioned explicitly the intermediate stack S_3 that the state goes through betwen S_2 and S_1. This is often sufficient to allow the Simplifier to discharge all VCs without the need for interactive proof.

4   Bounded Stack: Implementation / Refinement

Figure 5 shows a fragment of the stack package implementation, including the definition of the state and the definition of the Push procedure. The corresponding fragment in C is given in Figure 6. The state is in both cases defined as a set of two integer variables (for the size and capacity) together with an array variable. In SPARK a *range type* Ptrs is used, which is not possible in C.

In C we simply fill in the template of Figure 3 without touching the annotations. We consider a straightforward implementation of bounded stacks as structures containing fields for the capacity and size, as well as a dynamically allocated array. This requires providing, in addition to the C function definitions, appropriate definitions of the logical functions cap_of, top_of, and count_of, as well as of the predicate substack. count_of and cap_of simply return the values of structure fields. The most sophisticated aspect is the use of a universal quantifier in the definition of substack. Note also the use of the operator \at to refer to the value of a field of a structure variable in a given program state (not required when a single state label is in scope – it is implicit).

SPARK on the other hand has explicit support for refinement. Thus contracts can be written at a lower level using the state variables, as exemplified by the

```
package body Stack
--# own State is Capacity, Ptr, Vector;
is
    type Ptrs is range 0..MaxStackSize;
    subtype Indexes is Ptrs range 1..Ptrs'Last;
    type Vectors is array (Indexes) of Integer;

    Capacity: Ptrs := 0;
    Ptr: Ptrs := 0;
    Vector: Vectors := Vectors'(Indexes => 0);

    procedure Push(X: in Integer)
    --# global in out Vector, Ptr;
    --#        in Capacity;
    --# derives Ptr from Ptr & Vector from Vector, Ptr, X & null from Capacity;
    --# pre Ptr < Capacity;
    --# post Ptr = Ptr~ + 1 and Vector = Vector~[Ptr => X];
    is
    begin
        Ptr := Ptr + 1;
        Vector(Ptr) := X;
        --# accept F, 30, Capacity, "Only used in contract";
    end Push;
```

```
stack_rule(1) : cap_of(S) may_be_replaced_by fld_capacity(S) .
stack_rule(2) : count_of(S) may_be_replaced_by fld_ptr(S) .
stack_rule(3) : count_of(X) = count_of(Y) - Z may_be_replaced_by fld_ptr(Y) = fld_ptr(X) + Z.
stack_rule(4) : count_of(X) = count_of(Y) + Z may_be_replaced_by fld_ptr(X) = fld_ptr(Y) + Z.
stack_rule(5) : count_of(S) = cap_of(S) may_be_replaced_by fld_ptr(S) = fld_capacity(S).
stack_rule(6) : substack(X, Y) may_be_deduced_from
  [V=fld_vector(X), Z=fld_ptr(X)+1, Z may_be_replaced_by fld_ptr(Y), fld_vector(Y)=update(V, [Z], N)].
stack_rule(7) : substack(X, Y) may_be_deduced_from
  [fld_vector(X)=fld_vector(Y), fld_ptr(X)<fld_ptr(Y)].
stack_rule(8) : stack__top(X) = Y may_be_deduced_from
  [fld_vector(X) = update(Z, [fld_ptr(X)], Y)] .
```

Fig. 5. Stack SPARK implementation (fragment) and user-provided rules

Push procedure. Since there are no logical definitions as such in SPARK, the functions `cap_of` and `count_of` will be handled by the user rules `stack_rule(1)` and `stack_rule(2)` that can be applied as rewrite rules in both hypotheses and conclusions. The user rules 3 to 5 are auxiliary rules; their presence illustrates the limitations of the Simplifier in applying the previous 2 rewrite rules.

Refinement Verification in SPARK. Invoking the SPARK examiner with both package and body files will produce a set of verification conditions, establishing a correspondence between specification and implementation contracts in the classic sense of refinement: given a procedure with specification precondition P_s (resp. postcondition Q_s) and body precondition P_b (resp. postcondition Q_b), the VCs $P_s \implies P_b$ and $Q_b \implies Q_s$ will be generated, together with conditions for correctness of the procedure's body with respect to the specification (P_b, Q_b).

A crucial refinement aspect of our example has to do with the `substack` predicate. Note that there is no mention of the predicate at the implementation level, so we must now provide rules for inferring when a stack is a substack of another. Writing a rule based on the use of a quantifier (as we did in ACSL) would not help the Simplifier (although it could be used for interactive proof), thus we provide instead rule (6) for the specific case when X is a substack of Y that contains only one more element (`fld_vector` and `fld_ptr` correspond to the fields `Vector` and `Ptr` respectively in the stack body), and rule (7) regarding the case of two stacks represented by the same vector with different counters. These basically describe what happens in the `push` and `pop` operations.

In these rules we make use of the fact that SPARK arrays are logically modeled using the standard theory of arrays [14], accessed through the `element` and `update` operations. In particular the expression `update(V, [Z], N)` denotes the array that results from array `V` by setting the contents of the position with index `Z` to be `N`. Rule (8) concerns the top of a stack after an update operation at the `ptr` position. With these rules the Simplifier is able to discharge all VCs.

Verification of C code. Our C/ACSL file now contains a full implementation of the stack operations, based on the previously given contracts. Let us add to this a `swap` function (also shown in Figure 6). Running Frama-C on this file will generate verification conditions that together assert that the code of the stack operations and of the `swap` function conforms to their respective contracts. 38 VCs are generated, only 4 of which, labelled "pointer dereferencing", are not discharged automatically. These are safety conditions, discussed below.

```
typedef struct stack {
  int capacity;
  int size;
  int *elems;
} Stack;

int x, y;
Stack st;

/*@ axiomatic Pilha {
  @ logic integer cap_of{L} (Stack st) = st.capacity;
  @ logic integer top_of{L} (Stack st) = st.elems[st.size-1];
  @ logic integer count_of{L} (Stack st) = st.size;
  @ predicate substack{L1,L2} (Stack st) = \at(st.size,L1) <= \at(st.size,L2) &&
  @ \forall integer i; 0<=i<\at(st.size,L1) ==> \at(st.elems[i],L1) == \at(st.elems[i],L2);
  @ predicate stinv{L}(Stack st) =
  @ \valid_range(st.elems,0,st.capacity-1) && 0 <= count_of{L}(st) <= cap_of{L}(st);
  @ } */

/*@ requires count_of{Here}(st) < cap_of{Here}(st) && stinv{Here}(st);
  @ ensures cap_of{Here}(st) == cap_of{Old}(st) && count_of{Here}(st) == count_of{Old}(st)+1
  @ && top_of{Here}(st) == x && substack{Old,Here}(st) && stinv{Here}(st);
  @*/
void push (int x) {
  st.elems[st.size] = x;
  st.size++;
}

/*@ ensures x == \old(y) && y == \old(x);
  @*/
swap() {
  init(3); push(x);  push(y); x = top(); pop(); y = top(); pop();
}
```

Fig. 6. Stack C implementation (extract) and test function (`swap`)

Safety Checking.   Being able to write exception-free code is a very desirable feature in embedded and critical systems. In the stack example this is relevant for array out-of-bounds access, and again the two languages offer different approaches. An important feature of SPARK is that, using proof annotations and automatically generated safety conditions, programs can be shown statically not to cause runtime exceptions. The expression *runtime checks* (or *safety conditions*) designates VCs whose validity ensures the absence of runtime errors.

In the SPARK implementation the domain type of the array is a range type (as are the other state variables), which in itself precludes out-of-bounds access. The runtime errors that may occur concern precisely the range types: every use of an integer expression (in particular in assignments and array accesses) will generate conditions regarding the lower and upper bounds of the expression. For instance the instruction `Ptr := Ptr + 1` in the `Push` procedure generates a VC to check that `ptr + 1` lies within the range of type `Indexes`. Such conditions are generated and automatically discharged in both the `swap` and the refinement verification in a completely transparent way.

ACSL on the other hand treats array accesses (and pointer dereferencing in general) through special-purpose annotations. This is motivated by the very different nature of arrays in C – in particular they can be dynamically allocated and no range information is contained in their types. A `valid_range` annotation in a function precondition expresses that it is safe for the function to access an array in a given range of indexes. It should also be mentioned that a memory region separation assumption is used by default when reasoning about arrays.

Frama-C automatically introduces verification conditions for checking against out-of-bound accesses, thus the 4 VCs left unproved in our example. In order to address this issue we create a new predicate `stinv` that expresses a safety invariant on stacks (the count must not surpass the capacity, and array accesses should be valid within the range corresponding to the capacity). It suffices to include this predicate as precondition and postcondition in all operation contracts (with the exception of the precondition of `init`) for the safety conditions to be automatically discharged. The modifications are already reflected in Figure 6.

5   Conclusion

We are of course comparing two very different toolsets, one for a language with dynamic memory and 'loose' compilation, and another for a memory-bounded language with very strict compilation rules and side-effects explicitly identified in annotations (not to mention the refinement aspect). From our experience with SPARK and the study of published case studies the Simplifier does a very good job of automatically discharging safety conditions. The Simplifier has been compared with SMT solvers, and the relative advantages of each discussed [9].

While it would be unfair to compare SPARK with Frama-C in terms of the performance of safety checking (in particular because SPARK benefits from the strict rules provided by Ada regarding runtime exceptions), we simply state that safety-checking ACSL specifications requires an additional effort to provide specific safety annotations, whereas in SPARK runtime checks are transparently performed. On the other hand a general advantage of Frama-C is the multi-prover aspect of the VCGen: one can effortlessly export VCs to different provers, including tools as diverse as SMT solvers and the Coq [12] proof assistant. Finally, it is important to remark that unlike SPARK, to this date Frama-C has not, to the best of our knowledge, been used in large-scale industrial projects.

The situation changes significantly when other functional aspects are considered. Take this example from the Tokeneer project, a biometric secure system implemented in SPARK and certified according to the Common Criteria higher levels of assurance (http://www.adacore.com/tokeneer). We were quite surprised to find that the Simplifier is unable to prove C1 from H20:

```
H20: element(logfileentries__1, [currentlogfile]) =
        element(logfileentries, [currentlogfile]) + 1 .
-> C1: element(logfileentries, [currentlogfile]) -
        element(logfileentries__1, [currentlogfile]) = - 1 .
```

Simple as it is, our case study has shown that the Simplifier's ability for reasoning with logical functions and user-provided rules is quite limited. Also, our experiences with more 'algorithmic' examples involving loop invariants show that Frama-C is quite impressive in this aspect. For instance fairly complex sorting algorithms, involving nested loops and assertions with quantification, can be checked in Frama-C in a completely automatic manner, with no additional user-provided axioms or rules. In this respect it is our feeling that the SPARK technology needs to be updated or complemented with additional tools.

To sum up our findings, the effort that goes into verifying safe runtime execution is smaller in SPARK, whereas the situation seems to be reversed when the specification and automatic verification of other functional aspects is considered.

One aspect that our running example has not illustrated is related to *aliasing*. Reasoning about procedures with parameters passed by reference is typically difficult because such a procedure may access the same variable through different lvalues, for instance a procedure may access a global variable both directly and through a parameter. In SPARK such situations are rejected by the Examiner after data-flow analysis, so verification conditions are not even generated.

In C such programs are of course considered valid, but note that these situations can only be created by using pointer parameters, and it is possible to reason about such functions with pointer-level assertions. For instance, a function that takes two pointer variables may have to be annotated with an additional precondition stating that the values of the pointer parameters (not the dereferenced values) are different. We have stressed the importance of the use of state labels in ACSL; for reasoning about dynamic structures, serious users of Frama-C will also want to understand in detail the memory model underlying ACSL and the associated separation assumptions, which is out of our scope here.

Finally, we should mention that other tools are available for checking C code, such as VCC [4]. Many other verification tools exist for object-oriented languages; Spec# [2] is a good example.

Acknowledgment. This work was supported by project RESCUE, funded by FCT (PTDC/EIA/65862/2006).

References

1. Barnes, J.: High Integrity Software: The SPARK Approach to Safety and Security. Addison-Wesley Longman Publishing Co., Inc., Boston (2003)
2. Barnett, M., DeLine, R., Fähndrich, M., Jacobs, B., Leino, K.R.M., Schulte, W., Venter, H.: The Spec# Programming System: Challenges and Directions. In: Meyer, B., Woodcock, J. (eds.) VSTTE 2005. LNCS, vol. 4171, pp. 144–152. Springer, Heidelberg (2008)
3. Baudin, P., Filliâtre, J.-C., Marché, C., Monate, B., Moy, Y., Prevosto, V.: ACSL: ANSI/ISO C Specification Language. CEA and INRIA. Preliminary design, version 1.4 (October 29, 2008)
4. Cohen, E., Dahlweid, M., Hillebrand, M.A., Leinenbach, D., Moskal, M., Santen, T., Schulte, W., Tobies, S.: VCC: A practical system for verifying concurrent C. In: Urban, C. (ed.) TPHOLs 2009. LNCS, vol. 5674, pp. 1–22. Springer, Heidelberg (2009)
5. Conchon, S., Contejean, E., Kanig, J.: Ergo: a Theorem Prover for Polymorphic First-order Logic Modulo Theories, LRI, Univ. Paris-Sud/CNRS, and INRIA (2006)
6. Detlefs, D., Nelson, G., Saxe, J.B.: Simplify: a Theorem Prover for Program Checking. J. ACM 52(3), 365–473 (2005)
7. Filliâtre, J.-C., Marché, C.: The Why/Krakatoa/Caduceus Platform for Deductive Program Verification. In: Damm, W., Hermanns, H. (eds.) CAV 2007. LNCS, vol. 4590, pp. 173–177. Springer, Heidelberg (2007)
8. Hoare, C.A.R.: An Axiomatic Basis For Computer Programming. Communications of the ACM 12, 576–580 (1969)
9. Jackson, P.B., Ellis, B.J., Sharp, K.: Using SMT Solvers to Verify High-integrity Programs. In: AFM 2007: Proceedings of the second workshop on Automated formal methods, pp. 60–68. ACM Press, New York (2007)
10. Leavens, G.T.: Tutorial on JML, the Java Modeling Language. In: Stirewalt, R.E.K., Egyed, A., Fischer, B. (eds.) Proceedings of ASE 2007, p. 573. ACM, New York (2007)
11. Marché, C.: Jessie: an Intermediate Language for Java and C Verification. In: Stump, A., Xi, H. (eds.) Proceedings of PLPV 2007. ACM, New York (2007)
12. The Coq development team. The Coq proof assistant reference manual. LogiCal Project, Version 8.2 (2008)
13. Meyer, B.: Applying "Design by Contract". IEEE Computer 25(10) (1992)
14. Reynolds, J.C.: Reasoning about arrays. Commun. ACM 22(5), 290–299 (1979)

Static Versioning of Global State for Race Condition Detection

Steffen Keul

Dept. of Programming Languages, Universität Stuttgart,
Universitätsstr. 38, 70569 Stuttgart, Germany
steffen.keul@informatik.uni-stuttgart.de
http://www.iste.uni-stuttgart.de/ps/Keul

Abstract. The implementation of concurrent reliable software systems is very difficult. Race conditions on shared data can cause a program's memory state to become inconsistent and result in unpredictable behavior of the software. Much work has been published on analyses to identify access sites to shared data which do not conform to an accepted synchronization pattern. However, those algorithms usually cannot determine if a computation will use a consistent version of more than one shared data object. In this paper, we present a new static analysis algorithm to identify computations which can potentially load values that were stored independently of each other. These uses of global state are affected by race conditions and may yield undesired values during the execution of the program. We show applicability of an implementation of the analysis on several open-source systems.

Keywords: Concurrent Programming, Data Race Condition, Static Program Analysis.

1 Introduction

Concurrent programming is difficult due to subtle programming errors that are hard to find manually. Every interaction of one thread with shared memory needs to obey some global interaction protocol which the programmer has to keep in mind all the time. A violation of that protocol can introduce a race condition, possibly causing an inconsistent memory state. Special support from programming systems to specify and enforce the protocol is not widely available. Worse still, rigorous testing against concurrency bugs might prove in vain, because some of the issues only happen given very specific timing and data inputs, which might be extremely unlikely to encounter. For reliable concurrent software systems however, assuring the absence of harmful race conditions is essential to avoid intermittent misbehavior.

Today, there is a great number of analysis techniques to detect data races, both static and dynamic. Dynamic analyses are in general very precise, as they can identify issues that have happened (or may have happened given different scheduling) along the executed paths of execution [1], [2]. Unfortunately, dynamic

J. Real and T. Vardanega (Eds.): Ada-Europe 2010, LNCS 6106, pp. 111–124, 2010.

analysis can never come to the conclusion that a system is free of bugs, since it will always depend on specific input data into the system. To reach confidence about the absence of certain classes of race conditions, static analysis tools can be used. Static analysis can be conservative, meaning that all existing issues will be found, possibly including a number of false positive warnings.

Existing static race detection techniques usually identify all the places in the source code of a program where access conflicts might occur. Access conflicts occur, if two different threads access a common storage location, one of the threads writes to that location and there exists no ordering between the accesses. To prove the absence of access conflicts, many techniques verify that locking a common mutex variable provides mutual exclusion of the accesses [3], [4], [5], [6], [7], [8]. Artho et al. [9] analyze programs without access conflicts to verify that the sets of objects used inside of critical sections are consistent.

Other static analysis approaches use an extended type system to verify atomicity of functions, e.g. [10].

In this paper, we present a new approach that is able to identify uses of shared memory state that may be negatively influenced by a race condition. Our analysis technique focuses on the way in which global data is used by the program, taking mutex-based synchronization into account where it exists. This paper will refer to explicit mutex-lock and unlock functions, but the technique can be adapted to higher-level synchronization constructs like Java synchronized blocks or Ada protected units. In contrast to other work, we do not necessarily consider access conflicts to be programming errors, but identify calculations that are based on data which is not written into memory during an atomic operation.

The paper is organized as follows. In Section 2, we give some examples of concurrency issues to motivate this work. In Section 3 we outline how our intermediate representation is created, including an explicit representation of interprocedural, interthread data flow. In Section 4 we present the new analysis algorithm. Section 5 gives some measurements performed with an implementation of our algorithm, and Section 6 concludes.

2   Motivating Examples

Our work is motivated by the observation that data race detectors based on the lockset algorithm [5], [7], [8] produce undesired warnings in the following cases. We have encountered situations similar to the example in Listing 1 in industrial control devices. In this example, one thread thread1 repeatedly produces a new value and stores it to a shared variable g. The threads thread2, and thread3 repeatedly consume the value to perform some action. Both of the uses by thread2 and thread3 are conflict accesses because g can be assigned to and read concurrently without any synchronization. Assuming that reads and writes on g are performed atomically, thread2 would perform as expected. In thread3 however, there is a possibility that first the value of g is loaded, then a new value is written by thread1 and then that new value is read again by thread3. The product g*g is then calculated from sensor values of two different read-cycles which is unlikely to be intended semantics.

```
1  int g;
2
3  void *thread1(void *p)
4  {   while (1)  g = read_sensor_value();   }
5
6  void *thread2(void *p)
7  {   while (1)  act_1(5 * g + 17);   }
8
9  void *thread3(void *p)
10 {   while (1)  act_2(g * g);   }
```

Listing 1. Conflict accesses on g in thread2 and thread3, but only thread3 has an inconsistent expression

Using the traditional lockset algorithm, a static analyzer would warn about both calculations, in thread2 and in thread3. Our technique however would accept thread2 as intended by the programmer, because only one version of the global state is used during the calculation of its expression, but our technique would warn about the expression g*g in thread3 because the uses of shared variables (of g in this case) might stem from different versions of the global state.

A less obvious example is presented in Listing 2. Here, the assignments to g1 and g2 in Line 4 are both protected by locks m and n, respectively. Before the values of the global variables are used in line 13, both locks are acquired and might give a false sense of safety to a programmer. Since the assignments are not protected by a common lock, they can still be executed concurrently and, assuming atomic reads and writes, the reads in the main thread behave as if performed without locking. The program is free of access conflicts, but in contrast to traditional lockset-based data race checkers, our analysis is still able to identify the expression g1+g2 to be run on potentially inconsistent versions.

An important issue are concurrent updates of global state if the updated value depends on the previous state. The simplest example is the increment of a shared counter by several threads. If two threads t_1, t_2 perform the operation $g := g + c$ where g is a global variable and c is some constant, then these operations might be performed in a way that one increment is lost: Let g have the initial value g_0. t_1 loads the value g_0 of g into an register $r_{1,1}$. Then t_2 loads the current value g_0 of g into the register $r_{2,1}$ concurrently. Both perform the addition $r_{i,2} := r_{i,1} + c$. Then the results $r_{1,2}$ and $r_{2,2}$ are both stored back to g in arbitrary order. The resulting value of g is thus the value $g_0 + c$ although given a different interleaving, $g_0 + 2c$ might have resulted.

Traditional data race checkers would fail to discover the potential error however, if the code were executed with separate locking around the read and the store of the shared variable as in Listing 3. In this example, the shared variable has consistent protection, and there is no access conflict. Our technique is able to identify the stale update nonetheless by comparing the versions of global state of the left-hand side (LHS) of the assignment in Line 6 to its right-hand

```
1 void *thread1(void *p)          void *thread2(void *p)
2 {   while (...)              {   while (...)
3     {   mutex_lock(&m);          {   mutex_lock(&n);
4         g1 = ...;                    g2 = ...;
5         mutex_unlock(&m);            mutex_unlock(&n);
6 }   }                        }   }
7
8 int main()
9 {   create(thread1);  create(thread2);
10     while (...)
11     {   mutex_lock(&m);
12         mutex_lock(&n);
13         res = g1 + g2;
14         mutex_unlock(&n);
15         mutex_unlock(&m);
16 }   }
```

Listing 2. Free of data races, but the `mutex_lock`-calls around g1+g2 have no effect

```
1 pthread_mutex_lock(&m);
2   int local = global;
3 pthread_mutex_unlock(&m);
4 local += 17;
5 pthread_mutex_lock(&m);
6   global = local;
7 pthread_mutex_unlock(&m);
```

Listing 3. Nonatomic increments

side (RHS). Only if both sides have the same version then it is certain that no other assignment to the LHS can have occurred since calculating the RHS.

3   Program Representation

Our analysis tool uses knowledge about the syntactical structure of the program as well as its control flow and data flow. Therefore we compile the source code into the high-level graph representation IML [11]. In IML, the program is represented as a graph that contains a statement tree for every function, control flow graphs, and data flow edges from "assignment" to "read" nodes. IML is general enough to be able to represent programs from different source languages, like C, C++, Ada or Java.

The frontend that translates source code into our intermediate representation decides which accesses to variables are atomic assignments and atomic reads. Non-atomic updates of objects are explicitly represented as sequences of read and separate store. In our experiments, we simply assume all reads and writes of objects of primitive types to be atomic. The frontend's implementation can be adapted for architectures where this assumption is not valid.

3.1   Data Flow

We use a context-insensitive, flow-insensitive, but field-sensitive points-to analysis like the one by Pearce [12]. The points-to analysis associates a set of abstract objects with each dereference of a pointer value in the program.

In the program, there are certain actions that start a new thread during runtime of the program (using pthreads, calls to `pthread_create`). We associate an abstract thread with each of these start-sites. Starting from the thread's main function, call graphs for every abstract thread are created. Using points-to sets, we can then calculate the set of abstract objects accessed by every function. Propagating this set along the call graph, from callee to caller, gives the set of nonlocal variables accessed by a function.

Every nonlocal object that is used by functions of different threads is flagged as a shared variable.

In the next step, lockset analysis is performed. Lockset analysis calculates a set of mutex-locks held at a point in the program during any execution of the program. We define contexts of function calls to be the pair of the lockset, which is active at the call site and the abstract thread which executes the call. Thus lockset analysis is context-sensitive with respect to this notion of a context, but it does not incur the complexity of treating functions like inline code at every call site.

To model data flow caused by concurrent assignments, ψ-nodes are inserted into the intermediate representation. At all places in the program, where the value of a shared variable v is used, an explicit "read"-node exists in IML. If the read of v is an access conflict, then an artificial assignment to the shared variable is inserted into the control flow graph directly in front of the read-node. That assignment is called conflict-ψ-node. It takes the form $v := \psi(v_s, v_1, \ldots v_n)$, where v_s is later replaced by the sequentially reaching definitions of v and the $v_1, \ldots, v_n$ represent all possibly reaching definitions of v from concurrent conflict assignments.

If a read of a shared variable v is not an access conflict, then that read happens inside of a critical section protected by a mutex-lock. In this case, a section-ψ-node is created at all control flow entrances into the critical section. The section-ψ-node links the effect of concurrent updates into the sequential data flow of the critical section. Reads of a consistently protected shared variable inside a critical section are only reached by sequential data flow edges. In the critical section case, the ψ-node's arguments for potentially concurrent data flow $v_1, \ldots, v_n$ do not reference assignment-nodes in other threads directly, but so called link-out nodes. Link-out nodes are created at all exists of a critical section to represent the fact, that the critical section's assignments to shared variables become visible at the point of the link-out node. Note that at every entrance into or exit from a critical section, only one section-ψ-node or link-out node is created. The single node summarizes the data flow of all shared variables accessed in the critical section.

Once ψ-nodes are inserted, data flow links from definitions to their uses need to be calculated and stored into the intermediate representation. In our implementation, this is done by a transformation into SSA-form, as in [13].

Note, that the output of lockset-based data races checkers can be extracted from our intermediate representation, for shared variables which are read in at least one place: simply enumerate all conflict-ψ-nodes.

3.2   Summary Edges

To speed up the analysis, as described in Section 4.1, we need to efficiently propagate data flow facts across function call sites without re-analyzing the entire call graph rooted at that call site. Therefore, we add summary edges to the data flow graph. Summary edges have been used successfully in interprocedural slicing algorithms [14]. If inside of a callee function f, the value of parameter p reaches a set T of output parameters of f, then a summary edge is created at every call site for f from the copy-in node that corresponds to p to every copy-out node that corresponds to any node in T. Similarly, summary edges are created for nonlocal objects accessed inside of f as if they were passed as parameters.

4   Analysis Algorithm

In this section, we will explain our new analysis. It reasons about the versions of global state that are used in expressions. The analysis is performed in two successive phases: in the first phase, all expressions are annotated with the version of the global state they operate on. In the second phase, warnings are generated for suspicious constructs.

4.1   State-Version Analysis

In our program representation, the execution of a ψ-node identifies one unique observation of the global state. If two values stem from the same run-time instance of a ψ-node, then those two values were stored during execution of the same critical section. This property is ensured by the placement strategy for ψ-nodes. The state-version analysis uses this property to identify versions of global state with versions of the ψ-nodes whose values flow into the expressions.

We number all ψ-nodes in the program from 1 to n. The analysis uses the state space $\mathcal{L}$ to describe the visible global state at a point in the program:

$$\mathbb{V} = \{\bot, \top, \psi_1, \ldots, \psi_n\}$$
$$\mathcal{L} = \{s \mid s : \mathbf{Var} \to \mathbb{V}\}$$

In every state $m \in \mathcal{L}$, each abstract variable $v \in \mathbf{Var}$ of the program is mapped to its version from the set $\mathbb{V}$. The version can be either $\top$ if it is not influenced by any data flow originating in a different thread, $\bot$ if it can be influenced by more than one ψ-node, or $\psi_i \in \{\psi_1, \ldots, \psi_n\}$ if it can be influenced by only the most recent execution of the ψ-node with number i. Consequently, two variables a, b have a consistent version at a point in the program, if the analysis determines $(m(a) = m(b)$ and $m(a) \neq \bot)$ or $m(a) = \top$ or $m(b) = \top$.

Intraprocedural versioning. The intraprocedural analysis starts off with the optimistic assumption that a caller function does not propagate any versioned values into the callee function. This imprecision will be healed later during interprocedural analysis (see below in this section). Due to this, the functions can be analyzed separately in reversed topological order of the call graph. Before a caller function is entered, its callees will already be analyzed. An exception to this rule are cycles of the call graph which require iteration.

Consider, that versions of global state are created by either a ψ-node in a current function, or by a ψ-node in a callee function. Versions created in or propagated out of a callee are never equal to any version created in the current function, even if they originate from the same ψ-node (possible in case of recursion). Consequently, analysis of a call site can generate new versions of the global state. That information can be queried from the result of that function's analysis. The versions of nonlocal variables that are read in the callee, but not definitely updated, only need to be propagated across the call site using the summary edges (see Section 3.2).

The intraprocedural analysis is simple, if the ψ-nodes of the function are not contained in cycles of the control flow graph. In this case, every ψ-node can generate at most one version. If a ψ-node is contained in a cycle, then that node can generate a different version during every iteration of the cycle. To deal with a statically unknown number of different versions, the analysis simplifies the problem and tracks only the global version of the most recent execution of each ψ-node along every control flow path.

The data flow equations are solved by a standard monotone framework for an iterative forward data flow analysis. The initial value is $\iota \in \mathcal{L}$:

$$\iota = \forall v \in \mathbf{Var} : v \mapsto \top$$

At control flow confluence points, the states of the predecessor blocks $p_1, \ldots, p_n$ are joined by the meet operation $\sqcap \{p_1, \ldots, p_n\} = p_1 \sqcap \ldots \sqcap p_n$.

$$\forall x, y \in \mathbb{V} : x \diamond y = \begin{cases} \top, & \text{if } x = y = \top \\ \psi_x, & \text{if } x = \psi_x \wedge y \in \{\psi_x, \top\} \\ \psi_y, & \text{if } y = \psi_y \wedge x \in \{\psi_y, \top\} \\ \bot, & \text{otherwise} \end{cases}$$

$$a \sqcap b = \forall v \in \mathbf{Var} : v \mapsto a(v) \diamond b(v)$$

To determine the version of an expression, the versions $r_1, \ldots r_n \in \mathbb{V}$ of all variables that contribute values to the expression are joined using the operation $r = r_1 \diamond \ldots \diamond r_n$.

The intraprocedural analysis can be summarized by the following equations. We use $\text{in}(s)$ to denote the information that flows into a statement s and $\text{out}(s)$ for information that flows out of s. The set of predecessor statements of s is denoted $\text{pred}(s)$.

$$\text{in}(s) = \begin{cases} \iota, & \text{if } s \text{ is the function entry} \\ \sqcap_{p \in \text{pred}(s)} \text{out}(p), & \text{otherwise} \end{cases}$$

$$\text{out}(s) = \begin{cases} f_{:=} \left(\text{in}(s) \right), & \text{if } s \text{ is an assignment} \\ f_{\psi_i} \left(\text{in}(s) \right), & \text{if } s \text{ is the } \psi\text{-node with number } i \\ f_{\text{call}} \left(\text{in}(s) \right), & \text{if } s \text{ is a call site} \\ \text{in}(s), & \text{otherwise} \end{cases}$$

We distinguish between strong and weak updates of assignment-nodes. A strong update occurs, if the analysis can definitely decide that the left-hand side (LHS) abstract object of the assignment is a single object and the value is fully replaced by the assigned value. Weak updates happen whenever the LHS-object is not statically known to represent exactly one single object. This can happen in static analysis, for example, if assignments are made to array elements or to heap objects of which multiple instances might exist. At assignment-nodes, the version v_{RHS} of the expression on the right-hand side is calculated. If the assignment is a strong update, then the original version of the LHS can be killed and replaced by the new version. If the assignment is a weak update then the operation $\diamond$ is used to combine the versions of LHS and RHS.

$$f_{:=}(\text{pre}) = v \mapsto \begin{cases} pre(v) \diamond v_{\text{RHS}}, & \text{if weak update and } v \in \text{LHS} \\ v_{\text{RHS}}, & \text{if strong update and } v \in \text{LHS} \\ pre(v), & \text{otherwise} \end{cases}$$

A ψ-node ψ_i represents a potential assignment of the data flow originating in concurrent definitions to a set V of some variables. Each of the variables in V becomes consistent to the version ψ_i of the global state. But since the analysis only represents the most recent execution of a ψ-node, all variables $K = \mathbf{Var} \setminus V$ are not consistent to ψ_i anymore. This is reflected by setting all variables of K, which had the version ψ_i before, to $\bot$.

$$f_{\psi_i}(\text{pre}) = v \mapsto \begin{cases} \psi_i, & \text{if } v \in V \\ \bot, & \text{if } v \in K \wedge \text{pre}(v) = \psi_i \\ pre(v), & \text{otherwise} \end{cases}$$

Function calls are handled as follows. Let $\text{pre} \in \mathcal{L}$ denote the state that is active directly before the call site. That state is mapped to a new state $p' \in \mathcal{L}$ using summary edges (see Section 3.2). Thus, the state p' models the result of the call if all ψ-nodes inside of the callee are ignored. Similarly, let $R \in \mathcal{L}$ represent the meet of the results of the intraprocedural analysis of all possible callee functions without any influence from the caller. The following transfer function f_{call} calculates a conservative combination of p' and R. Any version propagated from the caller into the callee will always be different from any version that the caller produces. Therefore all variables reached by versions of the caller and by versions of the callee indicate that the callee only performs may-defs and leaves the variable in doubtable state. The variable's state is conservatively reduced to $\bot$. If the callee produces a different version of the same ψ-node (in case of recursion) then the version of the callee will always be newer, and the variables containing the older version are reset to $\bot$.

$$f_{\text{call}}(\text{pre}) = v \mapsto \begin{cases} \top & \text{if } p'(v) = R(v) = \top \\ \psi_j & \text{if } p'(v) = \top \wedge R(v) = \psi_j \\ \psi_i & \text{if } p'(v) = \psi_i \wedge R(v) = \top \wedge \{x \in \mathbf{Var}|R(x) = \psi_i\} = \emptyset \\ \bot & \text{otherwise} \end{cases}$$

It can be shown, that the transfer functions and meet operation only perform transitions that are monotonously decreasing with respect to the partial order defined here. For all states $x \in \mathcal{L}$, let $T_x = \{v|x(v) = \top\}$, let $\forall 1 \leq i \leq n : \Psi_{x,i} = \{v|x(v) = \psi_i\}$. The partial order of states is defined as:

$$a < b \Leftrightarrow (T_a = T_b \text{ and } \forall 1 \leq i \leq n : \Psi_{a,i} \subseteq \Psi_{b,i} \text{ and } \exists 1 \leq j \leq n : \Psi_{a,j} \subsetneq \Psi_{b,j})$$
$$\text{or } (T_a \subsetneq T_b \text{ and } \forall 1 \leq i \leq n : \Psi_{a,i} \subseteq \Psi_{b,i})$$

Since all operations are monotonous, and a single smallest state exists ($\forall v \in \mathbf{Var} : v \mapsto \bot$), and the condition $|\mathcal{L}| < \infty$ holds, the analysis is guaranteed to reach the largest fixed point.

Interprocedural analysis. As described in the previous paragraph, all functions are analyzed separately, based on the assumption that all of the function's input data have version $\top$. Versions that are created inside of a function are propagated to the function's caller, but the propagation from the caller into its callees has been omitted so far. This section will outline how context information is added to complete the analysis.

The fundamental observation is that no version created in a caller-function can be equal to a version created in one of its callees. The following algorithm is performed separately for every function in topological order of the call graph to produce the final result for a function. Inside of cycles of the call graph, the functions are processed in arbitrary order and the cycle is iterated until one iteration yields the same results as the previous one.

1. Use the state $c_c \in \mathcal{L}$ directly before a call site,
2. initialize all nodes inside of the callee to $\forall v \in \mathbf{Var} : v \mapsto \top$,
3. perform copy-in assignments for parameters and nonlocal objects accessed in the callee-function to map c_c into the callee, producing the state $c \in \mathcal{L}$,
4. for every $v_c \in \mathbf{Var}$: if $c(v_c) \neq \top$, then propagate the version $c(v_c)$ along the intraprocedural data flow edges in the callee-function. Assume this propagation reaches a data flow node, which identifies a variable v_s and its state $s \in \mathcal{L}$. Produce a new state for that node: $(v_s \mapsto c(v_c), \forall v \neq v_s : v \mapsto s(v))$,
5. calculate the interprocedural meet $\widehat{m}$ of the result of the intraprocedural analysis and the new states. In contrast to the intraprocedural meet operation $\sqcap$, a ψ_i originating from the intraprocedural analysis is never treated as equal to any ψ_j of the interprocedural analysis.

$$a \sqcap b = v \mapsto \begin{cases} \top, & \text{if } a(v) = b(v) = \top \\ \psi_a, & \text{if } a(v) = \psi_a \wedge b(v) = \top \\ \psi_b, & \text{if } b(v) = \psi_b \wedge a(v) = \top \\ \bot, & \text{otherwise} \end{cases}$$

Note that the number of different contexts identified by a state c_c before a call site might become very large. However, it is easily possible to use the $\sqcap$ operation on several different contexts to bound the number of contexts at the expense of a more conservative analysis result that produces more false positive warnings. Since the non-recursive functions are processed in topological order, all contexts for a callee function are available before that function is analyzed. Inside of cycles of the call graph, a viable option is to allocate only one context per function.

Figure 1 gives an example of a run of the analysis on an example function. Assume that another thread is executed concurrently to the function `caller`. That other thread acquires the mutex m, updates the value of the global variable g and releases m. In the example, ψ-nodes are already inserted. In line 6, the value of g is linked into the critical section. In lines 24 and 26, ψ-nodes represent the conflict uses of g. The function use is omitted, it can be assumed to have an empty implementation. In the "intra" column, the fixed point reached by the intraprocedural analysis is displayed. The column "inter" displays the states created by the interprocedural part of the analysis and the column "result" the final result after intra- and interprocedural information has been joined. The column "xpr" states the version of the expression calculated in the line of source code, if any. The column "xpr" is consulted during the warning-generation pass. Note that the last three columns depend on context. If there are more than one call site for f, and the active state before those call sites differs, then multiple instances of these three columns will be created.

Note that in line 14 the version of z is $\bot$ because the loop can have been exited by the break-statement in line 10. If that were the case, z's version might not be from the latest execution of the critical section. In contrast, the use of z in line 12 is always consistent with x's version.

In line 30, the previous version ψ_4 of the global variable g is propagated across the call-site using summary edges. Since f only performs may-defs to g, g still has the version ψ_4 directly after the call-site after the intraprocedural versioning. In the exit-node of f, g has the version ψ_1, therefore its version is reduced to $\bot$ in the interprocedural phase.

In line 18, no warning would be created after the intraprocedural phase. In that line x has version ψ_1 and y has version $\top$, which results in ψ_1 for the expression. Only after context-information is propagated across the assignment in line 17 the conflict becomes visible. In this case, the formal parameter q has version ψ_4 which is assigned to y and therefore two different versions are joined in the expression x + y. A similar effect happens on the return value of f. In the intraprocedural phase, both p and q have version $\top$, but after the interprocedural propagation, the return value's version is reduced to $\bot$.

	intra						inter						result						xpr
	x	y	z	g	p	q	x	y	z	g	p	q	x	y	z	g	p	q	
1 `int f(int p, int q)`																			
2 `{`	⊤	⊤	⊤	⊤	⊤	⊤	⊤	⊤	⊤	4	3	4	⊤	⊤	⊤	4	3	4	
3 `  int x, y, z;`																			
4 `  do {`	1	1	1	1	⊤	⊤	⊤	⊤	⊤	4	3	4	1	1	1	⊥	3	4	
5 `    mutex_lock(&m);`																			
6 `    /*g = `$\psi_1(g,\dots)$`*/`	⊥	⊥	⊥	1	⊤	⊤	⊤	⊤	⊤	⊤	3	4	⊥	⊥	⊥	1	3	4	1
7 `    x = g;`	1	⊥	⊥	1	⊤	⊤	⊤	⊤	⊤	⊤	3	4	1	⊥	⊥	1	3	4	1
8 `    y = g;`	1	1	⊥	1	⊤	⊤	⊤	⊤	⊤	⊤	3	4	1	1	⊥	1	3	4	1
9 `    mutex_unlock(&m);`																			
10 `    if (cond2) break;`																			⊤
11 `    z = x;`	1	1	1	1	⊤	⊤	⊤	⊤	⊤	⊤	3	4	1	1	1	1	3	4	1
12 `    use(x + z);`																			1
13 `  } while (cond1);`	1	1	⊥	1	⊤	⊤	⊤	⊤	⊤	⊤	3	4	1	1	⊥	1	3	4	⊤
14 `  if (x + z)`																			⊥
15 `    use(x + y);`	1	1	⊥	1	⊤	⊤	⊤	⊤	⊤	⊤	3	4	1	1	⊥	1	3	4	1
16 `  else {`																			
17 `    y = q;`	1	⊤	⊥	1	⊤	⊤	⊤	4	⊤	⊤	3	4	1	4	⊥	1	3	4	4
18 `    use(x + y);`																			⊥
19 `  }`																			
20 `  return p + q;`	1	1	⊥	1	⊤	⊤	⊤	4	⊤	⊤	3	4	1	⊥	⊥	1	3	4	⊥
21 `}`																			

	intra			inter			result			
	a	b	g	a	b	g	a	b	g	
22 `void caller()`										
23 `{`	⊤	⊤	⊤	⊤	⊤	⊤	⊤	⊤	⊤	
24 `  /*g = `$\psi_3(g,\dots)$`*/`	⊤	⊤	3	⊤	⊤	⊤	⊤	⊤	3	3
25 `  int a = g;`	3	⊤	3	⊤	⊤	⊤	3	⊤	3	3
26 `  /*g = `$\psi_4(g,\dots)$`*/`	3	⊤	4	⊤	⊤	⊤	3	⊤	4	4
27 `  int b = g;`	3	4	4	⊤	⊤	⊤	3	4	4	4
28										
29 `  use(a + b);`										⊥
30 `  use(f(a, b));`	3	4	⊥	⊤	⊤	⊤	3	4	⊥	⊥
31 `}`										

Fig. 1. Versioning analysis applied on example thread. Another thread performs updates on the shared variable g, protected by mutex m.

4.2 Suspicious Pattern Recognition

After version numbers have been annotated to the expressions of the program, Warnings are generated for suspicious ones. The warning generator traverses the statement trees of all functions in post-order. The statement tree contains simple nodes for accesses to variables and composite nodes for statements or expressions. A node can be marked to express that a warning has been generated for it. The version determined for a node, and its marking-state are propagated upwards in the tree.

Whenever a "read"-node on some shared variable is encountered, that shared variable's version is loaded. When a composite node is evaluated, its version is

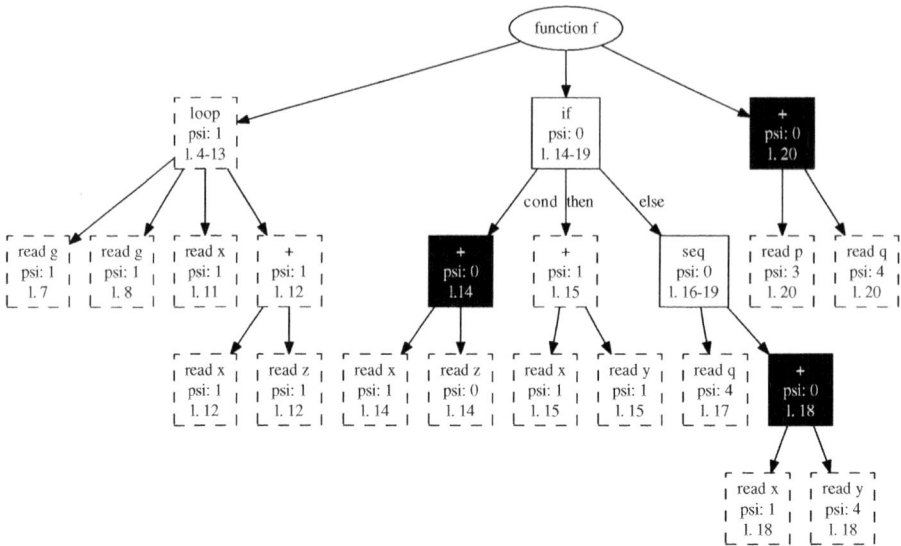

Fig. 2. Warning generation for the function f from Figure 1

calculated as the meet of all of its child nodes' versions. If the meet of only the unmarked child nodes of a composite node is ⊥ then a warning will be generated for the composite node. If a warning is created for a composite node or if all of its child nodes are marked, then the composite node will be marked.

The marking of tree nodes after a warning has been generated suppresses multiple warnings about the same issue. However, if for example, two statements from a sequence of statements generate individual warnings, then the warning about the entire sequence of statements might be suppressed. As a consequence, when inspecting source code, warnings must be considered within the individual syntactical context they were created for.

In Figure 2, the warning generation process is illustrated for the function f from Figure 1. The black nodes represent nodes that generate a warning. Nodes with solid borders do not generate warnings on their own, because of their children's marking. Nodes with dashed borders are considered intended code. They do not generate a warning and are ignored.

5   Empirical Results

We have implemented the algorithm described in the previous sections in the Bauhaus system [11]. We have used the analysis tool on different open source programs as shown in Figure 3. Manual inspection of the results for aget-0.4 showed that our tool was able to issue a warning about a race condition in a comparison in the function updateProgressBar, which can result in undesired output.

Tool	SLoC	results		efficiency		
		warnings	ψ-nodes	s. edges	intra	inter
aget-0.4	0.8k	10	39	<0.2s		
linuxdown	1.4k	29	109	<0.4s		
aaxine	46k	621	2,599	6.5s	0.8s	6.1s
clamd	66k	6,667	13,062	25s	92s	879s

Fig. 3. Measurements on different open source programs

In Figure 3 our measurements are presented. "SLoC" are measured using SLOCCount [15]. "warnings" is the number of warnings generated by the process explained in Section 4.2, "ψ-nodes" is the number of ψ-nodes inserted into IML, "s. edges" is the time needed to create summary edges, "intra" is the time for the intraprocedural analysis phase, "inter" the time for the fully context-sensitive interprocedural phase. Note that the interprocedural phase could be done much more efficiently if less contexts were distinguished as explained in Section 4.1.

The measurements show that our analysis runs fast on real programs. We expect to improve precision of the shared variable classification using escape analysis [16], resulting in better overall efficiency. At present, the number of false positive warnings is still too high for a complete manual inspection.

6 Conclusion

We have presented a new static analysis that identifies expressions in a concurrent shared-memory program which depend on potentially inconsistent global state. The analysis is able to find bugs, that previous techniques could not. It can handle atomic reads and writes of shared variables and the decision if an access is atomic can be configured by the frontend. The analysis supports mutex-synchronization or other schemes that can be transformed into an explicit data flow representation. Using the hierarchical warning generation, intuitive warnings can be generated. We have found that the analysis is very efficient and able to handle larger programs.

Acknowledgments. The author would like to thank Erhard Plödereder and the anonymous reviewers for valuable comments on an earlier version of this paper.

References

1. Savage, S., Burrows, M., Nelson, G., Sobalvarro, P., Anderson, T.: Eraser: a dynamic data race detector for multithreaded programs. ACM Trans. Comput. Syst. 15(4), 391–411 (1997)
2. Choi, J.-D., Lee, K., Loginov, A., O'Callahan, R., Sarkar, V., Sridharan, M.: Efficient and precise datarace detection for multithreaded object-oriented programs. In: PLDI 2002, pp. 258–269. ACM Press, New York (2002)

3. Kahlon, V., Sinha, N., Kruus, E., Zhang, Y.: Static data race detection for concurrent programs with asynchronous calls. In: ESEC/FSE 2009, pp. 13–22. ACM Press, New York (2009)

4. Raza, A., Vogel, G.: RCanalyser: A flexible framework for the detection of data races in parallel programs. In: Kordon, F., Vardanega, T. (eds.) Ada-Europe 2008. LNCS, vol. 5026, pp. 226–239. Springer, Heidelberg (2008)

5. Voung, J.W., Jhala, R., Lerner, S.: RELAY: Static race detection on millions of lines of code. In: ESEC-FSE 2007, pp. 205–214. ACM, New York (2007)

6. Pratikakis, P., Foster, J.S., Hicks, M.: LOCKSMITH: Context-sensitive correlation analysis for race detection. In: PLDI 2006, pp. 320–331. ACM, New York (2006)

7. Engler, D., Ashcraft, K.: RacerX: Effective, static detection of race conditions and deadlocks. In: SOSP 2003, pp. 237–252. ACM, New York (2003)

8. Sterling, N.: WARLOCK – a static data race analysis tool. In: Proceedings of the USENIX Winter 1993 Technical Conference, San Diego, CA, USA, pp. 97–106 (1993)

9. Artho, C., Havelund, K., Biere, A.: High-level data races. Software Testing, Verification and Reliability 13(4), 207–227 (2003)

10. Flanagan, C., Freund, S.N., Lifshin, M., Qadeer, S.: Types for atomicity: Static checking and inference for java. ACM Trans. Program. Lang. Syst. 30(4), 1–53 (2008)

11. Raza, A., Vogel, G., Plödereder, E.: Bauhaus - a tool suite for program analysis and reverse engineering. In: Pinho, L.M., González Harbour, M. (eds.) Ada-Europe 2006. LNCS, vol. 4006, pp. 71–82. Springer, Heidelberg (2006)

12. Pearce, D.J., Kelly, P.H.J., Hankin, C.: Efficient field-sensitive pointer analysis for c. In: PASTE 2004, pp. 37–42. ACM, New York (2004)

13. Staiger, S., Vogel, G., Keul, S., Wiebe, E.: Interprocedural static single assignment form. In: WCRE 2007, October 2007, pp. 1–10. IEEE Computer Society, Los Alamitos (2007)

14. Horwitz, S., Reps, T., Binkley, D.: Interprocedural slicing using dependence graphs. In: PLDI 1988, pp. 35–46. ACM, New York (1988)

15. Wheeler, D.A.: SLOCCount. v2.26, http://www.dwheeler.com/sloccount

16. Choi, J.-D., Gupta, M., Serrano, M., Sreedhar, V.C., Midkiff, S.: Escape analysis for java. SIGPLAN Not. 34(10), 1–19 (1999)

Using Hardware Support for Scheduling with Ada

Rod White

MBDA Missile Systems (UK) Ltd.
rod.white@mbda-systems.com

Abstract. Embedded hard real-time systems are often under severe pressure from a number of directions — limited processing capacity being a common issue. Having to handle a large number, or high rate, of external stimuli (interrupts) exacerbates the processor loading problem by compromising ideal processor behaviour through the disruption of performance enhancing features, such as of pipelines and cache memories. This paper reports on the use of Ada with a novel architecture that promotes the better utilisation of the processing resources for the "real" task of executing the application. The approach described in this paper is to use dedicated hardware facilities, a "Butler", to assist the processor in the management of events and the scheduling of tasks. Allied with a cooperative (non-preemptive) approach to scheduling the application, this allows the processing capacity available to the application to be increased by a significant factor. Whilst the approach is largely language independent its integration with the Ada tasking features provides for a very powerful and sympathetic platform for demanding and high-integrity applications.

1 Introduction and Scope

Embedded real-time systems are always under pressure in terms of space, weight and thermal constraints, and as if this was not enough there are ever increasing processing demands to provide enhanced functionality and higher integrity. Together these factors require that the maximum performance is extracted from the processing platform whilst ensuring deterministic behaviour.

An approach to addressing this problem, and the one that is described in this paper, is to offload key aspects of functionality to specialised hardware. Two contrasting approaches for the provision of such support are:

- Provide bespoke hardware that implements a key application specific function — an example here might be a dedicated fast Fourier transform block [1];
- Provide hardware that provides support to tasks common across the domain of real-time embedded systems — the classic example here would be the provision of a floating point co-processor [2].

The former approach can be an ideal solution for a specific subset of the domain of embedded real-time systems, however it suffers in the light of the need for

J. Real and T. Vardanega (Eds.): Ada-Europe 2010, LNCS 6106, pp. 125–138, 2010.

these systems to evolve over their lives, potentially rendering the specialised hardware obsolete. The latter approach, conversely, does not suffer from this problem as its function supports a more generalised, lower-level "need" of the system — it is thus the latter approach that is considered in this paper.

In this case, novel hardware is used to support the scheduling of threads/tasks and the related management of external events, with the goal being to reduce the processing overheads, and associated overall degradation in system performance often attributed to these functions, thereby maximising the available processing capacity for the "real" application. It has been developed and deployed in a number of systems over the last ten years. Whilst essentially language neutral, the approach described naturally integrates with the Ada tasking model and supports the provision of high performance, suitable for high integrity and safety critical applications.

Having a device to support the management of external events, and then integrating these with the internal (software-software) task interactions also directly supports the adoption of a cooperative (cf. preemptive) approach to scheduling the tasks of the application. As noted by Burns and Wellings [3] this cooperative approach in itself provides for an improvement in schedulability, reducing processor utilisation thus ensuring better margins on deadlines, also as observed here it also leads to additional benefits due to the reduction in disruption of the processor caches and pipelines.

The remainder of this paper is divided into five parts, addressing the following areas:

1. A brief survey of related work on hardware supported scheduling;
2. Description of the various forms of scheduling support devices;
3. The use and integration of the scheduling support device with Ada;
4. Practical results and issues;
5. Conclusions and opportunities for further enhancement.

2   Related Work

There have been a number of published accounts of the use of hardware supported scheduling for software systems. Most recently, for example by Nácul *et al.* [4], there has been a focus on hardware support for the scheduling of applications on symmetric multi-processor platforms. Earlier examples, are those by Nakano *et al.* [5], and Lai *et al.* [6]; in the latter case the hardware element of the scheduler is restricted to the management of the queues. Scheduling and communication functions are implemented in software.

In the Ada domain Burns and Wellings [3] note that there have been a number of examples of the use of hardware to directly support the execution of Ada programs. Perhaps the most notable here is the support provided to Ada tasking by ATAC described by Roos [7]; other examples of "Ada machines" being those from Runner and Warshawsky [8], and Ardö [9].

3 Scheduling Support Devices

The scheduling support device is not a single physical device — there have been several incarnations each "driven" by the technology of the processing platform; to-date the most important implementations are:

- Embedded as one of many functions in a semi-custom ASIC using asynchronous design techniques, tightly coupled to the processor;
- Implemented as logic and state machines in an FPGA coupled to the processor over a PCI bus;
- Implemented as a distributed solution across the two PowerPC processors embedded in a System-on-Programmable-Chip (SoPC) FPGA — in this case one of the processors is dedicated to handling the external events, with the other being reserved for the application and software-software scheduling controls. Communication between the two processors is through dual-ported shared memory.

Other, software only, versions have also been implemented to allow the same scheduling behaviour to be realised on non-embedded platforms and those where provision of the dedicated hardware support is not a practical or cost effective option — generally these are not platforms where the absolute real-time behaviour is important. The generic term used to describe these devices is a "Butler" [10]; so-called because it has a role very similar to that of the butler in a large house, it organises activities according to some protocol but defers to others for the final decisions, in this case the final decisions are made by a minimal software kernel.

3.1 Concept — Structures and Operations

Whilst each of the above technologies is quite different the fundamentals of operation remain constant across all of them. The basic structure of a Butler device consists of four groups of resources:

- A set of activities — schedulable items;
- A set of pollsets — groupings of activities which are considered to be at the same priority. Within each pollset a simple round robin approach to scheduling its activities is adopted;
- A set of stim-wait (or control) nodes — providing a pool of resources for each activity that allow it to wait for, and be stimulated by, particular events;
- A mechanism to determine the next activity to be executed.

The number of each of the above is dependent on the implementation technology, and the demands of the target applications; typically the device would allow for 64 .. 128 activities and pollsets, and 24 stim-wait nodes per activity. Each activity exists in the context of a pollset, which gives it an effective priority — multiple activities can be associated with a single pollset hence assigning them the same priority.

In addition to the structures a number of "instructions" are provided to manipulate these structures allowing a simple, software scheduler kernel to be layered over the device. These include:

- Suspend — causes the currently running activity to release control and make itself schedulable, this allows another activity at either a higher or the same priority (i.e. in the same pollset) to run if it is ready;
- Wait <*BitVector*> — causes the current activity to become blocked (setting the *Wait* bits defined in the *BitVector*), the *BitVector* determines which events can cause it to become schedulable again;
- Stim <*Activity, BitVector*> — sets the stim bits defined in the *BitVector* for the *Activity*, if there is a match between the *Stim* and *Wait* bits of any stim-wait node for the *Activity* it becomes schedulable;
- Next_Activity <*Activity*> — returns the next activity to be scheduled;
- Curract <*Activity*> — returns the number of the activity that is currently running (this is not maintained by the scheduler kernel as maintaining multiple copies of the information could lead to inconsistencies);
- AMI <*Boolean*>— *Anything More Important*, used with cooperative scheduling to determine if there is a ready activity at a higher priority than the current one;

Other instructions are provided for the initialisation of the Butler and to support "housekeeping" operations.

In addition to the above, each activity is associated with a "watchdog" timer that can be programmed to trigger if the activity executes for longer than a desired duration, these appear to provide direct support for an efficient implementation of the Ada.Execution_Time.Timers features introduced in Ada 2005 [11].

The Butler sets *Stim* bits in response to hardware events and the software Stim "instruction" described above, it evaluates these to determine if there are any stim-wait matches. When such matches are found, and the pollset (priority) of the activity with the match is higher than that currently scheduled, the AMI status is set *True* and, if in preemptive mode, the processor will be interrupted. At this point the actual activity to be scheduled is undecided, the decision is only finalised once a Suspend or Wait instruction has been executed. These cause the device to freeze the next activity selection logic and identify the highest priority ready activity. Where there are multiple ready activities in a single pollset the selection logic is conditioned by the last activity which executed in that pollset. The Next_Activity instruction returns the chosen activity and unfreezes the selection logic — any events that occurred between the Wait/Suspend and the Next_Activity instructions are now evaluated.

When no activity is schedulable the Next_Activity instruction returns the value Activity'Last (e.g. 64 or 128); this is a special case activity that is always considered to be schedulable. It is also the activity that the Butler considers to be "active" when the device is in a reset state — nothing else can run until a Suspend–Next_Activity sequence has been executed.

3.2 Use

The basic approach to using the device is to allocate each thread in the system to a separate activity, and organise the activities into pollsets according to the priorities of the associated threads. The activities are then all initialised and allowed to execute until they set a *Wait* condition for one of their set of stim-wait nodes, resulting in the activity becoming stopped; this state persists until a corresponding *Stim* bit is set. The *Stim* bit may be set by a request to the Butler either from another software thread through execution of a `Stim` instruction, by some external event such as an interrupt, or a timer expiring. Once a corresponding pair of *Stim* and *Wait* bits for an activity are both set the activity again becomes ready.

In a preemptive environment, if the priority of the ready activity is higher that that of the one currently executing the Butler support device will deliver an interrupt the processor, the service of which will force a context switch to the higher priority activity. The preempted activity will be made ready and returned to the end of its pollset, i.e. it will be eligible to run again only after all other ready members of its pollset.[1] This is clearly a different behaviour from that required in Ada where the preempted task is placed at the head of its priority queue — however the "normal" Ada behaviour can be obtained if all of the activities are simply placed in different pollsets (equivalent to a unique priority case).

Whilst a preemptive approach has been used successfully on some projects an alternative way of using the Butler is to adopt a cooperative, or non-preemptive, scheduling model; this approach results in "better" processor utilisation — a point which will be returned to later in the paper. When using a cooperative approach the application code is seeded with "calls" which will allow activities to be switched if certain conditions are satisfied. The density of the seeding of the application is dependent on the worst case responsiveness required to any event — the seeding process needs to be driven by experiment and measurement and is also discussed later in the paper.

Each of the seeded calls executes one of two primitive operations: in the first the activity will yield to any activity of higher priority than the current one — `Yield_To_Higher`; or, in the second, it will yield to any of higher or equal priority to the current activity — `Yield`. Generally the former is used as it results in the better utilisation of the processor, and provides a behaviour closer to that of fixed priority scheduling. In cases where the activities have unique priorities the `Yield` and `Yield_To_Higher` primitives are, of course, equivalent.

The activity with the value `Activity'Last`, as has already been mentioned, is always schedulable. In general this is mapped to some "Null" thread which in non-interruptible and simply loops repeatedly performing `Yield_To_Higher` operations.

---

[1] At the point of preemption it is not possible to know how many activities will run before the preempted one, the only safe assumption is that it will be the number of activities in the pollset minus one.

4 Integration with Ada

Several different integrations of the Butler with Ada have been successfully implemented. These range from a "bare" solution where only a minimal Ada runtime system is used; through an approach where a Ravenscar [12] run-time system is used simply to create the tasks contexts and provide the context switching service; and finally, to one where there is a "complete" integration of the device with a Ravenscar-like runtime. In the latter case the use of tasks and protected objects and protected procedures as interrupt handlers is fully supported; the reason for the runtime being described as Ravenscar-like is due to the task dispatching scheme being a bespoke, cooperative, round-robin one rather than the *FIFO_Within_Priorities* scheme, and the *Priority_Ceiling* approach to locking dictated by the Ravenscar profile. The term cooperative is used here to distinguish it from the non-preemptive approach defined for Ada 2005 where FIFO ordering is still required [11].

Rather than consider all of these integrations in some depth just the two extremes, the minimal runtime and full Ravenscar support, are discussed in more detail in the sections below.

4.1 Minimal Runtime System

Here a very restricted Ada runtime system is provided, the majority of the tasking system is not available, only the basic `delay until` construct is supported; this runtime is used in circumstances where the highest levels of safety integrity are required, for example DO178B level A [13], or DefStan 00-56 [14]. In other areas the runtime is also severely limited with no support for dynamic memory allocation in general and access types in particular — the runtime is derived from the GNAT "zero-footprint" runtime. In this case all of the scheduling services are provided by a support library (`scheduler.kernel`) with a very limited set of interfaces exposed to the application; these interfaces include support for:

- Thread creation;
- Thread wait — for any of a specific set of events;
- Signal event — to a particular thread;
- Yield — allowing any thread, which is ready and whose priority is at or above the current priority to run;
- Yield-to-higher — allowing any thread that is ready and whose priority is above the current priority to run;
- Delay until — absolute time;
- Mutex lock/unlock (only when preemptive dispatching is used).

There is no fine-grained control of priority provided with this approach; if mutual exclusion is required then processor level mutex operations are used — of course in a cooperative environment (the normal use of the solution), where there is no preemption, there is no need for explicit mutual exclusion controls, thus these are only required when used for a preemptive solution.

There is no support for protected operations in this minimal runtime system, posing the question: to what are external events mapped? In this case each external event is mapped to (one or more) Butler activities, and hence to corresponding threads. This might appear to be a rather "heavy-weight" approach but given the generally sporadic nature of the applications this is not the case.

In the absence of protected and suspension objects the inter-thread communications, and cross-stimulation, are encapsulated in a set of generic packages that, using the facilities of the scheduler kernel described earlier, provide a range of possible inter-thread interactions, both blocking and non-blocking. These interactions are the focus for most of the software-software `Wait` and `Stim` scheduling operations.

In the non-preemptive case the basic principle of operation is that all of the threads are created by calls to the scheduler kernel in the main subprogram, which has the lowest possible "priority". In the creation process all of the threads are made ready, once this is complete the main procedure enters an endless loop within which it performs a simple `Yield_To_Higher` operation allowing anything else to be run. This general sequence is shown in the code fragment below for the creation of two threads, each at different priority.

```
procedure Main is
begin
   Initialise_Kernel;  --  Ensures that the Butler is initialised
                       --  and that Activity'Last is the current activity
   Create_Thread (Activity_Ident   => Act_Id_1,
                  Pollset_Boundary => True,
                  Entry_Point      => Thread_1_Main'Access);
   Create_Thread (Activity_Ident   => Act_Id_2,
                  Pollset_Boundary => True,
                  Entry_Point      => Thread_2_Main'Access);

   --  All threads are now created but none have yet run
   --
   loop
      Yield_To_Higher; --  Allows the highest priority thread to
                       --  run, it will only return when there is
                       --  nothing else that is ready to run
   end loop;
end Main;
```

The `Yield` and `Yield_To_Higher` primitives are quite simple and are shown in the code fragments below.

```
procedure Yield is
   Current, Next : Butler.Activity_Id;
begin
   Butler.Suspend;
   Butler.Curract (Current);
   Butler.Next_Activity (Next);
   if Next /= Current then
```

```
        Switch_To (Next);   --  No point in switching to self...
     end if;
  end Yield;

procedure Yield_To_Higher is
   Current, Next : Butler.Activity_Id;
begin
   if Butler.AMI then
      Butler.Suspend;
      Butler.Curract (Current);
      Butler.Next_Activity (Next);
      Switch_To (Next);   --  If the priority is higher it cannot be self
   end if;
end Yield_To_Higher;
```

The advantage of this approach is that the interface from the application to the scheduler kernel is thin and hence introduces a very low processing overhead; the disadvantage is that whilst relatively simple to implement in a bare-board target it becomes somewhat more problematic to implement over an existing operating system in either host or target environments; making it difficult to replicate the bare-board scheduling behaviour in these environments.

4.2 Ravenscar-Like Runtime System

At the other extreme of the spectrum from the minimal runtime approach is that where a significant, but not necessarily full, Ada runtime is provided, allowing Ada to be used in a more "traditional" fashion. In this case the runtime used is a specially tailored variant of the GNAT Ada runtime that supported the Ravenscar profile.

At the application level the program comprises a number of tasks which interact through protected objects and suspension objects (as provided by the package Ada.Synchronous_Task_Control) — much as they would for any "standard" Ravenscar application. The fact that there is some special scheduler kernel is transparent to the application, as it is only the Ada runtime that is interfaced to the primitive scheduler operations. These operations are largely the same as those for the kernel when using the minimal runtime system described above, but in this case they are presented somewhat differently.

In this case the facilities provided by the scheduler kernel have to be presented in a manner compatible with the requirements of the Ada runtime system.[2] In this case a single "operating system" interface package is provided at the lowest level of the Ada runtime to provide a focus through which to interface to the underlying kernel. The sections below discuss each of the major Ada language (tasking) features and how they are realised using the scheduler kernel.

---

[2] Clearly the Ada runtime could be reformulated to match the scheduler primitives, but this route was not chosen as it was considered to be more difficult to implement.

Ada Tasks. The Ada tasks are implemented over the threads provided by the scheduler kernel; every task being associated with a unique thread, and each thread in turn being associated with a unique activity provided by the Butler. Thus there is a direct mapping from Ada task to Butler activity, with the priority of the activity (i.e. its pollset) determining the particular activity to be used.

Priority Inheritance. As noted above when a cooperative scheduling approach is used there is no need to provide mutual exclusion for resource access. When used in a preemptive environment the approach to providing mutual exclusion is dependent on the capabilities of the particular variant of Butler. Ideally the device supports the notion of temporary priority elevation allowing a ceiling inheritance protocol to be implemented; however with more primitive versions of the device this feature is not provided and a simple processor-based mutex is used — clearly this is far from ideal as it can lead to excessive blocking as in effect the "ceilings" are set unnecessarily high.

Protected Objects. There are two aspects to protected objects that require support from the underlying kernel: protected entries; and protected procedures attached to "interrupts". In the first case the entry uses a Butler stim-wait pair dedicated to the interface to the Ada runtime system.

The attachment of a protected procedure to an interrupt is effected by associating the procedure with its own particular Butler activity, this is "achieved" through the pragma `Attach_Handler`.

The use of Butler activities to support handlers mapped to protected procedures gives an opportunity to make the `Yield_To_Higher` and `Yield` operations more efficient. If the "core" of the operations shown above are replaced by the code fragment below it allows the invocation of the protected procedure to be reduced to what is, in effect, a procedure call, reserving the need to perform a context switch for the task switching case alone.

```
Suspend;
loop
   Curract (Current);
   Next_Activity (Next);
   exit when Type_Of (Next) = Thread;
   Invoke (Next);   --  Protected operation executed in context
                    --  of the current task
end loop;
Switch_To (Next);   --  New task
```

Where the procedure `Invoke` is:

```
procedure Invoke (Act : Activity_Id) is
begin
   Entry_Points (Act).all;      -- Execute the protected procedure
   Wait (Release_Mask (Act));   -- Make the protected procedure's
                                -- activity ''sleep'' again
end Invoke;
```

Suspension Objects. The `Suspension_Object`, which is provided by the package `Ada.Synchronous_Task_Control`, maps very directly onto the concept of the stim-wait node provided by the Butler — they are very similar concepts.

Delay Until. The `delay until` language construct is supported using the timers of the Butler. Unfortunately these only support relative delays, thus the absolute demands have to be converted (by the kernel) into this form.

Cooperative Scheduling Support Primitives. Clearly if the `Yield` operations are to be used in the application then these need to be provided in some way. There are two approaches that can be followed, either: provide a scheduler interface package that exposes the operations directly; or, use "standard" elements of the Ada language to obtain the desired effects.

The latter approach can only accommodate the yield operation a straightforward manner — this is achieved through the use of a `delay until` to either now, or some time in the past. This has the effect of placing the current task to the back of the ready queue for its priority and allows any ready thread of higher or equal priority to run. The `Yield_To_Higher` primitive is not supported directly; though, if the tasks have unique priorities the effect of `Yield` and `Yield_To_Higher` are identical.

The former approach could be improved if an extension to the runtime were to be provided to incorporate these facilities. In Ada 2005 there is the concept of extending the real-time features through a child package to `Ada.Dispatching`, so a package `Ada.Dispatching.Non_Preemptive` with a specification as shown below would allow the operations to be exposed in a useful manner retaining application independence from the scheduler.

```
package Ada.Dispatching.Non_Preemptive is

    procedure Yield;

    procedure Yield_To_Higher;

end Ada.Dispatching.Non_Preemptive;
```

Such a package has been suggested for inclusion in a future revision of the Ada language [15].

Advantages and disadvantages. Again as with the zero footprint runtime approach there are both advantages and disadvantages. The advantages are clearly that the application only makes use of the Ada tasking features for scheduling and inter-task interactions (notably the discussion is around the task and not the thread), and the mapping of the protected procedure to an activity and its dispatching as a simple procedure call is a very efficient solution. The use of these two features leads to an inherently more portable application.

On the other side of the coin there are two main disadvantages, these are:

– The runtime is bigger and the interactions with the scheduler are, when compared to those with the no runtime option, marginally less efficient;

– The provision of the yield operation is via a rather crude, and possibly obscure approach, and the yield to higher primitive is not provided at all, unless this is through a scheduler interface package; an approach which degrades the aforementioned advantage of portability.

Protected procedure "efficiency" is adversely affected by the lack of fine-grained priority management available in some variant of the hardware, hence this Ravenscar approach is best suited to environments utilising the more sophisticated devices.

5 Some Practical Results and Observations

In terms of results there are two main areas to consider: the effectiveness of the use of the device in place of a traditional software scheduler and hardware interrupt handler; and the impact of a cooperative scheduling approach over a preemptive one. Each of these areas is considered in the sections below. In all these cases the comparisons have to consider large applications, small detailed studies do not generally provide results that scale to bigger systems.

5.1 A Comparison of Hardware-Supported and Software-Only Approaches to Scheduling

The alternative, traditional approach considered here is one with tasks being managed in queues, and hardware events being fielded by relatively simple interrupt controllers with associated software interrupt handlers. Overall a significant improvement in processing performance has been observed across a number of systems where hardware assisted scheduling has been employed.

Providing precise figures for this improvement is not simple as there are a number of interacting aspects, the major two of which are: the lower levels of software overhead in the maintenance of the scheduler data structures; and, the "secondary" resultant impact on the effectiveness of the data and instruction caches. The impact of the latter should not be underestimated as relatively small changes to the caching effectiveness can have a significant impact on the available processing capacity.

In general the saving directly attributable to the hardware support is quite small, in the order of 1% of load; however there are further improvements when the cooperative approach is also used — this is described in the next section.

5.2 A Comparison of the Cooperative and Preemptive Approaches

At the extreme, in a system with no external events (including timers), these two approaches will lead to the same scheduling behaviour. However it would be highly unlikely that any real-time embedded system would exhibit those attributes.

The comparison is not a simple one, the differences between the two approaches are driven by a number of factors, the most significant of which are:

the rate of preemption driven context switches; and the degree to which the density of the yield points is excessive. The first of these is, in the general case, the dominant factor.

Preemption has two significant impacts on a modern processor: it disrupts the instruction pipeline; and causes the cache to be less effective. Whilst the former is a relatively straightforward effect the second is more complex especially where multi-level caches are used.

As an example of the possible savings, on one system changing from the cooperative to a preemptive model decreased the processor loading (as measured relative to the time spent in the "idle" activity) by 5%. This might not appear to be a significant saving but in a system where there are high levels of processor utilisation it can make the difference between the system working or failing, it should also be remembered that this saving is in addition to that achieved by simply having hardware support.

5.3   Issues of Seeding the Application with Cooperative Dispatching Points

Perhaps the biggest impediment to the use of the co-operative approach is the need to seed the application with calls to the `Yield_To_Higher` and `Yield` primitives. The required density of these calls relates to two factors: the speed of the processor, and the required responsiveness to any event. If the density of these calls is excessive then the benefits of the cooperative approach are eroded. Whilst this seeding might seem an onerous task in reality it only becomes problematic when the required responsiveness is very demanding — response times of the order of $30\mu s$ (using a relatively slow 133 MHz processor) are easily achieved whilst gaining significant benefits in available processing capacity.

Some experiments using the compiler to automatically implant the cooperative scheduling calls have been made. In general the results were mixed, overall the density was acceptable but there were areas of over- and under-seeding. At this time a simple automated approach does not seem possible, however the development of more sophisticated tools might be a possibility for the future.

6   Opportunities for Further Enhancements

As implementation technologies continue to evolve so too will the Butler type devices. The provision of multiple processor cores inside FPGAs present both a challenge and an opportunity. In the latter case FPGAs can provide a platform on which a more flexible scheduler can be constructed; whilst in the former there is the issue of scheduling applications distributed over many processors. Extensions to the Butler to coordinate the scheduling of tasks across a number of processors is one area that needs to be explored and developed if the technology is to remain relevant.

Leaving aside these more distant future issues there are several areas where, in the short term, the capability of the current scheduler can usefully be extended whilst retaining the advantages discussed earlier — in large degree these are inspired by the changes introduced in Ada 2005 [11]. There are three of particular interest: the provision of different scheduling policies; the use of the Butler's watchdog activity timers to support the concept of execution budgets; and the development of very low overhead design approaches based on the use of timers and protected procedures. Taking each of these in turn.

Support of additional scheduling policies. Clearly the support for a round-robin scheduling regime is rather limited if a more deterministic ordering is desired. Whilst the original hardware could only support this approach the more recent "softer" variants of the Butler have been adapted to support at least a FIFO-within-priorities approach. Equally the current lack of adherence to the Ada preemption semantics can also be corrected in these later variants.

Beyond this, support for an EDF mechanism is an interesting option as, if it can be implemented in an efficient manner, it should allow for better utilisation of the processors. This could be extremely useful given the levels of processor utilisation are already very high.

Execution time budgets. As noted earlier the Butler has a watchdog timer associated with the execution of each activity and this can trigger an interrupt if there is an overrun. This naturally maps on to the concept of execution time clocks provided in the package `Ada.Execution_Time.Timers`.

A low overhead design approach. Ada 2005 introduces the concept of pro-tected procedures being executed at some particular time, this is provided by the package `Ada.Real_Time.Timing_Events`. These protected procedures can be mapped onto the concept of a Butler activity that is controlled by some hard-ware timer. How useful this approach would be for real application needs more exploration, but combining these timers with protected procedures for other ex-ternal events, and using a cooperative approach to scheduling could allow for a very low overhead solution as it could completely eliminate the need for context switches, and allow simplification of the required runtime system.

7   Conclusions

The use of a hardware device to support the role of the scheduler has been shown to both be easy to integrate with an Ada runtime system, and reduce the overheads associated with task scheduling and interrupt handling. Significantly in its practical application reported here the greatest benefits are realised when a cooperative scheduling scheme is adopted.

The examples of use presented in this paper have focused on the issues in the context of no more than a Ravenscar profile, and in this case there is a high degree of compatibility. Attempting to extend the scope beyond Ravenscar to support more fully the Ada tasking model in general does not appear to be particularly straightforward, however this is not really a significant issue as the device was always designed with small platforms and high integrity applications in mind — neither of which are compatible with the full Ada tasking model.

References

1. He, H., Guo, H.: The realization of FFT algorithm based on FPGA co-processor. In: IITA 2008: Proceedings of the 2008 Second International Symposium on Intelligent Information Technology Application, Washington, DC, USA, pp. 239–243. IEEE Computer Society, Los Alamitos (2008)
2. Palmer, J.: The Intel®8087 numeric data processor. In: ISCA 1980: Proceedings of the 7th annual symposium on Computer Architecture, pp. 174–181. ACM, New York (1980)
3. Burns, A., Wellings, A.: Real-Time systems and Programming languages, 3rd edn. Addison-Wesley, Reading (2001)
4. Nácul, A.C., Regazzoni, F., Lajolo, M.: Hardware scheduling support in smp architectures. In: DATE 2007: Proceedings of the conference on Design, automation and test in Europe, San Jose, CA, USA, pp. 642–647. EDA Consortium (2007)
5. Nakano, T., Utama, A., Itabashi, M., Shiomi, A., Imai, M.: Hardware implementation of a real-time operating system. In: TRON 1995: Proceedings of the The 12th TRON Project International Symposium, Washington, DC, USA, pp. 34–42. IEEE Computer Society Press, Los Alamitos (1995)
6. Lai, B.C.C., Schaumont, P., Verbauwhede, I.: A light-weight cooperative multithreading with hardware supported thread-management on an embedded multiprocessor system. In: Proceedings of Asilomar Conference on Signals, Systems, and Computers (2005)
7. Roos, J.: A real-time support processor for ada tasking. SIGARCH Comput. Archit. News 17(2), 162–171 (1989)
8. Runner, D., Warshawsky, E.: Synthesizing Ada's ideal machine mate. VLSI Systems Design, 30–39 (October 1988)
9. Ardö, A.: Hardware support for efficient execution of ada tasking. In: Proceedings of the Twenty-First Annual Hawaii International Conference on Architecture Track, pp. 194–202. IEEE Computer Society Press, Los Alamitos (1988)
10. Campbell, E.R., Simpson, H.R.: Integrated circuits for multi-tasking support in single or multiple processor networks. Patent 6971099 (November 2005)
11. Taft, S.T., Duff, R.A., Brukardt, R.L., Ploedereder, E., Leroy, P. (eds.): Ada 2005 Reference Manual. Language and Standard Libraries, International Standard ISO/IEC 8652:1995(E) with Technical Corrigendum 1 and Amendment 1. Springer (2006)
12. ISO/WG9 Ada Rapporteur Group: Ravenscar profile for high integrity systems. Technical report (2007)
13. RTCA: Software considerations in airborne systems and equipment certification. Radio Technical Commission for Aeronautics (RTCA), European Organization for Civil Aviation Electronics (EUROCAE), DO178-B (1992)
14. UK Ministry of Defence: Defence standard 00-56: Safety management requirements for defence systems – issue 4. Technical report (2007)
15. AI05-0166-1: Yield for non-preemptive dispatching (2009)

Cache-Aware Development of High-Integrity Systems

Enrico Mezzetti[1], Adam Betts[2], José Ruiz[3], and Tullio Vardanega[1]

[1] University of Padua, Padova, Italy
{emezzett,tullio.vardanega}@math.unipd.it
[2] Rapita Systems Ltd., York, UK
abetts@rapitasystems.com
[3] AdaCore, Paris, France
ruiz@adacore.com

Abstract. The verification and validation requirements set on high-integrity real-time systems demand the provision of highly dependable figures for the timing behavior of applications. It is a well known fact that the adoption of hardware acceleration features such as caches may affect both the safeness and the tightness of timing analysis. In this paper we discuss how the industrial development process may gain control over the unpredictability of cache behavior and its negative effect on the timing analyzability of software programs. We outline a comprehensive approach to cache-aware development by both focusing on the application code and by exploiting specific compile-time and run-time support to control cache utilization.

1 Introduction

The development of High-Integrity Real-Time Systems (HIRTS) faces the obligation to attain extremely high verification and validation (V&V) coverage. One reflection of that requirement is that the V&V incidence on the total software development costs nears if not exceeds 60%. When high-integrity is a paramount concern, system validation is no longer limited to the functional dimension, but must instead also ascertain system correctness in the time, space and communication dimensions.

State-of-the-art approaches to the development and verification of HIRTS try to address both functional and non-functional system requirements as early in the development process as possible. Sound and early information on the timing behavior of the system is obtained by applying schedulability analysis techniques on an architectural model of the system instead of on the system implementation, and thus ahead of production.

A fundamental assumption behind this approach is that a most accurate correspondence must be preserved from system design throughout implementation to execution.

It therefore follows that in this development process no system or software design decisions should ever be made without being perfectly aware of their consequences. Unfortunately this strong requirement can only be satisfied in practice for simple processors and can hardly be guaranteed, for example, in the presence of complex hardware acceleration features like caches, complex pipelines and branch predictors.

Caches, in particular, may have disruptive consequences on the preservation of what stipulated in the schedulability analysis of the system, as they cause applications to

J. Real and T. Vardanega (Eds.): Ada-Europe 2010, LNCS 6106, pp. 139–152, 2010.

exhibit a disturbingly variable timing behavior. An uninformed use of caches may in fact hinder the determination, whether by analysis or measurement, of safe and tight bounds of the worst-case execution time (WCET) of tasks, which is an essential ingredient to schedulability analysis.

We therefore maintain that the industrial-level development process should embrace a cache-aware attitude so to regain control over the timing behavior of the system. In our opinion, a cache-aware development approach should aim at guiding the cache behavior by controlling the sources of cache-related variability.

In this paper we first reason on the impact of the application code on cache variability; we then introduce and partially evaluate a comprehensive approach to control the cache behavior, exploiting currently available tool, compiler and run-time support.

The rest of the paper is organized as follows: Section 2 introduces the current practice in industrial development processes with respect to timing analysis; Section 3 discusses the impacts of application code on the cache behavior; Section 4 elaborates our approach to restraining both statically and dynamically the cache behavior; in Section 5 we draw our conclusions.

2 Timing Analysis in Current Industrial Practice

Although no simple and exhaustive solution has yet been devised to cope with the inherent unpredictability of caches [1], several approaches have been proposed in the literature to derive safe and tight bounds of the WCET of tasks running on cache-equipped processors [2]. Some of these techniques have been successfully integrated into commercial tools, such as RapiTime [3] and aiT [4], and have been successfully applied in industrial case-studies [5,6].

This notwithstanding, software simulation and testing continue to be the common practice for obtaining WCET values, due in part to the limited diffusion of WCET tools and techniques in the industrial practice. Quite surprisingly, in most cases the WCET bounds are determined on the basis of past experience. A safety margin is then added to these WCET figures before they are given as input to schedulability analysis. Finally the WCET bounds are consolidated by testing, where a program (or part thereof) is executed and dynamically analyzed (measured) a number of times with a variety of inputs that represent selected configurations and/or operation modes. Safeness of timing and schedulability analysis thus relies on adequate test coverage and safety margins.

However, in the presence of hardware acceleration features like caches, those measurements are not necessarily safe, hence it is difficult to use them with confidence in schedulability analysis. The predictive value of scenario-based measurements is drastically reduced by the impact of caches in the timing behavior of a program [7]. In fact, the execution time behavior of a program in a cache-equipped processor depends at the same time on a complex set of interacting factors: execution history, memory layout and task interactions. The actual sources of cache variability and thus of potential unpredictability can be traced back to a set of cache-related impacts [1,7]:

– *Size impact:* if the program fits entirely in cache, most memory accesses lead to cache hits. However, if code or data is subsequently added then many more cache misses may ensue, resulting in degraded performance.

- *Sequential impact:* since cache contents depend on the history of program execution, and a program typically has multiple paths, the performance of a program can differ considerably depending on the path taken.
- *Concurrent impact:* when a task is interrupted or preempted, some of the cache lines it uses might be evicted by the higher-priority task or interrupt. In this case, memory accesses to the evicted program blocks on task resumption result in further cache misses. The voluntary suspension of a task incurs a particular case of concurrent impact as any other task or interrupt handler may change the cache state until its resumption.
- *Layout impact:* where code and data are placed in main memory influences the pattern of hits and misses. In particular, this can lead to a larger occurrence of conflict misses, which occur when memory blocks in the working set of a program compete for space in cache. When conflict misses are systematic, the WCET of a program can be greatly inflated.

Trying to simultaneously account for those impacts in a scenario-based measurement approach is very challenging and cumbersome. Moreover those factors may all change from test to operation, incurring insidiously different execution times.

Hence, HIRTS development cannot rely on an uninformed use of caches, for their uncontrolled effects on the timing behavior may invalidate the results of timing analysis and, in turn, dissipate the trustworthiness of schedulability analysis. Provided that none of the academic approaches alone can always produce a safe and tight WCET estimate, the only solution is to introduce a paradigm shift. Instead of ignoring the cache predictability problem and relying on some low-pedigree technique or "magic" tool that promises to solve the problem, the development process should be aware of the cache impact and try to ease system analyzability.

In the following sections we discuss two means to reduce cache-related variability: the first one consists in addressing predictability at the level of application code; the second focuses on taking explicit measures to (partially) governing the cache behavior.

3   Cache-Aware Coding

Several efforts to cope with cache predictability aim at devising a sound and computationally feasible analysis approach or try to avoid those hardware features or design choices that may incur less predictable behavior (e.g.: dynamic branch predictors, out-of-order execution, unpredictable cache replacement policies). Over and above the adoption of sound analysis approaches and hardware countermeasures, however, we must note that cache behavior is also highly affected by the actual program code, both in terms of performance and predictability. Let us now single out the specific dimensions in which the program code may impact the cache behavior.

Code patterns. Appropriate code structure contributes to improving WCET analysis by removing those unnecessary sources of overestimation that hamper both static analysis and hybrid measurement-based approaches to cache analysis. As observed in [7], the I-cache may be very susceptible to some critical code patterns (*cache-risk patterns*) that can incur a considerably variable cache behavior under some specific cache size, memory layout, execution path or patterns of preemption/suspension.

Besides these extreme instances, cache behavior is inherently affected by the fabric of the software program. Code patterns that display greater reference locality obviously attain better cache behavior in term of performance. With respect to I-cache, for example, low-level loops[1] highly benefit from the use of caches.

Devising good patterns for D-cache behavior is a more challenging issue: the idea of reference locality itself is not as intuitive as for instruction caches since it actually depends on how (and how often) data are accessed and reused. Data accesses are far more input dependent than instruction fetches: they not only depend on input-dependent control flow (as for instructions) but also on the input data as far as they directly influence the memory accesses (e.g.: an array index). A classification of data structures and access patterns from the standpoint of D-cache predictability is provided in [8].

Coding styles. More in general, coding styles may also affect, both negatively and positively, the tightness of timing analysis with respect to caches. We think that we should do all we can to avoid those code constructs that may yield to overestimation (e.g.: pointers, dynamic references, recursion, etc.). We should instead seek programming styles that favor, for example, more effective detection of infeasible paths, crucial for the tightness of WCET bounds, and reduce execution time variability. In general, coding styles also highly influence the amount of user intervention required by analysis tools: for instance, allowing automatic loop bound detection. For example simple enumeration-controlled *for-loops* are easier to bound than logically-controlled *while-loops* where the exit condition does not depend on a simple iteration variable.

However, it is worth noting that the final application code is obtained through a set of compiler transformations and optimizations which could be transparent to the programmer and may map the same code construct into differing machine code patterns. For example, the *switch-case* construct may be implemented as a sequence of conditional branches as well as through (less predictable) dynamic jumps via a table of indexes. Some studies [9,10] aim at devising WCET-aware compiler optimizations to be automatically applied at compile time.

Moreover, execution time variability stems from the predominant way of programming, which is typically geared to optimizing the average case, rather than the worst case. The idea behind some alternative programming paradigms, like the single-path programming approach [11], is very effective at avoiding overly different execution times between executions along alternative execution paths. Unfortunately, it suffers from serious drawbacks in term of both increased WCET and code size.

Generated vs. hand-written code. Automatically generated code typically differs from hand-written code in several respects. In the regard of the instruction cache, hand-written code is typically more cache-worthy than generated code, as the nature of human reasoning yields better reference locality in the code. Conversely, generated code is often characterized by the presence of long linear sequences of code that exploit no (or poor) temporal locality and typically pollute the cache.

Although hand-written code might seem to outperform the generated one in terms of cache performance, it is not the case with respect to code predictability and analyzability, where generated code often is much simpler to analyze (e.g.: by easing the detection

---

[1] Loops that neither contain any procedure call nor exceed the cache size.

of infeasible paths). In fact, code-generation engines usually produce structured code that follows a set of predefined code templates: analyzability thus depends on whether those templates are easy to analyze or not. Analysis tools can leverage this knowledge, which is certainly easier to acquire in that it suffices to focus on and understand just a limited set of recurring code constructs. Moreover, as code is typically generated from the specification of a model, information required to tighten the analysis results may be automatically derived from the model itself.

Automated code-generation facilities, which follow the Model-Driven Engineering (MDE) paradigm, are increasingly adopted in the industrial domain (e.g. SCADE [12], Matlab/Simulink [13]). As a matter of fact, industrial-quality HIRTS routinely integrate generated code from different modeling tools together with manual code.

To the best of our knowledge, however, no industrial-quality code generation engine exists that is expressly focused on generating predictable cache-aware code. Yet, some advanced software development suites do address the integration of WCET analysis tools in the development process (e.g. aiT integration into SCADE).

It is worth noting that both cache-aware code patterns and coding styles would be more easily enforced through automatic code-generation approaches (as well as compiler transformations), thus to preserve analyzability by construction.

Software architectures. From the standpoint of a component-based engineering approach, each software module is regarded as a component that concurs to the implementation of the overall system functionality. In this setting, the role played by software architectures is that of determining both the overall structure of the system and the pattern of tasks interleaving and interactions.

Accordingly, the timing behavior of each single component cannot be analysed in isolation, disregarding the impact of software architecture both in *static* (i.e. compile-time) and *dynamic* (i.e. run-time) dimensions.

Arguably therefore, software architectures affect the timing behavior of the overall system as they influence most sources of cache-related variability. In fact, the timing variability suffered by single components is at least related to three of the cache impacts discussed in Section 2: the layout, sequential, and concurrent impacts (Figure 1).

From the opposite point of view, one and the same component may incur variable timing behavior when immersed in distinct software architectures. In that light, software architectures should be evaluated over and above single components as a source of impact on cache behavior and a means to better control the overall system predictability.

In HIRTS, where addressing variability and predictability in an early stage of the development process is of utmost importance, cache-awareness should be regarded as a factor of choice between alternative architectures. Architectural *static impact* addresses the variability stemming from the static configuration of the system and can be traced back to sequential and layout impacts. Conversely, the *dynamic impact* relates to run-time variability and originates from the concurrent impact.

With respect to sequential and layout impact, each software architecture may incur and even demand changes in the code surrounding its constituting components, or may require the insertion of new code just inside those components (whether explicitly by the user or automatically by the compiler).

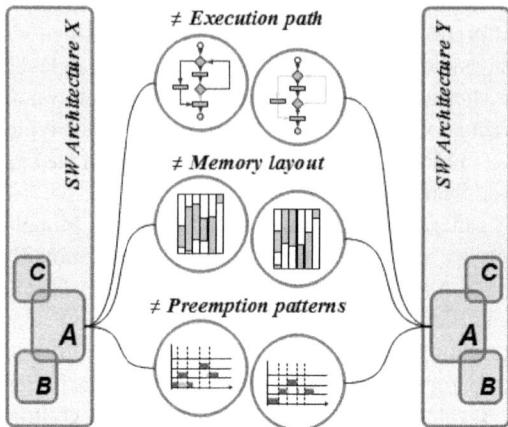

Fig. 1. Impact of SW architectures

Let us consider, for example, a software architecture that performs run-time monitoring through code instrumentation[2]. The execution time overhead incurred by the (more or less complex) instrumentation code is not limited to the time taken by the execution of the instrumentation points themselves but accounts for a variable cache behavior, stemming from a modified execution path and memory layout, which are no longer the same as that of the task in isolation. In particular, a tiny modification in the memory layout can incur a different amount of cache conflicts and, in turn, a considerably different timing behavior, as observed in [1].

When it comes to system run-time behavior, software architecture specifications determine the patterns of possible interrupts and preemptions, by way of synchronization protocols, resource access protocols, timer interrupts, and so forth. The resulting run-time variability perfectly matches our previous definition of concurrent impact.

For example, an HIRTS software architecture may include and require the use of execution-time timers (like those of Ada 2005 [14] and, similarly of POSIX [15]) to assure that tasks do not disobey at run time what was stipulated for the duration of their execution. Activating, suspending or resetting such timers would activate as many interrupts, and consequently trigger a particular concurrent impact.

A cache-aware architecture may reduce the cache variability with respect to each cache impact (e.g.: limiting the number of conflict misses and interferences), thus improving the precision of cache analysis and allowing a more predictable cache behavior.

4   Controlling the Cache Behavior

Besides the adoption of a proper programming approach, an uninformed use of caches may lead to uncontrolled variability in the timing behavior of a system. The cache

---

[2] A monitoring technique where each component is augmented with non-functional code tasked to collect the run-time traces of the component behavior to ensure that it conforms to certain bounding parameters.

impact taxonomy introduced in Section 2 is the cornerstone to attaining control over the cache behavior and increasing its predictability, as cache impacts well characterize the very sources of cache-related variability. We identified and implemented two different but complementary approaches to control statically and dynamically the cache behavior with a view at reducing the cache impacts and thus system variability.

The first method builds on statically restraining the layout impact by controlling the memory layout of a program. The second approach consists in controlling the cache utilization by deciding at run time whether and when a task is allowed to use the cache, thus affecting the extent of the concurrent impact in particular.

Both methods, of course, require some kind of aid from the compiler, as well as from dedicated support tools. To this extent, our approach specifically leverages on the Ada tool-chain by AdaCore and targets the LEON2 processor[3]. In the following sections, we describe those two methods and discuss the support they require, both in terms of compiler and support tools. Controlling the memory layout, in particular, relies on the availability of precise information on the program structure (i.e., its call graph).

4.1   Understanding the Program Structure

Collecting the call-graph information of a program is a fundamental step towards the analysis of its timing behavior. Unfortunately, some malign constructs, like indirect and dispatching calls, can make it considerably more difficult to gather sound and detailed information. Our approach builds on specific compiler support to devise the call graph information of a program.

A compiler typically collects information about subprogram calls for the code it processes. This information, together with control-flow analysis can be used to compute the full call graph for the application.

Leveraging the compiler's internals has a number of advantages. One of them is that it points directly at the user level constructs, making it much easier to understand the information than just having to do with plain references to the object code. It is also easy to port to different targets, and it works smoothly with any optimization level. Furthermore, a compiler has visibility on semantic information that can help tackle some challenging issues, such as for example, potential targets of an indirect call which can be determined based on subprogram profiles, actual references to subprograms, and visibility information.

A possible approach consists in devising compiler extensions[4] to generate per-unit call-graph information. One node is generated per subprogram, and one directed edge is generated to materialize a *may_call* relationship. The obtained information is then parsed to produce the complete call graph.

Indirect (including dispatching) calls, challenge static analysis because the target of these calls depend on the actual context of the execution. The approach followed here is to restrict the set of potential targets to those that could eventually be called at execution time. For dispatching calls we can create a global view of the class hierarchies and primitive operations and, with this information, we can later determine the list of

---

[3] http://www.gaisler.com
[4] Such extensions have been realized by AdaCore.

potential target primitive operations for a dispatching call. Likewise, for indirect calls (dereferences to values of access-to-subprogram types), the list of candidates is limited to those with a compliant profile and for which a reference has been taken.

4.2   Compute Better Code Organization

Caches introduce more jitter into a program's execution time profile because cache misses take much longer than cache hits – this variation complicates WCET analysis.

The cache impacts, introduced in Section 2 as those factors that contribute to execution time variation in the presence of caches, are quite difficult to analyse and cope with altogether. To a large extent, controlling the size and sequential impacts of the cache is very challenging and perhaps even impossible. However, careful placement of code and data in main memory can potentially avoid all conflict misses. This would eliminate, or at least alleviate, both the concurrent and layout impacts, bringing the following advantages: (1) a possible reduction in the WCET; (2) the prevention of sudden changes in the execution time profile of a program; and (3) the provision of absolute guarantees on the worst impact that cache misses can have on programs.

The layout mechanism implemented by a linker does not typically place code[5] with cache behaviour in mind, simply placing subprograms in consecutive memory locations according to the order in which they appear in the object files. This is clearly susceptible to inadvertent increases in the number of cache misses if either the ordering or the size of subprograms change between compilations, or indeed new subprograms are added. There is therefore a need to compute a cache-aware code layout *a priori* to the linking stage, and then force the subprogram address chosen by the layout algorithm onto the linker – this latter step can be achieved via a linker script.

Computation of a cache-aware code layout requires compiler support to emit, at a minimum, a list of all subprograms to be placed in memory and their sizes in bytes. One of the authors of this paper has worked on the development of an Instruction Cache Conflict Analyzer (ICCA) [16] tool which then computes such a layout through two different mechanisms.

The first uses a Genetic Algorithm (GA) to produce successive generations of layouts, each of which is evaluated in the manner depicted in Figure 2. Assuming a representative address trace of program execution has been collected (typically through simulation), this is remapped according to the address ranges specified in the new layout. This remapped address trace is then run through a cache simulator which records how many misses arose through conflicts in the cache, thus disregarding cold and compulsory misses. A layout with few conflict misses obtains a high fitness value, and subsequent generations (of layouts) are then produced through the normal crossover and mutation operators of GAs. This process iterates until a particular stopping criterion is satisfied, normally after a certain number of generations has evolved or a time budget has been exhausted.

---

[5] Controlling the data layout is not straightforward since some data locations are dynamically, rather than statically, computed, e.g. data on the stack and call-by-reference parameters. Instructions, on the other hand, are fixed and unmodifiable at compile time; for this reason, we focus exclusively on the code layout in the remainder of the discussion.

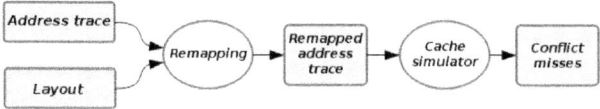

Fig. 2. Stages involved in evaluating a layout generated by the genetic algorithm

This mechanism has a few issues, however. In practical terms the evaluation of each generation of layouts can be quite slow, particularly as we want the representative address trace to be large so as to mirror actual program behaviour. That is, running each remapped trace through the cache simulator is expensive and may lead to termination of the GA after only a few generations, potentially leading to a layout not much better than the default one produced by the linker. A more crucial limitation of this approach is that it ignores structural properties of the program which have been resolved at compile time, such as the calling relation between subprograms and the control-flow graphs of each subprogram. The *structural* layout algorithm [17], on the other hand, takes advantage of this information. In a first step, it identifies frequently executed subprograms by eliciting loop bounds, either user annotated or automatically derived [18], and by taking account of overall program structure. The second step then proceeds to place subprograms with large frequencies into non-conflicting regions of memory, progressively fitting in less frequently code. However, observe that this algorithm assumes that there is compiler support in place to allow call graph and control-flow graph extraction.

Further complicating the layout algorithms is the fact that they may be subject to certain constraints. For example, as the software passes through various bug fixes, or new functionality is added, it may be critical that particular subprograms reside in the same location as they did in the previous layout because the software is already operational and patching must be kept to a minimum. In a similar vein, there may also be areas of memory where code should not be placed because, for example, they are reserved for interrupt handlers.

Limitations of cache-aware layouts. Although control of the layout is crucial to the goal of governing system timing behaviour, it is not without limitations. In particular, the following problems can arise in practice:

1. The accuracy of the structural layout is highly dependent on the accuracy of loop bounds. For many loop structures, the upper bound is not immediately obvious from simple inspection of the source code and is further complicated by dependencies on bounds between loops (so-called nonrectangular loops). In addition, static analysis techniques cannot automatically compute all bounds since this equates to solving the well-known Halting problem. All these properties create the possibility of the structural layout algorithm giving priority towards code which is executed less frequently than expected. One potential solution is to glean loop bounds during processing of a representative address trace, but this requires thorough testing to ensure confidence in the obtained bounds.
2. The structural layout only considers the static properties of the code, without consideration of dynamic properties such as mode-specific behaviour or infeasible

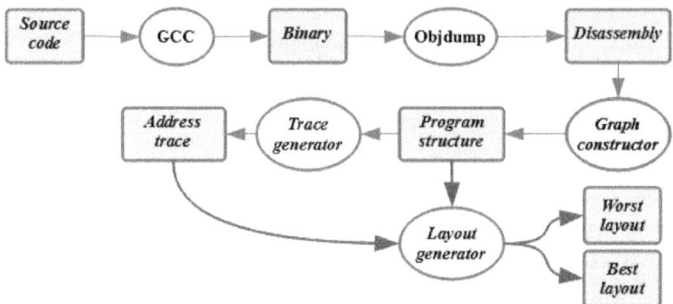

Fig. 3. Experimental framework to evaluate controlled code layout

paths. For example, in an application with many modes, it may be more desirable to ensure the group of subprograms in a particular mode of operation do not collide in the cache. However, deriving this type of flow information is extremely complicated.

3. Determining which program blocks collide in cache assumes a predictable cache replacement policy, such as Least Recently Used (LRU). Many caches, however, utilise pseudo-LRU or random replacement strategies, thus it is not possible in advance to deduce which memory accesses cause conflict misses.

4. The granularity of the computed layout is dictated by the level of linker support available. Most linkers only allow the addresses of subprograms to be specified, although in principle finer levels of granularity, e.g. at the loop level, would allow a better placement of code and therefore a better resolution of potential cache conflicts. A crude source-level solution is to place loops into individual subprograms, but this has the disadvantage of increasing stack overheads, not least violating sound coding guidelines.

Experimental Evaluation. In order to evaluate the effectiveness of a controlled layout in practice, we analysed a large-scale piece of software representative of part of the Attitude and Orbit Control System (AOCS) component of a typical satellite system. We used a bespoke cache simulator configured with the instruction cache settings found on a typical LEON processor; that is, size of 32 KiB, line size of 32 bytes, associativity of 4, and LRU replacement policy. The exact mechanics of the experimental framework are shown in Figure 3 and described as follows.

The source code was compiled using a standard GCC cross-compiler for the SPARC architecture, producing a binary that was subsequently disassembled using the *objdump* utility. In order to reconstruct the control-flow graphs and the associated call graph of the entire program — both of which are needed in the structural layout algorithm mentioned above — we developed a graph constructor tool, which reads SPARC disassembly and then writes these data structures to a program structure file. We also developed a tool to generate an address trace from the program structure file. This basically works by walking the control-flow graphs and dumping the addresses of the instructions contained in each traversed basic block to a file. When a basic block is encountered that leads to a subprogram call, a switch is made to the called control-flow graph; otherwise we randomly choose the next (successor) basic block to visit. In this case, the address trace generated contained 582,376 memory accesses.

The ICCA tool developed generates a best-case layout and a worst-case layout. The former is based on the structural information of the program and uses loop bounds obtained from a single parse of the address trace (its accuracy is therefore subject to one of the shortcomings noted above). On the other hand, the latter is computed by placing each subprogram on an 8 KiB (i.e. cache size divided by associativity) boundary in order to maximise the possibility that subprograms evict each other. For both layouts the address trace generated was remapped so that each memory reference corresponds to the new address in the new layout. Finally, we ran both the remapped address traces through the cache simulator, which records how many misses occurred.

Table 1. Comparison of layouts for the GNC task

Layout	Hits	Misses
Best layout	582,115	261
Worst layout	526,444	55,932

Table 1 reports the number of cache hits and misses for the Guidance and Navigation Control (GNC) task, which cyclically checks for the current satellite coordinates and computes the new direction. The GNC functional specification, excerpted from a real HIRTS application, involves 35 different sub-procedures. The reported results clearly underline that the best layout performs better than the worst layout as only 0.04% of memory accesses result in misses in comparison to 9.6%. Further inspection of these 261 misses reveals that most are due to compulsory misses, whereas the worst layout causes conflicts between subprograms and hence the degraded cache performance.

4.3 Dynamically Managing Cache Utilization

A cache-aware approach should also consider that allowing an unconditioned use of caches to all tasks is highly unlikely to be the best choice. Since not all the application code is worth of using the cache a naive policy would consist in favoring cache access to cache-worthy tasks. However, since HIRTS typically implement several functionalities at different criticality levels we may also consider that the most critical (or difficult to analyse) part of the system should not be affected by cache variability.

There are two main approaches to manage cache utilization, based on either restricting (partitioning) or controlling (locking) the cache behavior. As this paper reflects work that targets the LEON2 processor, which does not support partitioning, we focus on run-time management of the cache.

The run-time mechanism to enable/disable the cache will allow users to define the parts of the application that will execute with the cache enabled/disabled. A similar approach has been previously implemented by Universidad Politécnica de Madrid (UPM), as an extension to ORK+[19].

The status of cache enabled/disabled will be kept per-task, with the required machinery during context switches. It means that if task A decides to disable the cache for executing a given activity, if it gets preempted by task B, the context switch will enable the cache for task B (assuming that task B was executing with cache enabled), until control gets back to task A which will execute with the cache disabled until it decides to enable again the cache.

Both the data and instruction caches can be handled this way. We can either handle one of them or both at the same time, and the run time keeps track of the separate status of the two different blocks. By default, the caches are handled per-task, but it is also possible to change the behavior for all the tasks at the same time.

With respect to asynchronous interrupts, the cache status will be the same as that of the interrupted task. This behavior can be changed for all interrupts using the freeze on interrupt capability, by which the corresponding cache will be frozen when an asynchronous interrupt is taken. The execution of the interrupt handler will not evict any cache lines and when control is returned to the interrupted task, the cache state is identical to what it was before the interrupt.

The proposed interface for managing the cache is shown in Listing 1.1 below.

```
 1   package System.Cache_Control is
 2
 3       type Cache_Type is (Instruction , Data);
 4       --   The granularity of the operations can be on either the
 5       --   instruction or the data cache.
 6
 7       type Cache_State is (Disabled , Enabled , Frozen);
 8       --   The three different states for the cache
 9
10       procedure Enable_Cache
11          (Cache : Cache_Type; Partition_Wide : Boolean := False);
12       --   Enables the use of the indicated cache memory for the task
13       --   that performs the call. If Partition_Wide is set to True the cache
14       --   is enabled for the whole partition (all the tasks in the system).
15
16       procedure Disable_Cache
17          (Cache : Cache_Type; Partition_Wide : Boolean := False);
18       --   Disables the use of the indicated cache memory for the task
19       --   that performs the call. If Partition_Wide is set to True the cache
20       --   is disabled for the whole partition (all the tasks in the system).
21
22       procedure Enable_Cache_Freeze_On_Interrupt
23          (Cache : Cache_Type; Partition_Wide : Boolean := False);
24       --   The indicated cache will automatically be frozen when an asynchronous
25       --   interrupt is taken. If Partition_Wide is set to True then freeze on
26       --   interrupt is set for the whole partition (all the tasks in the system).
27
28       procedure Disable_Cache_Freeze_On_Interrupt
29          (Cache : Cache_Type; Partition_Wide : Boolean := False);
30       --   Disable the freeze on interrupt capability for the indicated cache. If
31       --   Partition_Wide is set to True then freeze on interrupt is set for the
32       --   whole partition (all the tasks in the system).
33
34       function Cache_Status (Cache : Cache_Type) return Cache_State;
35       --   Returns the cache status for the calling task
36
37       procedure Cache_Flush (Cache : Cache_Type);
38       --   Flush the indicated cache
39
40   end package System.Cache_Control;
```

Listing 1.1. Cache management package

The initial cache state for a task (that is whether instruction and data cache are activated or not) will be the cache state at the moment of the task activation (the state at system initialization for library-level tasks, and the state of the parent task when creating the new task).

Inhibiting the cache would be useful mainly in two different situations: first, when we want to reduce the interference, such as when we prevent background low-priority tasks from disrupting the cache contents (and therefore timing behaviour) of higher priority tasks; second, to prevent counterproductive cache evictions, such as those happening when there are parts of the code that do not take advantage of the cache (for example, when there is a long linear sequence of code) but would force useful cache contents out. Therefore, we can disable the use of the cache when we want to reduce the interference or when we do not take advantage of the cache.

5 Conclusions

The current industrial approach to timing analysis, which still relies on scenario-based measurements and safety margins, is arguably inadequate to cope with the timing variability incurred by caches. The industrial practice of HIRTS development cannot rely on an uninformed use of caches, but should instead embrace a cache-aware attitude.

In this paper we introduced a comprehensive and multifaceted approach to cope with cache-related variability that focuses on the properties of the application code and on compile- and run-time support to inform or partially control the cache behavior.

The application code should be regarded as a distinct source of cache unpredictability since code patterns, coding styles and software architectures, although at different granularity level, can effect the cache behavior. The adoption of cache-aware code patterns and coding styles, as well as the choice of cache-aware software architectures, greatly help cache analysis and reduce its inherent variability. Automated code generation engines should help in factorizing proper coding styles and patterns, to enforce cache-awareness and analyzability by construction.

A complementary approach consists in partially controlling the way the cache operates by limiting the sources of variability. We identified two dimensions in which to operate for the sake of improved predictability: forcing a cache-aware memory layout by minimizing the number of conflict misses and selectively enable/disable the cache on a per-task basis.

Unfortunately, cache-awareness is most effective when applied at the lowest level, near the machine code. This obviously contrasts with the trend in the industrial development process, where increasingly complex problems are dealt with at increasingly higher levels of abstraction. In our opinion, cache-awareness and predictability issues should be addressed – as early as possible – at higher levels of abstraction and then automatically translated to lower levels by exploiting proper tool support.

Although much work still has to be done in this direction, the ideas and approaches described in this paper provide supportive evidence that cache-awareness can be practically leveraged in the industrial development process.

Acknowledgments. The work presented in this paper was partially funded under ES-TEC/Contract 22167/09/NL/JK. For references [7,16] please refer to: Marco Zulianello, `marco.zulianello@esa.int`.

References

1. Mezzetti, E., Holsti, N., Colin, A., Bernat, G., Vardanega, T.: Attacking the sources of un-predictability in the instruction cache behavior. In: Proc. of the 16th Internat. Conference on Real-Time and Network Systems, RTNS 2008 (2008)
2. Wilhelm, R., Engblom, J., Ermedahl, A., Holsti, N., Thesing, S., Whalley, D., Bernat, G., Ferdinand, C., Heckmann, R., Mitra, T., Mueller, F., Puaut, I., Puschner, P., Staschulat, G., Stenströem, P.: The worst-case execution time problem: overview of methods and survey of tools. Trans. on Embedded Computing Systems 7(3), 1–53 (2008)
3. Rapita Systems Ltd: RapiTime tool, http://www.rapitasystems.com/rapitime
4. Absint GmbH: aiT WCET Analyzer, http://www.absint.com/ait/
5. Souyris, J., Le Pavec, E., Himbert, G., Borios, G., Jgu, V., Heckmann, R.: Computing the worst case execution time of an avionics program by abstract interpretation. In: Proceedings of the 5th Intl. Workshop on Worst-Case Execution Time Analysis (WCET) (2005)
6. Gustafsson, J., Ermedahl, A.: Experiences from Applying WCET Analysis in Industrial Set-tings. In: Proceedings of the 10th IEEE International Symposium on Object and Component-Oriented Real-Time Distributed Computing, ISORC (2007)
7. Vardanega, T., Bernat, G., Colin, A., Estevez, J., Garcia, G., Moreno, C., Holsti, N.: PEAL Final Report. Technical Report PEAL-FR-001, ESA/ESTEC (2007)
8. Lundqvist, T., Stentröm, P.: A Method to Improve the Estimated Worst-Case Performance of Data Caching. In: Proc. of the 20th IEEE International Conference on Embedded and Real-Time Computing Systems and Applications, RTCSA 1999 (1999)
9. Lokuciejewski, P., Falk, H., Marwedel, P.: Tighter WCET Estimates by Procedure Cloning. In: Proc. of the 7th Int. Workshop on Worst-Case Execution Time Analysis, WCET (2008)
10. Falk, H., Schwarzer, M.: Loop nest splitting for wcet-optimization and predictability im-provement. In: Proc. of the 6th Int. Workshop on Worst-Case Execution Time Analysis, WCET (2006)
11. Puschner, P.: The Single-Path Approach towards WCET-analysable Software. In: Proc. of the IEEE Int. Conference on Industrial Technology (2003)
12. ESTEREL SCADE Suite: http://www.estereltechnologies.com
13. Mathworks Simulink: http://www.mathworks.com/products/simulink
14. ISO SC22/WG9: Ada Reference Manual. Language and Standard Libraries. Consolidated Standard ISO/IEC 8652:1995(E) with Technical Corrigendum 1 and Amendment 1 (2005)
15. IEEE Standard for Information Technology: Portable Operating System Interface (POSIX) - Part 1: System Application Program Interface (API) - Amendment 4: Additional Real-time Extensions (1999)
16. Betts, A., Colin, A., Holsti, N., Gouy, Y., Garcia, G., Moreno, C., Vardanega, T.: PEAL2 Final Report. Technical Report PEAL-FR-001, ESA/ESTEC (2009)
17. Lokuciejewski, P., Falk, H., Marwedel, P.: WCET-driven Cache-based Procedure Positioning Optimizations. In: Proc. of the 20th Euromicro Conference on Real-Time Systems, ECRTS (2008)
18. Gustafsson, J., Ermedahl, A., Sandberg, C., Lisper, B.: Automatic Derivation of Loop Bounds and Infeasible Paths for WCET Analysis Using Abstract Execution. In: Proc. of the 27th IEEE International Real-Time Systems Symposium, RTSS (2006)
19. Universidad Politécnica de Madrid: GNAT/ORK+ for LEON cross-compilation system, http://polaris.dit.upm.es/~ork

Preservation of Timing Properties
with the Ada Ravenscar Profile

Enrico Mezzetti, Marco Panunzio, and Tullio Vardanega

Department of Pure and Applied Mathematics, University of Padova, Italy
{emezzett,panunzio,tullio.vardanega}@math.unipd.it

Abstract. Modern methodologies for the development of high-integrity real-time systems leverage forms of static analysis that gather relevant characteristics directly from the architectural description of the system. In those approaches it is paramount that consistency is kept between the system model as analyzed and the system as executing at run time. One of the aspects of interest is the timing behavior. In this paper we discuss how the timing properties of a Ravenscar compliant system can be actively preserved at run time. The Ravenscar profile is an obvious candidate for the construction of high-integrity real-time systems, for it was designed with that objective in mind. Our motivation was to assess how effective the Ravenscar profile provisions are to the attainment of property preservation. The conclusions we came to was that a minor but important extension to its standard definition completes a valuable host of mechanisms well suited for the enforcement and monitoring of timing properties as well as for the specification of handling and recovery policies in response to violation events.

1 Introduction

In recent years, methodologies for the development of high-integrity real-time systems have started to adopt styles that leverage forms of static analysis mostly based on an architectural description of the system. One of the core concerns of those development methodologies is to facilitate the early analysis of the design attributes that are critical to the computation, time, space and communication behavior of the system. The adopted architectural description language and the methodology that uses it should therefore permit the required forms of analysis to be performed as early as possible in the development process, typically much earlier than implementation and test on target.

This prerequisite is important, because when design attributes are used as input for system analysis, they later constrain system execution in order that the analysis assumptions can actually (continue to) hold true at run time. Ultimately therefore those design attributes turn into system properties. Preservation of properties at run time then becomes an essential provision to warrant consistency between the system as analyzed and the system during execution. In fact, any deviation that the system execution may incur at run time from the initial stipulations may invalidate the analysis results and cause undesirable consequences. Obviously, the nature of the attributes that the analysis techniques in use want set on the system determine how strict and taxing the preservation measures must be. A simple yet coarse analysis may demand little in the way of

J. Real and T. Vardanega (Eds.): Ada-Europe 2010, LNCS 6106, pp. 153–166, 2010.

run-time preservation capabilities, but it may also result in ineffective design. More sophisticated analysis costs more in both the intellectual gears required of the user and the support needed for preservation, but it also permits finer-grained control of the design.

In this paper we focus on how to ensure the preservation of timing properties at run time. This goal can be achieved with three distinct and complementary provisions:

1. enforcing the timing properties that are to stay constant during execution;
2. monitoring the timing properties that are inherently variable in so far as they are influenced or determined by system execution;
3. trapping and handling the violations of asserted properties.

In class 1 we include the provisions needed to enforce the period for cyclic tasks and the minimum inter-arrival time (MIAT) for sporadic tasks. Those values are stipulated as constants that feed schedulability and performance analysis and they must therefore be obliged as exactly as possible during execution. Needless to say, the granularity and accuracy of the software clock and the absolute vs. relative nature of delays have a tremendous influence on the degree of preservation that can be attained.

Provisions in class 2 concern the monitoring of the execution time of tasks and their deadlines. Both attributes are intrinsically variable, the latter because, while we may set deadlines as relative, when they take effect they are obviously absolute and thus depend on current time.

The ability to monitor those variable attributes is the prelude to being able to detect the violations of their bounds as well as identify the failing party. The bound assumed for task execution time is the worst-case value of it, known as WCET, which should not be overrun. Deadlines should not be missed, which we can detect by observing whether the jobs of tasks always complete before their respective deadline.

Those provisions belong in class 3, together with the ability to act on the violation event following some user-defined policy.

In this paper we discuss a practical strategy to attain the preservation of the timing properties of interest. We want this strategy to be effectively applicable under the constraints of the Ravenscar profile [1], which we regard as the most appropriate run-time infrastructure for high-integrity real-time systems.

We also contend that the ability to monitor the execution time of tasks is crucial in two distinct ways: it helps us adjudge the cause of a timing-related violation event with suitable accuracy and it permits to trigger the designated handling procedure with the least possible latency.

The ability to monitor execution time responds to two important yet basic needs:

– First, we must acknowledge that the worst-case execution time (WCET) of tasks is a most fundamental input to schedulability analysis. Designers are required to feed the analysis equations with a value that is both *safe*, that is, no less than the actual task WCET, and as *tight* as possible so as to avoid overly pessimistic analysis results. Unfortunately, obtaining bounds with both those two characteristics is a tough call for both the scientific community and the current industrial practice. Hence systems are statically analyzed on the basis of bounds that may prove unsafe in some possibly extreme scenarios of execution, whether normal or erroneous, and thus incur WCET overruns that invalidate the assurance of analysis.
The use of execution-time timers allows to promptly detect such overruns.

– Second, execution-time monitoring serves industrial developers most practical, effective and standard means to measure the execution of tasks in the most accurate and representative settings with respect to both hardware and operational scenarios. These measurements, when obtained through high-coverage verification and validation activities provide useful confirmatory evidence of the WCET bounds used in the analysis.

The remainder of the paper is organized as follows: in section 2 we briefly recall the essentials of the Ravenscar profile and account for its ongoing evolution; in section 3 we show how to enforce static timing properties; in section 4 we discuss how to monitor variable timing properties; in section 5 we propose some policies to detect and handle violation events; in section 6 we draw some conclusions.

2   The Ravenscar Profile

The Ravenscar profile (RP) [1] was one of the most prominent outputs of the 8th International Real-Time Ada Workshop (IRTAW), held in 1997. It was subsequently subject to minor refinements and clarifying interpretations during the 9th and 10th IRTAW in 1999 and 2002 respectively.

The RP has ever since received growing attention by the scientific, user and implementor community alike. Several industrial-quality implementations of it exist to date. Furthermore, with the 2005 revision of the Ada language it has also become a standard part of the language.

The rationale for the RP is to provide a restricted tasking model suited for the development of high-integrity real-time systems.

The Verification and Validation (V&V) activities for that class of systems include the use of static analysis to analyze the behavior of the system in the time and space dimensions. To best serve this need, the profile: excludes all Ada constructs that are exposed to non-determinism or unbounded execution cost; prescribes the use of a static memory model; and constrains task communication and synchronization to the use of protected objects under the ceiling locking protocol. The resulting run-time system can be implemented on top of a real-time kernel of little complexity – which is good for certification – and high space and time efficiency.

In our timing properties preserving architecture we use the following Ada constructs and features:

(i) the `delay until` statement, for the enforcement of the period of cyclic tasks and the MIAT of sporadic tasks (see section 3 for details);
(ii) `Timing_Event` declared at library level, for deadline monitoring (see section 4.1); and
(iii) execution-time timers for monitoring task WCET (see section 4.2).

`Timing_Events` and execution-time timers were introduced in the 2005 revision of the language, together with the standard definition of the RP. `Timing_Events` were – with definite benefit, as we shall see later – included in the Ravenscar profile, but under the restriction that they be declared at library level only [2]. Conversely, although the need to monitor the run-time behavior of tasks even under the Ravenscar constraints was evident, execution-time timers were excluded, for it was feared that the asynchronous nature of timer events would hamper the predictability of execution and cause a disturbing increase in the run-time overhead of implementations.

Interestingly, the cost-related element of the cautionary argument behind the exclusion of execution-time timers from the RP does not hold anymore: several industrial-quality implementations of the RP have recently been extended with (restricted) experimental support for it, e.g.: MarteOS [3] and ORK 2.1 [4]. The latter implementation is a real-time kernel developed by the Polytechnic University of Madrid, which targets the LEON2[1], a SPARC V8 processor. ORK 2.1 provides a lightweight implementation of execution-time timers, restricted to at most one per task. To facilitate use in high-integrity systems, ORK 2.1 provides a very comprehensive score of upper-bounds to the timing overheads of all its primitive services, including those for execution time monitoring.

Table 1 summarizes the run-time overhead incurred by the timer management procedures of the `Execution_Time` package.

Table 1. ORK 2.1 time overhead of `Execution_Time` procedures (in processor cycles)

Package	Procedure	Execution time
Execution_Time	Clock	435
Execution_Time	CPU_Time + Time_Span	58
Execution_Time	CPU_Time − Time_Span	58
Execution_Time	CPU_Time < CPU_Time	65
Execution_Time	CPU_Time ≤ CPU_Time	77
Execution_Time	CPU_Time > CPU_Time	73
Execution_Time	CPU_Time ≥ CPU_Time	51
Execution_Time	Split(CPU_Time, Seconds_Count, Time_Span)	1142
Execution_Time	Time_Of(Seconds_Count, Time_Span)	80

In spite of the negative effect caused the very poor clock registers provided in the LEON2 processor architecture, the overheads reported in Table 1 arguably demonstrate, from the standpoints of both implementation and execution, that the inclusion of execution-time timers can be afforded in the Ravenscar profile. The subsequent discussion will also show that the other concern, that of permitting asynchronous timer events to unduly occur during execution is defeated under the use that we propose.

Acknowledging this evidence, the 14th IRTAW held in October 2009 formalized an Ada Issue (AI) proposal for the inclusion of *execution-time timers* in the standard definition of the Ravenscar Profile. At the time of writing, that AI has been submitted to the approval of the Ada Rapporteur Group (ARG) for evaluation.

We look very favorably to this possible revision of the RP. As we discuss in the sequel in fact, the availability of execution-time timers is absolutely central to the suite of run-time mechanisms we need for the realization of detection and handling of time-related faults in a Ravenscar-compliant system.

There has been heated (yet amicable) discussion as to whether the RP should stay fixed as sanctioned in the Ada 2005 standard and let any extensions (as opposed to

---

[1] http://www.gaisler.com

general modifications) of it form a distinct profile. Our view in that regard is that if a language feature is deemed useful for the intent and purposes of the RP and its implementation incurs low-enough space and time overhead, then it should incrementally add to the standard RP instead of feeding a separate derivative profile.

3   Enforcement of Timing Properties

The first class of timing properties we described in section 1 comprises constant properties that can be enforced explicitly, like the task period in cyclic tasks and the MIAT in sporadic tasks.

The task period can be straightforwardly enforced with the use of an absolute delay, as supported by the `delay until` statement of Ada, which separates in time successive activations of jobs of that task, each job being represented by the inside of the outermost loop of task body.

To enforce the MIAT in sporadic tasks we need instead to combine the use of the absolute delay with a task structure that captures the software-generated release event associated to the task. It is worth noting that by adopting a two-staged strategy for the handling of hardware interrupts and sporadic tasks for the deferred (or second-level) part we attenuate – but not obliterate – the hazard occurring from interrupts occurring more frequently than stipulated.

For example, reference [5] defines tasks as a composition of four basic blocks (Figure 1) that mirrors HRT-HOOD [6]:

- a provided and required interface, respectively PI and RI;
- an operational control structure (OPCS), which implements the functional (sequential) behavior of each PI service;
- a thread, which implements the task behavior and thus executes PI services of the task, one per activation as required;
- an object control structure (OBCS), which operates as the synchronization protocol agent responsible for delivering the release event to the task, in conformance to the Ravenscar constraint that wants inter-task communication to be asynchronous via a protected object.

In that task structure, the PI of the task is entirely delegated to the OBCS: each invocation of that PI is therefore addressed to the OBCS, which reifies it into a *request descriptor* and posts it in a dedicated application-level queue.

The release event of a sporadic task is determined by the occurrence of two subordinate conditions: the task has woken up from its MIAT-long suspension; and at least one invocation request is pending in the OBCS queue. When the latter condition is true, the guard to the corresponding entry in the OBCS opens and the thread may fetch with mutual exclusion guarantees the request descriptor from the OBCS queue. The thread then interprets the descriptor to determine which PI must be executed, and calls the designated service in the OPCS (see listing 1).

Cyclic tasks can be reconciled with this structure by requiring that at every periodic release they use a protected procedure to fetch a request descriptor from their OBCS. This provision enables the cyclic task structure to allow the execution of commanded operations instead of just the nominal periodic operation. In the latter case the request descriptor would take a default value, but explicit invocations of the cyclic task PI would cause non-default request descriptors to be deposited in the queue of the corresponding OBCS. Interestingly, the latency of execution of the commanded operation would not undermine its ultimate utility, for it would be bounded by the task period.

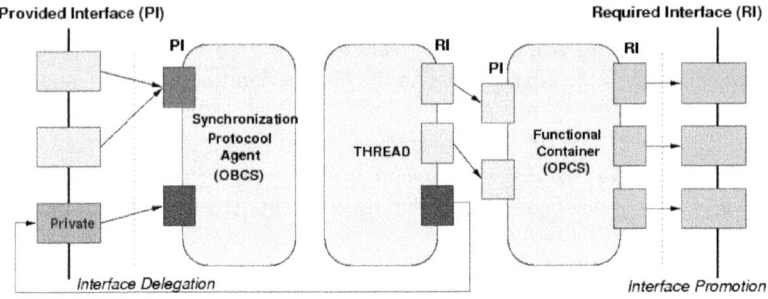

Fig. 1. Compositional task structure

Listing 1. Task structure for the enforcement of period or MIAT

```
1  loop
2    <fetch a request from OBCS and decode it>;
3    <invoke the required service in OPCS>;
4    Next_Time := Next_Time + Milliseconds (Interval);
5    delay until} Next_Time;
6  end loop
```

Much like many other real-time constructs, the efficacy of the delay until statement depends on the accuracy of the implementation of hardware and software clocks, and on the precision of the hardware timer. The lack of proper hardware support may negatively affect the accuracy of clocks and thus of absolute delays, as described in [7].

4 Monitoring of Timing Properties

Modern development approaches employ static analysis techniques to predict the timing behavior of the system model. Unfortunately, however, the values set for the task timing attributes that depend on run-time behavior – most notably, the worst-case execution time – may be exceeded. This is because the problem is difficult and prone to inaccurate reasoning or inadequate means. The consequences of a WCET overrun misbehavior may be dire, in that a number of tasks may miss their deadlines.

Let us now focus on the monitoring of deadlines, task WCET and blocking time induced by the use of the Ceiling Locking protocol to warrant mutual exclusion for shared critical sections.

4.1   Deadline Monitoring

Schedulability analysis ascertains whether every job of a task can complete its execution before the applicable deadline, which can be either absolute or relative to the release time of the task.

Since the expiration of an absolute deadline intrinsically is a time event, timing events can effectively be used to perform deadline monitoring.

In Ada 2005 the `Timing_Event` is a lightweight mechanism that executes a protected procedure at a specific time instant, without the need to employ a dedicated task. The code to be executed at the given time is specified in a `Timing_Event_Handler`. `Timing_Events` are triggered by the progression of the hardware clock. Implementations may execute the protected procedure directly in the context of the interrupt service routine that acknowledges the clock interrupt. This is in fact an implementation advice in the Ada specification.

Listing 2. Deadline-monitored task

```
1  loop
2     Set_Handler (Deadline_Event,
3                      Milliseconds (Rel_Deadline),
4                      Deadline_Miss_Handler);
5     <task operations>;
6     Next_Time := Next_Time + Milliseconds (Interval);
7     Cancel_Handler (Deadline_Event, isSetHandler);
8     delay until Next_Time;
9  end loop;
```

At each new task release, a timing event can be armed to expire at the absolute deadline of the task invoking the `Set_Handler` procedure (see listing 2). If the task was able to complete its activation before its deadline, the timing event would be cleared using the `Cancel_Handler` procedure. Otherwise, the timing event would be fired and the designated handler would be executed.

Unfortunately, very little can be learned from the detection of a deadline miss, for the violation event is not directly related with the actual cause of it. A deadline miss could in fact be incurred by a WCET overrun of the monitored task itself, or by greater interference from higher priority tasks (each element of it being a possibly marginal WCET overrun), or even by the blocking caused by the resource access protocol, when a lower priority task holds a resource with ceiling priority higher than that of the monitored task. As a consequence, no other useful operations can be performed for the handling of a deadline miss than just logging the event for the purposes of information integration over time.

4.2   WCET Monitoring

The provisions that enable the monitoring of execution time of tasks are probably the single most useful mechanism to ensure the preservation of timing properties. In Ada 2005, `Execution_Time.Timers` provide a simple yet efficient mechanism to monitor the execution time of tasks, to detect WCET overruns and to react in a timely fashion to a violation event.

Execution-time clocks were first introduced in the POSIX 1003.1d standard [8] as a means to cater for information on the run-time behavior of tasks. Execution-time clocks have subsequently been included in the 2005 revision of Ada [2]. The inclusion of execution-time timers in the Ada language standard is very good news indeed. Previously in fact, the industrial need for monitoring the execution time of tasks or for measuring execution time in general could only be responded to by resorting to vendor-specific solutions, realized in whether hardware or software.

The `Execution_Time` package associates a `Clock` to a designated task, which is used for measuring the CPU time actually consumed by the task execution. (To tell the truth, the language standard permits the measured value to include the execution time of interrupt handlers occurred during the execution of the task. This may obviously cause the resulting value to be pessimistically inaccurate. To rectify this discrepancy the 14th IRTAW formulated an implementation advice to treat the execution time of interrupt handlers separately from that of the preempted tasks.)

A `Timer` realizes a mechanism on top of an execution-time clock (thus related to a single task) which triggers a `Timer_Handler` procedure when the task has consumed a given amount of CPU time.

Listing 3. WCET-monitored task

```
1   loop
2       Set_Handler (WCET_Timer,
3                       Milliseconds (WCET),
4                       WCET_Violation_Handler);
5       <task operations>;
6       Next_Time := Next_Time + Milliseconds (Interval);
7       delay until Next_Time;
8   end loop;
```

Every individual task can be attached to a timer that monitors the CPU time that is consumed by the task. At each task activation the timer is set to expire whenever the task exceeds its allotted CPU time (which is meant to be its WCET). In the event of a WCET overrun the `Timer_Handler` procedure is immediately executed. In contrast with deadline monitoring, the handler need not be cancelled on self-suspension because a suspended task does not consume CPU time. Since the timer that has fired a handler on a violation event is directly attached to the overrunning task, a detected WCET overrun is always correctly ascribed to the actual culprit.

Under fixed-priority preemptive dispatching, a WCET overrun may cause a missed deadline not only in the overrunning task itself, but also on lower priority tasks owing to greater interference.

4.3   Blocking Time Monitoring

A task that executes longer than stipulated inside the critical section of a shared resource may cause a subtle case of timing fault. In fact, the *response time equation* (1) of any task τ_i is determined by three additive factors: the WCET C_i of τ_i itself; the worst-case interference due to the execution of higher priority tasks including kernel overheads (I_i); and the *blocking time*, which is computed as the longest time the task of interest can be prevented from executing by lower priority tasks (B_i) in force of the resource access protocol in use.

$$R_i = C_i + B_i + I_i \tag{1}$$

In order to determine the blocking time factor that applies to every individual task we must therefore compute an estimate for the longest execution time of each critical section and then apply specific filtering scheme that depends on the resource access protocol in use. It is worth noting in this regard that the `Ceiling_Locking` policy, which is prescribed in the Ravenscar profile, provides a minimized bound for the blocking time factor value and guarantees that each task can be blocked at most once per activation and just before release.

This notwithstanding, detecting and diagnosing this kind of timing fault can prove quite cumbersome. The mere fact that a task executes longer than expected inside a critical section does not necessarily incur a WCET overrun in any affected task (the running task and that may suffer blocking from it) as the task execution as a whole may even out this violation. Consequently, to cope with this kind of fault we cannot simply rely on WCET monitoring through `Timers`.

As we inferred earlier on, a blocking-time violation can affect task schedulability in a subtler way than just causing WCET overruns in them. In fact, whereas WCET overruns only affect the schedulability of the faulty task or of lower priority ones, the overrun in a critical section may cause a missed deadline even for higher priority tasks whose priority is lower than or equal to the ceiling of the used shared resource.

An interesting study [9] targeting Real-Time Java describes an elegant approach to directly monitor blocking time. The proposed solution leverages the inherent property of the `Ceiling_Locking` policy, which ensures that blocking may occur only once per task activation and just before its release. The essence of the proposal revolves around using a kernel-level timer to measure the time duration that a task is prevented from execution owing to priority inversion. Due to the lack of standard support for it, however that approach is currently not feasible in our context.

An alternative approach consists in measuring the execution time actually spent within shared resources instead of monitoring the blocking time incurred from their use. The worst-case blocking time term B_i in equation (1) depends on the adopted synchronization protocol; with the `Ceiling_Locking` policy prescribed by the Ravenscar profile – which has the same worst-case behavior as the priority ceiling protocol [10]) – the worst-case blocking time B_i induced on task τ_i amounts to the duration of the longest critical section executed by lower priority tasks in a shared resource with a ceiling priority higher than or equal to the priority of τ_i.

Unfortunately, to monitor the time a task executes inside a shared resource we cannot use the Ada `Timers`, for they are associated to only one task and this attachment is statically fixed at timer creation. Hence we cannot define a timer that can be reassigned to the tasks that enter a given critical section.

To circumvent the lack of direct language support, one might possibly resort to using the execution-time clocks on which `Timers` are based. An execution-time clock can in fact be used to measure task execution in any given code region. One could thus query the CPU time consumed by the task of interest before and after the critical section and then calculate the difference (see listing 4).

Listing 4. Time monitoring of execution in shared resource

```
1   Time_In := Execution_Time.Clock;
2   <beginning of critical section CS>;
3   <end of critical section CS>:
4   Time_Out := Execution_Time.Clock;
5   if Time_Out - Time_In > CS_WCET then
6       <violation handling>;
7   end if;
```

If the CPU time spent executing in the critical section is longer than estimated we may have a blocking-time violation for the higher priority tasks that contend for the same resource. This can be determined by comparing the consumed CPU time against the amount of blocking that the overruning task is predicated to induce on higher priority tasks; if that is the case, then we do have a violation event to treat.

Unfortunately however this approach suffers from at least two serious defects. First, the scheme shown in listing 4 would not be able to promptly detect a WCET overrun inside a critical region, but only after the task has finished executing in the shared resource and has released it, which may *not* actually occur in the case of serious programming or execution error. Furthermore, in contrast with the Timer_Handler procedure in Timers, the handling mechanism would not be executed at interrupt level but at the priority of the overrunning task, which is immediately preempted by higher priority tasks, perhaps even of those it was blocking. This implies that the handling of the fault is further deferred, possibly after the preempting task has already missed its deadline. Finally, this approach also adds considerable time and space overhead to the monitoring framework of the architecture.

5   Handling of Timing Faults

Several policies can be adopted to try to remedy a detected timing fault. The handling type may depend on: the severity and frequency of the timing fault; the criticality of the affected system function; system requirements. In fact, for several high-integrity real-time systems, the only recovery operation admissible on the detection of a severe fault requires to either terminate the program and enter some safe mode, or else switch to a hot redundant computer, if available.

We now enumerate the fault handling policies that can be used when a timing violation is detected at run time. Those policies can be applied in the face of occasional or even recurrent overruns of modest or even important gravity. Some of the proposed treatments simply contribute information for fault identification and diagnosis. Other treatments permit to effect a recovery action, which is able to mitigate or remedy the effects of the timing fault.

However, as we further discuss, all of those policies are unable to remedy *permanent overrun* situations that arise from a task getting stuck executing forever in a loop.

Error logging. This is the simplest and most basic treatment: the WCET violation event is simply logged. Although the logging does not remedy the problem, the log can be used to inform some designated fault handling authority, which can then apply some system- or partition-wide policy.

Integration of WCET. When designers perform schedulability analysis based on Response Time Analysis [11], they determine the worst-case response time of each task and thus earn confidence that tasks meet their deadline. As we mentioned earlier on, the robustness of the analysis results depends on the safeness of the WCET bounds that are fed to the equations.

Sensitivity analysis (for example in the flavor described in [12]) instead is a theory that is able to calculate how long the execution of a task can exceed its WCET while still maintaining the overall system schedulable. In essence, provided that all the remaining timing parameters stay fixed, we are able to statically calculate the maximum amount of tolerance the system can admit for single violations of WCET.

We can leverage this information to realize some WCET overrun handling policies.

Let us call ΔC_x the allowable excess execution time for task τ_x that we determine using sensitivity analysis. When task τ_i should ever incur a WCET overrun, perhaps because the estimated WCET bound C_i was too optimistic, we can permit the task to execute until $C_i + \Delta C_i$ without fearing consequences for system schedulability. The timing fault incurred when execution time exceeds C_i should however be always notified to the fault management authority so that it can set an upper bound on the number of times the violation is allowed before escalating to other handling policies (such as e.g., degraded mode, safe mode, etc...).

If a task should frequently incur WCET overruns that do not exceed ΔC_i, an obvious alternative strategy would consist in directly increasing the WCET bound that is monitored by the execution-time timer of the task. The increment that integrates the WCET can be applied to one and the same task multiple times as long as it does not exceed ΔC_i. Unfortunately, if we wanted to apply this policy to more than one task at a time, we would need to recalculate the ΔC_x increment factor for all tasks τ_x.

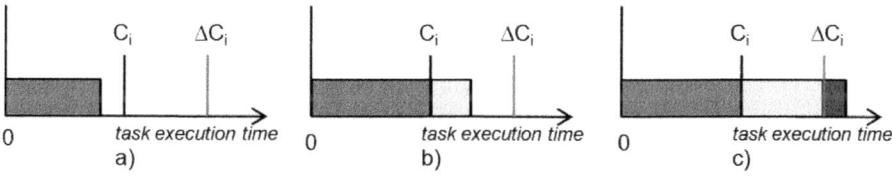

Fig. 2. a) Nominal execution of a task; b) The task overruns the WCET bound used in the schedulability analysis; the overall system however is still schedulable; c) The task overruns the WCET bound and the sensitivity analysis bound; the overall system is not schedulable anymore

The theory presented in [13] has potential for application in our context. That work in fact formalizes the class of "weakly hard real-time systems" and supports it with a suite of schedulability equations that are able to ascertain whether a task set meets "any n in m deadlines" (with $m \geq 0$ and $0 \leq n \leq m$), or "any row n in m deadlines".

In [14] instead, the authors leverage on [13] to determine the ΔC_i of a task in a weakly hard real-time system under EDF. Unfortunately, this theory is only able to predict the ΔC_i of a single task under the assumption that all other system parameters stay fixed. This limitation notwithstanding, an extension of that theory that was able to account for shared resources and fixed priority preemptive scheduling would be an interesting candidate for application in our context.

Period or MIAT change. Increasing the period or MIAT of a periodic or sporadic task that is frequently overrunning its WCET may help one mitigate the effects on affected tasks. If a sustainable schedulability analysis theory [15] was used (as for example Response Time Analysis), then this relaxation of the system parameters is guaranteed to preserve the overall system schedulability.

Task inhibition via OBCS. If tasks are realized with the compositional structure described in section 3, it is possible to set the guard of the OBCS entry to false so as to prevent any further release of an overrunning task. In order to make the mechanism compliant to the RP, the guard of the entry shall be expressed as a simple Boolean variable; this is simple to achieve as the guard can be set by a designated protected procedure that can be invoked by the fault handling authority. The solution applies directly to sporadic tasks – and cyclic tasks alike – and it is reversible in that the guard can be set to true again anytime the fault handling policy deems it safe.

The applicability of the latter two policies is contingent on the system requirements: the system should be able to operate with degraded performances or without the functions in which the faulty tasks is involved; this assessment includes the evaluation of producer-consumer relationships in which the faulty task is involved. Table 2 recapitulates the possible policies and their essential characteristics.

Table 2. Techniques against WCET overruns

Technique	Recovery Action	Ravenscar Compliance
Error Logging	○	yes
Integration of WCET	*	yes
Period/MIAT change	●	yes
Inhibition via OBCS	●	yes

Symbols: ● = the technique can be used as (part of) a recovery action;
* = the technique can be part of a recovery action in a limited number of situations;
○ = the technique does not remedy the timing fault.

The occurrence of a *permanent overrun* is an extremely severe situation to cope with. For this situation to occur, a task must be stuck executing forever in a loop. In that situation in fact, the rules of fixed-priority preemptive dispatching will never permit lower priority tasks to ever execute again.

A fault of this kind is extremely delicate for Ravenscar systems, since the RP does not provide for any mechanisms that permit to directly cope with it.

Task termination would be no solution, not only because it is explicitly excluded by the RP, but also because of its inherent exposure to massive extents of non-determinism and its disruptive costs to kernel implementation and verification.

The use of dynamic priorities and/or asynchronous task control could be advocated to mitigate or remedy the problem. The former feature would be used to decrease the priority of the offending task to the lowest possible value: this solution is however not satisfactory for data integrity in so far as the task would stay eligible for execution and may consume data when the CPU has no other tasks to execute. The latter would not be able to force tasks stuck in a critical section to yield as the task in question shall first release the resource before asynchronous task control can take effect.

In the case the system was not able to direct perform ultimate maintenance on itself, patching part of the software (in actual fact, the functional part of offending tasks) while continuing reduced operation may become the only applicable non-disruptive course of action. The inhibition of designated tasks by setting the corresponding OBCS entry guard to false would permit to safely replace the faulty OPCS.

As a conclusion, there is still an open area of investigation for a practical and effective handling policy for this kind of severe faults. However it should be clear that due to the high-integrity nature of the real-time systems in which the RP is used (and thus to the extensive V&V campaigns they are subject to), we can assume that the probability of occurrence of permanent overruns is negligible.

6   Conclusion

In this paper we discussed the importance of preservation of properties at run time for state-of-the-art development methodologies. As the analysis of systems is applied in earlier design stages, it becomes imperative to ensure that the system at run time does not deviate from what was predicated by analysis. In our work we focused on run-time preservation of timing properties. We centered our approach on the adoption of a subset of the Ada language known as the Ravenscar profile (RP), which facilitates the design of systems that are by definition amenable to static analysis in the time and space dimensions. We described a framework for the enforcement and monitoring of timing properties which also allows to perform a set of fault handling and recovery actions.

The framework requires only three time-related constructs of the Ada language: the *delay until* statement, timing events and execution-time timers. The first two constructs already belong in the RP. The inclusion of execution-time timers in the RP, which at the time of this writing, is under evaluation by the Ada Rapporteur Group, would make the RP satisfactorily fit for monitoring WCET as well as providing the mechanisms to react to violation of that property.

Our study singled out two areas that need further investigation:

1. the monitoring of blocking time, which currently has no practical and satisfactory solution in Ada; it would be interesting to investigate the feasibility of a solution inspired to the proposal described in [9]. Alternatively, we might want to allow execution-time timers to be used for measuring the duration of critical sections.
2. permanent WCET overruns (caused for example by a task stuck in an endless loop) are critical in a Ravenscar system, since the profile does not provide any effective mechanism to cope with this situation; however, thanks to the intensive V&V campaigns that are routinely required by the high-integrity nature of the systems of our interest, we can assume that the occurrence of these faults has a negligible probability to occur.

In conclusion, we contend that in the context of high-integrity real-time systems the Ravenscar Profile is an excellent candidate to be used as the cornerstone of a development methodology. The RP in fact guarantees the development of statically analyzable systems and provides adequate means to ensure property preservation from design to implementation and eventually at run time.

References

1. Burns, A., Dobbing, B., Romanski, G.: The Ravenscar Tasking Profile for High Integrity Real-Time Programs. In: Asplund, L. (ed.) Ada-Europe 1998. LNCS, vol. 1411, p. 263. Springer, Heidelberg (1998)
2. ISO SC22/WG9: Ada Reference Manual. Language and Standard Libraries. Consolidated Standard ISO/IEC 8652:1995(E) with Technical Corrigendum 1 and Amendment 1 (2005)
3. Aldea Rivas, M., González Harbour, M.: MaRTE OS: an Ada Kernel for Real-Time Embedded Applications. In: Strohmeier, A., Craeynest, D. (eds.) Ada-Europe 2001. LNCS, vol. 2043, p. 305. Springer, Heidelberg (2001)
4. Universidad Politécnica de Madrid: GNATforLEON cross-compilation system, http://polaris.dit.upm.es/~ork
5. Bordin, M., Vardanega, T.: Automated Model-Based Generation of Ravenscar-Compliant Source Code. In: Proc. of the 17th Euromicro Conference on Real-Time Systems (2005)
6. Burns, A., Wellings, A.J.: HRT-HOOD: A Structured Design Method for Hard Real-Time Ada Systems. Elsevier, Amsterdam (1995)
7. Zamorano, J., Ruiz, J.F., de la Puente, J.A.: Implementing Ada.Real_Time.Clock and Absolute Delays in Real-Time Kernels. In: Strohmeier, A., Craeynest, D. (eds.) Ada-Europe 2001. LNCS, vol. 2043, p. 317. Springer, Heidelberg (2001)
8. IEEE Standard for Information Technology: Portable Operating System Interface (POSIX) - Part 1: System Application Program Interface (API) - Amendment 4: Additional Real-time Extensions (1999)
9. dos Santos, O.M., Wellings, A.J.: Blocking Time Monitoring in the Real-Time Specification for Java. In: The 6th International Workshop on Java Technologies for Real-Time and Embedded Systems, pp. 135–143 (2008)
10. Sha, L., Lehoczky, J.P., Rajkumar, R.: Solutions for Some Practical Problems in Prioritized Preemptive Scheduling. In: Proc. of the 7th IEEE Real-Time Systems Symposium, pp. 181–191 (1986)
11. Joseph, M., Pandya, P.K.: Finding Response Times in a Real-Time System. The Computer Journal 29(5), 390–395 (1986)
12. Bini, E., Di Natale, M., Buttazzo, G.: Sensitivity Analysis for Fixed-Priority Real-Time Systems. Real-Time Systems 39(1-3), 5–30 (2008)
13. Bernat, G., Burns, A., Llamosí, A.: Weakly Hard Real-Time Systems. IEEE Trans. Computers 50(4), 308–321 (2001)
14. Balbastre, P., Ripoll, I., Crespo, A.: Schedulability Analysis of Window-Constrained Execution Time Tasks for Real-Time Control. In: Proceedings of the 14th Euromicro Conference on Real-Time Systems, pp. 11–18 (2002)
15. Baruah, S., Burns, A.: Sustainable Scheduling Analysis. In: Proceedings of the 27th IEEE Real-Time Systems Symposium, pp. 159–168 (2006)

Towards the Definition of a Pattern Sequence for Real-Time Applications Using a Model-Driven Engineering Approach*

Juan Ángel Pastor, Diego Alonso, Pedro Sánchez, and Bárbara Álvarez

Division of Systems and Electronic Engineering (DSIE)
Technical University of Cartagena, Campus Muralla del Mar, E-30202, Spain
juanangel.pastor@upct.es

Abstract. Real-Time (RT) systems exhibit specific characteristics that make them particularly sensitive to architectural decisions. Design patterns help integrating the desired timing behaviour with the rest of the elements of the application architecture. This paper reports a *pattern story* that shows how a component-based design has been implemented using periodic concurrent tasks with RT requirements. The Model-Driven Software Development (MDSD) approach provides the theoretical and technological support for implementing a pattern-guided translation from component-based models to object-oriented implementations. This work has been done and validated in the context of the development of robotic applications.

1 Introduction

There is a well established tradition of applying *Component Based Software Development* (CBSD) [19] principles in the robotics community, which has resulted in the appearance of several toolkits and frameworks for developing robotic applications [15]. The main drawback of such frameworks is that, despite being *Component-Based* (CB) in their conception, designers must develop, integrate and connect these components using *Object-Oriented* (OO) technology. The problem comes from the fact that CB designs require more (and rather different) abstractions and tool support than OO technology can offer. For instance, the lack of explicit "required" interfaces makes compilers impossible to assure that the components are correctly composed (linked). Also, component interaction protocols are not explicitly defined when using an OO language. Moreover, most of these frameworks impose the overall internal behaviour of their components, and therefore they lack of formal abstractions to specify it. In this way, framework components have so many platform-specific details that it is almost impossible to reuse them among frameworks [12]. In particular, robotic systems are reactive systems with RT requirements by their very nature, and most of the frameworks for robotics do not provide mechanisms for managing such requirements. The *Model-Driven Software Development* (MDSD) paradigm [18] can provide the

* This work has been partially supported by the Spanish CICYT Project EXPLORE (ref. TIN2009-08572), and the Fundación Séneca Regional Project COMPAS-R (ref. 11994/PI/09).

J. Real and T. Vardanega (Eds.): Ada-Europe 2010, LNCS 6106, pp. 167–180, 2010.

theoretical and practical support to overcome the above drawbacks. MDSD is starting to catch the attention of the robotics community [6] mainly due to the very promising results it has already achieved in other application domains (e.g., automotive, avionics, or consumer electronics, among many others) in terms of improved levels of reuse, higher software quality, and shorter product time-to-market [13].

In our opinion, it is needed a new CBSD approach for robotic software development that: (1) considers components as architectural units, (2) enables components to be truly reusable among frameworks (by separating their design from the implementation details), and (3) considers application timing requirements. In the context of the robotics domain and the aforementioned technologies (CBSD and MDSD), the authors have defined the *3-View Component Meta-Model* (V^3CMM) [10] as a platform-independent modelling language for component-based application design. V^3CMM is aimed at allowing developers to model high-level reusable components, including both their structural and behavioural facets. Such behavioural facets are modelled by means of state-charts and activity diagrams. Though these diagrams abstract designers away from run-time issues (such as the number of tasks, the concurrency model, etc.), these details must be realised in further steps. The problem then is how to translate V^3CMM models into executable code that, on the one hand, reflects the behaviour of the original V^3CMM models, and, in the other hand, is organised in a set of tasks compliant with the application-specific timing requirements.

This paper describes the approach we have taken for solving this problem, and the results we have obtained so far. This approach revolves around the definition of a framework that provides the required run-time support, and a set of 'hot-spots' where a model-to-code transformation will integrate the code generated from the V^3CMM models describing the concrete application. The patterns that have been selected to design such framework are described as a *pattern story* [8].

In short, the main contributions of the work presented in this paper are:

– An object-oriented interpretation of CBSD architectural concepts.
– A framework supporting such interpretation and taking into account timing requirements.
– A rationale of the framework design following a pattern story.

The remainder of this paper is organised as follows. Section 2 provides a general overview of the overall approach of the paper. Section 3 describes the patterns that comprise the architecture of the developed framework. Section 4 is devoted to detail the main issues of the dynamic of the applications generated using the framework. Section 5 relates this work with other proposals found in the literature. And finally, Section 6 discusses future work and concludes the paper.

2   General Overview of the Approach

The proposed development process starts with the modelling of the application architecture using the V^3CMM language. For the purpose of this paper any language enabling the modelling of components (such as UML, SysML or other UML profiles) could have been used. The reasons why we decided to develop a new modelling language (V^3CMM) are outside the scope of this paper and are described in [4], but, for the curious reader, they are mainly related to keeping a strong control over the concepts considered in the language and their semantics, and for easing model transformations.

V^3CMM comprises three complementary views, namely: (1) a *structural* view, (2) a *coordination* view for describing the event-driven behaviour of each component (this view is based on UML state-charts), and (3) an *algorithmic* view for describing the algorithm executed by each component depending on its current state (this view is based on a simplified version of UML activity diagrams). V^3CMM enables describing the architecture (structure and behaviour) of CB applications, but provides no guidelines for developing implementations. Therefore, as stated in the introduction, it is necessary to provide designers with tools that enable them to generate the program code from these high level abstractions. This code must take into account application-specific timing requirements, and reflect the behaviour of the original V^3CMM models.

The most important and challenging implementation issue is related to the implementation of real-time constraints in the framework structure, and among it, how many tasks must be created and how to distribute the component activities among them. Taking into account that each system might need a different task scheme (e.g. number of tasks, periods, deadlines, etc.), and that even given a system, this scheme can greatly vary (due to different execution resources, varying timing requirements, change of algorithms, etc.), a very flexible solution is required. This solution should allow task derivation from V^3CMM models, and specifically from the coordination view, since this view models both the concurrent behaviour (in the form of orthogonal regions), and the timing requirements of the algorithms (i.e. execution time, period, deadline, etc.) executed by the component.

Fig. 1 shows the pursued ideal solution, where it is possible to 'arbitrarily' allocate the activities associated to the states of the state-chart of a V^3CMM component to a set of tasks. It is worth clarifying that, in the rest of the paper, when we mention 'activity' we really mean activity diagram. The solution must not force a direct one-to-one relationship between components and execution tasks, but instead allow for more flexible schemes. In a given system, activities allocation would be driven by the RT requirements of each activity, the selected scheduling algorithms, different heuristics, execution platform constraints, etc. As these requirements, algorithms, heuristics and constraints could greatly differ from system to system, a great flexibility is then required for allocating activities to tasks. The proposed solution (see Fig. 2), detailed in the following section, considers that application code can be classified into the following three sets:

CS1. Code that provides a run-time support compliant with the domain specific requirements. Normally, this involves making trade-offs among the requirements of the application domain. For instance, in domains where hard real-time is usually needed (e.g. robotics, embedded systems, avionics, etc.), CS1 code should support characteristics such as different concurrency policies, real-time scheduling, event processing and signalling, reliability, memory management, etc., even at the cost of sacrificing other characteristics.

CS2. Code that provides an OO interpretation of the V^3CMM concepts. For instance, how components and ports are mapped to objects, state-charts implementation, port communication issues, etc.

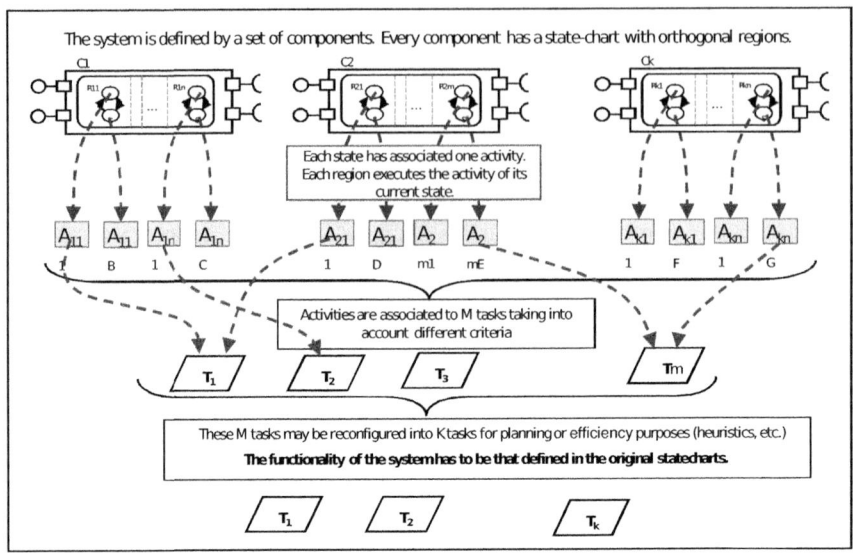

Fig. 1. Ideal scenario for allocating activities to tasks

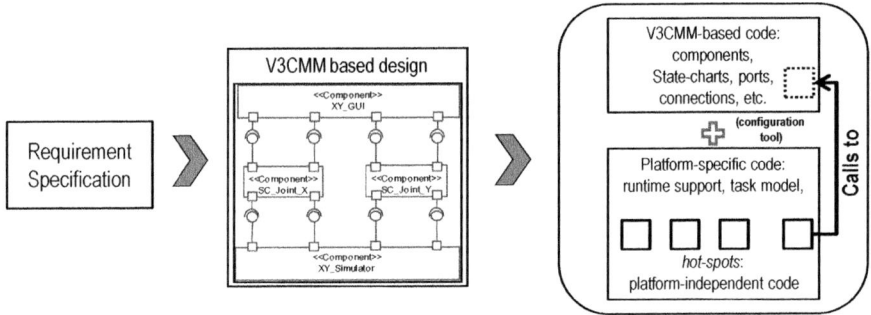

Fig. 2. Global view of the development process

CS3. Code corresponding to the application functionality, described by V^3CMM models.

These three code sets are arranged in a way that code sets CS1 and CS2 constitute a framework, where CS3 must be integrated in order to obtain the final application. The hot-spots for specialising the framework are defined in CS2. CS2 also serves for minimising the coupling between CS3 and CS1, enabling their separate evolution and reuse. As long as the interpretation of the V^3CMM concepts (CS2) remains the same, it would be possible to reuse the run-time support (CS1) in different applications (CS3). And, even more interesting, it would be possible to select a given run-time support (CS1) for the same application functionality (CS3), depending on the application domain requirements. CS1 and CS2 have been designed and implemented manually, following a set of design patterns, while CS3 is automatically generated from the V^3CMM models and integrated in the framework by means of a model transformation.

3   Global Architecture of the Generated Applications

This section explains how the framework design (shown in Fig. 3) has been obtained starting from its main requirements. Some of the most important patterns that comprise the pattern story are highlighted in the figure by the classes that fulfil the roles defined by such patterns. The correspondence between the classes and the code sets will be described at the end of the section where it will be better understood. Due to space limitations, this section is focused on the three main challenges that were faced when designing the framework, namely: how to allocate state activities to tasks, how to implement state-charts, and finally how to manage the component internal data.

Among the aforementioned challenges, the main one is how to allocate the activities associated to the states of the state-charts to different tasks. In order to achieve it, the COMMAND PROCESSOR architectural pattern [7] and the highly coupled COMMAND pattern have been selected. The COMMAND PROCESSOR pattern separates service requests from their execution. For this purpose, the pattern defines a task (the command processor) where the requests are managed as independent objects (the commands). Each activity associated to a state is implemented as a separate command, which can be allocated to any command processor. The roles defined by these two patterns are realised by the classes **Activity_Processor** and **State_Activity**, respectively (see Fig. 3). The COMMAND PROCESSOR pattern provides the required flexibility, since it imposes no constraints over activity subscription, number of activities, activity duration, concurrency scheme, etc. Nevertheless, this pattern has the following liabilities:

- It leads to a large number of subclasses since it is necessary to define a subclass of **State_Activity** for each and every activity defined in the V^3CMM models. As these subclasses will be generated by the model transformation, it is not a relevant drawback for this work.
- Loss of performance due to the additional indirection levels. This loss is paid off given the obtained flexibility.
- The component internal data can be simultaneously accessed by activities belonging to the same component but allocated to different tasks by the implementation. It will be necessary to synchronize such concurrent accesses, as detailed below.

The second challenge is how to interpret and implement state-charts in a way that enables its integration in the scheme defined by the aforementioned COMMAND PROCESSOR pattern. Providing an implementation that considers all the possibilities offered by hierarchical states and orthogonal regions is an extremely complex issue, which can be afforded by following different techniques [16]. In our case, we decided that both regions and states should be treated homogeneously, and their activities allocated to different command processors without knowing (or caring about) their type. This need is fulfilled by using a simplified versions of the COMPOSITE pattern. The roles defined by this pattern are realised by the classes **State, Orthogonal_Region**

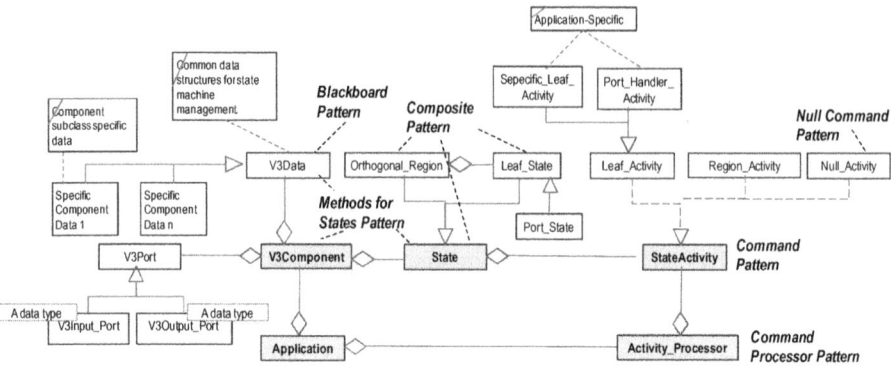

Fig. 3. Simplified class diagram of the generated code

and **Leaf_State**. The state-chart is managed following the METHODS FOR STATES pattern [7], where the instances of the classes representing the state-chart are stored in a hash table, while orthogonal regions store the keys of their leaf states in order to manage them. To shorten the implementation of the first working version of the framework, we only considered orthogonal regions comprising non-hierarchical states. In spite of this limitation, a broad range of systems can be still modelled.

The distinction between states and regions led us to define specific subclasses of **State_Activity**. Basically, we needed two hierarchies of subclasses: activities associated to leaf states (represented by the root class **Leaf_Activity**), and activities associated to regions (represented by the class **Region_Activity**). The latter is aimed at managing the region states and transitions, and thus is provided as part of the framework. The formers are related to (1) the activities defined in the V³CMM models, which are generated by the model transformation and are represented by **Specific_Leaf_Activity** subclasses, and (2) activities to manage ports, which are also provided by the framework and are represented by **Port_Handler_Activity** subclasses. Following the NULL OBJECT pattern, the **Null_Activity** class has been defined in order to smoothly integrate those states that have no associated activity.

The third and last challenge covered in this paper is how to provide concurrent access to the component internal data. This data is organised following the BLACKBOARD pattern. The idea behind the blackboard pattern is that a collection of different tasks can work cooperatively on a common data structure. In this case, the tasks are the command processors mentioned above, and the data comprise input/output port information and the hash table that stores state information. The main liabilities of the BLACKBOARD pattern (i.e. difficulties for controlling and testing, as well as synchronization issues in concurrent applications) are mitigated by the fact that each component has its own blackboard, which maintains a relatively small amount of data. In addition, it is possible to optimize the access to the blackboard in some important cases. For instance, the hash table that stores the component state is accessed following a *1-writer/n-readers* scheme.

The full pattern story comprises eighteen patterns, from which only the most important ones from the point of view of the global architecture have been described. There are other patterns, such as OBSERVER, COPIED VALUE, DATA TRANSFER OBJECT, TEMPLATE METHOD, STRATEGY, PROXY, etc., which are not shown in the figure since the roles defined by them cannot be clearly identified in Fig. 3 and there is no space left to explain how they have been used in the framework design.

The classes shown in Fig. 3 fall into the code sets described in the previous section as follows:

CS1: Run-time support. This set comprises the classes **Activity_Processor** and **State_Activity**, which have been manually coded.

CS2: Interpretation of V^{3}CMM concepts. This set comprises almost the rest of the classes shown in Fig. 3: **State_Activity, Leaf_State, Orthogonal_Region, State, Port_State, V3Input_Port, V3Output_Port, Region_Activity, Leaf_Activity, V3Data,** and **V3Component**. Notice that **State_Activity** is the link between CS1 and CS2. Classes **V3Input_Port** and **V3Output_Port** are defined as generics (or templates), which are instantiated with the concrete messages types the ports exchange. The classes comprising CS2 have been manually coded, and define the main framework hot-spots. Although the framework is mainly specialised by sub-classing them (and therefore it can be considered a white-box framework), it provides some concrete subclasses. These subclasses, which are enumerated below, are defined for implementing the port behaviour, and are meant to be directly instantiated.

  – **Port_State**: concrete leaf states modelling the state of a given port.
  – **Port_Handler_Activity**: concrete strategies for managing input ports. By default, port to port communication is implemented following the asynchronous without response policy, since it is the basic block for distributed systems and for designing more complex interaction schemes.
  – **Region_Activity**: concrete strategy for managing orthogonal regions.

CS3: Application functionality. This set integrates (1) new subclasses of the hotspots defined in CS2, and (2) instances of these new subclasses and of the classes comprising CS1 and CS2. All these classes and instances are automatically generated by a model-to-code transformation from the V^{3}CMM models. The most relevant elements of this set, generated for each component, are:

  – Data types representing the messages exchanged by components through their ports.
  – Instances of the **V3Input_Port** and **V3Output_Port** generic classes with the concrete messages that the ports exchange. Notice that these instances represent only the static structure of ports. Their dynamic behaviour is defined in the item below.
  – New orthogonal regions (instances of **Orthogonal_Region**), added to the original state-chart in order to manage the behaviour of the component ports. These orthogonal regions comprise leaf states (instances of **Port_State**), as well as the activities corresponding to these states (instances of **Region_Activity** and **Port_Handler_Activity**, respectively). This design decision provides regularity and flexibility to the framework, since (1) all regions, both those derived from the V^{3}CMM models and those added to manage ports, are treated homogeneously by the command processors, and (2) ports handling is explicit and can be allocated to different tasks, depending on the timing requirements.

– A subclass of **V3Data** comprising the specific component data as described previously.
– An instance of the class **V3Component**. This object acts as a container for all the previous elements.

Finally, when all the components have been generated, the transformation connects the components ports, creates a set of command processors, and allocates activities to them.

4   Allocation of Activities to Tasks

This section deals with relevant aspects of the application dynamics and with the criteria followed by the transformation to allocate activities to command processors. From a dynamic point of view, it is important to remark that command processors can execute activities defined in the state-charts of different components. Among

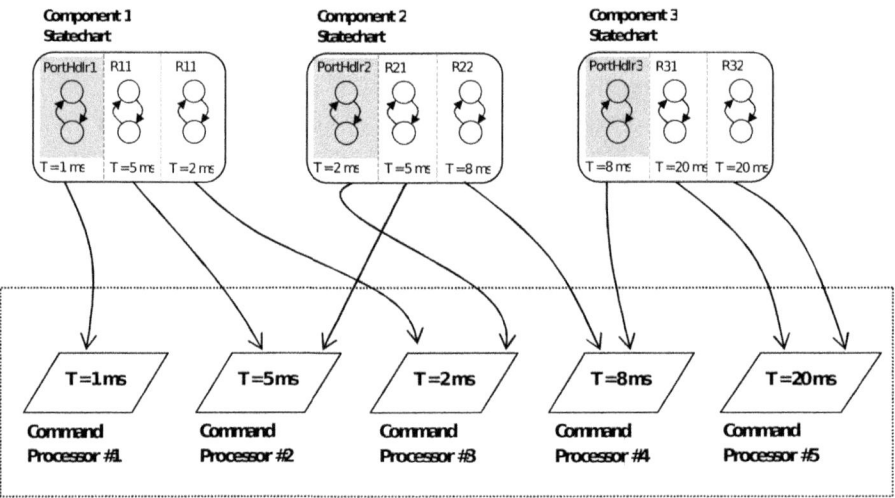

Fig. 4. Sample allocation scenario. From state-charts to command processors

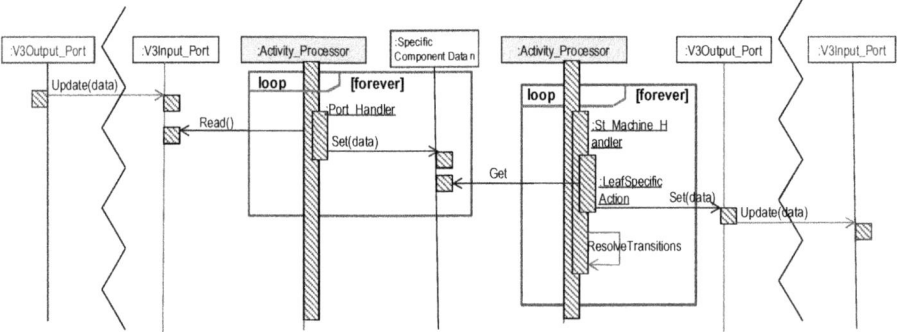

Fig. 5. A sequence diagram with a typical execution scenario

the many feasible possibilities for allocating activities to command processors, the main criteria is based on activity periods, since it facilitates the further schedulability analysis of the command processors. Fig. 4 shows a sample allocation scenario from the activities defined in state-charts to the tasks defined in command processors. This scenario comprises three components, each of them associated to a state-chart with three orthogonal regions, including the region added for port management (the shaded one). For the shake of simplicity, the example assumes that all the activities associated to the states contained in a given region have the period of its associated region activity. Notice that command processors 2 and 3 access the internal data corresponding to component 2 concurrently.

A typical execution scenario is shown in the sequence diagram of Fig. 5, which comprises the communication among three components. A **V3Input_Port** object stores the data received from an output port. Then, a task (i.e. an **Activity_Procesor**) will asynchronously put this data into a **V3Data** object (global to the component). Afterwards, another task will asynchronously process the incoming data depending on the current component state. As a consequence of this processing, state transitions in one or more regions of the component may occur. Moreover, this processing includes the execution of the activities of the set of current active states, and the updating of new data in output ports (sub-program **set(data)** in Fig. 5).

Code listing 1 shows an excerpt of the Ada specification of the **Activity_Procesor**, which has been implemented as a generic package, while code listing 2 shows the body of the task corresponding to a command processor. The main characteristics of this generic package are the following:

- The priority of the task contained in the package body is assigned according to both the timing requirements of the subscribed activities and the chosen scheduling algorithm. As this data is known before the transformations generate the code, it is possible to derive the priority of each **Activity_Processor**. Thus, a fixed priority static scheduling algorithm can always be used if required.
- The transformation takes into account that a task may include activities with different periods. The period assigned by the transformation to each task (**Activity_Processor**) is equal to the lowest period of its subscribed activities.

Listing 1. Code excerpt of the specification of the **Activity_Processor** generic package

```
1   generic
2      Listener          : access I_Activity_Processor_Listener 'Class;
3      Name              : Unbounded_String;
4      Worker_Priority   : System.Any_Priority;
5   package Common.Activity_Processor is
6      function Get_Name return Unbounded_String;
7      procedure Set_Priority (Priority : System.Any_Priority);
8      function Get_Priority return System.Any_Priority;
9      procedure Start;
10     procedure Stop;
11     procedure Set_Period (Period: Time_Span);
12     function Get_Period return Time_Span;
13     procedure Add_Activity (Act : access I_State_Activity 'Class);
14     procedure Del_Activity (Act : access I_State_Activity 'Class);
15  end Common.Activity_Processor;
```

Listing 2. Code excerpt of the body of the **Activity_Processor** generic package showing the task corresponding to a command processor

```
1    task body Worker is
2            Next_Exec   : Time := Clock;
3            Iterator    : P_Dll.Cursor;
4            Element     : State_Activity_All;
5    begin
6            Suspend_Until_True (Start_Lock);
7            while Continue loop
8                    delay until Next_Exec;
9                    Next_Exec := Next_Exec + Period;
10                   Iterator := Activity_List.First;
11                   while (P_Dll.Has_Element (Iterator)) loop
12                           Element := P_Dll.Element (Iterator);
13                           Element.Execute_Tick;
14                           P_Dll.Next (Iterator);
15                   end loop;
16           end loop;
17   end Worker;
```

It is important to highlight that activities may execute periodically or not. When activities are sporadic, the period attribute represents the minimum separation between two consecutive executions. The activities are executed in the same order as they have been subscribed to the **Activity_Processor**, although any alternative policy could have been chosen. Tasks are executed by the operating system according to the chosen scheduling algorithm.

– The sub-program **Add_Activity** enables subscribing activities to tasks.

This design assumes that activities are defined to have an execution time as short as possible to simplify scheduling. When an algorithm includes a big number of iterations or considers a continuous control action, then the activity should be divided into a set of sub-activities with a bounded execution time (for example, an algorithm step or a discrete control action).

The framework design requirements impose many constraints to the flexibility provided by the COMMAND PROCESSOR pattern. These constraints are mainly enforced by the real-time nature of the application domain. Some examples of the impact of these requirements are that command processors do not spawn new tasks to execute subscribed activities (which is permitted by the pattern), and that it is not allowed subscribing activities to command processor or modifying periods at execution time, to mention a few.

In order to validate the framework we have developed (1) several case studies, and (2) a tool to monitor the execution of each application and to change the number of command processors, and the allocation of activities to tasks. The tool enables us to experiment with the number of command processors and different activities allocation criteria, by reconfiguring the application generated by the transformation. The case study shown in this paper corresponds to a Cartesian robot, developed in the context of a research project (European Union's Fifth Framework Programme, Growth, G3RD-CT-00794) [10]. Fig. 6 shows an excerpt of the state-chart corresponding to the controller of one of the robot joints, and the part of the aforementioned configuration tool in charge of configuring command processors.

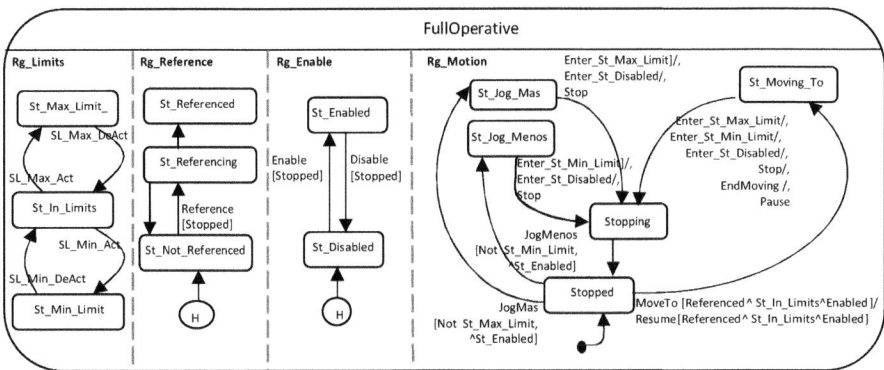

a) State-chart modelling the behaviour of a joint of the Cartesian robot.

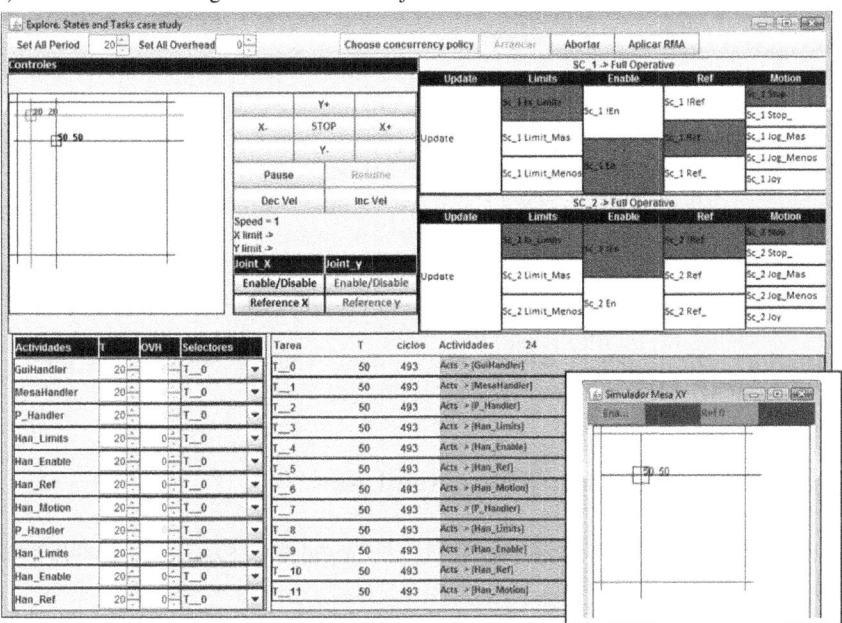

b) Configuration tool. The left part enables users to set activity periods, an estimated execution time, and to allocate activities to tasks. The right part shows, for each task, its execution period, number of execution cycles, and the activities allocated to it.

Fig. 6. Case study of a Cartesian robot and the reconfiguration tool

5   Related Work

As said in the introduction, there is a well established tradition of applying CBSD principles for developing robotic applications. However, there are not many initiatives for applying MDSD principles to robotic software development. In general, existing robotic frameworks cannot be considered to be model-driven, since they have no meta-model foundation supporting them. Among the main examples of applying the

MDSD approach to robotics is the work related to the Sony Aibo robot presented in [5]. Another initiative, described in [11], revolves around the use of the Java Application Building Center (jABC) for developing robot control applications. Although jABC provides a number of early error detection mechanisms, it only generates Java code and, thus, its applicability to systems with real-time requirements is rather limited. Finally, Smartsoft [17] is one of the most interesting initiatives for applying a MDSD approach to robotic software development. Nevertheless, as far as we know, none of these initiatives considers real-time issues.

The current state of the application of MDSD to robotic software development contrasts with what happens in other similar domains, where big efforts are being carried out in this line. For instance, the ArtistDesign Network of Excellence on Embedded Systems Design [1] and the OpenEmbeDD [3] project address highly relevant topics regarding real-time and embedded systems, while the automotive industry has standardised AUTOSAR [2] for easing the development of software for vehicles.

As Buschmann et al. [7] states, not all domains of software are yet addressed by patterns. However, the following domains are considered targets to be addressed following a pattern-language based development: service-oriented architectures, distributed RT and embedded systems, Web 2.0 applications, software architecture and, mobile and pervasive systems. The research interest in the RT system domain is incipient and the literature is still in the form of research articles. A taxonomy of distributed RT and embedded system design patterns is described in [9], allowing the reader to understand how patterns can fit together to form a complete application. The work presented in this paper is therefore a contribution to the definition of pattern languages for the development of this kind of systems with the added value of forming part of a global MDSD initiative.

6   Conclusions and Future Research Lines

This paper has described an approach to provide a run-time support (framework) to a component-based approach for modelling RT applications. To do that, it has been necessary to provide an OO interpretation of the high-level architectural concepts defined in V^3CMM (components, ports, state-charts, etc.), taking into account real-time requirements. The proposed solution is not general nor closed to future improvements, but it is a stable and validated starting point for further development.

The adoption of a pattern-driven approach has greatly facilitated the design of such framework. In addition, the selected patterns have been described like a pattern story. A further step would be the definition of a *pattern sequence*, which comprises and abstracts the aforementioned pattern story, so that developers can use it in other applications as long as they share similar requirements. With several pattern stories and pattern sequences it would be possible to define a true *pattern language* for a given domain, which gives a concrete and thoughtful guidance for developing or refactoring a specific type of system. The greatest difficulties in reporting this story have been how to synthesize in a few pages the motivations for choosing the patterns that have been used, and the lack of consensus about the best way of documenting pattern stories.

The characteristics of the Ada language that have revealed most useful for the development of the framework have been its mature concurrency facilities, strong typing, the generics mechanism, and the flexibility provided by packages in order to organise and encapsulate component structure. In addition, the new container library has proven very useful for implementing the internal blackboard of each component. The main difficulty comes from the fact that Ada is an extensive language and requires a deep understanding of the its mechanisms in order to successfully combine them.

Regarding future research lines, we are currently working on extending the framework with additional capabilities following a pattern-driven approach. Among these extensions, it is worth mentioning the following: (1) component distribution, (2) testing and adding heuristics for activities allocation and task grouping, (3) refining and improving the patterns used for implementing hierarchical and timed state-charts, and (4) comply with the Ravenscar profile for designing safety-critical hard real-time systems. Assessing timing requirements fulfilment in an automated way is also very important, and thus we plan to study strategies to generate analysis models for different scheduling analysis tools. The usage of the UML profile for MARTE [14] as a mechanism to formalize the models involved is also an approach to be explored.

References

[1] ArtistDesign - European Network of Excellence on Embedded Systems Design (2008-2011), http://www.artist-embedded.org/
[2] AUTOSAR: Automotive Open System Architecture (2008-2011), http://www.autosar.org/
[3] OpenEmbeDD project, Model Driven Engineering open-source platform for Real-Time & Embedded systems, (2008-2011), http://openembedd.org/home_html
[4] Alonso, D., Vicente-Chicote, C., Ortiz, F., Pastor, J.: V^{3}CMM: a 3-View Component Meta-Model for Model-Driven Robotic Software Development. Journal of Software Engineering for Robotics (JOSER) 1(1), 3–17 (2010)
[5] Blanc, X., Delatour, J., Ziadi, T.: Benefits of the MDE approach for the development of embedded and robotic systems. Application to Aibo. In: Proc. of the 3rd National Conference on Control Architectures of Robots (2007)
[6] Bruyninckx, H.: Robotics Software. The Future Should Be Open. IEEE Robot. Automat. Mag. 15(1) (2008) ISSN 1070-9932
[7] Buschmann, F., Henney, K., Schmidt, D.: Pattern-Oriented Software Architecture. A Pattern Language for Distributed Computing, vol. 4. John Wiley and Sons Ltd., Chichester (2007) ISBN 0471486485
[8] Buschmann, F., Henney, K., Schmidt, D.: Pattern-Oriented Software Architecture. On Patterns and Pattern Languages, vol. 5. John Wiley and Sons Ltd., Chichester (2007) ISBN 0471486485
[9] Dipippo, L., Gill, C.: Design Patterns for Distributed Real-Time Embedded Systems. In: Real-Time, Springer, Heidelberg (2009) ISBN 0387243577
[10] Iborra, A., Alonso, D., Ortiz, F.J., Franco, J.A., Sánchez, P., Álvarez, B.: Design of service robots. IEEE Robot. Automat. Mag., Special Issue on Software Engineering for Robotics 16(1) (2009), doi:10.1109/MRA.2008.931635, ISSN 1070-9932
[11] Jorges, S., Kubczak, C., Pageau, F., Margaria, T.: Model Driven Design of Reliable Robot Control Programs Using the jABC. In: Proc. Fourth IEEE International Workshop on Engineering of Autonomic and Autonomous Systems EASe 2007, pp. 137–148. IEEE, Los Alamitos (2007)

[12] Makarenko, A., Brooks, A., Kaupp, T.: On the Benefits of Making Robotic Software Frameworks Thin. In: Proc. of the IEEE/RSJ Int. Conf. on Intelligent Robots and Systems (IROS 2007). IEEE, Los Alamitos (2007)

[13] OMG: MDA success stories (2008), Available online: http://www.omg.org/mda/products_success.html

[14] OMG: UML Profile for MARTE: Modeling and Analysis of Real-Time Embedded Systems, formal/2009-11-02 (2009), http://www.omg.org/spec/MARTE/1.0

[15] Robot Standards and Reference Architectures (RoSTa), Coordination Action funded under EU's FP6: http://wiki.robot-standards.org/index.php/Current_Middleware_Approaches_and_Paradigms

[16] Samek, M.: Practical UML Statecharts in C/C++, Second Edition: Event-Driven Programming for Embedded Systems. Newnes (2008), ISBN 0750687061

[17] Schlegel, C., Hassler, T., Lotz, A., Steck, A.: Robotic software systems: From code-driven to model-driven designs. In: Proc. International Conference on Advanced Robotics ICAR 2009, pp. 1–8. IEEE, Los Alamitos (2009)

[18] Stahl, T., Völter, M.: Model-Driven Software Development: Technology, Engineering, Management. Wiley, Chichester (2006)

[19] Szyperski, C.: Component software: beyond object-oriented programming. A-W, 2nd edn. (2002), ISBN 0201745720

Scheduling Configuration of Real-Time Component-Based Applications[*]

Patricia López Martínez, Laura Barros, and José M. Drake

Departamento de Electrónica y Computadores, Universidad de Cantabria,
39005-Santander, Spain
{lopezpa,barrosl,drakej}@unican.es

Abstract. This paper proposes a strategy to manage the scheduling of real-time component-based applications that is fully compatible with the concept of component viewed as a reusable and opaque software module. The strategy is used on top of the RT-CCM technology, which extends the OMG's LwCCM technology with the purpose of building real-time distributed component-based applications that can be executed on embedded platforms and with heterogeneous communication services. The strategy is based on three services included in the RT-CCM framework, which are implemented by the containers of the components, and are in charge of supplying the threads and the synchronization artifacts that the business code of a component requires to implement its functionality. During the components configuration process, these services are used to assign the values that lead to a schedulable application to the scheduling parameters of these threads and synchronization mechanisms, without having to know the internal code of the components. The assigned values are obtained from the analysis of the real-time model of the application, which is built based on metadata provided by the components and the elements of the platform.

1 Introduction

The aim of component-based development is to build applications as assemblies of reusable software components that satisfy three characteristics: isolation (components are atomic units of deployment), composability (they should be composable with other components) and opacity (neither the environment nor other components or a third party can modify their codes) [1]. Several strategies have been proposed to apply this component-based paradigm to the development of real-time systems. This work relies on the RT-CCM (*Real-Time Container Component Model*) technology [2], which was initiated in former european projects [3][4], and which results from applying two extensions to the LwCCM (*Lightweight CORBA Component Model*) specification [5]:

- The interactions between components are generalized by specialized components, called connectors. They provide the communication mechanisms in their code,

---

[*] This work has been funded by the EU under contract FP7/NoE/214373 (ArtistDesign); and by the Spanish Government under grant TIN2008-06766-C03-03 (RT-MODEL). This work reflects only the author's views; the EU is not liable for any use that may be made of the information contained herein.

J. Real and T. Vardanega (Eds.): Ada-Europe 2010, LNCS 6106, pp. 181–195, 2010.

allowing the components to implement only the business logic. They do not have to be based on CORBA, as it is required in LwCCM.

• The interface and the implementations of a component include metadata related to their temporal behaviour, which are used to predict the temporal behaviour of the applications in which the component takes part.

RT-CCM presents two outstanding features: 1) The internal architecture of the components can be arbitrarily complex, and 2) the components incorporate all the informa-tion that is required to generate automatically the code of the containers and the connectors that adapt their codes to the corresponding platforms. As Figure 1 shows, an RT-CCM component is delivered as a package that includes, together with the code, the metadata that describe its functionality (described through the set of required and provided ports), its temporal behaviour, its configuration properties and its instantiation requirements. These metadata must be enough to generate the component container and the required connectors without modifying or accessing the internal code.

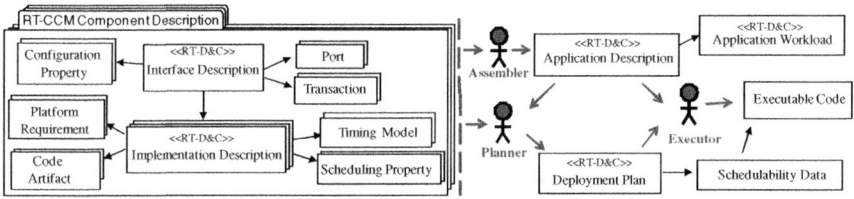

Fig. 1. Information provided by an RT-CCM component on parameters

For defining these metadata, RT-CCM relies on the RT-D&C extension [6]. The OMG's D&C specification [7] formalizes the formats and the contents of the documents that are used to describe a component and a component-based application. These documents are used by the application designers (*Assembler* and *Planner*) as a guide for accessing to the different pieces of information that are provided by the components and managed during the design and deployment process. RT-D&C extends D&C with the real-time metadata that are required to predict, analyse and configure the temporal behaviour of a component-based application during its design process.

The purpose of the real-time design of an application is to schedule the execution of its activities in order to satisfy the temporal requirements imposed on its specification. In traditional real-time design strategies, the designer has several means of getting a suitable scheduling for the application: (i) defining the concurrency level, i.e. the number of threads available for the execution of the application activities; (ii) assigning these activities to the threads in which they are scheduled; (iii) choosing the synchronization mechanisms required to coordinate the execution of the different threads; or (iv) assigning the policies and the scheduling parameters which are used as the basis to decide which thread accesses to the processing, synchronization or communication mechanisms when several threads compete for them.

When a component-based strategy is applied, the designer manages the application at a higher level of abstraction. All the previous aspects are related with the internal code of the components, so they are unknown and inaccessible for the designer due to the opacity required for managing the components. In this case, the designers can control or configure the execution only by means of the information included in the deployment plan. Through the deployment plan, the planner chooses concrete implementations for each instance that forms the application, assigns concrete values to their configuration parameters, maps the instances to the nodes and selects the communication mechanisms used for each connection between components. In a real-time application, the deployment plan must also include all the information required to configure the execution of the application so that the specified timing requirements are met.

This work presents the design process of a real-time component-based application according to the RT-CCM technology, which requires the explanation of:

- The mechanisms that have been introduced in the framework to control the scheduling of the applications.
- The models that describe the temporal behaviour of the individual components, which are used to generate the reactive model of the complete application. This final model serves as the basis to evaluate the scheduling configuration.
- The timing metadata that are associated to the components and to the deployment plans in order to configure the application scheduling in an opaque way, and based on the results extracted from the analysis.

Related work. Several works aim to achieve temporal predictability for the applications based on the metadata provided by the components. The temporal models and the associated composition process are well defined in [8], however the applied analysis is focused on performance, and it does not offer a way of configuring the temporal behaviour of the components based on the analysis results. Its concept of component is similar to ours: a reusable module that can offer a complex functionality by implementing different services and responses to events. Other approaches, specially focused on control systems [9][10], are based on lower granularity components that implement basic passive functions. In this case, the real-time design consists in composing and mapping them to the environment threads and assigning priorities to each thread. Similar to our approach, CIAO [11] implements the LwCCM specification and uses D&C to configure and deploy applications. It offers capacity for configuring real-time characteristics of the applications by using RT-CORBA features. However, they do not follow any strategy to obtain this information from the analysis. The configuration is made directly on the deployment plan based on the designer expertise.

2   An RT-CCM Application Example

Figure 2 shows the components architecture and a possible deployment of the ScadaDemo application: an RT-CCM application that is used along the paper as an example to introduce the proposed concepts[1]. Its functionality consists in supervising a set of analog environment magnitudes, and storing statistical data about them in a logger. The operator can choose the magnitudes to supervise through the keyboard, and he can also choose one of them to be periodically refreshed in the monitor.

---

[1] Since this paper deals with the real-time design strategy and the schedulability configuration mechanisms, for reasons of space, the used example is monoprocessor, although RT-CCM is specially focused on distributed applications and the same strategy can be applied to them.

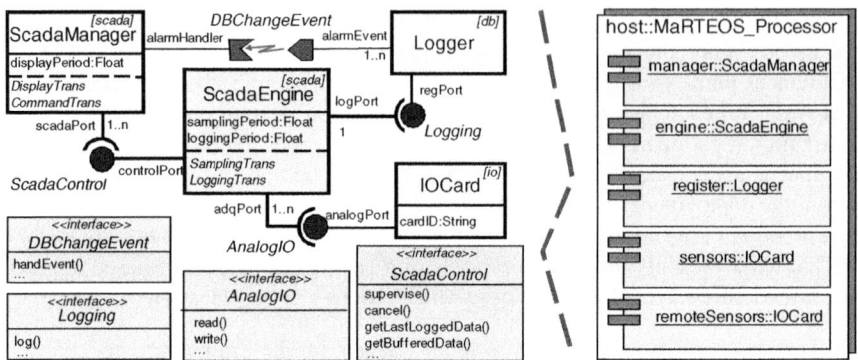

Fig. 2. Architecture (left side) and deployment (right side) of the ScadaDemo application

The application is built by assembling instances of four different types of components, organized in a three-tier architecture. The data tier is composed by leaf components: *IOCard*, which manages the acquisition cards used to read the analog signals, and *Logger*, which allows registering data with timing marks in a permanent data base. The business logic tier is formed by a component of *ScadaEngine* type, which implements a standard SCADA (Supervisory Control and Data Acquisition) functionality. It supervises periodically (with a configurable period) a set of magnitudes, processes statistically the values read through the *adqPort* port, and registers the obtained results through the *logPort* port. Finally, the presentation tier is implemented by the *ScadaManager* component, which implements the specific functionality of this application, processing the commands introduced by the operator and displaying periodically the results of one of the magnitudes. Figure 2 shows also the basic functionality of each component type, by defining their provided and required ports, called facets and receptacles respectively, together with the interfaces that these ports implement.

In RT-CCM, the functionality of an application is specified in a reactive way, as the set of transactions that it executes concurrently in response to external or timed events. In this case, there are four transactions, three of them with timing requirements:

1. Sampling transaction: Represents the periodic (*samplingPeriod* period) activity through which the value of each magnitude is read and statistically processed.
2. Logging transaction: Every *loggingPeriod* period (higher than *samplingPeriod*) the information of all the supervised magnitudes is registered in the logger.
3. Display transaction: The information about one of the magnitudes is updated in the monitor every *displayPeriod* period.
4. Command transaction: The commands introduced by the operator are attended and executed, without timing requirements.

3 Threads and Components

The business code of a component implements the set of services offered through the component facets, and the responses to the events that the component attends. In the

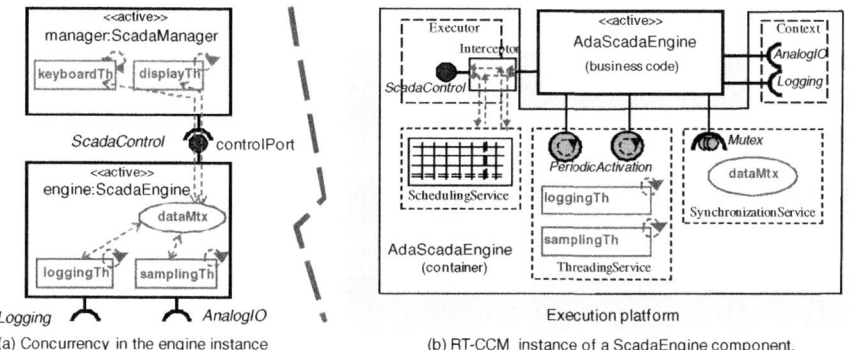

(a) Concurrency in the engine instance

(b) RT-CCM instance of a ScadaEngine component.

Fig. 3. Threads that concur in the engine instance of the ScadaDemo application

general case, this code requires to be concurrently executed by multiple threads, which are created either by the component itself or by other components that invoke its services. As a consequence, the code of a component must include internal synchronization mechanisms to guarantee mutually exclusive access to the shared resources, and to synchronize the threads that concur in it.

As an example, Figure 3 (a) shows the four threads that concur in the *engine* instance (of ScadaEngine component type) during the execution of the ScadaDemo application. Two of them are internal to the component: *samplingTh*, which reads periodically the supervised magnitudes, and *loggingTh*, which registers periodically the statistical values in the logger. The other two threads come from invocations made by the *manager* instance (of ScadaManager component type) in the *controlPort* facet: *keyboardTh* modifies the list of variables to supervise, and *displayTh* requires the information about the magnitude to display. The four threads require access to some internal data hold by the component, so they are synchronized by a mutex called *dataMtx*.

The real-time design and schedulability analysis of component-based applications require knowledge about these threads, their associated synchronization mechanisms and the activities that they execute. Besides, configuring the scheduling of an application requires that the parameters that control the scheduling of the different elements can be assigned by the configuration and launching tools. To make the inherent opacity of components compatible with the real-time design process, in RT-CCM the creation and management of threads and synchronization artifacts have been extracted from the code of the components. They are implemented by the containers, whose codes are known and accessible by the tools.

RT-CCM uses three elements to facilitate the scheduling of the threads in that opaque way, without knowing the code of the components:

- Four new port types have been defined. They are used by the business code of the components to access to the threads and the synchronization mechanisms provided by the container.
- The activities assigned to each thread and the points in which these threads synchronize their flows are described by the real-time model of the component.

- Interceptors are used to establish the scheduling parameters with which each service invoked in a component is executed, based on the concrete transaction and the point inside the transaction in which the invocation is made.

The new types of ports defined in the RT-CCM technology are:

- *PeriodicActivation* ports: For each port of this type declared by a component, the container (by means of the *ThreadingService*) creates a thread that periodically executes the *update()* method offered by the port. The activity executed by this method must have a finite duration (lower than the activation period).
- *OneShotActivation* port: For each port of this type declared by a component, the container creates a thread that executes the *run()* method offered by the port once, when the component is activated. The method execution can have an arbitrary duration, which can last the complete active life of the component.
- *Mutex* port: For each declared port of this type, the container (by means of the *SynchronizationService*) creates a mutex, which the component can manage through the *lock()* and *unlock()* methods invoked on it through the port.
- *ConditionVariable* port: For each port of this type the container (by means of the *SynchronizationService*) creates a condition variable, which the component can use to suspend and activate the internal threads, through the *wait()* and *notify()* methods invoked on it through the port.

Figure 3(b) shows the ports through which the *AdaScadaEngine* implementation, the Ada 2005 implementation of the ScadaEngine component used in the ScadaDemo example, requires the two internal threads, *samplingTh* and *loggingTh* ports, and the mutex, *dataMtx* port, which it needs to implement its functionality.

In RT-CCM a component is a complex module whose temporal response is not defined by its own code in the general case, since this temporal behaviour depends on the temporal behaviour of other components that it uses, and on the final execution platform. Therefore, the aim of the real-time model of a component is not to describe the temporal behaviour of the component as an isolated module, but to provide the information about the component that is required to predict the temporal behaviour of any application in which it may be used. Each component implementation has its own real-time model, which basically contains the declaration of the processing and synchronization resources that the component uses to implement its offered services and its responses to external or timed events. The execution of a component service or the response to a received event are described as the execution of a set of activities ordered by control flow relations (sequential, fork, branch, merge and join). Each activity is described by enumerating the resources that it uses and the corresponding usage times.

In RT-CCM these models are formulated according to CBSE-MAST [12], an extension of the MAST [13] modelling methodology. It incorporates parameterization and composability to the components models, which facilitate their composition into full reactive models able to be analysed with the MAST set of tools. The modelling concepts used in MAST are almost the same as the ones proposed in the SAM (*Schedulability Analysis Modelling*) chapter of the OMG's MARTE [14] profile. Figure 4 represents the real-time model of the AdaScadaEngine implementation. The model includes the SchedulingServers that describe the *samplingTh* and *loggingTh* threads that

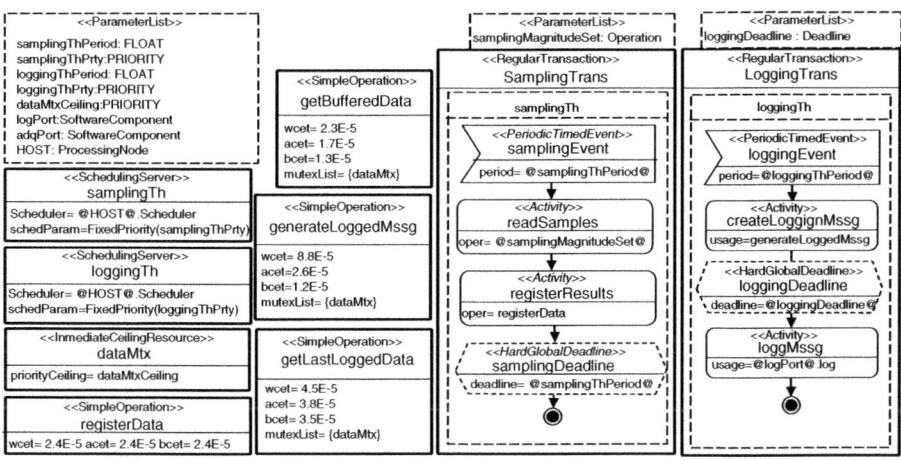

Fig. 4. Elements of the real-time model of the AdaScadaEngine implementation

the component uses internally. The model states that they are scheduled by the scheduler of the processor in which the component is installed (HOST reference) and they are managed according to a fixed priority preemptive scheduling policy. The model declares a SharedResource to describe the *dataMtx* mutex, which uses a priority ceiling policy. The models of the *getBufferedData* and *getLastLoggedData* real-time services, offered through the controlPort facet, are also included. Besides, the model describes as transactions, the two periodic activities executed internally in the component, *SamplingTrans* and *LoggingTrans*. They correspond to the code executed in the two update() methods of the two declared PeriodicActivation ports. Each transaction defines the SchedulingServer in which it is scheduled (*samplingTh* and *loggingTh* respectively), the generation pattern of the triggering events, the sequence of activities that are executed in response to those triggering events, and the timing requirements that must be met in each execution. Finally, the model includes some internal operations that are used to describe the transactions activities, as for example *registerData*.

The real-time model of a component is parameterized in three different aspects:

- The real-time model of the processor in which the component is executed is not known at development time, so it is referenced through the HOST predefined parameter. The execution times of the internal activities of the component are formulated as normalized execution times, so only in the context of an application deployment, when the processor and its processing capacity are known, the actual physical execution times can be obtained.
- The resources usages generated by those component activities that consist in invoking services on other components (via receptacles) can not be specified at component development time. The model includes only a reference to the port and the service invoked. Only in an application, when the concrete connected component is known, the actual resource usages can be evaluated. This is the case e.g. of the invocation of the *log* method (in *logPort*) in the *LoggingTrans* model.

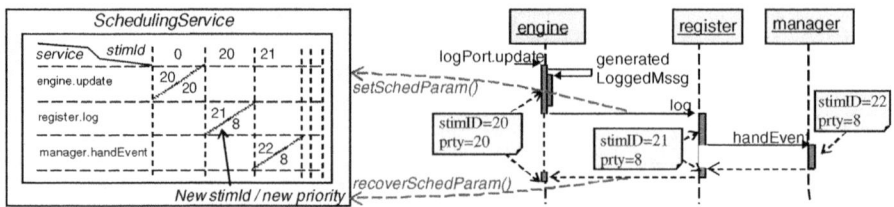

Fig. 5. Management of scheduling parameters in RT-CCM

- There are some characteristics of the real-time model that are declared as parameters to adapt them to the specific situation in which the component is instantiated in a concrete application context. In the example, the *samplingThPeriod* and *loggingThPeriod* are parameters of the real-time model since different values can be assigned to them according to the concrete application context.

To get a more flexible scheduling of the applications, the execution of the services and the responses to events that the components manage can be scheduled according to parameters (priorities, preemption levels, etc.) that depend on the concrete transaction and the internal state of the transaction in which they are executed [15]. To make this scheduling easier, each of the transactions executed in the application are associated with an independent thread when they are sequential, or with a set of threads when they are concurrent. When the timing requirements are assigned to the finalization of the last activity of the transaction, the scheduling can be associated to the threads, making all the activities to execute with the same scheduling parameters. However, when the requirements are associated to intermediate points of the transaction, the scheduling parameters must be independently assigned for each activity.

In RT-CCM, this kind of management of the scheduling parameters in an activity-based manner, is managed by means of interceptors. This mechanism [16] is used to manage non-functional aspects, by invoking environment services before and after the execution of a service in a component. In RT-CCM, before a component service is executed, the interceptor calls the *setSchedParam()* method in the *SchedulingService* of the container. This method receives as argument an identifier (called stimId) of the transaction and the transaction state, which is used to modify the scheduling parameters of the invoking thread and the value of stimId. When the service execution ends, the interceptor invokes the *recoverSchedParam()* method, which recovers the value of stimId and the scheduling parameters that the thread had when the invocation was made. To clarify this concept, Figure 5 shows the scheduling management in the case of the Logging transaction of the ScadaDemo example. The *update()* method of the loggingTh port of the *engine* instance (which maps the Logging transaction) is started with stimId = 20 and priority = 20. The invocation of the *log* service in the *register* instance is made with that value of stimId. When the interceptor associated to this service invokes *setSchedParam()*, according to the configuration of the SchedulingService established for the application, the priority of the invoking thread is set to 8 and the stimId value is changed to 21 (in order to distinguish other invocations made inside the *log* service, as the *handEvent* invocation on the *manager* instance). When the execution of *log* ends, the initial values for the stimId and the priority are recovered, by invoking the *recoverSchedParam()* method.

4   Real-Time Components Description

An RT-CCM component is described by means of the descriptors formalized in the RT-D&C specification. According to it, the information that describes a component is split up in two parts: the component interface and the component implementations.

The RT-D&C's ComponentInterfaceDescription contains the information about the functionality, connectivity and configurability of the component that is common to all its possible implementations. It provides the information required by the assembler to decide if a component is useful in the application that is being designed. In real-time applications, some specific aspects of this description must be remarked:

- The functionality of a real-time application is described by means of a reactive specification, which defines the external or timed events to which the application responds, the activities that constitute these responses and the timing requirements that must be met. As a consequence, the RT-D&C descriptor for a component interface must include metadata declaring the kind of responses to the events that the component can attend, i.e. the transactions generated in the component.
- The connectivity of the components must be described not only from the functional point of view (based on interfaces compatibility) but also from the real-time models composability point of view. Some metadata must be included to guarantee that an assembly of components leads to a real-time composed component, i.e. a component for which a temporal behaviour model can be generated. With that aim, in RT-D&C, each facet declares the operations for which the component provides a real-time model, and each receptacle declares the operations whose real-time models are needed by the component. In an application, a facet of a component can be connected to a receptacle of another component only if all the real-time models of operations required by the facet are provided by the receptacle.

The RT-D&C's ComponentImplementationDescription contains the specific information of an implementation of the component interface. The planner obtains from it the information that he requires to decide the deployment of an instance of the component in a concrete node of the platform. In case of a real-time component, it has to include metadata that allow the planner to configure the application scheduling:

- Declaration of the threads required by the component to implement its functionality, formulated as activation ports.
- Declaration of the synchronization artifacts required by the component to manage concurrent accesses to its internal data, formulated as synchronization ports.
- Declaration of the scheduling configuration parameters. Each implementation can declare the priorities, preemption levels, priority ceilings, etc. that must be configured to control the scheduling of the threads and the synchronization mechanisms required by the component.

Besides, the implementation description must include the reactive model that describes the temporal behaviour of the component. This model must include:

- Temporal behaviour models of the services offered through the facets. Each model describes the sequence of activities executed when the service is invoked.

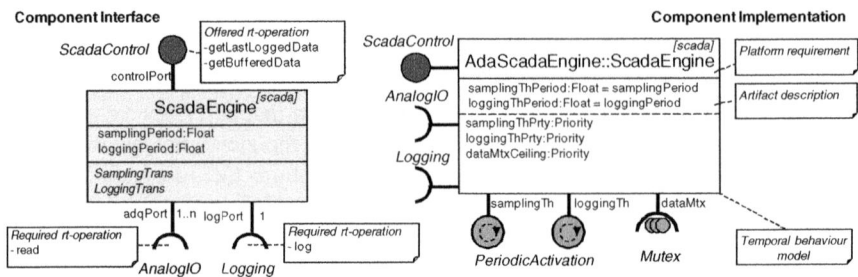

Fig. 6. ScadaEngine interface and AdaScadaEngine Implementation

- Temporal behaviour models of the transactions initiated by the component in response to external or timed events. They are described also as the sequence of activities executed in them, together with the triggering patterns and the timing requirements imposed on their execution.

Figure 6 shows the elements that constitute the interface of the ScadaEngine component, and the description of the AdaScadaEngine implementation. The ScadaEngine interface description includes the following elements:

- The *controlPort* facet that implements the *ScadaControl* interface. The component declares that it offers associated real-time models for the *getBufferedData* and *get-LastLoggedData* services.
- For implementing its functionality, the component needs to be connected to at least one component implementing the *AnalogIO* interface through the *adqPort*. It requires that the connected component offers a real-time model for the *read* service. It declares another required port, *logPort*, which must be connected to a component implementing the *Logging* interface. In the case of real-time applications, the connected component must provide a temporal model for the *log* service.
- The component defines two configuration parameters, *samplingPeriod* and *loggingPeriod*, for adapting its business behaviour to the corresponding application.
- The component responds to two different events, through the *SamplingTrans* and *LoggingTrans* transactions. These transactions map the ones required by the application that were identified in section 2 (Sampling and Logging transactions).

The description of the AdaScadaEngine implementation specifies:

- The requirements that the component imposes on a processor to be instantiated.
- The description of the artifacts which hold the implementation code, and the way in which they have to be instantiated and executed.
- The description of the activation ports. As it was said in Section 3, the AdaScadaEngine implementation requires two threads, which execute the *update()* method of the corresponding *samplingTh* and *loggingTh* ports.
- The description of the synchronization ports. The AdaScadaEngine implementation requires a mutex, which is accessed through the *dataMtx* port.
- Implementation configuration parameters: due to the periodic activation ports, two new parameters appear at this level, *samplingThPeriod* and *loggingThPeriod*,

which describe the activation periods for the ports. They take values directly from the corresponding samplingPeriod and loggingPeriod parameters.

- Scheduling configuration parameters: The implementation introduces three scheduling parameters (also due to the activation and synchronization ports), *samplingThPrty*, *loggingThPrty* and *dataMtxCeiling*, which are used to controlytyuthe scheduling of the internal activities of the component.
- The reference to the file in which the reactive temporal model of the component is described, whose main elements were introduced in section 3. As shown in Figure 4, its parameters correspond to the implementation and scheduling configuration parameters defined in the component implementation (*sampling/loggingThPeriod, sampling/loggingThPrty and dataMtxCeiling*).

5 Real-Time Design of a Component-Based Application in RT-CCM

Figure 7 shows the artifacts and the actors involved in the process of development of an application based on the RT-CCM technology. The *assembler* is a domain expert who implements the functionality of the application by assembling instances of the available components, based on the metadata provided by their interfaces. He generates the description of the application as a composed component. The *planner* decides the processor in which each instance is going to be instantiated, selects the appropriate implementation for each instance and chooses the communication mechanism to use for each connection between instances. The planner describes the application as a deployment plan. Finally, the *executor* generates the executable codes for each node, transfers and installs them in the corresponding nodes and starts the application.

When the designed application has real-time requirements, some specific characteristics are added to this process:

- The specification of the application has a reactive nature, so the assembler must build the application choosing firstly those components that have the capacity to manage the events to which the application responds. This is the cause of selecting e.g. the ScadaEngine component in the ScadaDemo example, since it implements two of the required transactions. Then, he may have to choose other components to satisfy the connectivity requirements of the chosen components, as it happens with the IOCard and Logger components in ScadaDemo, which are chosen to fulfil the functionality of the ScadaEngine component.
- The assembler must formulate the real-time requirements of the application in the context of one or several workloads, i.e. he must specify the generation patterns for the events that lead the execution of the application, and the timing requirements that must be satisfied during the execution.
- The assembler builds the application ensuring that it implements the functional specification. However, he can not guarantee that the timing requirements are going to be met, since the timing behaviour of the application depends on the execution platform and the concrete component implementations chosen. He can only assure that a real-time model of the application can be obtained, by checking the composability of the real-time models of the components involved.

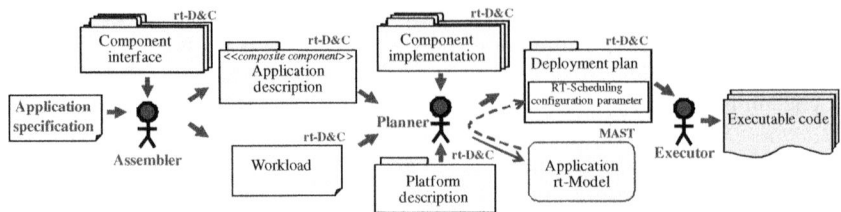

Fig. 7. Development process of an RT-CCM component-based application

- The planner is responsible of making the application schedulable. Besides assigning instances to nodes and choosing the concrete implementations, he must assign values to the scheduling parameters of the components and the platform resources so that the timing requirements of the application are met.

This last aspect is identified as the real-time design of a component-based application. It is a complex task, which requires having the temporal behaviour model of the complete application, in order to use it as the basis for applying real-time design algorithms and tools. These tools are used to obtain optimal values for the scheduling parameters and to analyse the schedulability of the application, certifying the fulfilment of the timing requirements. Figure 8 shows the final model that results from the deployment of the ScadaDemo application shown in Figure 2, with a workload that corresponds to a situation in which three magnitudes are supervised with a sampling period of 10 ms, a logging Period of 100 ms and a display period of 1s. The processor considered in this case has a speedFactor = 0.5 (i.e. with half the capacity of the processor taken as reference for specifying the normalized execution times in the real-time models of the components) [13][14] and its scheduler uses a fixed priority policy.

The real-time model of the application is automatically generated by a tool that takes as inputs the deployment plan, and the descriptor of the execution platform. The model is built by identifying the component instances that form the application and composing the temporal models that they include in their descriptions. In this final model, all the references and parameters are solved since all the connections between components are known and also the capacity of the platform. Although the generation of the real-time model of the application is guided by the metadata and the parameterized models included in the component packages, the result is a conventional real-time model, which can be analysed with standard real-time design and analysis tools. In our case, the tools provided by the MAST environment are used.

The results obtained from the real-time design process in RT-CCM are:

- The initial priority for all the threads required by the components.
- The priority ceilings that must be assigned to each required mutex.
- The priority of execution of each invocation received in a component service in the context of the transaction in which the invocation is made. The tool generates the sequences of stimId values that identify univocally each received invocation.
- The stimId values that the active components must use to identify each transaction that is triggered on them. They are given to the threads that execute the activation ports of the components.

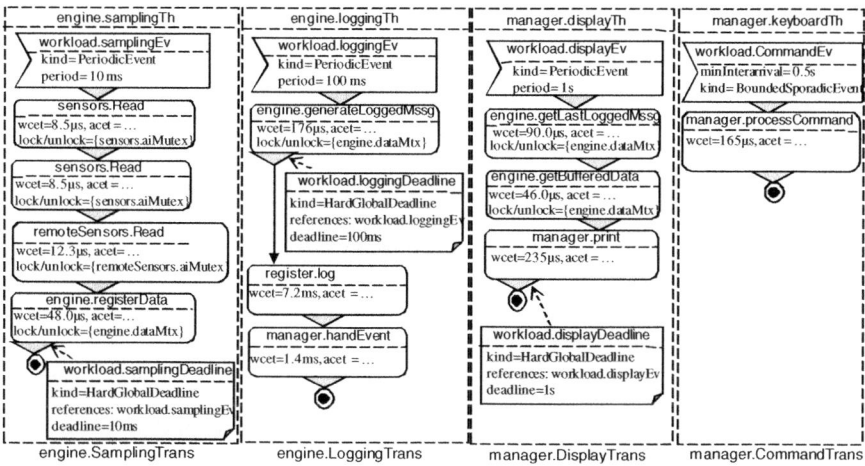

Fig. 8. Real-time model of the deployed ScadaDemo Application

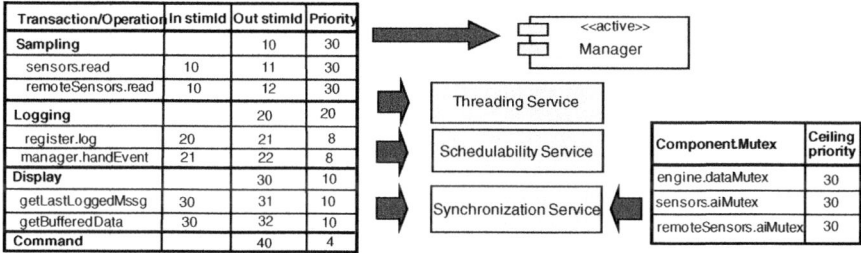

Fig. 9. Schedulability configuration results in the ScadaDemo example

The tables in Figure 9 show the priority assignment obtained for the ScadaDemo example. The Sampling and Display transactions have deadlines associated to the end of the transaction, so the assigned priority is the same for all the activities executed in them. However, the Logging transaction has a deadline associated to an intermediate state, so the activity *register.log*, which is executed after it, receives a lower priority than the rest of the transaction. Based on this information, the launching tool that starts the application execution by instantiating the components, configures the platform services in each node with the following information:

- The ThreadingService receives the initial priority and stimId with which each thread provided to a component through an activation port must start its execution. Each stimId identifies univocally one transaction.
- The SynchronizationService receives the configuration parameters for each of the synchronization artifacts required by the components (e.g. mutex ceilings).
- The SchedulingService of each node receives the tables with the mappings between stimId and priority values, which are used to configure each invocation made on a component service.

With this strategy, the RT-CCM technology satisfies the objective of configuring the scheduling of an application respecting the opacity of the components.

6 Conclusions

The strategy proposed in this paper allows the designer of a real-time component-based application to configure its scheduling, satisfying the opacity requirement typical of the components paradigm. The strategy is applied on top of the RT-CCM technology, which uses a container/component model to extract the scheduling management from the business code of the components. The management of all the aspects related with the application scheduling are carried out by a set of services included in the components containers. Besides, the technology relies on an extension of the D&C specification, which incorporates metadata about the temporal behaviour of components and platforms. These metadata allow the designers of the applications to analyse their temporal behaviour, or to extract from this analysis the scheduling configuration parameters to be assigned to the component instances, through the services, in order to guarantee the fulfilment of the timing requirements of the application.

References

[1] Crnkovic, I., Larsson, M.: Building Reliable Component-Based Software Systems. Artech House Publishers (2002)
[2] López, P., Drake, J.M., Pacheco, P., Medina, J.L.: An Ada 2005 Technology for Distributed and Real-Time Component-based Applications. In: Kordon, F., Vardanega, T. (eds.) Ada-Europe 2008. LNCS, vol. 5026, pp. 254–267. Springer, Heidelberg (2008)
[3] IST project COMPARE: Component-based approach for real-time and embedded systems, http://www.ist-compare.org
[4] IST project FRESCOR: Framework for Real-time Embedded Systems based on Contracts, http://www.frescor.org
[5] OMG.: CORBA Component Model Specification. formal/06-04-01 (April 2006)
[6] López Martínez, P., et al.: Real-time Extensions to the OMG's Deployment and Configuration of Component-based Distributed Applications. OMG's 9th Work. Distributed Object Computing for Real-time and Embedded Systems, Arlington, VA, USA (2008)
[7] OMG: Deployment and Configuration of Component-Based Distributed Applications Specification, version 4.0, formal/06-04-02 (April 2006)
[8] Bondarev, E., de Withy, P., Chaudron, M.: CARAT: a Toolkit for Design and Performance Analysis of Component-Based Embedded Systems. DATE Europe Conference (2007)
[9] Åkerholm, M., et al.: The SAVE approach to component-based development of vehicular systems. Journal of Systems and Software 80 (May 2007)
[10] Angelov, C., Sierszeckiy, K., Zhou, F.: A Software Framework for Hard Real-Time Distributed Embedded Systems. In: Proc. 34th Euromicro Conf. Software Engineering and Advanced Applications, Parma (August 2008)
[11] Kavimandany, A., Gokhale, A.: Automated Middleware QoS Configuration Techniques for Distributed Real-time and Embedded Systems, April 2008. Real-Time and Embedded Technology and Applications Symposium. IEEE Computer Society Press, Los Alamitos (2008)

[12] López, P., Drake, J.M., Medina, J.L.: Real-Time Modelling of Distributed Component-Based Applications. In: Proc. of 32h Euromicro Conf. on Software Engineering and Advanced Applications, Croatia (August 2006)

[13] González Harbour, M., et al.: MAST: Modeling and Analysis Suite for Real-Time Applications. In: Proc. of the Euromicro Conference on Real-Time Systems (June 2001)

[14] OMG: UML Profile for Modeling and Analysis of Real-Time and Embedded systems (MARTE), OMG doc. formal/2009-11-02 (November 2009)

[15] Gutiérrez García, J.J., González Harbour, M.: Prioritizing Remote Procedure Calls in Ada Distributed Systems. ACM Ada Letters XIX(2), 67–72 (1999)

[16] OMG: Quality of Service for CORBA Components, ptc/06-04-05 (April 2006)

The Evolution of Real-Time Programming Revisited: Programming the Giotto Model in Ada 2005

Andy Wellings and Alan Burns

Department of Computer Science, University of York
Heslington, York YO10 5DD, UK
{andy,burns}@cs.york.ac.uk

Abstract. Kirsch and Segunupta in a recent paper have argued that several generations of real-time programming models for use in digital control systems can be identified: the Physical-Execution Time (PET) model, the Bounded-Execution-Time (BET) model, the Zero-Execution Time (ZET) model and the Logical-Execution-Time (LET) model. They classify Ada as belonging to the BET model and claim that a LET model, as supported by the Giotto language, is superior. Whilst historically one can recognise different approaches to programming real-time systems, this paper refutes the argument that general-purpose real-time languages like Ada (or Real-Time Java) neatly slot into a BET model. Instead, we suggest that the real issue that the LET model addresses is the ability of a programming model to give composable abstractions that allow programs to have bounded input and output jitter. Languages like Ada (and many real-time operating systems) have mechanisms that easily allow this to be achieved. Using Ada as an example, we show two different ways. Each of which has advantages and disadvantages.

1 Introduction

Kirsch and Sengupta [4] have evaluated the suitability of various approaches to programming digital control systems and use this to draw some conclusion about the evolution of real-time programming models. They argue that "digital control is defined by a set of abstractions that are real-time programmable and mathematically tractable in the context of the dynamics of physiochemical processes". The claim is that these abstractions constitute "a precise definition of the real-time problem". Essentially, the action of a component of a control system is governed by two equations: the output equation and the state equation. The component periodically reads input signals (measurements from sensors, input for other components etc) and uses the two equations to compute the component's output (actuator commands, output to other components etc) and to update its state. Ideally, the computation and interaction happens in zero time or with a constant delay. There is no communication with other tasks except via the input and output at the beginning and end of each task's iteration. This restrictive communication model, however, is not appropriate for systems where more dynamic interactions between tasks are required. Hence, their requirements should be viewed only in the context of control systems.

J. Real and T. Vardanega (Eds.): Ada-Europe 2010, LNCS 6106, pp. 196–207, 2010.

Using the above statement of requirements, Kirsch and Sengupta contend that languages like Giotto and Esterel are in some sense superior to languages like Ada or Real-Time Java (or C/C++ with support from real-time operating systems). In this paper we refute this claim. We show that their evaluation is mainly based on the requirement to support composability of systems. Essentially this requires the ability to be able to specify timing requirements on components and to ensure when systems are composed these requirements are met.

The paper is structured as follows. In section 2 we review the different generations of real-time programming models presented by Kirsch and Sengupta. In section 3 we classify the main requirements for real-time programming in this area, and re-interpret Kirsch and Sengupta requirements. Then in section 4 we consider the Giotto model in the context of these requirements. We show that the main strength of Giotto is that it allows composability of tasks with input and output jitter requirements. Section 5 shows how these input and output jitter requirements can easily be met in Ada. Finally we draw our conclusions.

2   The Evolution of Real-Time Programming

Kirsch and Sengupta [4] contend that as real-time programming has drawn closer to the computing abstractions of digital control, the real-time programming models have evolved from the physical-execution-time (PET) and bounded-execution-time (BET) programming models to higher-level programming models such as the zero-execution-time (ZET) and logical-execution-time (LET) models.

According to Kirsch and Sengupta, the PET programming model was developed to program control systems on processor architectures with simple instructions that have constant execution time. The programmer designed a sequence of (usually) assembly instructions and could not use any concurrency. The sequential nature of the resulting program and the predictability of the early assembly instructions resulted in fixed delays between input and output. However, as systems became more complex and processor architectures less predictable in the temporal domain, composability of components became difficult and the PET model needed to be replaced.

The emergence of operating system and real-time scheduling facilitated the development of the BET model. The aim of the BET model is to handle concurrency and real time. Each component could now be represented as a task that had a period and a deadline (usually the same as the period). The task was required to finish its execution in the worst-case by its deadline. Hence the "execution time" of the task was *bounded* by its deadline. Worst-case execution time analysis and schedulability theory could be used to guarantee that each task's execution time (response time) was bounded. Whilst composability of tasks is supported by schedulability analysis, the BET model is criticised by Kirsch and Sengupta[4] for its lack of I/O composability. Essentially their argument is that the response time of a task can vary considerably from its best-case to its worst case. Similarly, the start time of a task will depend on whether higher priority (or earlier deadline) tasks are runnable at its release time. Hence, if input is read at the beginning and output written at the end of a task's execution then input and output will suffer significant jitter. This jitter will also vary when new tasks are added. Consequently, they claim that the BET model does not support I/O composability.

To counteract the I/O composability problem, the ZET model was introduced. The fundamental assumption underpinning this computational model is the *ideal* (or *perfect*) **synchronous hypothesis** [1]:

Ideal systems produce their outputs synchronously with their inputs.

Hence all computation and communication is assumed to take zero time. Clearly, this is a very strong, and unrealistic, assumption. However, it enables the temporal ordering of I/O events to be determined more easily. During implementation, the *ideal synchronous hypothesis* is interpreted to imply 'the system must execute fast enough for the effects of the synchronous hypothesis to hold'. What this means, in reality, is that following any input event, all associated outputs must occur before any new input could possibly happen. The system is then said to 'keep up' with its environment. Although a ZET complier can guarantee the unchanged I/O behavior of old tasks with the addition of new tasks by executing all I/O operations together, it takes no advantage of the scheduling facilities of real-time operating systems – as it accepts multiple tasks but produces a sequential program to be executed by the operating system.

Finally, Kirsch and Sengupta claim that the LET model is the most recent of the real-time programming models. In the LET model a task computes logically from reading input to writing output for some given amount of time that is called its logical execution time. The task is guaranteed to read the input at the start of its release and provide the output at the end of its logical execution time. Actually the task may complete its computation before the end of the time, but the output will not be made available until this time. During its logical execution time, the task may be preempted by other tasks and resumes execution again, however it will be guaranteed (by schedulability analysis) that the task will offer the output if it meets its deadline, which is the end of the logical execution time.

Throughout their discussions Kirsch and Sengupta give example languages that they claim fit the models. For example they claim Ada and Java fit the BET model, Esterel and Lustre fit the ZET model and Giotto fits the LET model. The implication is that languages that support the "higher-level" models are more suited to programming digital control systems. Hence, Giotto is a superior language for digital control systems than say Ada or real-time versions of Java.

We contend in this paper that Kirsch and Sengupta arguments are rather simplistic and do not distinguish between the *expressive power* of a language, and its *ease of use*. We will show that Ada has the expressive power to meet the real-time requirements implied by the LET model. *Ease of use* is, inevitably, subjective. A language that has higher-level abstractions is however likely to be easier to use but only if those abstractions match closely the abstractions needed by the programmer. Any slight variation may make the programs more difficult to write. We will show that the LET model is only partially successful in meeting its own goals, and that for large systems I/O composability becomes more difficult to bound effectively. We show how having a more flexible model allows the programmer to exercise better control.

3   Requirement for Real-Time Programming Models

To facilitate the specification of the various timing constraints found in real-time applications, it is useful to introduce the notion of **temporal scopes**[5][2]. Such scopes identify a collection of statements with an associated timing constraint. The possible attributes of a temporal scope (TS) are illustrated in Figure 1, and include

1. deadline – the time by which the execution of a TS must be finished;
2. minimum delay – the minimum amount of time that must elapse before the start of execution of a TS;
3. maximum execution time – of a TS;
4. maximum elapse time – of a TS.

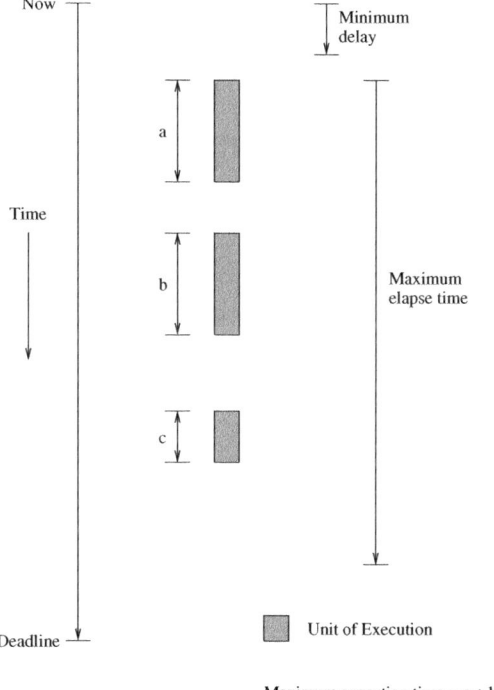

Maximum execution time = a + b + c

Fig. 1. Temporal scopes

Temporal scopes with combinations of these attributes are also possible and, for some timing constraints, a combination of sequentially executed temporal scopes is necessary. For example, consider a simple control action that reads a sensor, computes a new setting and outputs this setting via an actuator. To get fine control over when the sensor is read (input jitter), an initial temporal scope with a tight deadline is needed. The output is produced in a second temporal scope which has a minimum delay equal to the first scope's deadline but a later deadline – see code example below. If there is a need to also control output jitter then a third temporal scope could be added which has a long 'minimum delay' and a short time interval before its deadline.

Temporal scopes can themselves be described as being either **periodic** or **aperiodic**. Typically, periodic temporal scopes sample data or execute a control loop and have explicit deadlines that must be met. Aperiodic, or **sporadic**, temporal scopes usually arise from asynchronous events outside the embedded computer. These scopes have specified response times associated with them.

In many real-time languages, temporal scopes are, in effect, associated with the tasks that embody them. Tasks can be described as either periodic, aperiodic or sporadic depending on the properties of their internal temporal scopes. Most of the timing attributes given in the above list can thus be satisfied by:

1. running periodic tasks at the correct rate;
2. completing all tasks by their deadline.

The problem of satisfying timing constraints thus becomes one of scheduling tasks to meet deadlines, or **deadline scheduling**.

Here, we focus on periodic activities as that is the focus of the LET model. A task that is sampling data may be composed of a number of temporal scopes:

```
loop
    start of 1st temporal scope
        ...  -- input activities
    end of 1st temporal scope
    start of 2nd temporal scope
        ...  -- processing
    end of 2nd temporal scope
    IDLE
    start of 3rd temporal scope
        ...  -- output activities
    end of 3rd temporal scope
end;
```

The input activities of this task take place in the first temporal scope and hence the deadline at the end of this scope regulates the maximum input jitter for the task. The input data may already be available in buffers for the task, or the task may need to read input registers in the sensor's device interface. The second temporal scope incorporates whatever computations are needed to calculate the task's output values (no input or output takes places in this scope). The third scope is concerned with the output action. Here the IDLE interval is important; it is measured from the beginning of the loop and constrains the time before the output can be produced by the task. The deadline on this final temporal scope places an upper bound on the time of the output phase.

Although it would be possible to incorporate this sequence into a single task, scheduling analysis places restrictions on the structure of a task. Specifically, a task must only have one idle (delay) statement (at the beginning of the execution sequence) and one deadline (at the end). So, for illustration, assume the control task has a period of 100ms, a constraint on input jitter of 5ms, a constraint on output jitter of 10ms and a deadline of 80ms. The three necessary tasks would take the form:

```
task periodic_PartA;
  ...
begin
  loop every 100ms
    start of temporal scope
      input operations
      write data to a shared object
    end of temporal scope - deadline 5ms
  end;
end;

task periodic_PartB;
  ...
begin
  loop every 100ms
    start of temporal scope
      IDLE 5ms
      read from shared object
      computations
      write data to a shared object
    end of temporal scope - deadline 70ms
  end;
end;

task periodic_PartC;
  ...
begin
  loop every 100ms
    start of temporal scope
      IDLE 70ms
      read from shared object
      output operations
    end of temporal scope - deadline 80ms
  end;
end;
```

Note that as now the tasks are concurrent the second temporal scope must also have an IDLE statement in order to stop it executing too soon.

4   Giotto

In order to understand the LET model better, this section considers in more detail the Giotto language.

Giotto [3] is a domain-specific high-level research programming language for control applications. As such, its focus is on the composability of components and the control of input and output jitter.

The basic functional unit in Giotto is the **task**, which is a periodically executed section of code. Several concurrent tasks make up a **mode**. Tasks can be added or removed by switching from one mode to another.

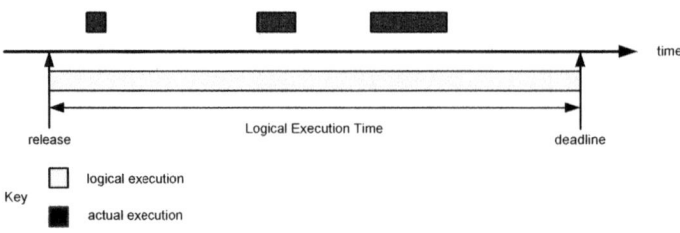

Fig. 2. The Logical Execution Time model

Tasks communicate with each other via typed **ports**. Ports are either *input* or *output*. The values of a task's input ports are set when the task is released. The value of its output ports are only made available to other tasks when the task's deadline has been reached. Hence, tasks are not allowed to communicate with each other during their execution. The code responsible for copying data from one task's output port to another task's input port is called a **driver**. Drivers are also responsible for reading from sensors and writing to actuators.

Driver code takes a bounded amount of execution time and is assumed to execute (effectively) instantaneously. Tasks are assumed to take a non-negligible amount of time to process the data in their input ports and produce their output data. Hence, Giotto is similar to Esterel in that driver code satisfies the synchronous hypothesis. Unlike Esterel, application code does not need to support this hypothesis. Instead, the model is referred to as a Logical Execution Time (LET) model. This model is depicted in Figure 2. In terms of temporal scopes that were introduced in Section 3, a LET task and its associated driver code can be considered as a sampling task that consist of three temporal scopes. The first and third scopes control the input and output jitter, and are executed by the driver code.

There are various versions of Giotto, below the main characteristics of a program are shown using pseudo code. Here, the program simply monitors two sensors: temperature and pressure, in order to keep the system within some specified limits (by outputing values to two actuators: a pump and a heater).

```
sensor
  port temperature type integer range 10 .. 500
  port pressure type integer range 0 .. 750
actuator
  port heater type (on, off)
  port pump type integer 0 .. 9
input
  T1 type integer range 10 .. 500
  PI type integer range 0 .. 750
output
  TO type (on, off)
  PO type integer 0 .. 9

task temperature input TI output TO temperature_controller
task pressure input PI output PO pressure_controller
```

```
driver temperature_sensor
  source temperature destination TI function read_temperature
driver pressure_sensor
  source pressure destination PI function read_pressure
driver heater_actuator
  source TO destination heater function write_heater
driver pump_actuator
  source PO destination pump function write_pump

mode normal period 20 ports TO, PO
  frequency 2 invoke temperature driver temperature_sensor
  frequency 1 invoke pressure driver pressure_sensor
  frequency 2 update heater_actuator
  frequency 1 update pump_actuator
start normal
```

Giotto is more concerned with the architecture of the program rather than the details of a task's or driver's code. It focuses on the declaration of ports (sensors, actuators, input and output), tasks and drivers. The above code shows that there are two sensors and two actuators and the type of their associated data. Associated with each sensor is a driver that is responsible for taking the data from the devices' registers and placing the values in the input ports of the two tasks. Similarly, drivers are responsible for taking the data from the output ports of the two tasks and writing the values to the actuators' device registers.

The scheduling of the system is specified using the mode construct. In this simple example, a single mode is defined (called `normal`). The system is time triggered with a period of 20 milliseconds. The schedule consists of the frequencies of the two tasks within this period – hence task `temperature` runs every 10 milliseconds, `pressure` every 20 milliseconds. The tasks inputs are associated with the appropriate drivers. Similarly, the actuators have associated drivers. The semantics of the statement are that the drivers associated with the `invoke` statement must be scheduled at the release time of the task according to the synchronous hypothesis. The drivers associated with the `update` statement are scheduled at the deadlines of the tasks (here equal to their periods). A task in Giotto is composable with other tasks but only if it can be shown that the system is *time safe*. In other words, some form of schedulability analysis must be undertaken by the designer before deployment.

Giotto is a good example of a language targeted to the characteristics of a particular application domain. Its restrictive communication model, however, means that it is not appropriate for systems where more dynamic interactions between tasks are required. For example, where the task's computation can takes various branches depending on values in a real-time database, and it is difficult to efficiently extract all these routes into different tasks (they would need to be in different modes).

5   Controlling Input and Output Jitter in Ada

In many real-time application areas, particularly control systems, real-time tasks have the simple structure reflected in the LET programming model. In many applications, controlling jitter is performed by the I/O device itself. These "smart" sensors and actuators can perform their I/O operations at particular points in time with minimum latency. However where these are not available, the application must implement the necessary requirements.

Few industrial strength real-time languages explicitly have facilities to directly specify jitter requirements (i.e. constraints). There are, however, several ways by which the programmer can use other real-time mechanism to meet the requirements.

Section 3 showed how a jitter-constrained task could be transformed into two or three tasks each with its own deadline. Then by judicial use of scheduling parameters or temporal scopes, the required behavior could be achieved. This is trivial to do in Ada. However, the main disadvantage of the approach is that it is rather heavy in its use of Ada tasks, requiring a task to execute a small bounded piece of code. In situations where it is necessary to undertake a small computation periodically and with minimum jitter (for example, just reading the sensor value), a timing event can be used instead and is more efficient. It is this approach that is considered in detail in the next subsection.

5.1   Controlling I/O Jitter in Ada Using Timing Events

The input and output from and to sensors and actuators is a good example of where small amounts to computations are constrained by jitter requirements. Consider again the periodic control activity. It reads a sensor, performs some computation based on the sensor value and writes a result to an actuator. In order to ensure that the environment does not become unstable, the control algorithm requires that the sensor be read every 100 milliseconds (for example); the variation in the time at which the sensor is read each cycle (input jitter) is a maximum of 5 millisecond. The output should be written to the actuator within a deadline of 80 milliseconds, and the output jitter no more than 10 milliseconds. Figure 3 illustrates these timing constraints.

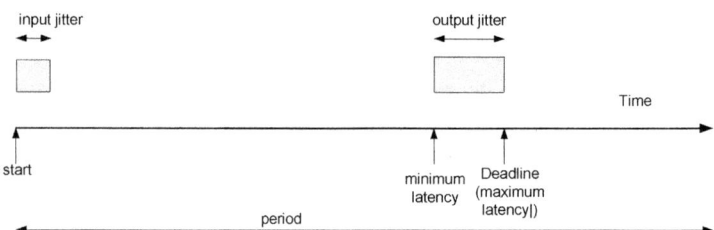

Fig. 3. A simple task with input and output jitter constraints

One way to satisfy a tight time constraint in Ada is to use timing events in conjunction with a task. First, the time constraint on the input can be implemented by the following protected type:

```
protected type Sensor_Reader is
  pragma Interrupt_Priority (Interrupt_Priority'Last);
  procedure Start;
  entry Read(Data : out Sensor_Data);
  procedure Timer(Event : in out Timing_Event);
```

```
private
  Next_Time : Time;
  Reading : Sensor_Data;
  Data_Available : Boolean := True;
end Sensor_Reader;

Input_Jitter_Control : Timing_Event;
Period : Time_Span := Milliseconds(40);
```

The procedure Start is used to initiate the first sensor reading. The routine then sets up the next reading using the Input_Jitter_Control timing event. The timer will call the Timer procedure at the appropriate time. This will take the next sensor reading, and set up the next event. The control algorithm simply calls the Read entry, which becomes open every time new data is available. The body of the protected type is given below.

```
protected body Sensor_Reader is
  procedure Start is
  begin
    Reading := Read_Sensor;
    Next_Time := Clock + Period;
    Data_Available := True;
    Set_Handler(Input_Jitter_Control, Next_Time, Timer'Access);
  end Start;

  entry Read(Data : out Sensor_Data) when Data_Available is
  begin
    Data := Reading;
    Data_Available := False;
  end Read;

  procedure Timer(Event: in out Timing_Event) is
  begin
    Reading := Read_Sensor;
    Data_Available := True;
    Next_Time := Next_Time + Period;
    Set_Handler(Input_Jitter_Control, Next_Time, Timer'Access);
  end Timer;
end Sensor_Reader;
```

The repetitive use of timing events is an effective solution for this type of requirement. A similar approach can be used for the control of the output.

```
protected type Actuator_Writer is
  pragma Interrupt_Priority (Interrupt_Priority'Last);
  procedure Start;
  procedure Write(Data : Actuator_Data);
  procedure Timer(Event : in out Timing_Event);
private
  Next_Time : Time;
  Value : Actuator_Data;
end Actuator_Writer;

Output_Jitter_Control : Timing_Event;
```

Here, the Start routine is called 26 milliseconds (that is, 30 - 4 milliseconds) after starting the sensor data collection timer.

```
SR.start;
delay 0.026;
AW.start;
```

where SR and AW are instances of the two protected types.

Finally, the control algorithm task can be given. Note that it contains no 'delay until' statement. The rate is controlled by the opening and closing of the Read entry.

```
task type Control_Algorithm (Input : access Sensor_Reader;
                             Output : access Actuator_Writer);
task body Control_Algorithm is
  Input_Data : Sensor_Data;
  Output_Data : Actuator_Data;
begin
  loop
    Input.Read(Input_Data); -- blocking operation
    -- process data;
    Output.Write(Output_Data); -- non-blocking operation
  end loop;
end Control_Algorithm;
```

The use of timing events to represent a periodic activity is appropriate for small execution times or when minimum jitter on the periodic activity is required.

5.2 Revisiting the Three-Tasks System

The main disadvantage of the solution presented in the previous section is that the code is always executed at interrupt priority level and hence has a temporal interference on the rest of the program. Furthermore, all input and output is treated with the same urgency and requiring the same (or similarly small) amount of computational time. Indeed, these are exactly the same criticism that can be levelled at the LET model. There is no ability to specify the required I/O latency itself. The processing of some sensor reading may be able to tolerate the extra noise introduced by the input jitter.

To have more control it is necessary to revert to the three tasks approach. Each task can then be given its own deadline and scheduled so that they start at different offsets from one and other. The flexibility afforded by Ada allows this and other solutions (for example, a single tasks which dynamically changes its priority) to be programmed.

6   Conclusions

In this paper we have re-examined the claims made by Kirsch and Sengupta concerning the evolution of real-time programming languages. Firstly, we noted the restrictive communication model, imposed by the LET model is not appropriate for systems where more dynamic interactions between tasks are required. Hence any claim made must be tempered by this constraint. Secondly, we show that there are two derived requirements from Kirsch and Sengupta's arguments.

- Tasks (components) of a system that have deadline constraints must be composable. That is a task that meets its deadline in one system should be capable of moving to another system without change and still meet its deadline (it is *time safe* in Giotto terminology). We claim it is the role of schedulability analysis to support composability and to show that tasks are indeed time safe.

- I/O operations within systems must also be composable. This mean that when systems are composed, the time at which input and output occurs must be the same. Adding new tasks should not significantly change this. We claim that bounding input and output jitter is a common problem for all real-time systems, and one that can be solved by a variety of means. We have shown two approaches in Ada to achieving bounded (tight) I/O jitter.

Ada 2005 has the expressive power to meet the requirements for control systems identified by Kirsch and Sengupta. Its also has the flexibility to allow programmers to tailor their solutions to an actual system requirements rather than those imposed by some idealized model of the class of systems.

References

1. Berry, G.: Real time programming: Special purpose or general purpose languages. In: Ritter, G.X. (ed.) Proceedings of Information Processing 1989. Elsevier Science Publishers, Amsterdam (1989)
2. Burns, A., Wellings, A.J.: Real-Time Systems and Programming Languages, 4th edn. Addison-Wesley, Reading (2009)
3. Henzinger, T.A., Horowitz, B., Kirsch, C.M.: Giotto: A time-triggered language for embedded programming. In: Henzinger, T.A., Kirsch, C.M. (eds.) EMSOFT 2001. LNCS, vol. 2211, pp. 166–184. Springer, Heidelberg (2001)
4. Kirsch, C.M., Sengupta, R.: The evolution of real-time programming. In: Lee, I., Leug, J.Y.-T., Son, S.H. (eds.) Handbook of Real-Time and Embedded Systems, pp. 11-1–11-23. Chapman and Hall/CRC (2007)
5. Lee, I., Gehlot, V.: Language constructs for distributed real-time programming. In: Proceedings of the Real-Time Systems Symposium, pp. 56–57. IEEE Computer Society Press, Los Alamitos (1985)

AdaStreams: A Type-Based Programming Extension for Stream-Parallelism with Ada 2005

Gingun Hong[1], Kirak Hong[1], Bernd Burgstaller[1], and Johann Blieberger[2]

[1] Yonsei University, Korea
[2] Vienna University of Technology, Austria

Abstract. Because multicore CPUs have become the standard with all major hardware manufacturers, it becomes increasingly important for programming languages to provide programming abstractions that can be mapped effectively onto parallel architectures.

Stream processing is a programming paradigm where computations are expressed as independent actors that communicate via data streams. The coarse-grained parallelism exposed in stream programs facilitates such an efficient mapping of actors onto the underlying hardware.

In this paper we propose a type-based stream programming extension to Ada 2005. AdaStreams is a type-hierarchy for actor-specification together with a run-time system that supports the execution of stream programs on multicore architectures. AdaStreams is non-intrusive in the sense that no change of an Ada 2005 programming language implementation is required. Legacy-code can be mixed with a stream-parallel application, and the use of sequential legacy code with actors is supported. Unlike previous approaches, AdaStreams allows creation and subsequent execution of stream programs at run-time.

We have implemented AdaStreams for Intel multicore architectures. We provide initial experimental results that show the effectiveness of our approach on an Intel X86-64 quadcore processor. The initial release of our work is available for download at [1].

1 Introduction

For the past three decades, improvements in semi-conductor fabrication and chip design produced steady increases in the speed at which uniprocessor architectures executed conventional sequential programs. This era is over, because power and thermal issues imposed by laws of physics inhibit further performance gains from uniprocessor architectures. To sustain Moore's Law and double the performance of computers every 18 months, chip designers are therefore shifting to multiple processing cores. The IBM Cell BE [12] processor provides 9 processing cores, Microsoft's Xbox CPU [2] has 3 cores, and more than 90% of all PCs shipped today have at least 2 cores. According to a recent survey conducted by IDC [13], all PCs (desktops, mobile and servers) will be multi-cores in 2010, with quad and octal cores together already constituting more than 30% market share. For programming languages it becomes therefore increasingly important to provide programming abstractions that work efficiently on parallel architectures.

J. Real and T. Vardanega (Eds.): Ada-Europe 2010, LNCS 6106, pp. 208–221, 2010.

Many imperative and early object-oriented languages such as Fortran, C and C++ were designed for a single instruction stream. Extracting parallelism that is sufficiently coarse-grained for efficient multicore execution is then left to the compiler. However, sequential applications usually contain too many dependencies to make automated parallelization feasible within the static analysis capabilities of compilers. Ada, C# and Java provide thread-level concurrency already as part of the programming language itself. Thread-level concurrency allows the expression of task-parallelism (performing several distinct operations – tasks – at the same time), data-parallelism (performing the same task to different data items at the same time) and pipeline parallelism (task parallelism where tasks are carried out in a sequence, every task operating on a different instance of the problem) [19] already in the source code.

Because threads execute in a shared address space, it is the programmer's responsibility to synchronize access to data that is shared between threads. Thread-level concurrency plus synchronization through protected objects, monitors, mutexes, barriers or semaphores [14,11] is commonly referred to as thread and lock-based programming. In addition to the difficulties of writing a correct multi-threaded program, thread and lock-based programming requires the programmer to handle the following issues.

1. Scalability: applications should scale with the number of cores of the underlying hardware. Encoding a programming problem using a fixed set of threads limits scalability.
2. Efficiency: over-use of locks serializes program execution, and the provision of lock-free data structures is difficult enough to be still considered a publishable result. Programs are likely to contain performance bugs:[1] cache coherence among cores is a frequent source of performance bugs with data that is shared between threads. False sharing [19] is a performance bug where data is inadvertently shared between cores through a common cache-line.
3. Composability: composing lock-based software may introduce deadlocks and performance bugs.

It is therefore important to identify programming abstractions that avoid the above problems. Pipeline parallelism is so common in parallel programs that it was selected as a distinguished parallel programming pattern [20]. Because pipeline parallelism operates on a conceptually infinite data stream, it is often called stream parallelism.

Stream-parallel programs consist of a set of independent actors that communicate via data streams. Actors read from their input channels, perform computations and write data on their output channels. Each actor represents an independent thread of execution that encapsulates its own state. Actors are self-contained, without references to global variables or to the state information of other actors. The self-containedness of actors rules out any dependencies except those implied by communication channels: an actor can execute if sufficient data is available on its input channels and if the output channels provide enough

---

[1] Bugs that prevent an otherwise correct program from executing *efficiently*.

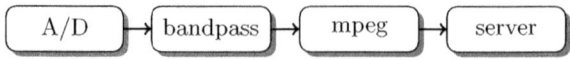

Fig. 1. Example stream program

space to accommodate the data produced by the actor. Because of this lack of dependencies stream programs provide a vast amount of parallelism, which makes them well-suited to run on multi-core architectures.

Fig. 1 depicts an example stream program that consists of an A/D converter, a bandpass filter, an mpeg-encoder and a network server that provides an mpeg data-streaming service. The application domain for stream parallelism includes networks, voice, video, audio and multimedia programs. In embedded systems, applications for hand-held computers, smart-phones and digital signal processors operate on streams of voice and video data.

Despite its large application domain, stream-parallelism is not well-matched by general purpose programming languages; mainly because actors and streams are not provided at the language level. As a consequence, programmers need to devise their own abstractions, which are then prone to lack readability, robustness and performance. A programming language implementation that is not aware of stream parallelism most likely will not be able to take advantage of the abundance of parallelism provided by stream programs.

The contributions of this paper are as follows.

- We present a type-based stream programming extension for Ada 2005. Our extension lifts the abstraction level for the development of stream programs. Actors are expressed as tagged types and conveniently connected via a single method call.
- We provide design and implementation of a run-time system for Ada 2005 that allows the execution of stream programs. Our run-time system manages the data channels between actors, load-balances and schedules actors among the parallel execution units of a processor, and provides the complete stream program execution infrastructure.
- Unlike previous approaches, we allow the dynamic creation of stream graphs. Instead of applying heuristics, we profile stream programs to load-balance actors among the parallel execution units of a processor.
- The initial release of AdaStreams is available for download at [1].

The remainder of this paper is organized as follows: in Sec. 2 we provide background information and survey related work. In Sec. 3 we introduce the type-based programming abstractions for stream-parallelism proposed for Ada 2005. In Sec. 4 we describe the design and implementation of the run-time system required to support applications that use our programming abstractions for stream parallelism. Sec. 5 contains our evaluation of AdaStreams on the Intel x86-64 architecture. We draw conclusions and outline future work in Sec. 6.

2   Background and Related Work

A survey on programming languages that include a concept of streams can be found in [22]. For example, Lustre [8] is a synchronous dataflow programming language used for safety-related software in aircrafts, helicopters, and nuclear power plants. However, it supports only a limited number of data types and control statements. Esterel [5] improves on the number of control statements and is well-suited for control-dominated synchronous systems. Both languages require a fixed number of inputs to arrive at the same time before a stream node executes.

StreamIt [24] uses syntax similar to Java and is more flexible than its predecessors. A StreamIt programmer constructs a stream graph consisting of filters which are connected by a fixed number of constructs: Pipelines, SplitJoins, and FeedbackLoops. Two types of splitters are supported: Duplicate and RoundRobin. A FeedbackLoop allows to create cycles in the stream graph. In contrast to its predecessors, StreamIt supports a dynamic messaging system for passing irregular, low-volume control information between filters and streams.

We do not consider specification languages like SDL [4] here because in this paper we are interested more in implementing systems than in designing systems.

Our approach differs from Kahn process networks [15] which allow data-dependent communication. Leung et al. show in [18] how Kahn process networks can be mapped onto parallel architectures using MPI for communication.

Summing up, our approach for AdaStreams goes beyond that of StreamIt because we allow dynamic creation of stream graphs. Messaging can be done via standard Ada features such as protected objects. In contrast to the languages mentioned above, the whole spectrum of data types available in Ada can be used for streaming. However, currently we do not provide predefined structured stream graphs like StreamIt does with its Pipelines, SplitJoins, and Feedback-Loops. The filters, splitters and joiners provided by the AdaStreams library are sufficient to generate structured graphs. For example, Fig. 3(d) shows how a feedback loop can be constructed with AdaStreams. As explained in [23], it is yet not entirely clear whether structured stream graphs are sufficient for all possible applications. Our plan with AdaStreams is to survey the stream graph patterns arising from real-world applications and build higher-level stream graph constructs from commonly occurring patterns.

Stream programs expose an abundant amount of explicit parallelism already in the source code. Actors (i.e., stream graph nodes) constitute independent units of execution that interact only through data channels. Actors may be stateless or encapsulate state. Despite this amount of parallelism it is still a challenging task to schedule a stream program on a parallel architecture. The obvious solution of assigning an Ada task to each filter and to model communication via producer-consumer style bounded buffers induces too much context-switch and synchronization overhead for all but the largest filters. In fact filters often contain only a small amount of computation, which makes it hard to maintain a high computation-to-communication ratio with stream programs. StreamIt and AdaStreams require that the amount of data consumed and produced by an

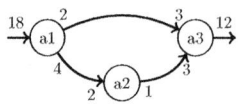

Actor	Iterations
a1	3
a2	6
a3	2

Fig. 2. Example: SDF and minimal steady-state schedule

actor is known *a priori*. Stream graphs with this property employ synchronous data-flow (SDF). Figure 2 depicts an SDF example stream graph. The numbers associated with each input and output of an actor denote the number of data items consumed and produced during one actor execution. For example, Actor a2 consumes two data items and produces one data item per execution. Conceptually, an SDF graph repeatedly applies an algorithm to an infinite data stream. An SDF graph is executing in steady-state if the amount of data buffered between actors remains constant across repeated executions. The table in Fig. 2 depicts the number of iterations required for each actor such that the above SDF graph stays in steady state. E.g., Actor a1 has to be executed three times, resulting in 3×2 data items on channel a1→a3. Actor a3 will consume those 6 data items during its two executions. Computing the steady state for SDF graphs has been studied in [17][2]. StreamIt uses a variant of this algorithm for structured SDF graphs [16]. An SDF graph is scheduled based on its steady state. The scheduler consists of two phases, one bootup-phase to bring the system into steady state, and the steady-state schedule itself.

The stream programming paradigm is also applied in Google's recently-released systems programming language "Go" [10]. Go provides co-routines that communicate via channels.

3   A Type-Based Programming Abstraction for Stream Parallelism with Ada 2005

To add a stream programming abstraction to the Ada programming language, the following approaches are conceivable: (1) extend the core language itself through language extensions, (2) provide a compiler extension for streaming constructs, or (3) provide a programming library that the user can link with standard Ada application code. AdaStreams is strictly a library. Although language extensions are attractive, they create a high barrier to adoption, especially in commercial settings. A library-based extension allows re-use of legacy code, opens up a migration path and does not require programmers to step out of their accustomed programming environment. Moreover, a library lowers the entry barrier for language researchers and enthusiasts who want to work in this area themselves. We felt that at this stage the stream programming paradigm is still in the state of flux, which suggests to choose a library as a light-weight approach to begin with. Ada provides excellent support for packages, types and

---

[2] Note that a steady state for a given SDF graph need not exist in general.

generic programming, which facilitates library creation. A library-only solution is of course not perfect. We had to omit features that require compiler support, like filter fusion/fission to improve load-balancing of stream programs on multi-core architectures. However, libraries have been successfully applied to extend programming languages, as demonstrated by the POSIX threads library [7] and by the Intel Thread Building Blocks [21].

Fig. 3 shows the three actor programming primitives that AdaStreams provide: filters, splitters and joiners. Together, these primitives are sufficient to generate arbitrary stream graph structures. Fig. 3(d) shows how a loop can be constructed from a joiner, a filter and a splitter.

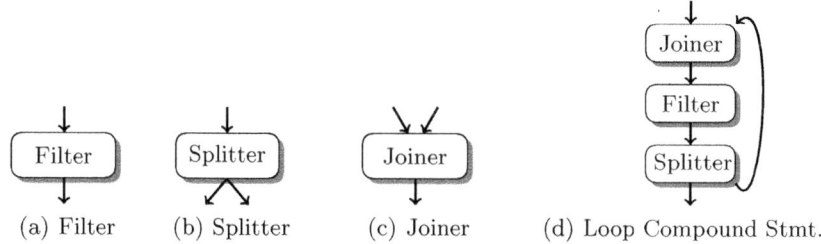

(a) Filter   (b) Splitter   (c) Joiner   (d) Loop Compound Stmt.

Fig. 3. Three AdaStreams stream-graph primitives and one compound statement

Each AdaStreams filter has an input and output type. That way filters are allowed to convert data, which allows the generation of heterogeneous stream graphs. Splitters and joiners are restricted to a single type. Types are used during stream graph creation to ensure type compatibility of adjacent stream graph primitives. Users may define arbitrary types by extending our abstract tagged root type `Root_Data_Type` as depicted in Fig. 4.

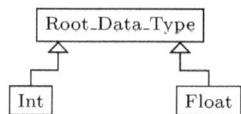

Fig. 4. Root data type hierarchy

We chose a hierarchy of tagged types depicted in Fig. 5 to represent stream program actors. The abstract type `Base_Filter` at the root of this hierarchy contains the commonalities among actors. Types `Filter`, `Splitter` and `Joiner` are generic types parameterized by the respective input or input and output types from the root data type hierarchy.

Type `Base_Filter` is depicted in Fig. 6. Every actor has to provide a primitive operation named `Work` (line 5) which encodes the actor's computation. The `Base_Filter` record can be extended by actors that need to keep state information across invocations of the work function.

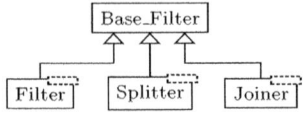

Fig. 5. Type hierarchy for AdaStream filters

```
1    with Root_Data_Type;
2    package Base_Filter is

3      type Base_Filter is abstract tagged private;
4      type Base_Filter_Ptr is access all Base_Filter'Class;

5      procedure Work (f: access Base_Filter) is abstract;

6      procedure Connect(f: access Base_Filter;
7                        b: access Base_Filter'Class;
8                        out_weight: Positive := 1;
9                        in_weight: Positive := 1) is abstract;

10     function Get_In_Type(f: access Base_Filter)
11                    return Root_Data_Type.Root_Data_Type'Class is abstract;
12     procedure Set_In_Weight (f: access Base_Filter; in_weight : positive) is abstract;
13   private
14     type Base_Filter is abstract tagged null record;
15   end Base_Filter;
```

Fig. 6. Base_Filter type

Every actor needs a `Connect` operation (lines 6–9) to attach its streamgraph successor(s). The arguments to the `Connect` operation are the downstream successor (line 7) and the number of output data items (line 8) of this actor plus the number of input data items (line 9) of the downstream successor. For example, to connect actors X and Y via edge $X \xrightarrow{1\ 2} Y$, operation `X.Connect(Y,1,2)` would be used by the AdaStreams library user. In the case of multiple successors (i.e., with splitters), the `Connect` operation must be invoked for each successor. The successor's `Set_In_Weight` operation is invoked from within `Connect` to communicate the `in_weight` argument value to the successor. `out_weight` and `in_weight` of stream-graph edges are used to compute the steady state schedule as outlined in Sec. 2.

At run-time, operation `Connect` checks that the data types used in the filters to be connected are equivalent. Operation `Get_In_Type` (lines 10 and 11 in Fig. 6) is used to retrieve the input type of the downstream actor. If the data types differ, exception `RTS.Stream_Type_Error` is raised. Hence we combine a type secure approach with dynamic creation of arbitrary stream graphs.

Filters, splitters, and joiners (see Fig. 3) specific to a chosen root data type can be instantiated from the generic packages `Filter`, `Splitter`, and `Joiner`. These packages are parameterized by the respective input or input and output types.

The generic package for filters is depicted in Fig. 7. AdaStreams filters provide primitive operation `Pop` to retrieve a single data item from a filter's input stream.

```
1    with Root_Data_Type, Base_Filter;
2    generic
3        type In_Type is new Root_Data_Type.Root_Data_Type with private;
4        type Out_Type is new Root_Data_Type.Root_Data_Type with private;
5    package Filter is
6        type Filter is abstract new Base_Filter.Base_Filter with private;
7        procedure Work(F: access Filter) is abstract;
8        procedure Push(F: access Filter; Item: Out_Type);
9        function Pop(F: access Filter) return In_Type;
10       ...
11   private
12       type Filter is abstract new Base_Filter.Base_Filter with record
13           In_Var : aliased In_Type;
14           Out_Var : aliased Out_Type;
15           In_Weight : Positive;        -- # data items Work() pops per invocation
16           Out_Weight : Positive;       -- # data items Work() pushes per invocation
17       end record;
18   end Filter;
```

Fig. 7. Generic package providing the AdaStreams filter type

Likewise, operation `Push` allows a filter to write a data item onto the output stream. Operations `Push` and `Pop` are to be used within a filter's `Work` operation. As already mentioned, by overriding the abstract primitive operation `Work` of a filter, the user implements the actual behavior of the filter. The `Work`-operations of splitters and joiners are provided by our implementation: splitters partition the incoming data stream into sub-streams, joiners merge several incoming data streams of the same type into a single stream.

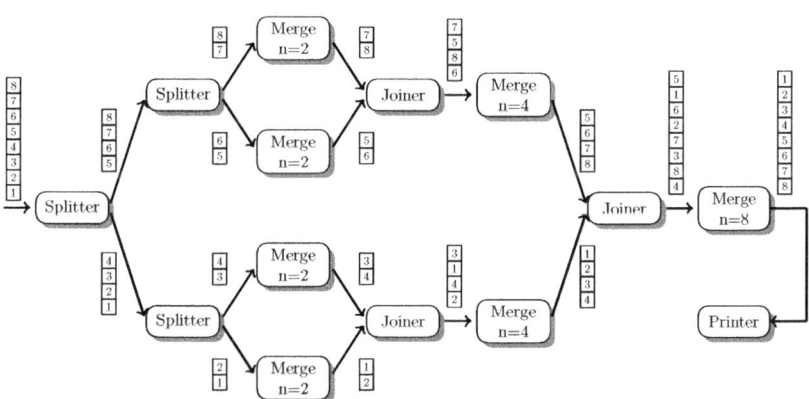

Fig. 8. The merge filters in the merge sort benchmark, with N=8

Fig. 8 shows a stream-parallel version of the Mergesort algorithm for $N = 8$ data items. During each steady-state execution (aka iteration) of this stream program, 8 data items are popped from the input stream, sorted, and pushed onto the output stream. We chose this example because it showcases the dynamic creation of stream-graphs depending on user input data (parameter N). The Mergesort example is implemented as follows:

1. First the stream data type is declared by extending the `Root_Data_Type`. In our case it is an integer type (see Fig. 9). The implementation of the operations for this type are not shown since they are straight-forward.
2. Next the filters needed for Mergesort are defined by extending the standard filter type. We need a filter for the source of the stream to be sorted. This is filled via a random number generator. In addition we need a Merger for doing the actual work and a Printer to display the final result. Splitters and joiners are also defined as shown in Fig. 10. Note that for space-considerations we had to move the implementations of the above filter's `Work`-operations to the paper's accompanying technical report [9].
3. Procedure Main[3] uses the recursive function `SetUp_MergeSort` to setup the stream graph needed by Mergesort. This is done in a standard way. A reference to this can be found in almost any book on algorithms and data structures. An example of the stream graph for $N = 8$ items to be sorted is shown in Fig. 8. Runtime arguments of Main are the number of CPUs to use and the number of iterations of the stream graph.

```
1    package Root_Data_Type.Int is

2        type Int is new Root_Data_Type with record
3          I : Integer;
4        end record;

5        function "+" (Left, Right : Int) return Int;

6        function "<=" (Left, Right : Int) return Boolean;

7    end Root_Data_Type.Int;
```

Fig. 9. Root_Data_Type.Int

```
1    with Root_Data_Type.Int, Base_Filter, Filter, Splitter, Joiner;
2    package UserFilters is
3        package Int_Filter is new Filter (Root_Data_Type.Int.Int, Root_Data_Type.Int.Int);
4        package Int_Splitter is new Splitter (Root_Data_Type.Int.Int);
5        package Int_Joiner is new Joiner (Root_Data_Type.Int.Int);

6        type Merger (aValue : Integer) is new Int_Filter.Filter with record
7          N : Integer := aValue;
8        end record;
9        procedure Work (F : access Merger);
10
11       type Source is new Int_Filter.Filter with null record;
12       procedure Work (F : access Source);

13       type Printer is new Int_Filter.Filter with null record;
14       procedure Work (F : access Printer);
15   end UserFilters;
```

Fig. 10. Mergesort_Filters

---

[3] Shown in the paper's accompanying technical report [9].

4   The AdaStreams Run-Time System

We implemented the AdaStreams run-time system (RTS) as an Ada package that must be compiled and linked with applications that wish to use the AdaStreams library. Package RTS contains several child packages as shown in Fig 11 and exports only two procedures, as depicted in Fig 12. Procedure `Connect` is used by our generic implementations of filters, splitters and joiners. The `Connect` operations from the `Base_Filter` type hierarchy invoke `RTS.Connect` to inform RTS about connections between actors. Child-component RTS.Stream_Graph maintains the stream-graph topology from calls to `RTS.Connect`.

After the stream graph has been created, the RTS client calls `RTS.Run` to execute the stream graph on `NrCPUs` for `NrIterations`. At this stage RTS executes the following steps:

1. The steady-state for the given stream graph is calculated as outlined in Sec. 2. We use a thin binding to the GiNaC C++ symbolic algebra package [3]. Package RTS.Stream_Graph sets up a system of linear equations that models the input-output behavior of the stream graph. The solution to this equation system denotes the steady state iterations for each actor. For a stream graph that has no steady state RTS raises exception Invalid_Stream_Graph. This is not a limitation of our framework but a manifestation of a defective stream graph structure: due to sample rate inconsistencies any schedule for such a graph will result either in deadlock or unbounded buffer sizes [17].

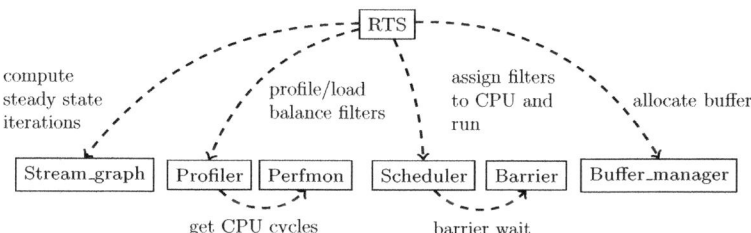

Fig. 11. Component diagram for the AdaStreams run-time system

```
1    with Base_Filter;
2    package RTS is
3        Stream_Type_Error : exception;
4        -- Raised with connections of type-incompatible filters.

5        Invalid_Stream_Graph : exception;
6        -- Raised for a stream that has no steady state.

7        procedure Connect(From : Base_Filter.Base_Filter_Ptr;
8                          To : Base_Filter.Base_Filter_Ptr;
9                          Out_Weight : Positive := 1;
10                         In_Weight : Positive := 1);

11        procedure Run (NrCPUs : Positive; NrIterations : Natural);
12   end RTS;
```

Fig. 12. RTS run-time system package specification

2. Buffers representing the data channels are allocated between adjacent actors. The size of a buffer is computed as the data type size times the input or output rate times the number of steady-state iterations.
3. A boot schedule to bring the stream graph into steady state is computed and executed on the actors. During this bootup phase the actors are profiled to determine the execution times of their work functions. Profiling uses the x86-64's hardware cycle counters exported by the clock library from [6] (again we use a thin binding). Based on the execution times the actors are allocated to CPUs using a simple but fast greedy algorithm: actors are sorted from largest to smallest work function execution time. CPU allocation happens then in a round-robin fashion from the sorted list of actors.
4. For every CPU a scheduler from package RTS.Schedulers is created and the corresponding actors are registered with the scheduler. A scheduler is an Ada task that maintains a list of registered actors together with the corresponding numbers of steady-state iterations. Invocation of a scheduler's Run entry initiates execution of the registered actors' work functions.
5. Stream graph execution is initiated with the schedulers.

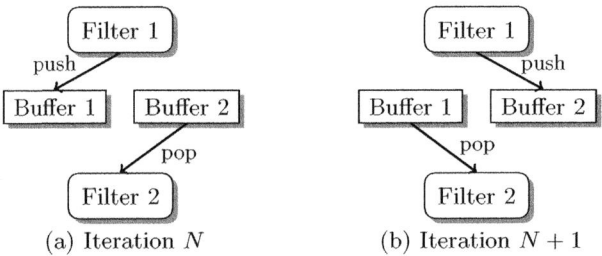

(a) Iteration N (b) Iteration $N+1$

Fig. 13. Double-buffering applied with data channels

There is no need for synchronization of actor execution within a single CPU, because schedulers invoke work functions sequentially. However, across CPUs schedulers need to be synchronized. It is worth noting that we require only a single barrier (implemented as a protected object) for scheduler synchronization. As depicted in Fig. 13, we actually employ two buffers between adjacent actors. Two buffers ensure that both the reader and the writer have their own buffer and need not synchronize with each buffer access. After every steady state iteration schedulers synchronize on the barrier and swap the read and write buffers before the next iteration. Barriers with double buffering reduce synchronization overhead among schedulers and keep the computation-to-communication ratio of stream programs high.

5   Experimental Results

We devised the following Ada benchmark programs to conduct an initial evaluation of the AdaStreams library:

Table 1. Characteristics of benchmark programs implemented with AdaStreams

Benchmark	Filters	Splitters	Joiners
Synthetic	58	1	1
Mergesort	33	15	15
Matrix Multiply	44	5	5
Block Matrix Multiply	31	7	7

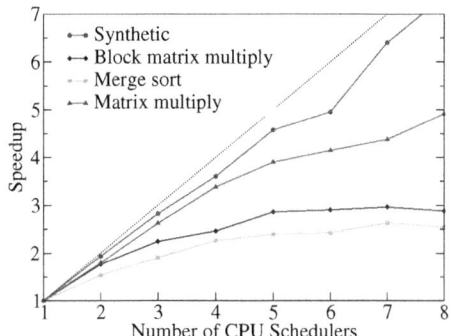

Fig. 14. Scalability of stream benchmark programs

1. Synthetic: this is a synthetic benchmark that uses a busy wait loop to spend CPU cycles. In this benchmark each work function spins for one second before pushing a single data item. Consequently, this benchmark has a very high computation-to-communication ratio.
2. Mergesort: this benchmark uses a stream of random integers, reads N elements from the stream and outputs the N elements in sorted order (as outlined in Sec. 3).
3. Block matrix multiply: Block matrix multiply splits each matrix in the stream into blocks and multiplies blocks with small communication overhead. Blocks are added and combined.
4. Matrix multiply: multiplies two square matrices. It transposes one of them and multiplies two matrices in parallel.

Table 1 shows the characteristic features of our benchmark stream programs. All benchmarks were compiled with the 64-bit version of GNAT GPL 2009 (20090511). To determine the scalability of the AdaStreams implementation with respect to the number of CPU cores, we executed all benchmarks on an Intel x86-64 server with two Xeon 5120 quadcore CPUs. As expected, the synthetic benchmark with its high workload scaled best. Matrix multiply also scaled very well, with a speedup of a factor of almost 5 with 8 CPU cores. Block matrix multiply achieved a speedup of almost three times with more than four cores. The work functions of Mergesort show very fine-grained parallelism; under those circumstances scalability was reasonable. It should be noted that scalability of stream programs was achieved without changing even a single line of source code—mapping of actors to different numbers of CPU cores was all transparently handled by the AdaStreams library.

6 Conclusions and Future Work

In this paper we have proposed a type-based stream programming extension to Ada 2005. AdaStreams is a type-hierarchy for actor-specification together with a run-time system that supports the execution of stream programs on multicore architectures. AdaStreams is non-intrusive in the sense that no change of an Ada 2005 programming language implementation is required. Legacy-code can be mixed with a stream-parallel application, and the use of sequential legacy code with actors is supported. Unlike previous approaches, AdaStreams allows dynamic creation of stream programs. Messaging (known from StreamIt) can be done via standard Ada features such as protected objects. The whole spectrum of data types available in Ada can be used for streaming. Each AdaStreams filter has an input and output type. That way filters are allowed to convert data, which allows the generation of heterogeneous stream graphs. Splitters and joiners are restricted to a single type.

We have implemented AdaStreams for Intel multicore architectures. We provide initial experimental results that show the effectiveness of our approach on an Intel X86-64 quadcore processor. The initial release of our work is available for download at [1].

Our plan with AdaStreams is to survey the stream graph patterns arising from real-world applications and build higher-level stream graph constructs from commonly occurring patterns. We will investigate improvements to our greedy actor allocation algorithm.

References

1. AdaStreams Web Site, http://elc.yonsei.ac.kr
2. Andrews, J., Baker, N.: Xbox 360 System Architecture. IEEE Micro 26(2), 25–37 (2006)
3. Bauer, C., Frink, A., Kreckel, R.: Introduction to the GiNaC Framework for Symbolic Computation within the C++ Programming Language. J. Symb. Comput. 33(1), 1–12 (2002)
4. Belina, F., Hogrefe, D.: The CCITT-Specification and Description Language SDL. Computer Networks 16, 311–341 (1989)
5. Berry, G., Gonthier, G.: The Esterel Synchronous Programming Language: Design, Semantics, Implementation. Sci. Comput. Program. 19(2), 87–152 (1992)
6. Bryant, R.E., O'Halloran, D.R.: Computer Systems: A Programmer's Perspective. Prentice-Hall, Englewood Cliffs (2003)
7. Buttlar, D., Farrell, J., Nichols, B.: PThreads Programming. O'Reilly, Sebastopol (1996)
8. Caspi, P., Pilaud, D., Halbwachs, N., Plaice, J.: Lustre: A Declarative Language for Programming Synchronous Systems. In: POPL 1987, pp. 178–188 (1987)

9. Hong, G., Hong, K., Burgstaller, B., Blieberger, J.: AdaStreams: A Type-based Programming Extension for Stream-Parallelism with Ada 2005. Technical Report TR-0003, ELC Lab, Dept. of Computer Science, Yonsei University, Seoul, Korea (March 2010), http://elc.yonsei.ac.kr

10. Google. The Go Programming Language Specification, http://golang.org (retrieved November 2009)

11. Herlihy, M., Shavit, N.: The Art of Multiprocessor Programming. Morgan Kaufmann, San Francisco (2008)

12. IBM Redbooks. Programming the Cell Broadband Engine Architecture: Examples and Best Practices (August 2008), http://www.redbooks.ibm.com

13. IDC. PC Semiconductor Market Briefing: Re-Architecting the PC and the Migration of Value (June 2008), http://www.idc.com

14. ISO/IEC 8652:2007. Ada Reference Manual, 3rd edition (2006)

15. Kahn, G.: The Semantics of a Simple Language for Parallel Programming. In: Rosenfeld, J.L. (ed.) Information Processing, Stockholm, Sweden, August 1974, pp. 471–475. North Holland, Amsterdam (1974)

16. Karczmarek, M., Thies, W., Amarasinghe, S.: Phased Scheduling of Stream Programs. SIGPLAN Not. 38(7), 103–112 (2003)

17. Lee, E.A., Messerschmitt, D.G.: Static Scheduling of Synchronous Data Flow Programs for Digital Signal Processing. IEEE Trans. Comput. 36(1), 24–35 (1987)

18. Leung, M.-K., Liu, I., Zou, J.: Code Generation for Process Network Models onto Parallel Architectures. Technical Report UCB/EECS-2008-139, EECS Department, University of California, Berkeley (October 2008)

19. Lin, C., Snyder, L.: Principles of Parallel Programming. Addison Wesley, Reading (2008)

20. Mattson, T.G., Sanders, B.A., Massingill, B.L.: Patterns for Parallel Programming. Addison Wesley, Reading (2007) (3rd printing)

21. Reinders, J.: Intel Threading Building Blocks. O'Reilly, Sebastopol (2007)

22. Stephens, R.: A Survey of Stream Processing. Acta Informatica 34, 491–541 (1997)

23. Thies, W.: Language and Compiler Support for Stream Programs. PhD thesis, Massachusetts Institute of Technology (February 2009)

24. Thies, W., Karczmarek, M., Amarasinghe, S.P.: StreamIt: A Language for Streaming Applications. In: Horspool, R.N. (ed.) CC 2002. LNCS, vol. 2304, pp. 179–196. Springer, Heidelberg (2002)

A Comparison of Generic Template Support: Ada, C++, C#, and Java™

Benjamin M. Brosgol

AdaCore; 104 Fifth Ave., New York NY 10011 USA
brosgol@adacore.com

Abstract. *Generics* (also known as *templates*) have become a standard feature of modern programming languages, offering parameterization by data types and possibly other entities. Generics support efficient type-safe container data structures, general-purpose algorithms, and other reusable components. However, the approaches in different languages vary widely in syntax, semantics, and usage. This paper summarizes the design of generics in Ada, C++, C#, and Java and compares them with respect to expressiveness, implementation model / run-time efficiency, and interaction with object-oriented programming and other features.

Keywords: generic programming, templates, Ada, C++, C#, Java.

1 Introduction

One of the fundamental software engineering principles is *abstraction*: the ability to generalize from specific instances and identify a common pattern that can be parameterized. Run-time parameterization (subroutine definition and invocation) has been a staple of programming languages since the earliest days of computing, and translation-time parameterization (macro definition and instantiation) followed soon thereafter. Macros, however, are rather unstructured, since instantiation simply involves text substitution and expansion. It was only in the 1970s, with the groundbreaking work on languages such as CLU [1] and Alphard [2], that researchers recognized that translation-time parameterization could be generalized and made more reliable and robust. Instead of a mechanism based on text substitution, the language could enforce syntactic and semantic checks on the content to be expanded, and allow parameters to be specified in terms of program entities such as types. A well-known example is a "container" data structure (list, stack, queue, etc.) that can be parameterized by element type. The resulting mechanism came to be known as *generics* or *templates*, and it is sometimes referred to more fancily as *parametric polymorphism*.

Generics resemble macros in that each instantiation replicates the template, either conceptually or actually, with formals replaced by actuals. However, generics are distinct from macros in at least two important ways.

- The generic template is checked for syntactic and semantic correctness; it is not simply raw source text that gets expanded. Thus all uses of generic formal parameters must be consistent with their declaration, or compilation will fail.

J. Real and T. Vardanega (Eds.): Ada-Europe 2010, LNCS 6106, pp. 222–237, 2010.

- Instantiations are checked to ensure that their arguments (actual generic parameters) match their corresponding formal parameters.

Generics offer several advantages.[1] An obvious benefit is *reuse*; without generics, the developer of a component has two main choices:

1. Use macros and a preprocessor. But text substitution and expansion are at the wrong semantic level: names in the generic template would be interpreted based on the scope of the instantiation rather than the scope of the generic's definition, contrary to standard block structure conventions.
2. For container-like data structures, define the component to take a general element type (`Object` in many object-oriented languages, `void*` in C) and apply casts when extracting elements. This approach adds run-time cost for type checking and means that errors are detected late.

This second point brings up another benefit of generics: *type safety*. With generics, a data structure such as a queue can be guaranteed to only contain elements of some specific type. It is not possible to insert an integer and then remove it and treat it as having some other type. A corollary benefit is thus *efficiency*: with an appropriate implementation model, type safety can be guaranteed at compile time. There should be no need for run-time checks to ensure that the data in the queue has the correct type.

Generics are heavily used in the definition of standard libraries. Examples are the I/O and containers packages in Ada, the Standard Template Library in C++, and the containers class libraries in C# and Java.

Different languages, however, take different approaches to realizing generics. The main distinctions stem from design decisions in several areas:

- *Expressiveness / Basic Semantics*
  - Which kinds of entities can be made generic? Does instantiation need to be explicit, or can it be implicit?
  - Which kinds of formal parameters are allowed for a generic entity, and what are the rules for matching a formal parameter by an actual parameter at an instantiation?
  - What establishes an instantiation's legality and how it may be used?
  - If a formal parameter to a generic is a type, how may it be used in the template? Can a formal type parameter be constrained so that the matching actual type parameter needs to supply specific operations?
  - Are recursive instantiations permitted?
- *Implementation Model*
  - Does each instantiation of a generic yield a separate expansion, or can different instantiations (in particular with different arguments) share common code?
  - Are there run-time costs associated with generics?
  - When are errors detected?

---

[1] There are also some drawbacks. Generics introduce syntactic and semantic complexity, and, if misused, may lead to "code bloat" in implementations that expand the template separately for each instantiation. They also generally require special tool support, for example in a debugger.

    ○ How is separate compilation handled?
- *Feature Interactions*
    ○ How do generics interact with Object-Oriented Programming, overload resolution, name binding, and other language features?

The remainder of this paper will summarize how these issues are addressed in practice by four specific languages: Ada [3], C++ [4], C# [5], and Java [6]. These are not the only languages that support generics (others include Modula-3 and Delphi) but they are used heavily and illustrate the breadth of approaches.

Length constraints prevent inclusion of complete examples. Please refer to the companion web site [7] for full listings of examples in the four languages.

Earlier work comparing generic programming features in different languages includes [8], which omits Ada, and [9], which omits C#.

2   Ada

Among the languages covered in this paper, Ada is the only one that supported generics from its earliest release. Ada's model is significantly different from the other languages, principally because Ada has distinct features for modularization and data typing. A class in C++, C#, or Java would be modeled in Ada by a (tagged) type declared in a package.

2.1   Expressiveness / Basic Semantics

- *Which kinds of entities can be made generic? Does instantiation need to be explicit, or can it be implicit?*

Ada allows packages and subprograms to be generic. Types themselves are not generic, but a type declared in a generic package has some of the properties of generic types in other languages.

Instantiation must be explicit and has the effect of declaring a non-generic package or subprogram. Implicit instantiation was rejected because of semantic complexity and readability concerns [10]. Also, implicit instantiation is most useful for generic types (classes) but in Ada types are not generic.

- *Which kinds of formal parameters are allowed for a generic entity, and what are the rules for matching a formal parameter by an actual parameter at an instantiation?*

Ada has a rich facility for generic parameterization. Formal generic parameters may be types, subprograms (including operator symbols), objects (values or variables), and instances of generic packages. Formal types come in a variety of flavors, reflecting the fact that different categories of types (integer types, access types, ...) have different operations available. Instantiations may make use of default values and named associations. Unlike C++ (which requires constants), Ada allows run-time evaluable expressions in actual parameters for formal objects.

If a unit needs to be parameterized by type, the designer chooses the appropriate category (for example, `digits <>` for floating-point types) and can provide additional formal subprogram parameters for operations that are not automatically available based on the type's category but that are needed within the generic template.

• *What establishes an instantiation's legality and how it may be used?*

An instantiation's legality may depend on the full generic specification rather than just whether the parameters match. However, embodying a principle that has come to be known as the *contract model*, an instantiation's legality does not depend on the generic body. In general, Ada prohibits usage of features in a generic body if such features could make some instantiations illegal.

An instance of a generic unit can be used in the same manner as a non-generic unit. Unavailability problems with an instance's subprograms, which are possible in C++ (see below), do not arise in Ada.

• *If a formal parameter to a generic is a type, how may it be used in the template? Can a formal type parameter be constrained so that the matching actual type parameter needs to supply specific operations?*

A formal type may only be used in ways that are allowed for every type in its category, unless the required operations are provided as additional generic formal parameters.

• *Are recursive instantiations permitted?*

No. The error will be detected at compile time.

2.2 Implementation Model

• *Does each instantiation of a generic yield a separate expansion, or can different instantiations share common code?*

The Ada rules allow both expansion-based and code-sharing implementations. During Ada's early years, code sharing (for instantiations of the same generic with different actual parameters) was especially useful because generics were the only way to pass subprograms as parameters. The subject attracted considerable attention (e.g., [11]), and the code sharing optimization was provided by several compilers.

Code sharing in general, however, is very difficult to implement. With the provision of subprograms as run-time parameters in Ada 95 (and also the emergence of hardware with greater code space capacity), this space optimization became less critical, and today nearly all Ada compilers use the expansion model.

• *Are there run-time costs associated with generics?*

Generic instantiation in Ada is purely a compile-time activity, but in some cases run-time checks may be generated (for example to ensure that an expression supplied as an actual parameter satisfies the subtype constraints of a formal generic object parameter).

• *When are errors detected?*

All static semantic errors in generic templates, and all mismatch errors at instantiations, are caught at compile time. However – and this is an issue also in C++, C#, and Java – it is possible for an instantiation to be legal, but to generate an illegal overloading of some subprogram P that the compiler only detects at points of P's invocation. One example (with analogs in C++ and C#) is a generic package that declares subprograms P(X1:T1) and P(X2:T2) where T1 and T2 are formal generic parameters, and the generic is instantiated with the same type as actual parameter for both.

As noted above, run-time checking may be needed for formal object parameters. Also, a generic body must be elaborated before any instantiation, or else an "access before elaboration" exception will be raised at run time.

• *How is separate compilation handled?*

Generic units may be separately compiled, as may their instantiations. Ada's requirement for explicit instantiation has the benefit of the programmer controlling code sharing. A simple conceptual model is that each instantiation expands to a separate body of code. A linker optimization can eliminate those subprograms that are not called.

2.3 Feature Interactions

• *How do generics interact with Object-Oriented Programming, overload resolution, and other language features?*

Object-Oriented Programming. The main interaction with OOP concerns the extension of tagged types declared in generic packages. Ada addresses this issue through generic child packages: a type declared in a generic child can extend a tagged type declared in the generic parent package.

Any of the generic packages in the hierarchy may contain a dynamically bound invocation for a primitive subprogram of one of the tagged types, and it will work with the standard effect in the instantiated package.

With non-generic OOP (a tagged type in a non-generic package specification), a derived type may appear in either a child or a client ("with"ing) unit. If a tagged type is declared in a generic package, then the derived type may only be declared in a child.

Overload Resolution / Name Binding. Generics themselves are not overloadable, but instances of a generic subprogram may be overloaded.

An important issue is how to resolve a (statically bound) subprogram invocation in the generic template when some of the actual parameters of the subprogram are of a generic formal type T. When the subprogram can be resolved as one of the other generic formal parameters, then that is the interpretation. Otherwise, if it is an operation defined for T based on T's type category (e.g., "=" for a formal private type) then the built-in (primitive) version of the operation is used. If neither of these resolutions is possible, the subprogram invocation is illegal.

3 C++

Although not in the initial version of C++, templates were always considered essential for parameterization of container classes. A minimal facility was added in 1990, based on experience with prototype implementations of early design proposals, and several enhancements have appeared subsequently. The key goals for C++'s template facility were "notational convenience, run-time efficiency, and type safety. The main constraints were portability and reasonably efficient compilation and linkage" [12, p. 339].

3.1 Expressiveness / Basic Semantics

• *Which kinds of entities can be made generic? Does instantiation need to be explicit, or can it be implicit?*

Function and class (or struct) templates are allowed. Instantiation may be either explicit or implicit. Explicit instantiation must be managed carefully, since multiple instantiations of the same template with the same arguments can cause linker errors due to duplicate definitions.

When a function template's implicit instantiation is invoked, the type arguments to the instantiation may be omitted if they can be deduced from the run-time parameters:

```
template <typename T> void foo(T t) ...
...
foo(100); // Equivalent to foo<int>(100)
```

Member functions of templates must be defined as function templates themselves, and they are only instantiated if called. Implicitly instantiating a class template does not automatically instantiate all member function definitions.

• *Which kinds of formal parameters are allowed for a generic entity, and what are the rules for matching a formal parameter by an actual parameter at an instantiation?*

Templates may have type parameters (identified by the keyword `typename` or `class`), nontype parameters, and template parameters. At an instantiation, a template's type parameter is matched by a type argument, a nontype parameter is matched by a constant value, and a template parameter is matched by a template argument.

Any type (built-in, class, struct, etc.), except class types defined within functions, may be supplied as an argument for a type parameter.

The type of a template's nontype parameter must be an integral or enumeration type, a pointer type (for example a pointer-to-function type), or a reference type. The matching argument must be a constant value of the corresponding type. Since instantiating a class template with an argument produces a specific type, restricting nontype arguments to constants ensures that the compiler can determine when two instantiations denote the same type. However, a side effect is that string literals are not allowed as arguments for templates, since different occurrences of the same literal may be at different addresses.

A template's template parameter `TT` is matched by a template argument whose parameters correspond to (i.e. have the same types as) the parameters of `TT`. Such parameters facilitate template composition.

• *What establishes an instantiation's legality and how it may be used?*

A class template instantiation's legality depends only on whether the arguments match the formal parameters. However, instantiating a member function from the class instance will fail if the member function invokes a function that is not available for the argument type. For example, consider a class template with a type parameter `T` and a member template function `Foo()` that uses some operation for `T`. Unless the template takes an additional parameter (a pointer-to-function for the required operation), instantiating `Foo` with an argument type `TT` will fail if `TT` does not have the needed operation.

The absence of a generic "contract model" makes software maintenance difficult, since there is no way for the author of a template to know whether an implementation change will cause errors when existing instantiations are recompiled.

• *If a formal parameter to a generic is a type, how may it be used in the template? Can a formal type parameter be constrained so that the matching actual type parameter needs to supply specific operations?*

A template's type parameter may be used as a regular type inside the template. C++ has no syntax for establishing constraints on a type parameter; if additional operations are needed this will either be part of the informal contract of the template (documented in comments) or else supplied as explicit pointer-to-function parameters to the template.

• *Are recursive instantiations permitted?*

Yes, for example using non-type parameters such as ints. Templates in C++ in effect provide a compile-time functional language, with iteration realized through recursive instantiation (template specialization [12, p. 373] terminates the recursion). This style, referred to as *metaprogramming*, can be used to obtain highly-optimized performance (see for example [13, p. 314]) but can be rather opaque.

3.2 Implementation Model

• *Does each instantiation of a generic yield a separate expansion, or can different instantiations share common code?*

C++'s design philosophy encourages sharing of separate instantiations with the same arguments, whether within the same translation unit or across translation units, but this is not consistent in practice. Because of the lack of a "contract model", sharing instantiations with different arguments is more difficult than with Ada.

• *Are there run-time costs associated with generics?*

Template expansion and argument/parameter matching are purely compile-time (or link-time) activities. Run-time efficiency was a major goal for the C++ design, and techniques such as template specialization can be used to optimize performance (e.g. by specifying pass-by-value parameters rather than const references for particular types).

• *When are errors detected?*

Errors, especially instantiations with types that do not provide needed operations, are detected during compilation (or linking), at the point of instantiation or function invocation. Thus, unlike Ada, C#, and Java, such errors are not detected during compilation of the template definition.

• *How is separate compilation handled?*

It is natural for the template declaration (the interface, without function bodies) to be placed in a header file (.hpp). An issue is whether the template body (the "template definition") should be in the same header file, similar to an inline function, or in an implementation file (.cpp).

Placing the template definition in the header file, referred to as the "inclusion model" in [13], is common practice. A program that needs the template can simply #include the header file. However, template definitions typically require further #includes, and the closure of all of these #includes can result in considerable code bloat and/or excessive compilation time. Also, the definition needs to be bracketed by #ifndef/#define and #endif brackets to avoid duplication of definition in #includeing translation units.

An alternative is to place the template declaration in a .hpp file and the definition in a .cpp file (the "separation model"). The translation unit using the template #includes the .hpp file. This raises the issue of how the implementation locates the corresponding `.cpp` file. One technique is to mark the declaration(s) and definition with the `export` keyword. However, this mechanism is not uniformly supported by current compilers, and in general the inclusion model is used. Precompiled headers can help reduce compilation cost.

3.3 Feature Interactions

• *How do generics interact with Object-Oriented Programming, overload resolution, and other language features?*

Object-Oriented Programming. Template classes can form inheritance hierarchies, in the same way as regular classes. A template class may derive from non-template classes and/or from template classes. Here's an example adapted from [12, p. 346]:

```
template <typename T> class Vector   /* ... */ ;
template <typename T> class OrderedVector : Vector<T>   /* ... */ ;
```

However, if `TC<T>` is a template class with a class parameter, and `T2` derives from `T1`, it does not necessarily follow that `TC<T2>` derives from `TC<T1>`. I.e., template instantiations are not *covariant*. The rationale is straightforward. If a `List<Subclass>` reference `ref` were assignable to a `List<Superclass>` variable `vbl`, then through `vbl` it would be possible to add `Superclass` objects to `ref`.

Overload Resolution / Name Binding. Function templates may be overloaded, and the names used inside template definitions may likewise be overloaded.

The name binding rules are complex [12, pp. 368ff], since three different contexts are involved: the template definition, the argument type declaration, and the template use / instantiation. The complications are especially intense for the names that depend on a template argument.

Other Features. There are a number of "corner case" pathologies. For example, an instantiation `SomeTemplate<int, Vector<int>>` is illegal because the ">>" at the end is parsed as a shift operator. The programmer must insert a space between the brackets, e.g. `SomeTemplate<int, Vector<int> >`.

4   C#

Generics were added to C# (and to the .NET infrastructure) in Version 2, with the goals of type safety, time efficiency (no boxing /unboxing or casts) and space efficiency (avoidance of code duplication).

4.1 Expressiveness / Basic Semantics

• *Which kinds of entities can be made generic? Does instantiation need to be explicit, or can it be implicit?*

C# allows declarations of generic types (classes, interfaces, structs, and delegates) and generic methods. It does not permit generic properties, events, indexers, operators, constructors, or finalizers, but these entities may be declared within generic types.

Instantiation is implicit, but a "using alias" directive can simulate an explicit instantiation (for example to create a shorthand name).

- *Which kinds of formal parameters are allowed for a generic entity, and what are the rules for matching a formal parameter by an actual parameter at an instantiation?*

The only kind of formal parameter that a generic entity can take is a type.

Unless otherwise constrained (see below), instantiation with both value types (such as the predefined type `int`) and reference types is permitted. However, instantiation with pointer types is not allowed.

- *What establishes an instantiation's legality and how it may be used?*

Although an instantiation's legality is based only on the matching of parameters (including satisfying constraints on the formal), ambiguous overloadings may result that are only detected at method invocation. This is similar to Ada's semantics, described above.

- *If a formal parameter to a generic is a type, how may it be used in the template? Can a formal type parameter be constrained so that the matching actual type parameter needs to supply specific operations?*

Type parameters may be constrained so that they can only be instantiated with types having particular characteristics. Type constraints include whether a type is a reference type or a value type, whether it derives from a specific class or implements a particular interface (or interfaces), and whether it supplies an accessible no-arg constructor.

If the generic requires a type parameter to have a specific method available, then the type parameter can be constrained to derive from some specific type that includes that method, or to implement an interface that declares that method.

Constraints that are not enforceable at compile time can be checked at run time through the use of reflection in a static constructor. An example (checking that a type parameter is an enum) appears in [5, p. 390].

- *Are recursive instantiations permitted?*

Since C# generics can only take type parameters, "metaprogramming" in the style of C++ is not supported. However, the definition of a generic type or method may contain instantiations of the same generic. The caching / code sharing mechanism prevents unbounded expansion.

4.2 Implementation Model

- *Does each instantiation of a generic yield a separate expansion, or can different instantiations share common code?*

The language rules were designed to allow code sharing. All instantiations with reference types can share a single code body. Each instantiation with a specific value type has its own expansion (instantiations with the same value type share the same body).

- *Are there run-time costs associated with generics?*

With the standard C# implementation model, instantiation itself is performed at run time, through the "just-in-time" (*JIT*) compiler, when control reaches the point of instantiation. Instantiations are cached to perform code sharing as described above.

Alternatively, instantiations can be precompiled to native code through Microsoft's NGEN utility, also with code sharing. NGEN will process all instantiations, since it does not know which ones are required at run time and which ones are not.

With either approach there is no run-time overhead (boxing, casts, etc).

• *When are errors detected?*

Errors are detected during compilation, potentially in three different contexts: an illegal construct in the generic itself, an illegal instantiation (non-matching argument), or usage of an ambiguous construct resulting from an instantiation

• *How is separate compilation handled?*

No special rules. The compiler produces special intermediate language for generics, and also outputs generic-specific information in the metadata.

4.3   Feature Interactions

• *How do generics interact with Object-Oriented Programming, overload resolution, and other language features?*

Object-Oriented Programming. Generic classes can participate in inheritance hierarchies. As with C++, generics are not covariant.

Overload Resolution / Name Binding. Method overloading within a generic type definition results in some complex semantics. For example:

```
class Gen<T>{
  Foo(T t){...}
  Foo(int i){...}
}
...
Gen<int> x = new Gen<int>();
x.Foo(0); // Which Foo?
```

The C# rules (similar to C++) dictate that the "more specific" method (here the one with an explicit `int` parameter) is selected. Such preferencing rules can cause maintenance problems. If the version with an explicit `int` parameter was introduced during program maintenance, the invocation of `Foo` will silently change meaning when recompiled. In the analogous examples in Ada and Java, the call on `Foo` would be ambiguous.

Other Features. Since information about generics is retained in the compiled assembly, run-time reflection and introspection are permitted.

5   Java

Generics were introduced in Java 5 to support type-safe collections and general-purpose methods in an upwards-compatible fashion (i.e., not requiring any changes to Java Virtual Machine implementations, and easing the migration path for developers who had previously used non-generic solutions). Upwards compatibility comes at a price, however; as observed in [14, p. 1], generics are "sometimes controversial" and have left "a few rough edges". They also introduce a run-time cost (casts implicitly inserted by the compiler). These issues result from Java's model of "type erasure" where all traces of genericity in the source disappear in the generated byte codes.

5.1 Expressiveness / Basic Semantics

• *Which kinds of entities can be made generic? Does instantiation need to be explicit, or can it be implicit?*

Classes, interfaces, methods, and constructors can be defined as generic.

Instantiation is implicit, similarly to C++ and C#. Instantiating a generic class or interface is referred to as *type invocation* and results in a *parameterized type*.

A unique aspect of Java's generic model is that instantiations of the same generic class Gen<T> with different type arguments, say Gen<T1> and Gen<T2>, do not produce different classes. Instead they yield the same *raw type* Gen as described below. Consequently all of the instantiations share the same static fields. This effect is generally undesirable (e.g. preventing the common style of maintaining an instantiation-specific counter to keep track of the number of constructed objects).

• *Which kinds of formal parameters are allowed for a generic entity, and what are the rules for matching a formal parameter by an actual parameter at an instantiation?*

The only formal parameter permitted is a type (Java refers to this as a *type variable*.) A matching actual parameter is a reference type that satisfies all specified constraints (see below).

Although primitive types are not allowed, Java's "boxing" rules allow uses of generic instantiations with primitive values; the compiler will implicitly allocate an actual object of the relevant type (for example an Integer for an int value).

• *What establishes an instantiation's legality and how it may be used?*

Instantiation legality is based only on parameter matching. Problems with unavailability of operations, as in C++, do not arise. However, as with the other languages, instantiations may yield ambiguous overloadings that make certain method invocations illegal.

• *If a formal parameter to a generic is a type, how may it be used in the template? Can a formal type parameter be constrained so that the matching actual type parameter needs to supply specific operations?*

Java allows the specification of type constraints (*bounds*) to ensure that the needed operations on the formal type parameter are available. This is accomplished by specifying that a formal type extends some other type (possibly one of the other generic formal parameters) and/or implements any number of interfaces.

• *Are recursive instantiations permitted?*

Analogous to C#, Java does not support metaprogramming in the style of C++, but a generic class may contain an instantiation of itself.

5.2 Implementation Model

• *Does each instantiation of a generic yield a separate expansion, or can different instantiations share common code?*

Java's type erasure model ensures that all instantiations share the same code. The erasure of a generic type yields the *raw* type, which is obtained by replacing each formal parameter (type variable) by Object if it does not have an "extends" bound, and by its first bound otherwise.

• *Are there run-time costs associated with generics?*

The compiler generates implicit casts, since the erasure of a generic class loses instantiation-specific information. Thus:

```
Stack<String> ss = new Stack<String>();
ss.Push("Hello");      // compiled as ss.Push((String)"Hello");
String s = ss.Pop();   // compiled as String s = (String)(ss.Pop());
```

Also, since type parameters must be reference types, using primitive values such as ints incurs boxing/unboxing overhead.

• *When are errors detected?*

Static semantic errors in the definition of the generic are caught at compile time. These errors include invocation of operations that are not consistent with the formal parameter's constraints, and declaring potentially ambiguous method overloadings (see below). Some ambiguities are detected (at compile time) when an attempt is made to invoke an ambiguous method from an instantiation.

For upwards compatibility, Java permits converting from a parameterized type to its underlying non-generic (*raw*) type. However, type errors might then remain undetected until run time (for an example see [15, p.165]).

• *How is separate compilation handled?*

Compilation of a generic produces a (non-generic) raw type. Run-time reflection will not recover the generic-related information.

5.3   Feature Interactions

• *How do generics interact with Object-Oriented Programming, overload resolution, and other language features?*

Object-Oriented Programming. Similarly to C++ and C#, Java allows generic types to extend other types (either non-generic or generic), subject to the usual rule that a class can extend only one superclass but can implement an arbitrary number of interfaces.

Also like C++ and C#, generic classes are not covariant: if C2 extends C1, and Gen<T> is a generic class, then it does not follow that Gen<C2> extends Gen<C1>. Thus a Gen<C2> reference cannot be assigned to a Gen<C1> variable, nor may it be passed as an argument to a method taking a Gen<C1> parameter. Sometimes, however, these operations make sense and should be allowed. For example, consider the following hypothetical generic collection class:

```
public class Mob<T>{
    public addAll( Mob<T> m){...} // Add m's elements to this
}
...
Mob<C1> m1 = new Mob<C1>();
Mob<C2> m2 = new Mob<C2>();
m1.addAll(m2);   // Illegal
}
```

The method invocation is illegal since m2 is not a Mob<C1>. In order to allow such invocations, the declaration of addAll's parameter must be changed so that it accepts not only a Mob<T> but also a Mob<U> for any class U in the type hierarchy rooted at T. The form is called a *wildcard* and has the following syntax:

```
public class Mob<T>{
    public addAll( Mob<? extends T> m){...}
// Add m's elements to this
}
```

The example above – m1.addAll(m2); – will now succeed. As a shorthand, the common case <? extends Object> can be abbreviated as <?>.

Wildcards are also useful in the other direction. If we are "consuming" elements from a collection Mob<C2>, then the target may a Mob<C1> where C1 is either C2 or any of its superclasses. Java has a wildcard form for this purpose also, with the syntax <? super T>.

A wildcard may be used for a formal parameter and/or result type of a method in a generic class or interface, and also as the type of a declared variable.

Overload Resolution / Name Binding. Outside of generics, Java's overloading rules forbid declaring two methods with the same name and the same signature. Java's erasure model requires strengthening this rule for generics; for example the following is illegal:

```
public class Gen<T1, T2>{
    public void Foo(T1 : t1){...}
    public void Foo(T2 : t2){...}
}
```

Although the two declarations of Foo have different signatures, they have the same "erasure signatures" (obtained by replacing the type name by its corresponding bound), and declaring two methods in the same generic type with the same erasure signature is prohibited. (Here it is as though each declaration of Foo had a parameter of type Object.)

The example above would be legal in Ada, C++, and C#, as would an instantiation with the same type argument for both parameters. The illegality would be an attempt to invoke Foo from such an instantiation.

Java's rules are somewhat analogous to Ada's model of "assuming the worst" in a generic declaration, although motivated by different factors. For Ada the issue is enforcement of the "contract model", and for Java the issue is consistency with type erasure.

Other Features. Java's erasure model results in a number of restrictions. A formal type parameter of a generic type cannot be used as the type of a static field, nor may it be referenced within a static method or static constructor. It is also prohibited in constructors for objects or arrays. Other restrictions are listed in [16, p. 268].

6   Conclusions

Each of the language designs has approached generics in a unique fashion, yielding both advantages and drawbacks. Tables 1 through 3 summarize the comparison.

Table 1. Generics Comparison Summary, Part 1

	Generic entities	*Generic parameters*	*Instantiation*	*Constraints allowed on formal types?*
Ada	• Packages • Subprograms	• Types • Subprograms • Objects • Package instances	• Explicit	• Yes
C++	• Classes, structs • Functions	• Types • Constant values • Templates	• Implicit	• No
C#	• Types • Methods	• Types	• Implicit	• Yes
Java	• Classes, interfaces • Methods	• Reference types	• Implicit	• Yes

Table 2. Generics Comparison Summary, Part 2

	Contract model?	*Recursive intantiation / "metaprogramming"?*	*Code sharing? (same generic, different arguments)*
Ada	• Yes	• Neither	• Implementation dependent, but generally no
C++	• No	• Both	• Implementation dependent, but generally no
C#	• No	• Recursion: yes • Metaprogramming: no	• Yes for reference types, no for value types
Java	• Yes	• Recursion: yes • Metaprogramming: no	• Yes for all types

Table 3. Generics Comparison Summary, Part 3

	Avoidance of run-time overhead	Error detection	Instantiation covariance
Ada	• Yes	• Compile time, generally early (at point of generic declaration or instantiation) but some only at uses of instantiation	• Not applicable
C++	• Yes	• Compile or link time, late (at uses of instantiation)	• No
C#	• Yes (after JIT compilation of instantiation)	• Compile time, generally early but some only at uses of instantiation	• No
Java	• No (compiler generates implicit casts)	• Mixed. Some caught at compile time, analogous to Ada; others at run time (class cast exceptions)	• No, but may be modeled through wildcards

In brief:

- *Ada* provides the most precise and explicit interface for a generic unit, and the requirement for explicit instantiations makes the programmer's intent clear. But the separation of the class concept into two features (package and tagged type) complicates the interaction between generics and OOP (generic hierarchies), and the number and variety of generic formal types can be confusing.
- *C++* provides considerable expressive power and flexibility, and allows the programmer to fine-tune performance. But the interface for a generic template is broad and implicit, allowing errors in a template definition to remain undetected until triggered by an instantiation. And the semantics for name resolution in templates is complex.
- *C#* allows expression of constraints on a type's operations, and it offers a straightforward approach for code sharing. But arguments to a generic are restricted to types (no constants, for example), and the preferencing rules for name resolution in generics are complicated.
- *Java* provides a solution that is upwards compatible with earlier versions of Java and the JVM, and its "erasure" model ensures code sharing. But performance is compromised (implicit casts are generated to ensure type safety, requiring run-time checks), and the semantics can be counterintuitive (e.g., different instantiations sharing static data).

Given the tradeoffs among different goals (generality, early error detection, run-time efficiency, code space compactness, upwards compatibility) it is not surprising that none of the languages is uniformly superior to the others. However, languages evolve over time, and new languages will undoubtedly be designed. Perhaps the "lessons learned" from user and implementer experience will lead to new insights and approaches that bring reuse with fewer tears.

Acknowledgements

The author is grateful to Bob Duff, Ed Falis, and Ed Schonberg from AdaCore for their review of an early version of the paper, and to the anonymous referees for their commments and suggestions.

References

1. Liskov, B., et al.: CLU Reference Manual. Springer, Heidelberg (1983)
2. Wulf, W.A., London, R.L., Shaw, M.: Abstraction and verification in Alphard: Introduction to language and methodology. USC Information Sciences Institute (1976)
3. ISO/IEC JTC1/SC 22/WG 9. Ada Reference Manual – ISO/IEC 8652:2007(E) with Technical Corrigendum 1 and Amendment 1 – Language and Standard Libraries (2007)
4. International Organization for Standardization. ISO/IEC 14882:2003, The C++ Standard Incorporating Technical Corrigendum 1 (2003)
5. Ecma International. C# Language Specification – ECMA-334, 4th edn. (June 2006)
6. Gosling, J., Joy, B., Steele, G., Bracha, G.: The Java Language Specification, 3rd edn. Addison-Wesley, Reading (2005)
7. Brosgol, B.M.: Companion Examples: A Comparison of Generic Template Support (November 2009), http://www1.adacore.com/ brosgol/ae2010/examples.html
8. Garcia, R., et al.: A comparative study of language support for generic programming. In: Proc. OOPSLA 2003. ACM, New York (2003)
9. Khalifa, A.A.: Generics: Ada 95 vs C++ vs Java 1.5. Master's thesis, Univ. of Jyväskylä, Finland (2005), https://jyx.jyu.fi/dspace/handle/123456789/12351?show=full
10. Ichbiah, J.D., Barnes, J.G.P., Firth, R.J., Woodger, M.: Rationale for the Design of the Ada Programming Language (1983)
11. Bray, G.: Implementation implications of Ada generics. ACM SIGAda Ada Letters III(2) (1983)
12. Stroustrup, B.: The Design and Evolution of C++. Addison-Wesley, Reading (1995)
13. Vandevoorde, D., Josuttis, N.M.: C++ Templates: The Complete Guide. Addison-Wesley, Reading (2007)
14. Naftalin, M., Wadler, P.: Java Generics and Collections. O'Reilly, Sebastopol (2007)
15. Flanagan, D.: Java in a Nutshell, 5th edn. O'Reilly, Sebastopol (2005)
16. Arnold, K., Gosling, J., Holmes, D.: The Java Programming Language, 4th edn. Addison-Wesley, Reading (2006)

Towards Ada 2012: An Interim Report

Edmond Schonberg

AdaCore Inc.
schonberg@gnat.com

Abstract. The Ada Rapporteur Group (ARG), following the instructions of ISO/IEC JTC1/SC22/WG9 is preparing an update to the Ada 2005 standard. This paper presents a snapshot of the more important language enhancements under discussion. Even though these enhancements are not yet in their final form, and will not become part of the proposed new standard until approved by ISO, the description that follows is an accurate reflection of the main directions in which the language is evolving. However, the names of packages, subprograms, and formal parameters, as well as some details of the syntax might change from what is presented here.

1 Introduction

The WG9 committee, after discussions with the ARG and with members of the Ada community, has instructed the ARG to complete the Amendment to Ada 2005 [1] so that ISO standardization of the new version can be completed by 2012. This is a relatively short horizon. but it matches the interval between previous releases, demonstrates that the language continues to evolve, and at the same time places a bound on the changes to the language, and ensures that they do not present an undue implementation burden on existing compilers.

This paper is an informal survey of the more important enhancements that the ARG is discussing. These enhancement are grouped as follows:

- Section 2 discusses enhancements directly related to correctness, namely the introduction of more powerful assertion mechanisms in the language: pre- and postconditions, global assertions, type invariants, are other mechanisms that encourage the programmer to better specify the meaning of the code they write, and allow the run-time to verify that this meaning is in fact obeyed.
- Section 3 discusses enhancements to the Containers library.
- Section 4 presents language enhancements that contribute to expressiveness and readability: conditional expressions, case expressions, more powerful membership tests, and corresponding iterator forms. Most of these are syntactic enhancements whose semantics is intuitive and fit well in Ada. One addition in this category has a larger import because it reverses an early design decision that had been controversial ever since Ada 83: functions will now have in and in out formal parameters.
- Section 5 discusses visibility mechanisms: more powerful use clauses, and integrated packages that provide better access to declarations in nested packages.

J. Real and T. Vardanega (Eds.): Ada-Europe 2010, LNCS 6106, pp. 238–250, 2010.

- Section 6 presents concurrency and real-time enhancements that address the multicore revolution.
- Section 7 mentions other minor syntactic enhancements that simplify the programming task and polish some awkward corners of the language.

Each one of the enhancements we describe corresponds to one or more Ada Issues (AIs). We must emphasize that our descriptions are informal, and reflect the state of affairs as of this writing (March 2010). Please refer to the database at the Ada Information Clearinghouse (see *http://www.ada-auth.org/AI-SUMMARY.HTML*) where the interested reader will find up-to-date descriptions and a full list of Amendment AIs.

2 Program Correctness

The enhancements in this area address the familiar issue of "programming by contract" (see [2] for a modern discussion). They provide the programmer with tools to specify formally the intent of a construct. This formal description can then be verified/enforced at execution time, or even confirmed statically by analysis tools. Such contract specifications allow compilers and other tools to catch errors in usage or implementation earlier in the development cycle. They also provide valuable documentation of the intended semantics of an abstraction.

2.1 Aspect Specifications (AI05-0183)

Assertions about the behavior of subprograms, types, and objects are *aspects* of the corresponding entities, and a uniform syntax will be available to specify these, as well as more familiar operational and representational attributes of various kinds of entities. Thus the notion of aspect generalizes the familiar Ada concept of attribute. The properties of these attributes can be specified with representation clauses (for example size representation clauses) or with pragmas (for example pragma Pack). These specifications are unified with the new notion of *aspect*:

```
aspect_specification ::=
        with aspect_mark [=> expression] { , aspect_mark [=> expression] }
```

An aspect specification can appear in object definitions, type declarations, all manner of subprogram declarations, component declarations and entry declarations.

2.2 Pre- and Postconditions for Subprograms (AI05-0145)

These aspects are predicates, i.e. boolean expressions that must be True on entry to (resp. on exit from) the subprogram to which they apply. The declaration of the function Pop for the canonical Stack data type might be as follows:

```
function Pop(S : in out Stack) return Elem
   with
     Pre  => not Is_Empty(S),
     Post => not Is_Full(S);
```

A postcondition often needs to refer to the value of an in out parameter or of a global object before the subprogram is executed. The attribute 'Old, applied to any nonlimited entity, denotes its value on entry to the subprogram. Similarly, the attribute 'Result denotes the value returned by a function.

2.3 Type Invariants (AI05-0146)

From a contractual point of view, the visible behavior of a private type is described indirectly through the pre- and postconditions that apply to the primitive operations of the type. Other contractual details of an abstraction are better described directly as properties of the type itself.

The new aspect notation allows us to write:

```
type T (...) is private
   with Invariant => Is_Valid(T);

type T2 (...) is abstract tagged private
   with Invariant'Class => Is_Valid(T2);

function Is_Valid (X : T) return Boolean;
```

Note that Is_Valid is referenced before its declaration. This may seem like a break from the Ada canonical linear order of elaboration, but in fact it corresponds to the rule that aspects are elaborated at the point the entity to which they apply is frozen (this is the point at which all the characteristics of the type must be known). In most cases this means the end of the enclosing library package declaration.

An invariant can be type-specific, or class-wide, in which case it applies to all extensions of the type. An invariant is checked on exit from any visible subprogram that is a primitive operation of the type.

2.4 Global In/Out Annotations (AI05-00186)

In order to more fully specify the semantics of a program, it is necessary to indicate what effect subprograms may have on the environment, that is to say enclosing scopes and library-level entities. Global in/out annotations indicate what objects global to a given subprogram S are read or modified by an execution of S. The aspects in, out and in out can specify the following:

```
<object_name> -- the named object, and all of its subcomponents
null          -- the empty set (the subprogram is pure)
others        -- the universal set (all globals may be affected)
others in pkg -- all objects declared or whose designated type is declared in pkg
```

There are additional annotations to indicate that all objects designated by a particular access type, or by access types defined in the current package, may be accessed or modified. Annotations for generic formal parameters are also available. This rather heavy machinery is indispensable if we want to specify to the compiler the possible effect of a subprogram call, without having to rely on global program analysis tools.

3 Containers

Container libraries have become ubiquitous in modern programming environments. The enhancements in this area provide abstractions with better storage properties, task-safety, and useful search properties. There is one common advantage of standardized containers that is worth emphasizing: memory management of collections of values is handled by the container operations, not directly by the user. Storage allocation and reclamation are behind the scene, thus freeing the programmer from some of the more delicate and error-prone aspects of low-level programming. This is particularly important when indefinite types, such as class-wide types, are involved.

3.1 Bounded Containers (AI05-0001)

In their more general form containers place objects and auxiliary data structures in the heap. Even though most heap management is hidden from the programmer, thanks to the use of controlled types, such heap usage is forbidden in high-integrity environments, which renders 2005 containers virtually useless in this realm of application. Ada 2012 introduces bounded variants of containers (vectors, lists, maps) that have a fixed capacity and so can be stack-allocated. The new container types are all discriminated types, constrained by capacity. The bounded containers are not themselves controlled types, which allows for a lighter implementation. (Of course, if the element type of a bounded container is controlled, the container itself will have to be finalized.)

This AI also adds to the Ada library several general purpose packages for case-insensitive operations on strings for sorting and for hashing.

3.2 Holder Containers (AI05-0069)

In Ada 2005 it is not possible to declare a variable of an indefinite type without giving it an initial value that fixes its constraints once and for all. The holder container is a wrapper that can hold a single value of some (possibly indefinite) type. This value can be queried and modified, thus providing the equivalent of a variable of an indefinite type.

3.3 Synchronized Queues (AI05-0159)

Queues were omitted from the 2005 Container library, because they were considered trivial to write, and too elementary to be included in a language standard. However, queues that are task-safe are somewhat more complex, and it is worthwhile to standardize an efficient version of such shared data-structures. Ada 2012 introduces a synchronized interface Queue, declared in package Ada.Container.Synchronized_-Queues, and several generic packages that implement that interface:

    Bounded_Synchronized_Queues
    Unbounded_Synchronized_Queues
    Bounded_Priority_Queues
    Unbounded_Priority_Queues!

The flexibility of Synchronized interfaces (which can be implemented by tasks or by protected types) is put to good use here: each of these packages is parameterized by an instantiation of Synchronized_Queues. For example:

```
with Ada.Containers.Synchronized_Queues;
generic
  with package Queues is new
    Ada.Containers.Synchronized_Queues (<>);
package Ada.Containers.Unbounded_Synchronized_Queues is
  pragma Preelaborate;

  type Queue is synchronized new Queues.Queue with private;
private
     -- not specified by the language
end Ada.Containers.Unbounded_Synchronized_Queues;
```

3.4 Multiway Trees (AI05-0136)

Trees are the quintessential dynamic data structures, and ones for which hiding storage management activities in the implementation is particularly worthwhile. The Container library will now include a very general tree structure, a multiway tree, where each internal node has a vector of descendant nodes, so that there is easy navigation from a node to its siblings and to its ancestors. Search and insertion operations on this structure must have a complexity of O (Log (N)).

4 Functions, Expressions, Control Structures

The enhancements in this group aim to simplify programming in the small: more expressive function declarations, new expression forms, better notation for existing constructs. Most of these can be considered syntactic sugar, that is to say shortcuts to common program fragments that can be written in today's Ada. The first enhancement in this group, however, has a deeper semantic impact.

4.1 In Out Parameters for Functions (AI05-0143)

Ever since Ada 83, functions have had only in parameters, with the justification that they were intended to be the equivalent of mathematical (pure) functions with no side effects. However functions can modify global variables, and thus have arbitrary side effects for which there is no syntactic indication. In Ada 2012, functions will have both out and in out parameters, to indicate more explicitly the way in which a function call may affect the state of the program.

4.2 Dangerous Order Dependences (AI05-0144)

This in turn highlights a weakness in the way Ada specifies (or fails to specify) the order of evaluation of expressions and parameters in calls. If functions have in out parameters, there is a greater danger that side effects make the evaluation of an expression non-deterministic. To alleviate the problem, Ada 2012 mandates static checks that make many common order-dependences illegal. For example, if F is a function with an in out parameter, the expression:

$$F (Obj) + G (Obj)$$

has an illegal order-dependence because the result may be different depending on the order in which the operands of this expression are evaluated. Similarly, the new rules force a compiler to reject aliasing between two actual parameters of an elementary type, when one of the formals is not an in parameter. The checks mandated by AI05-0144 can be made linear in the size of the expression (call or assignment). These checks depend on a static definition of when two names denote the same object, or when one name denotes a prefix of another name. Unlike more rigorous verification systems such as Spark [3], the checks proposed by this AI cannot be complete, given that arbitrary side effects may be present through global variables; they do nevertheless eliminate the most egregious examples of order-dependences. Ada will remain free of idioms that rely on a particular order of evaluation, such as the celebrated C idiom for copying strings:

```
(while *p++ = *q++);
```

4.3 Conditional and Case Expressions (AI05-0147 and AI05-0188)

The chief purpose of these syntactic shortcuts (familiar from other programming languages, such as C++ and various functional languages) is to simplify writing pre- and postconditions, as well as type invariants. These are often complex predicates which would have to be written as off-line functions, thus making them more opaque. Conditional and case expressions allow these predicates to be directly attached to the declaration of the entity to which they apply:

```
procedure Append (V : Vector; To : Vector)
   with Pre =>
     (if Size (V) > 0 then
          Capacity (To) > Size (V) else True);
```

It is frequently the case that predicates impose a check in one case but not in the other, so the trailing else True can be omitted in that case:

```
procedure Append (V : Vector; To : Vector)
   with Pre =>
     (if Size (V) > 0 then Capacity (To) > Size (V));
```

Conditional expressions can also be useful to simplify existing code involving if statements, though here tastes may differ. For example, there might be a definite advantage in rewriting an if statement if both of its branches control two subprogram calls that differ only in one actual parameter, e.g.:

```
Eval (X + Y, F (if Cond then 1 else 0));
```

instead of

```
if Cond then
    Eval (X + Y, F (1));
else
    Eval (X + Y, F (0));
end if;
```

The semantics of conditional expressions is identical to that of short-circuit expressions. Conditional expressions are static if the condition and both dependent expressions are static.

Case expressions stand in the same relation to case statements as conditional expressions to if statements. The well-understood advantage of case expressions is that the compiler can verify that all cases are covered. Thus a case expression is safer than a conditional expression with a series of tests.

4.4 Iterators (AI05-0139)

Traversing a collection is an extremely common programming activity. If the collection is described by one of the library containers, iteration over it can be described by means of the primitive operations First and Next.   These operations typically use cursors to provide access to elements in the collection. However, it is often clearer to refer directly to the elements of the collection, without the indirection implied by the presence of the cursor. This AI will make it possible to write, for example:

```
for  Cursor in Iterate (My_Container) loop
    My_Container (Cursor) := My_Container (Cursor) + 1;
end loop;
```

as well as:

```
for Element of My_Container loop
    Element := Element + 1;
end loop;
```

This syntactic extension is obtained by means of a predefined interface Basic_Iterator, a function with special syntax that provides the equivalent of indexing a container with a cursor, and an implicit "dereference" operation that retrieves an element of the container when presented with a reference to such an element:

```
generic
   type Cursor is private;
   No_Element : in Cursor;
package Ada.Iterator_Interfaces is

   type Basic_Iterator is limited interface;
   function First (Object : Basic_Iterator) return Cursor;
   function Next (Object: Basic_Iterator;
                  Position: Cursor) return Cursor;
   type Reversible_Iterator is
      limited interface and Basic_Iterator;
   function Last (Object : Reversible_Iterator)
```

```
    return Cursor;
  function Previous (Object   : Reversible_Iterator;
                     Position: Cursor) return Cursor;
end Ada.Iterator_Interfaces;
```

An instantiation of this package is present in every predefined container, but the user can instantiate such a generic and provide special-purpose First and Next functions to perform partial iterations and iterations in whatever order is convenient. The familiar keyword **reverse** can be used to determine the direction of iteration.

4.5 Extended Membership Operations (AI05-0158)

The current machinery to define subtypes has no provision for declaring a subset of the values of a scalar type that is not contiguous. Membership in such a subset must be expressed as a series of tests:

```
type Color is (Red, Green, Blue, Cyan,
               Magenta, Yellow, Black);
Hue : Color;
   ...
if Hue = Red or else Hue = Blue or else Hue = Yellow then ...
```

The proposed membership notation allows sequences of values to appear as the right operand:

```
if Hue in (Red |  Blue | Yellow ) then ...
```

Once this notation is introduced, it can be extended to any non-limited type:

```
if Name in ("Entry" | "Exit" | Dict("Urgence") | then ...
```

4.6 Quantified Expressions (AI05-0176)

Invariants declared over containers are often expressed as predicates over all the elements of the container. The familiar notation of Set Theory provides the model for introducing quantified expressions into Ada:

> Quantified_Expression ::= Quantifier Iterator "|" Predicate
>
> Quantifier ::= **for all** | **for some**
> Iterator ::= defining_identifier **in** expression
> Predicate ::= Boolean_expression

For example, a postcondition on a sorting routine might be written as:

```
for all J in A'First .. Index'Pred (A'Last) |
           A (J) <= A (Index'Succ (J));
```

We have departed from the standard notation and rejected the use of *exists* as a new keyword, because it is in common use in existing software. Instead, the non-reserved word **some**, appearing after keyword **for**, specifies that the expression is existentially quantified. For example, the predicate Is_Composite applied to some positive integer might be (inefficiently) described thus:

(**for some** J **in** 2 .. N /2 | N **mod** J = 0)

The iterator forms proposed in AI05-0139 will also be usable in quantified expressions.

5 Visibility

The AIs in this category try to simplify the programming task by providing simpler ways for names to denote specific entities, and by allowing wider uses for entities of certain kinds.

5.1 Use All Type (AI05-0150)

The Ada community has been divided over the use of use clauses ever since Ada 83. Certain style guides forbid use clauses altogether, which forces programmers to qualify all names imported from another unit. To lighten this rather heavy burden, which among other things forces the use of the awkward notation P.".+", the use type clause introduced in Ada 95 provides use-visibility to the operators of a type defined in another unit, so that infix notation (X + Y) is legal even when the type of X and Y is not use-visible. AI05-0150 extends this visibility to all primitive operations of a type (including the literals of an enumeration type). If the type is tagged, this is extended as well to subprograms that operate on T'Class.

5.2 Issues of Nested Instantiations (AI05-0135 and Others)

It is common for a library package P to contain an instantiation of some other package Inner, in order to export a type T declared within Inner. This is often done by means of a derived type DT, which inherits the operations of T and makes them available to a client of P. However, this derivation is a programming artifact (in the vernacular, a kludge) and it is desirable to find a more direct way of re-exporting the entities declared in an inner package. A related issue is that of private instantiations: a package declares a private type PT and needs to declare a container of objects of this type. The instantiation cannot appear in the same package before the full declaration for PT, which leads to a contorted architecture. The ARG is examining several proposals to simplify these programming patterns, including integrated packages (whose contents are immediately visible in the enclosing package) and formal incomplete types for generic units.

5.3 Incomplete Types Completed by Partial Views (AI05-0162)

In many situations we declare an incomplete type in order to provide an access type used in some other construct. The completion of the incomplete type must occur within the same declarative part. For purposes of information hiding, we may want to complete the incomplete declaration with a private type, but this is currently forbidden by the language. This AI proposes that the completion of an incomplete type declaration may be any type declaration (except for another incomplete one). Type declarations can thus be given in three parts: an incomplete type declaration, a private type declaration, and finally a full type declaration.

5.4 Incomplete Parameter and Result Types (AI05-0151)

Limited with_clauses make it possible to describe mutually recursive types declared in separate packages, by providing incomplete views of types. If such an incomplete view is tagged, then it can be used as the formal in a subprogram declaration and even in a call, because it is known to be passed by reference. This AI extends the use of untagged incomplete types obtained through limited views, so they can be used as parameter types and result types, as long as the full view of the type is available at a point of call.

6 Concurrency and Real Time

Most programming languages are proposing new constructs to make proper use of the multicore chips that will dominate the hardware landscape of the next decade. The International Real-Time Ada Workshop has proposed a number of language extensions to simplify the programming of such architectures [4].

6.1 Affinities (AI05-0167)

The first requirement is a mechanism to describe the set of available processing cores in a chip, and to specify a mapping (partitioning) between tasks and cores. In existing operating systems, this mapping is often described as the "affinity" of the task, and the control of task affinities in multiprocessor systems is as important as the control of priorities. This is achieved by means of the following child packages of System (only the outlines are provided):

```
package System.MultiProcessors is
   Number_of_CPUs : constant Positive := <implementation-defined>;
   type CPU is range 1 .. Number_of_CPUs;
   Default_CPU : constant CPU := <implementation-defined>;
   type CPU_Set is array (CPU) of Boolean;
end System.MultiProcessors;

with Ada.Task_Identification; use Ada.Task_Identification;
with Ada.Real_Time;          use Ada.Real_Time;
package System.Multiprocessors.Dispatching_Domains is
   type Dispatching_Domain is limited private;
   System_Dispatching_Domain: constant Dispatching_Domain;
   function Create(PS: CPU_Set) return Dispatching_Domain;
   function Get_CPU_Set(AD : Dispatching_Domain) return CPU_Set;
   procedure Assign_Task (AD : in out Dispatching_Domain;
                          T  : Task_Id :=  Current_Task);
   procedure Delay_Until_And_Set_CPU
         (Delay_Until_Time : Ada.Real_Time.Time; P : CPU);
```

```
private
   type Dispatching_Domain is new CPU_Set;
   System_Dispatching_Domain : constant Dispatching_Domain :=
                                    (others => True);
end System.Multiprocessors.Dispatching_Domains;
```

Needless to say, the implementation of these operations depends on the availability of lower-level constructs in the underlying operating system. The paper by Sáez and Crespo [5] indicates that at least on GNU-Linux operating systems their implementation is relatively straightforward today.

6.2 Extending the Ravenscar Profile to Multiprocessor Systems (AI05-0171)

The Ravenscar profile [6] has been extremely successful for real-time applications, and is in wide use today. This AI proposes its extension to multi-processor systems, to facilitate the construction of deterministic and analyzable tasking programs that can be supported with a run-time system of reduced size and complexity. The proposed extensions to the Ravenscar profile depend on the partitioning facilities described above, but forbid dynamic task migration and require that a task be on the ready queue of a single processor.

6.3 Barriers (AI05-0174)

Barriers are basic synchronization primitives that were originally motivated by loop parallelism. Operating systems such as POSIX already provide barriers, where a set of tasks is made to wait until a specified number of them are ready to proceed, at which time all of them are released. The effect of a barrier can be simulated with a protected type, but only with substantial overhead and potential serialization, so a new mechanism is needed. This mechanism is provided by means of a new package:

```
package Ada.Synchronous_Barriers is
   type Barrier(Number_Waiting : Positive) is limited private;
   procedure Wait_For_Release (The_Barrier : in out Barrier;
                               Last_Released : out Boolean);
end Ada.Synchronous_Barriers;
```

When a variable of type Barrier is created with Number_Waiting = N, there are no waiting tasks and the barrier is set to block tasks. When the count reaches N, all tasks are simultaneously released and the "Last_Released" out parameter is set in an arbitrary one of the callers, which then performs cleanup actions for the whole set. Note that this is different from the Ada 2005 proxy model for a protected operation: there the task that modifies the barrier executes sequentially, in some unspecified order, the pending actions of all tasks queued on the barrier.

6.4 Requeue on Synchronized Interfaces (AI05-0030)

The introduction of synchronized interfaces is one of the most attractive innovations of Ada 2005: a concurrent construct may be implemented by means of an active entity (a task) or a passive one (a protected object), both of which may include queues to enforce mutual exclusion. However, only functions and procedures are allowed as primitive operations of interfaces. It is desirable to support the construction of concurrent algorithms that involve requeue statements, where the construct on which the requeue is to take place may be either a task or a protected object. This AI proposes a pragma to indicate that a given interface operation may allow requeuing, as the following example demonstrates:

```
type Server is synchronized interface;
procedure Q(S : in out Server; X : Item);
pragma Implemented (Q, By_Entry);
```

The pragma can also take the parameters By_Protected_Procedure and By_Any.

7 Syntactic Frills

The AIs in this category address small programming irritants in the syntax of the language, and simplify the programming of common idioms.

7.1 Labels Count as Statements (AI05-0179)

One of the most common uses of gotos in Ada is to provide the equivalent of a "continue" statement in a loop, namely to skip part of the body of the loop and start the next iteration. The following pattern will be familiar:

```
loop
   ...
   if Cond then
      goto Continue;
   end if;
   ...
   <<Continue>> null;
end loop;
```

The null statement is only noise, forced by the current rule that a label is part of a statement. The rule proposed in this AI is that a label by itself is a valid constituent of a statement sequence. This simple rule was chosen, instead of the more contentious introduction of a new reserved word **continue** to be used as a new statement form.

7.2 Pragmas Instead of Null (AI05-0163)

Programmers have found the current rules for pragma placement confusing and error-prone. The syntactic rules concerning them have been simplified, so that they can appear in an otherwise empty sequence of statements, without requiring the presence of an explicit null statement to make the sequence legal.

8 Conclusions

The Ada 2012 amendment strikes a balance between conflicting requirements:

- On the one hand, the evolution of software engineering suggests new language features to facilitate the construction of ever-more-complex systems.
- On the other hand, the large established software base mandates that all new constructs be upward compatible, easy to describe and relatively easy to implement.
- Finally, the Ada community expects the language to evolve, reflecting the development of software methodologies and the evolution of other languages in the same domain.

Time will tell how well the proposed amendment navigates between these constraints. Some partial implementations of the new features are appearing in existing compilers, which will allow language enthusiasts to experiment with them early on. We trust that the Ada community will welcome the new face of the language.

Acknowledgements

This paper summarizes the collective work of the ARG. Particular thanks are due to John Barnes and Tullio Vardanega, for many helpful suggestions for improvements. Remaining errors and omissions are the author's sole responsibility.

References

[1] Tucker Taft, S., Duff, R.A., Brukardt, R.L., Ploedereder, E., Leroy, P.: Ada Reference Manual. LNCS, vol. 4348. Springer, Heidelberg (2006)
[2] Fowler, M.: UML distilled, 3rd edn. Pearson Education, Boston (2004)
[3] Barnes, J.: High Integrity Software. In: The SPARK approach to Safety and Security, Pearson Education, Boston (2003)
[4] Special issue of Ada Letters on the proceedings of IRTAW-14, Portovenere, Italy (2009) (in press)
[5] Sáez, S., Crespo, A.: Preliminary Support of Ada2012 in GNU/Linux systems: Ada-Europe 2010. LNCS (2010) (these proceedings)
[6] Burns, A., Dobbing, B., Vardanega, T.: Guide for the use of the Ada Ravenscar Profile in High Integrity Systems. Ada Letters XXIV(2), 1–74 (2004)

Managing Transactions in Flexible Distributed Real-Time Systems[*]

Daniel Sangorrín[1], Michael González Harbour[2],
Héctor Pérez[2], and J. Javier Gutiérrez[2]

[1] Graduate School of Information Science
Nagoya University, Nagoya, Japan
`dsl@ertl.jp`
`http://www.ertl.jp`
[2] Computers and Real-Time Group
Universidad de Cantabria, 39005 - Santander, Spain
`{mgh,perezh,gutierjj}@unican.es`
`http://www.ctr.unican.es/`

Abstract. This paper describes the design and implementation of the Distributed Transaction Manager (DTM), a service that provides remote negotiation of contracts representing resource reservations in real-time distributed applications. We assume that there is an underlying middleware which can be used by the application to negotiate contracts locally: processor contracts have to be negotiated in the same processor where they will run, and network contracts have to be negotiated in a processing node connected to the specific network that will be used. In addition, the paper proposes the integration of the DTM in a distribution middleware based on CORBA and Ada's Distributed Systems Annex (DSA) which supports advanced scheduling mechanisms based on contracts. The use of the distribution middleware enhances some implementation aspects of the DTM and provides new capabilities as, for example, routing messages through different networks.

Keywords: flexible scheduling, real-time, distribution middleware, CORBA, Ada DSA, communications.

1 Introduction

The evolving complexity of real-time systems has lead to the need for using more sophisticated scheduling techniques, capable of simultaneously satisfying multiple types of requirements such as hard real-time guarantees and quality of service requirements, in the same system. To better handle the complexity of these systems,

---

[*] This work has been funded in part by the Spanish Ministry of Science and Technology under grant number TIN2008-06766-C03-03 (RT-MODEL), and by the IST Programme of the European Commission under project FP6/2005/IST/5-034026 (FRESCOR). This work reflects only the authors' views; the EU is not liable for any use that may be made of the information contained herein.

J. Real and T. Vardanega (Eds.): Ada-Europe 2010, LNCS 6106, pp. 251–264, 2010.

instead of asking the application to interact directly with the scheduling policies, scheduling services of a higher level of abstraction are being designed, usually based on the concept of resource reservations [1]. The FRESCOR European Union project [2] in which we have participated was aimed at investigating these aspects by creating a contract-based scheduling framework.

Future development of real-time distributed systems will be supported by high-level models as the one defined in the standard OMG Specification MARTE (Modelling and Analysis of Real-Time Embedded Systems) [3]. This standard includes the *end-to-end flow* as a basic entity for modelling the behaviour of distributed systems. This is the new name for the *transaction*, a set of interrelated operations with a timing constraint between its start and its completion (not to be confused with the meaning that the same word has in the domain of databases). In the context of this paper a distributed transaction consists of a sequence of activities that can be either task jobs in the processors or messages in the networks. This paper explores new trends in managing transactions for flexible scheduling systems.

Although the support for contracts defined in the FRSH API (FRESCOR framework application interface) [4] is enough to negotiate contracts locally, it puts a burden on the application to manage the negotiation process of a whole distributed transaction. The first objective of this work is to propose and implement a Distributed Transaction Manager (DTM) that extends the negotiation capabilities defined in FRSH to allow remote negotiations and renegotiations of contracts, and a centralized management of the results of the negotiation process. The implementation platform for the DTM is a FRESCOR environment using the C language and MaRTE OS [5] with RT-EP [6][7] and CAN [8] real-time networks. All of these resources have implementations supporting adaptive resource reservations with contracts.

In previous works we proposed mechanisms for the integration of middleware and advanced scheduling services, such as contract-based reservations, with transactions. In [9] some initial ideas were given to allow a distribution middleware to manage complex scheduling parameters specified by an application in a way that minimizes overhead. In that work, a proposal to integrate a generic technique to express complex scheduling and timing parameters of distributed transactions was presented. The implementation of these ideas over PolyORB [10][11] ported to MaRTE OS [5] was presented in [12]. PolyORB is a distribution middleware by AdaCore [13] which supports several distribution standards. Finally, in [14] we extended this generic technique and proposed it to be integrated as a part of the Distributed Systems Annex of Ada (DSA).

The first implementation of the transaction manager described in this paper limits its capabilities just to the management of remote contracts, and as a proof of concepts it was implemented directly over the network services (RT-EP and CAN Bus) [7][8]. We are now implementing a second version to provide a full support for the transactional model integrated with the capabilities of a distribution middleware. This proposal will be fully implemented in PolyORB over MaRTE OS. Currently we have implemented the key issues in order to check the feasibility of the proposal.

The document is organized as follows. Section 2 describes the specification of the Distributed Transaction Manager and gives the details on its main services. Section 3 deals with the architecture of the implementation of the DTM. The model of the transaction and its implementation in the middleware is presented in Section 4.

Section 5 proposes the integration of the DTM in distribution middleware based on standards. The extension of the DTM protocol to provide full support for the transactional model as well as some issues of the implementation of the DTM in PolyORB are pointed out in sections 6 and 7, respectively. Finally, Section 8 draws the conclusions and considers future work.

2   Specification of the Distributed Transaction Manager

The Distributed Transaction Manager (DTM) is a distributed application responsible for negotiation of distributed transactions in a FRESCOR contract-based scheduling framework implementation. FRESCOR contracts provide a resource reservation framework that, as such, provides protection among the different software components running on top of it, facilitating the independence of their development and execution. But the framework produced in FRESCOR goes well beyond the capabilities of other resource reservation frameworks by providing adaptive reservations that can make use of spare capacity available; management of QoS parameters expressed at the application level; an integrated management of multiple schedulable resources including CPUs or networks; management of time-protected shared objects; integration with component-based design methods; off-line schedulability analysis and simulation tools that allow the application developer to reason about the timing behaviour of the application before it is built; and an API called FRSH that makes the application independent of the underlying operating system, networks and scheduling policies. Unlike other adaptive QoS approaches [15], the FRESCOR framework guarantees the minimum budget requested via a schedulability analysis of the system.

The requirements of an application or application component are written as a set of contracts, which are negotiated with the underlying implementation. To accept a set of contracts, the system has to check as part of the negotiation if it has enough resources to guarantee all the minimum requirements specified, while keeping guarantees on all the previously accepted contracts negotiated by other application components. If as a result of this negotiation the set of contracts is accepted, the system will reserve enough capacity to guarantee the minimum requested resources, and will adapt any spare capacity available to share it among the different contracts that have specified their desire or ability for using additional capacity. As a result of the negotiation process initiated by the application, if a contract is accepted, a virtual resource is created for it representing an adaptive resource reservation.

The objective of the Distributed Transaction Manager is to allow in distributed systems the remote management of FRESCOR contracts, including capabilities for remote negotiation and renegotiation of resource reservation contracts, and management of the coherence of the results of these negotiation processes. In this way, FRESCOR provides support for distributed global activities or transactions consisting of multiple actions executed in processing nodes and synchronized through messages sent across communication networks.

Fig. 1 shows the overall DTM architecture as viewed from the application. The DTM has been designed as a layer between the application and the FRSH API in order to avoid increasing the complexity of the FRSH implementation. The DTM is

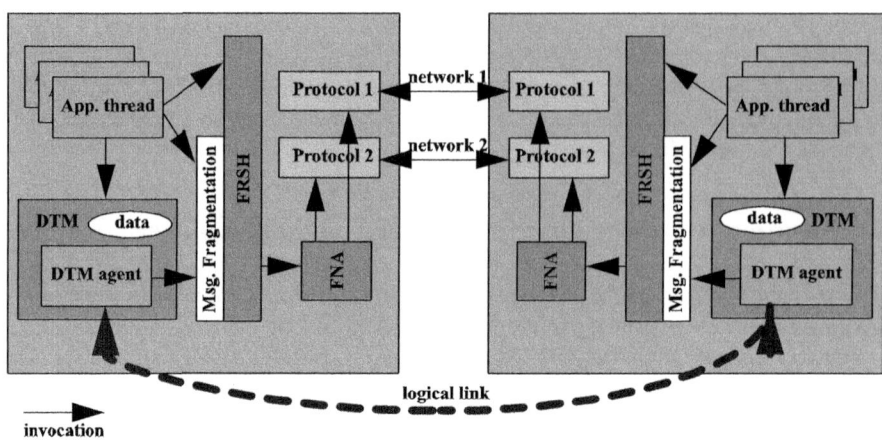

Fig. 1. Role of the DTM in the FRESCOR application architecture

instanced at every node in the system. Each instance stores necessary data for the negotiation process and a *DTM agent*, which will listen to negotiation messages either from
the local node or from remote nodes, will perform the requested actions, and will send
back replies when required.

The remote negotiation process requires bidirectional communication, either direct
or through other nodes acting as routers, between the node requesting the negotiation
and the node performing it, because the requester needs to get the results of the negotiation. As the level of resource reservations required for supporting the routing operations is difficult to configure in general, the DTM may use a static routing mechanism
that utilizes the resource reservations assigned by the system designer to this service.

It is expected that in some networks the DTM messages, specially those containing
contracts, will not fit into the maximum size of a packet. For these cases, a fragmentation layer is deployed between the DTM implementation and the FRSH distribution
services. This layer is independent of DTM and can be used by the application to send
large messages as can be seen in Fig. 1.

The services that the DTM offers to the application are defined by the DTM API
[7][8]. The main services are briefly described as follows:

- **Assignment of Resources to the Transaction Manager.** This service allows the
  application to specify the resource reservations made locally for the operation of
  the transaction manager itself. Some processing bandwidth must be reserved for
  the DTM manager thread responsible of executing the DTM services. In addition,
  network bandwidth must be reserved for the messages that the DTM agents must
  exchange among them. In this way, the framework will guarantee that the
  manager does not overrun the capacity assigned for its execution.
- **Initialization of the Transaction Manager.** In order to use the services of the
  transaction manager it is necessary to ensure that the DTM agents and their data
  structures have been initialized in all nodes. Otherwise, a message sent to a
  remote node to request some service could be lost if nobody is at the other side to
  store and process that message. This service implies creating at each node the

necessary data structures and threads to implement the transaction manager, and synchronizing the initialization with all the nodes involved in the system, by waiting until all of them are initialized.

- **Creation and Management of a Transaction.** This service allows the application to specify the set of contracts that compose a transaction and the nodes where they have to be negotiated. Transactions may require that the periods of all or some of the virtual resources associated to it be the same, to achieve synchronized behaviour. This requirement will be specified by the application when a contract is added to a transaction, and will cause the negotiation process to reach a consensus on the common period to be used for those virtual resources requiring a synchronous period.
- **Negotiation of a Transaction.** This service implies:
  - Checking the consistency of the transaction.
  - Negotiating contracts in remote nodes. This is accomplished by sending a message to each involved DTM agent, with the corresponding contracts. Each DTM agent does the local negotiation and reports back to the original DTM agent the results of the negotiation.
  - Negotiating local contracts.
  - Collecting the results of the remote negotiations.
  - Making a decision based on the results. If one or more of the results implied that a contract was rejected, the whole transaction will be rejected. If all the contracts were accepted and one or more contracts require synchronous periods it is necessary to find out which is the most restrictive period, which will then become the synchronous period of the transaction.
  - Communicate the final decision to all the implied DTM agents, which in turn will adjust the periods of the contracts when necessary, to match the synchronous transaction period.

3   Architecture and Implementation of the DTM without Distribution Middleware

The implementation of the Distributed Transaction Manager in FRESCOR is a decentralized architecture in which the transactions can be created and negotiated from any processing node. Each DTM agent contains a global data structure where the information about the negotiations is kept. This data structure contains information about whole transactions that were created in the corresponding processing node, and also partial information about the parts of those transactions that were created remotely but have been negotiated locally.

The DTM agent contains multiple threads, as can be seen in Fig. 2. One of them, called the *DTM manager thread* is in charge of performing the actions related to the management and negotiation of transactions. The other threads, called the *DTM acceptor threads*, are in charge of listening to messages arriving through the different networks, coming from other remote DTM agents. Fig. 2 also shows the parts that would be replaced with the services provided by the middleware and that will be discussed in Section 5.

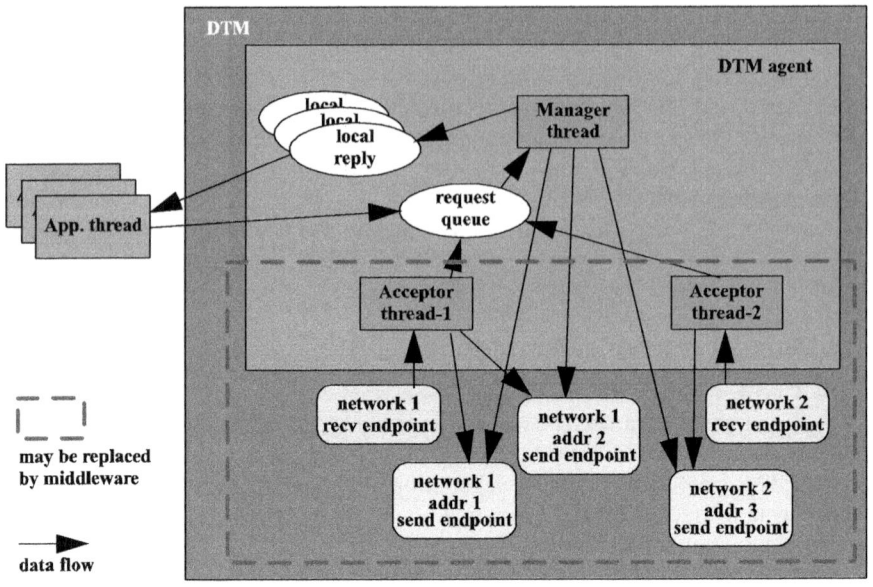

Fig. 2. Internal architecture of a DTM agent

The DTM acceptor threads perform two different services:

- *Routing*: when the DTM message arriving at the acceptor thread is addressed to a different node, it resends that message through the appropriate network according to a static routing table.
- *Handling*: when the DTM message arriving is addressed to the current node, the message type is checked, and a request is queued for the *DTM manager thread*.

The DTM manager thread waits for the arrival of DTM messages at the DTM request queue. To minimize the service times, this is a prioritized queue. When a DTM message arrives, either from a DTM acceptor or directly from a local thread in the application, the DTM manager processes that message. Depending on the type of message, new requests to other remote nodes may be necessary, in which case the manager will have to wait to get the replies from the DTM request queue. Once the request is serviced, a reply is correspondingly sent to the local thread or to a remote node.

The DTM agent contains one send endpoint per connected node through which it can send messages. This send endpoint is bound to the virtual resource that was specified by the application. The DTM agent also contains one receive endpoint per connected network, which is used to receive remote DTM messages.

When a local application thread invokes one of the services that requires intervention of the manager thread, a request is enqueued in the DTM request queue. The local application thread is then put in a *local reply* object, which is a synchronization object where it will wait until the DTM manager sends a reply. Since concurrent invocation of the DTM services is possible, a pool of these synchronization objects is needed. The number of elements in this pool is configurable. Local reply objects will be identified through a handle value.

To avoid deadlocks, processing of local and remote DTM messages by the manager thread is preemptible. While a requesting application thread is waiting in the local reply object, the manager will continue to process other messages. Between the manager thread making a remote negotiation request and receiving the reply from the remote node it will also continue to process other DTM messages. The implementation allows concurrent negotiations being requested by multiple nodes.

4   Transactional Model in Middleware

In this section we summarize the architecture of the transactional model that we will use. This model was proposed in [14] to be included in the DSA, and it defines an interface to allow the middleware and the applications to manage event associations and the scheduling of the different components of a transaction. A distributed transaction is defined to relate parts of an application consisting of multiple threads executing code in multiple processing nodes, and exchanging messages through one or more communication networks. The scheduling parameters must be defined not only for processing tasks but also for the message streams in the communication networks. Two kinds of schedulable entities are defined:

- The *handler tasks* intended to execute remote calls in the processing nodes. These handlers are created explicitly with the appropriate scheduling information.
- The *endpoints* or communication points are used to transport messages through the network with specific scheduling parameters associated with the endpoint. The endpoints are also created explicitly with static scheduling parameters.

In this transactional model, external events trigger the transactions. The only explicit operation that is required from the application code is to set an identifier for each of those events (the *Event_Id*). The rest of the transaction elements, including the communication endpoints, the handler tasks, and all the scheduling parameters, can be described as a part of a configuration operation. Once the task at the beginning of the transaction has set the initial event, all the subsequent activities (including the task's activity itself) are scheduled according to the associated event defined for each part of the transaction. This *Event Id* is set internally by the middleware at the *transformation points* defined at the following actions: setting the initial event, the start of the execution of an RPC Handler, and the reception of the reply by a task waiting for a synchronous RPC.

Pre-configured scheduling parameters will be used according to the *Event_Id* for each application task or RPC Handler. Setting the initial *Event_Id* parameter is sufficient to enable the middleware to identify the particular point in the transaction and therefore the scheduling parameters required in each case. This model also allows an RPC Handler to be shared among different transactions executing in turn with different scheduling parameters.

5 Integration of the DTM with Distribution Middleware

As described in previous sections, the DTM is essentially a distributed application that contains an agent in every node. The agents listen to incoming local or remote messages, perform the requested actions, and send back the replies. This architecture was initially implemented directly over the network communication primitives, but could alternatively be implemented using different distribution standards (e.g. CORBA [16], DDS [17], or Ada DSA [18]), thus simplifying the complexity of the communication among agents.

The presence of distribution middleware implements part of the functionality inherent to DTM. In particular, this architecture could benefit from using a standard distribution model in the following aspects:

- *Simplicity of the protocol and the DTM application.* The current architecture implements a specific communication protocol which requires the management of all the data involved in the remote request (i.e. source node, destination node, size of contracts...). However, middleware could manage the distribution aspects in a transparent way for the user (e.g., using the IOR in CORBA [16] or the topic subscription in DDS [17]).
- *Initialization.* The initialization process in the DTM assures that every agent in the distributed system is ready to send and receive requests. In this case, a static approach has been proposed where the user has to specify all the connection paths within the system. This model could be replaced by a more dynamic approach like that used in DDS, where the discovery of new entities is made at runtime through the built-in topics (DDS entities to provide information to the application). Those special entities must also have another network contract associated, to limit the overhead introduced by the discovery process. Despite that neither CORBA nor DSA do not specify any mechanism to assert the initialization of entities, a solution based on the CORBA Naming Service [19] will be proposed in Section 7. Although this solution is intended to use a CORBA service, it could be also applied to DSA by means of the interoperable platform provided by PolyORB.
- *Removal of the Acceptor Tasks.* The two services provided by those entities could be replaced by middleware:
  - *Handling.* It is the process of listening for incoming remote calls, processing them with the appropriate scheduling parameters and notifying any new requests to the local DTM agent. In this case, the same functionality could be provided by the RPC Handler tasks.
  - *Routing Service.* In this context, routing means the capacity to interconnect different networks in systems where nodes are not connected directly.
  - *Fragmentation services.* Although this service could be developed as a new FRESCOR service, most distribution standards implicitly integrate it (e.g., GIOP in CORBA [16] or the DDS Interoperability Wire Protocol [20]), so the use of middleware would avoid the inclusion of unnecessary extra features into the framework.

However, a general purpose middleware could not satisfy all the requirements imposed by the DTM (e.g., complete support for the transactional model or a resource reservation scheduler). Our previous work with GLADE [9] and PolyORB middlewares [21], which aimed to provide support for different scheduling policies and the distributed transaction, facilitates the transition to the integration by introducing:

- *Full support for the transactional model.* Our model manages internally all the transaction-related details: identification of the transaction, mapping between incoming and outgoing events in the transformation points [14] and the assignment of the appropriate scheduling parameters for each element of the transaction.
- *Transaction identification.* The identification of a transaction is performed through the *Event_Id* parameter, which is then interpreted by the middleware [9]. New transactions activated through the DTM will be required to have specific *Event_Ids* defined. This association could be automatically managed by middleware and will be discussed in the next section.
- *Routing.* As we pointed out before, this service should be included as part of the middleware to limit the overhead that would be incurred by crossing all the implementation layers up to the application level. Our approach focuses on the routing through the *Event_Id*. Once the routing node has identified the event parameter and thus the ongoing transaction, it inquiries the middleware whether the invoked object is located in the local node or not. If not, the implementation will route the same incoming message through the pre-configured send endpoint.

Finally, another minor enhancements could be introduced in the DTM:

- Removal of the restriction of waiting for a specific transaction. The current API requires the user to specify the name of the transaction whose negotiation is waiting for. Such restriction could be easily solved in Ada through the use of an empty string as the default value for this parameter in the API function. This could be useful in dynamic systems where a pool of threads are supplying different services (e.g., a multimedia system providing video and regular voice calls) and thus different transactions could be executed.
- Processing of different requests using the same RPC Handler. The proposed internal management of the middleware implementation allows that a single RPC handler task could process several requests corresponding to different transactions, since the handler task is just bound to a particular endpoint and not to a single event. The same applies now to the Acceptor Tasks because in the new implementation they become regular RPC Handler tasks.

6   Extension of the DTM Protocol to Provide Support for the Transactional Model

The current version of the transaction manager limits its capabilities just to the management of remote contracts. However, once integrated within the middleware, the automatic deployment of the complete transaction becomes desirable: after accepting each new transaction in the system, the user should set only the initial *Event_Id* parameter while the middleware would automatically direct the remote call through the appropriate endpoints and RPC handlers transparently using the negotiated contracts.

This automatic deployment requires an extension of the protocol used by the DTM to enable the middleware to create and automatically set up handlers and endpoints. In particular, the new integrated version would require:

- *The specification of the full transaction.* In addition to the contract-related parameters, the transaction flow should be specified by the user. A possible solution consists of making use of a configuration language. Through the use of this language, middleware can bind the scheduling parameters, identified by their contract's name, to the associated flow (e.g., the appropriate *Event_Ids*). Furthermore, the definition of *RPC_Handlers* requires differentiating these contracts from those related to regular application tasks which are not bound to any receive endpoint.

- *Choosing unused Event_Ids.* Since any node can start a new negotiation, the maintenance of a list of all the events being used along the distributed system would increase the complexity and the overhead introduced by the agents. The proposed solution is based on the reservation of a certain amount of *Event_Id* values per node. This permits that each node that starts a negotiation, can safely select all the *Event_Ids* to be used in the transaction flow. Then, this extra information would be sent with the contract's data in the same *DTM_REQ_NEG_SET* message (see Fig. 3). This approach matches most of the requirements imposed by small and medium-size distributed systems.

- *Choosing unused ports.* Middleware should select an unused port in those nodes where the receive endpoints must be created, and then this new information will be sent back to the root node (e.g. the node which started the negotiation) in the *DTM_REP_NEG_SET* message (see Fig. 3). However, the root node must share this information with those nodes specified in the transaction flow and could include it in the *DTM_REQ_STATUS* (see Fig. 3) message which informs that the transaction has been accepted. Only then, the middleware could create the handlers and the endpoints with the appropriate parameters to enable the communication.

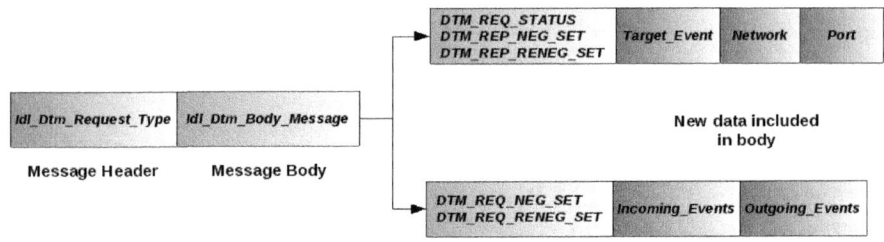

Fig. 3. DTM Protocol Extended

7   Implementation of the DTM in PolyORB

Nowadays, CORBA is considered a very mature technology to build distributed systems within the industry. However, a variety of problems still need to be addressed for systems with timing requirements [12]. Bringing the FRESCOR framework to a

CORBA-compliant middleware will enable to establish timing protection for the real-time distributed application components, that is, no tasks will be allowed to overrun their assigned and guaranteed budget execution time, or use more communication bandwidth than the reserved allocation. However, there could be systems that are part of a dynamic environment and thus the system requirements could not be completely known in advance at configuration time. In such systems the DTM emerges as a new mechanism to manage the negotiations and their results within all the nodes involved in the new distributed transaction. This section describes how to integrate this tool within the CORBA model and, in particular, in the PolyORB middleware.

The remote data types and services provided by the DTM must be described through the IDL language [16]. In particular, this has required the definition of:

- *Send_Message:* A remote call interface used to exchange the different kinds of messages between the DTM agents.
- *Idl_Dtm_Message*: A record used to store a generic message unit data. It consists of a header, indicating the message type, and a body, storing the specific data associated to a particular message type.

  - *Idl_Dtm_Request_Type*: An enumeration type to differentiate each of the 15 different types of messages to manage the initialization, the negotiation process and the status results.
  - *Idl_Dtm_Body_Message*: The specific data associated to a particular *Idl_Dtm_Request_Type*. Internally, it is an IDL union type which is mapped to a mutable discriminated Ada record [22] and therefore not optimized for memory requirements. However, the transmission of data is not affected by this kind of structure since the middleware will only send the amount of data strictly required through the network.

- Exchanged data types: Each kind of message has different data structures which will be exchanged between the agents. All of them must be described in IDL, including those consisting of complex types such as the contracts.

The initialization process may be configured statically as proposed in the original DTM or can make use of the CORBA Naming Service [19]. Each agent should register its IOR on it when it becomes ready to start or accept requests, and get the IOR from the remaining agents to assert that they are also in the ready state.

The *Routing Service* has been implemented in PolyORB within the GIOP protocol as shown in Fig. 4. Middleware requires to retrieve the *Event_Id* parameter stored in the GIOP *Service Context* field for any incoming message to identify the ongoing transaction. Once the transaction has been identified, the scheduling parameters can be updated if required and the middleware will try to locate the remote operation in the local node. If the location fails, then the message is routed through the appropriate send endpoint. Currently the implementation only supports routing using the same protocol personality (e.g., a FRESCOR network using RT-EP and CAN).

Fig. 4 represents a general overview of the DTM integrated into PolyORB. The current version is partially developed and uses PolyORB-CORBA, FRSH contracts for the scheduling policy, and RATO tasking policy (which supports the explicit creation of handler tasks and their association with endpoints) [21]. For the moment, it

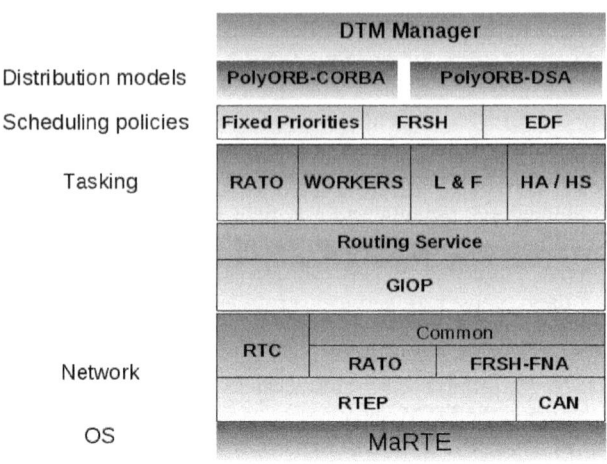

Fig. 4. DTM Manager integrated with middleware

only implements the basic contract parameters to specify the timing requirements and the proposed DTM protocol. A future version will integrate the PolyORB-DSA personality and any other resources managed by the framework.

We have evaluated the DTM over a platform consisting of four 800 Mhz embedded nodes connected through a 100 Mbps Ethernet with GNAT GPL 2008, MaRTE OS 1.9 and the modified version of PolyORB 2.4. Three tests have been run for two, three and four processing nodes. The tests consist of 10 independent asynchronous transactions, each one negotiating one contract for each processing node and one contract for each link over the network. Table 1 shows the times measured for these three tests. As it can be seen, the distributed negotiation process takes less than 20 ms for two processing nodes. In the cases of three and four processing nodes, this time is not increased significantly despite the higher overhead in the network and the extra negotiations of contracts. In spite of the fact that the DTM specification might seem at first complex and heavy we have found that we can get good performance time measurements.

Table 1. DTM metrics to negotiate one transaction using middleware (times in μs)

Num. of Nodes	Max	Avg	Min	Std. deviation
Two nodes	19508	19383	19133	111
Three nodes	25546	25219	24470	330
Four nodes	33255	32713	32565	199

8   Conclusions and Future Work

The paper presents the Distributed Transaction Manager (DTM) to extend the negotiation capabilities of the flexible contract-based scheduling framework defined in the

FRESCOR European Project. The DTM is intended as a middleware layer that allows the application components to perform remote negotiations and renegotiations of contracts, and a centralized management of the results of the negotiation process. The DTM has been successfully implemented in the FRESCOR framework demonstrating its usefulness.

As an extension of the basic capabilities, another implementation of the DTM has been proposed using a general purpose distribution middleware based on the CORBA and Ada DSA standards. This implementation provides full support for the transactional model and takes advantage of the distribution middleware to develop the DTM internals in a simpler way that is also more platform independent. It also extends some capabilities as for example the specification of the full transaction or the routing service that interconnects different networks over the standard layer of GIOP.

This features designed for DTM over the distribution middleware have been partially implemented. In the short term we plan to complete this implementation and evaluate its benefits and performance.

References

1. Aldea, M., et al.: FSF: A Real-Time Scheduling Architecture Framework. In: Proc. of the 12th IEEE Real-Time and Embedded Technology and Applications Symposium, RTAS 2006, San Jose, CA, USA (2006)
2. FRESCOR project web page: http://www.frescor.org
3. Object Management Group. A UML Profile for MARTE: Modeling and Analysis of Real-Time Embedded systems, Beta 2 OMG Document Number: ptc/2008-06-09 (2008)
4. FRESCOR Architecture and contract model for integrated resources II. Deliverable (D-AC2v2), http://www.frescor.org
5. MaRTE OS web page, http://marte.unican.es/
6. Martínez, J.M., González Harbour, M.: RT-EP: A Fixed-Priority Real Time Communication Protocol over Standard Ethernet. In: Vardanega, T., Wellings, A.J. (eds.) Ada-Europe 2005. LNCS, vol. 3555, pp. 180–195. Springer, Heidelberg (2005)
7. FRESCOR Distributed Transaction Manager - proof of concept. Deliverable (D-ND5v1), http://www.frescor.org
8. FRESCOR Distributed Transaction Manager - Prototype Demonstration. Deliverable (D-ND5v2), http://www.frescor.org
9. López Campos, J., Javier Gutiérrez, J., González Harbour, M.: Interchangeable Scheduling Policies in Real-Time Middleware for Distribution. In: Pinho, L.M., González Harbour, M. (eds.) Ada-Europe 2006. LNCS, vol. 4006, pp. 227–240. Springer, Heidelberg (2006)
10. PolyORB web page, http://polyorb.objectweb.org/
11. Vergnaud, T., Hugues, J., Pautet, L., Kordon, F.: PolyORB: a Schizophrenic Middleware to Build Versatile Reliable Distributed Applications. In: Llamosí, A., Strohmeier, A. (eds.) Ada-Europe 2004. LNCS, vol. 3063. Springer, Heidelberg (2004)
12. Pérez, H., Gutiérrez, J.J., Sangorrín, D., Harbour, M.G.: Real-Time Distribution Middleware from the Ada Perspective. In: Kordon, F., Vardanega, T. (eds.) Ada-Europe 2008. LNCS, vol. 5026. Springer, Heidelberg (2008)
13. AdaCore Technologies, The GNAT Pro Company, http://www.adacore.com/
14. Tijero, H.P., Gutiérrez, J.J., Harbour, M.G.: Support for a Real-Time Transactional Model in Distributed Ada. In: Proceedings of the 14th International Real-Time Ada Workshop (IRTAW 14), Portovenere (Italy). ACM Ada-Letters, New York (2009)

15. Loyall, J.P., Rubel, P., Schantz, R., Atighetchi, M., Zinky, J.: Emerging Patterns in Adaptive, Distributed Real-Time, Embedded Middleware. In: OOPSLA 2002 Workshop - Patterns in Distributed Real-time and Embedded Systems, Seattle, Washington (2002)
16. Object Management Group. CORBA Core Specification. OMG Document, v3.0 formal/02-06-01 (2003)
17. Object Management Group. Data Distribution Service for Real-time Systems. OMG Document, v1.2, formal/07-01-01 (2007)
18. Tucker Taft, S., Duff, R.A., Brukardt, R.L., Ploedereder, E., Leroy, P. (eds.): Ada 2005 Reference Manual. LNCS, vol. 4348. Springer, Heidelberg (2006)
19. Object Management Group. Naming Service Specification. OMG Document, v1.3 formal/04-10-03 (2004)
20. Object Management Group. The Real-time Publish-Subscribe Wire Protocol. DDS Interoperability Wire Protocol Specification. OMG Document, v2.1, formal/2009-01-05 (2009)
21. Pérez Tijero, H., Javier Gutiérrez, J.: Experience in integrating interchangeable scheduling policies into a distribution middleware for Ada. In: Proceedings of the ACM SIGAda Annual International Conference on Ada and Related Technologies, SIGAda 2009, Saint Petersburg, Florida, USA (2009)
22. Object Management Group. Ada Language Mapping Specification. OMG Document, v1.2 formal/01-10-42 (2001)

An Efficient Implementation
of Persistent Objects

Jacob Sparre Andersen

Jacob Sparre Andersen Research & Innovation
Vesterbrogade 148K, 1. th.
1620 København V
Danmark

Abstract. Persistent objects form a general and very useful method for storing internal program data between executions of a program. And as [1] points out, Ada is an excellent language for implementing persistent objects. This paper introduces a low-impact, efficient implementation of persistent objects based on storage pools and the "POSIX.Memory‑Mapping" API [2]. The performance and reliability of the implementation is compared with serialisation.

1 Introduction

There are two basic ideas behind this paper. The one is that memory-mapping is an extremely fast I/O method. The other is that Ada storage pools allow us to control where in virtual memory dynamically allocated objects are stored. These two ideas combined allow us to make dynamically allocated objects be stored in a part of virtual memory which is mapped to a file, and thus automatically stored. Binding an access type to a specific storage pool takes only a single attribute definition clause, making this technique very easy to use.

In section 2 an interface for managing persistent objects is presented. In section 3 the actual implementation is described. In section 4 a comparison to other techniques for implementing persistence, including an experimental comparison with serialisation, is presented. Finally, in section 5, we conclude and point to possible future enhancements of this technique. The full source code of the system, as well as demonstration programs is available from `http://www.jacob-sparre.dk/persistence/`.

2 An Interface for Persistent Objects

The concept of persistent objects is about maintaining a collection of objects created by an application from one execution of the application to the next. Two of the techniques devised for this purpose are serialisation, where the objects are written to a file represented as a stream, and storage in a database, where the objects in the process memory are simply buffers for data stored in a relational database.

J. Real and T. Vardanega (Eds.): Ada-Europe 2010, LNCS 6106, pp. 265–275, 2010.
© Springer-Verlag Berlin Heidelberg 2010

The reader is pointed to [3] for a general and thorough presentation of persistent objects in relation to Ada. The persistent objects technique presented in the following gives the programmer something close to *orthogonal* persistence, with the major limitation that it only works on explicitly allocated objects.

2.1 Package Specification

The package "Persistent_Storage_Pool" declares a descendant of "System.Storage_Pools.Root_Storage_Pool". All objects allocated on a storage pool of this type will be persistent.

```
package Persistent_Storage_Pool is
   type Instance is new System.Storage_Pools.
      Root_Storage_Pool with private;
```

The package also declares the abstract tagged type "Root_Object", and a function to access the root object of a storage pool:

```
   type Root_Object is abstract tagged null record;
   subtype Root_Class is Root_Object'Class;
   type Root_Name is access all Root_Class;
   [...]
   function Root (Pool : Instance) return Root_Name;
```

The root object of a persistent storage pool is the starting point for the collection of persistent objects. I.e. if one wants to make a tree structure of objects persistent, one will make the root node of the tree the root object of the persistent storage pool. Notice that the root object of a storage pool is the object referred to by "System.Storage_Pools.Root". Other objects in the "System.Storage_Pools.Root_Class" are only persistent if they are allocated in the storage pool.

A persistent storage pool object is activated by a call to one of the procedures "Create" and "Load". "Create" takes four arguments: the storage pool to activate, a file name, an initial value for the root object, and the number of storage elements to allocate for the pool:

```
   procedure Create
      (Pool           : in out Instance;
       As             : in     String;
       Initial_Value  : in     Root_Class;
       Size           : in     System.Storage_Elements.
          Storage_Count);
```

"Load" manages with two arguments: the storage pool to activate, and the name of the file to load it from:

```
   procedure Load (Pool : in out Instance;
                   From : in     String);
```

Before "Create" or "Load" has been called on a persistent storage pool object, all operations on the pool will raise "Ada.IO_Exceptions.Status_Error".

The specifications of "Allocate", "Deallocate" and "Storage_Size" are in the private part of the package.

Notice that there is no "Close" operation, since that easily would result in dangling pointers. A persistent storage pool is only closed and deallocated as the program terminates. This is done by the operating system.

2.2   Use

Using this system for making objects persistent is actually quite simple:

- An object of the persistent storage pool type is declared.
- For each type of object which should be persistent, an access type is declared as using the persistent storage pool object as its storage pool.
- A storage pool root type is derived from "Persistent_Storage_Pool.Root_ Object".
- Finally the persistent storage pool is created or loaded from a file.

```
with Persistent_Storage_Pool;
    [...]
    Persistent : Persistent_Storage_Pool.Instance;
    [...]
    type Some_Reference is access all Some_Class;
    for Some_Reference'Storage_Pool use Persistent;
    [...]
    type Another_Reference is access all Another_Class;
    for Another_Reference'Storage_Pool use Persistent;
    [...]
    type Root is new Persistent_Storage_Pool.Root_Object
        with [...];
    [...]
    Create_or_Load (Pool => Persistent , [...]);
```

2.3   Example

The demonstration program makes a single-linked list persistent by allocating its elements in a persistent storage pool object. First the pool object is declared:

```
    Storage_Pool : Persistent_Storage_Pool.Instance;
```

and then the access type for the nodes in the list is hooked up with the pool object:

```
    type Reference is access all Object;
    for Reference'Storage_Pool use Storage_Pool;
```

To access the head of the list, a descendant of "Persistent_Storage_Pool.Root_ Object" is declared:

```
type Root is new Persistent_Storage_Pool.Root_Object
   with
   record
      First : Reference;
   end record;
```

Now we either create a new pool:

```
Create (Pool            => Storage_Pool,
        As              => Argument (2),
        Initial_Value => Root'(First => null),
        Size            => 100);
```

or load an existing one:

```
Load (Pool => Storage_Pool,
      From => Argument (2));
```

(We see that the name of the storage pool file is passed to the demonstration program as the second command line argument.)

Then we can find the tail of the linked list as usual:

```
Tail := Root_Reference (Storage_Pool.Root).First;
while Tail.Next /= null loop
   Tail := Tail.Next;
end loop;
```

And when we allocate a new object as the new tail of the linked list:

```
Tail.Next := new Object'(Data => "Tofta_Teld",
                         Next => null);
```

it automatically ends up in the persistent pool.

3   Implementation Using Memory-Mapped Files

3.1   Memory-Mapped Files

To understand memory mapped files, we can start with a quote from the POSIX specification of the function "mmap" [4]:

> The mmap() function shall establish a mapping between a process' address space and a file.

The actual copying of data between disk and RAM is handled by the operating system. Essentially the mapped file is assigned as swap space to its part of the process' address space. This gives us the possibility of saving some copying between disk and RAM; if the operating system for example already has "swapped" the file to disk, saving the data has zero cost – they are already in the file.

The POSIX specification of "mmap" gives us an implicit guarantee that the mapped file will contain an exact copy of the process memory once "unmap" has been called (i.e. once the program has stopped).

For the purpose of the technique presented in this paper, a very important feature of "mmap" and "POSIX.Memory_Mapping.Map_Memory" is that it is possible to ask the operating system to map a file to a specified part of the process address space. I.e. when we map a file into memory, we can have it placed at the same address as last time, thus maintaining the validity of pointers pointing to specific locations in the memory mapped file.

Without this feature, we would need to be able to implement relative access types[1] in Ada, to make the technique feasible. Since POSIX does not guarantee that we always will be allowed to map a file to the address we request, it would broaden the possible use of the technique, if Ada allowed us to implement relative access types. The use of address space layout randomisation is likely to create problems for this technique, so a future-proof version of this technique will require relative access types.

Although this implementation is using the Ada POSIX API, it is likely that memory mapping implementations in non-POSIX operating systems will work equally well. According to [5] "Most modern operating systems or runtime environments support some form of memory-mapped file access", so even if your target platform isn't POSIX compatible, it is likely that the technique can be used without too many modifications.

3.2 Implementation Technique

Besides declaring access types to use a persistent storage pool, the core of the technique lies in the procedures "Create" and "Load", which take care of asking the operating system to map a file to memory.

procedure Create. The first step in creating a persistent storage pool is to create and open a file for it. With the POSIX Ada API this is done with "POSIX.IO.Open_Or_Create".

The second step is to allocate the requested space for the storage pool in the file. This is done using "POSIX.IO.Seek" together with an instantiation of "POSIX.IO.Generic_Write"[2].

The third step is to map the file into memory (at an address chosen by the operating system) with "POSIX.Memory_Mapping. Map_Memory":

```
Pool.Address := Map_Memory (Length      => Pool.Size ,
                            Protection  => Allow_Read
                            + Allow_Write ,
                            Mapping     => Map_Shared ,
                            File        => Pool.File ,
                            Offset      => 0);
```

---

[1] I.e. access types, where the system address corresponding to an access type can be modified with a fixed offset at run-time.

[2] A more general implementation might extend the size of the storage pool automatically, when needed.

The fourth step is to store the basic parameters of the storage pool in the storage pool itself. Since the storage pool at this point is mapped into memory, this can be done by placing an object in the storage pool memory space with:

```
Header : Persistent_Storage_Pool.Header;
pragma Import (Ada, Header);
for Header'Address use Pool.Address;
```

and then copy the parameters to the "Header" object:

```
Header := (Key       => Persistent_Storage_Pool.Key,
           Address   => Pool.Address,
           Allocated => Conversions.Storage (Header'
             Size),
           Root      => null);
```

Finally we allocate space for the root object in the storage pool, and copy the initial value of the root object there.

procedure Load. The first step in loading a persistent storage pool is to open the file it is stored in. With the POSIX Ada API this is done with "POSIX.IO. Open".

The second step is to load the basic parameters for the storage pool from the file with an instantiation of "POSIX.IO.Generic_Read".

The third step is to check that the memory area, where it was last time, is not occupied. This is done with the function "mincore()" (which unfortunately isn't in POSIX yet). If this check fails, "Load" will raise the exception "Storage_Error"[3].

The last step is to map the file into the memory area where it was last time, so references will continue to point to the same objects. Like in procedure "Create", this is done with "POSIX.Memory_Mapping.Map_Memory".

In between these steps, there are various consistency checks on the loaded data. If these checks fail the exception "Persistent_Storage_Pool.Bad_Pool_ Format" will be raised.

4   Comparison with Other Techniques

To test the actual impact of this technique, two test programs have been made. Both of them create or load a network of objects, and then explore it. The only difference between the two programs is which persistence implementation they use to avoid creating the network, if it already has been created. One of these programs (B) uses Ada.Streams to implement persistence following the pattern described in [6], while the other one (C) uses the technique presented in this paper to implement persistence.

---

[3] The expected reason for this check to fail, is that the operating system uses address space layout randomisation. In that case, the solution could be to let "POSIX.Unsafe_Process_Primitives.Exec" rerandomise the address space, since it is likely that a new random layout will not occupy the relevant memory area.

4.1   Speed

Figure 1 shows how much time it takes to run programs B and C in the mode where they create a network from scratch and write it to disk. The measurements appear to be dominated by the time it takes to create the network. Since program C uses the operating system to save the data, measuring the time inside the program would not be fair to program B. As we can see from the graph, there appears to be a small, but significant speed difference in favour of program C, although the large error bars on a few of the data-points make the case a bit muddled.

Figure 2 shows how much time it takes to run programs B and C in the mode where they load a network from disk and explore it. Here we can see that for large numbers of objects, program C is significantly faster than program B. The two fitted lines are linear with a small offset. For large network sizes this corresponds to program C being approximately 8 times faster than program B.

No measurements have been made of loading a network, modifying it, and then saving the modified network. Since program B has to rewrite the whole network, it is likely that program C will be significantly faster for this combination of actions.

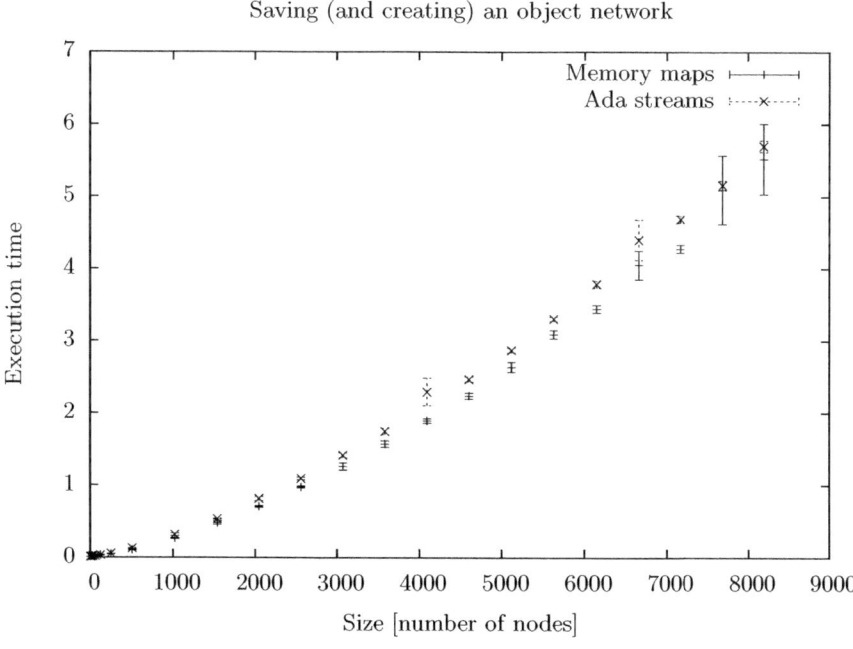

Fig. 1. Comparing the writing speed of program C (Memory maps) and program B (Ada streams). Error bars correspond to 95% confidence intervals.

Loading an object network

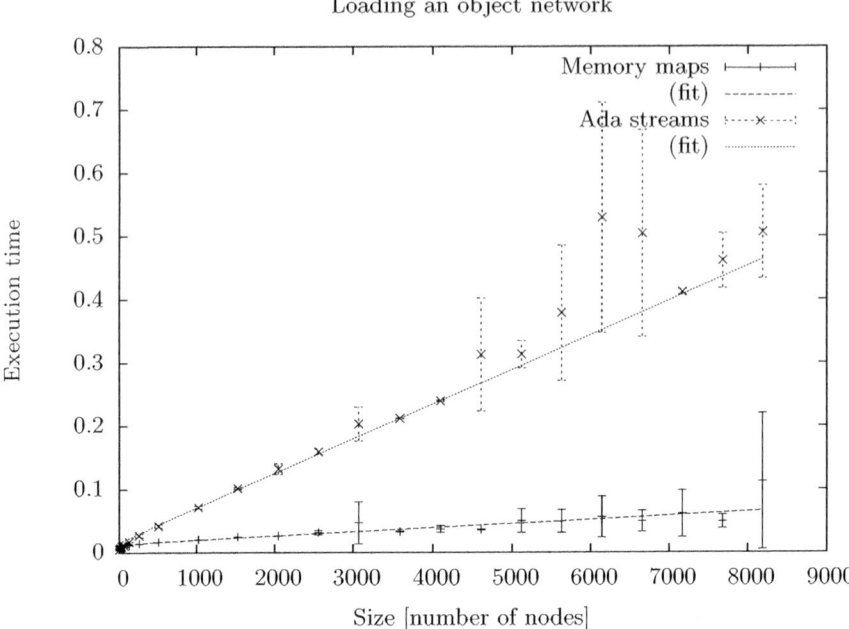

Fig. 2. Comparing the reading speed of program C (Memory maps) and program B (Ada streams). Error bars correspond to 95% confidence intervals. Linear functions are fitted to the measurements.

4.2   Persistence Manager

Using memory maps to implement persistence moves a bit of the responsibility from the application to the operating system.

One could claim that this reduces the risk of loosing data, since the operating system will take care of saving the persistent objects, if the application dies[4]. The down-side of this is that the application may die while the persistent data are in an inconsistent state, leaving the data inconsistent for the next time the application is executed. A safe implementation should therefore either maintain the persistent data constantly in a consistent state, or maintain a flag in the persistent data, which indicates if the data are consistent or not.

4.3   Shared Data

Memory maps can be shared between several processes, such that several instances of the same program can operate on the same persistent data structure.

---

[4] The guarantee that the mapped file will contain an exact copy of the process memory once "unmap" has been called (i.e. once the program has stopped) is only implicit in the POSIX specification of "mmap" [4].

Although this requires that the programmer implements the appropriate locking using primitives supplied by the operating system[5], it is still an improvement over stream-based and other load-work-store type persistence implementations.

4.4 System Calls

System calls have a large impact on the performance of applications on practically all architectures, since the CPU has to switch from the application/user context to an operating system context.

Using memory maps reduces the number of system calls needed to implement persistence to a fixed number per execution of the application, no matter how much data is being stored[6].

Implementing persistence using serialisation (streams) will result in a number of system calls which will scale linearly with the number of objects being stored. Inserting a buffering stream between the serialisation routine and the operating system, will reduce the number of system calls. With a careful implementation a buffering stream may even use as few system calls as using memory-mapped files.

4.5 Virtual Memory

To understand the performance of I/O implementations on a modern operating system, it is necessary to remember that modern operating systems work with the concept of virtual memory. Virtual memory is **not** the same as RAM. Virtual memory should rather be seen as a unified address space, where the operating system freely moves the actual data around between disk (swap), RAM and CPU caches. At the same time, the operating system maintains RAM caches with parts of files. Each process has its own virtual memory, and when data are copied from an operating system controlled resource, such as a disk, to a process, there is a performance cost since the operation requires both a context switch and moving data around.

Virtual memory, disk based swap space, and RAM cached files make it hard to make an exact estimate of how large a volume of data is copied between disk and RAM. What we can do is estimate the minimal volume of data copied around. For a traditional persistent object system it is $O(N)$ whereas the implementation presented here is $O(1)$, since the only data the operating system is required to copy is the fixed size head of the persistent storage pool file. In practise we will of course expect the process to access some of the objects in the persistent storage pool, and then they will have to be copied as well. But since we use a memory map, the whole process of managing which parts of the persistent storage pool are in RAM, and which are on disk is handled by the operating system. – This is not likely to be the dominant performance cost, since moving data around is a relatively cheap process.

---

[5] Ada protected objects cannot be shared in this way, if one wants their semantics to be preserved.

[6] Extending the persistent storage will require some system calls.

4.6 Dangling References

If a persistent object contains a reference (access) to a non-persistent object, the referenced object will have disappeared the next time the persistent storage pool is loaded, resulting in a dangling pointer.

The technique presented here requires that all references from persistent objects are references to persistent objects. Currently this is checked manually, and thus a potential source of errors. A source code analyser, such as AdaControl [7], should be extended to make this check automatic.

Serialising objects using Ada streams pose a similar challenge, but in this case the tool presented in [6] appears to be able to solve the problem in an automated fashion.

4.7 Storage Format Stability

When a program is recompiled, the layout of data types, type tags, etc. may change. Since Ada uses name based type equivalence, this makes sense. Unfortunately this (and name based type equivalence) will make a persistent storage pool from one version of a program unusable for another version of the program, such that programs cannot rely on this technique for long-term storage. For long-term storage – i.e. data which should persist beyond the life-time of a specific version of a program – it is still necessary to use a documented, implementation-independent storage format.

Implementing persistence using streams, does not automatically solve the problem of saving in an implementation-independent file format, but it is probably easier than with memory-mapped files.

5 Conclusion and Future Work

We have demonstrated a technique for handling persistent objects in Ada. The technique works on existing Ada compilers without any modifications.

We have demonstrated that the technique is significantly faster than the most prominent competing technique for implementing persistent objects.

We have demonstrated that persistence can be implemented at the cost of adding a single attribute definition clause to each persistent object access type in an application.

Altogether the technique presented here delivers faster I/O and less impact on the code of the program using it, compared to serialisation.

Although the technique does not **require** external tool support, the use of the technique will be safer with tool support. An obvious choice would be to add the required rule to AdaControl.

We have not yet demonstrated that the technique works on major non-POSIX operating systems. Nor have we solved the problems which address space layout randomisation may introduce.

The big drawback of the technique is that it isn't guaranteed to work on all operating systems with an Ada compiler.

There are thus three steps, which together will improve the benefit of using the presented technique in the areas of safety, reliability and portability:

- Extend AdaControl to check that persistent objects only contain access types which refer to objects in the same persistent storage pool.
- Extend how Ada handles access types, so we can create relative access types, and thus avoid the problems address space layout randomisation may introduce.
- Move the handling of memory-mapped files into the Ada standard.

The first of these steps is easy, the second is difficult, and the third does not seem all that likely to happen.

References

1. Card, M.P.: Why Ada is the right choice for object databases. CrossTalk (1997)
2. IEEE: IEEE STD 1003.5: 1990, Information Technology – POSIX Ada Language Interfaces Part 1: Binding for System Application Program Interface, as amended by IEEE STD 1003.5b: 1996, Amendment 1: Realtime Extensions (1996)
3. Crawley, S., Oudshoorn, M.: Orthogonal persistence and Ada. In: Proceedings of the conference on TRI-Ada 1994, pp. 298–308. ACM, New York (1994)
4. The Open Group Base Specifications: mmap (2004), http://www.opengroup.org/onlinepubs/000095399/functions/mmap.html
5. Wikipedia, the free encyclopedia: Memory-mapped file (2010), http://en.wikipedia.org/wiki/Memory-mapped_file
6. García, R.G., Strohmeier, A., Keller, L.: Automatic Serialization of Dynamic Structures in Ada. Technical report, École Polytechnique Fédérale de Lausanne, Infoscience (2003)
7. Adalog: AdaControl (2009), http://www.adalog.fr/adacontrol2.htm

Author Index

GPSR Compliance

The European Union's (EU) General Product Safety Regulation (GPSR) is a set of rules that requires consumer products to be safe and our obligations to ensure this.

If you have any concerns about our products, you can contact us on ProductSafety@springernature.com

In case Publisher is established outside the EU, the EU authorized representative is:

Springer Nature Customer Service Center GmbH
Europaplatz 3
69115 Heidelberg, Germany

Batch number: 09490872

Printed by Printforce, the Netherlands